Re-membering the Reign of God

Postcolonial and Decolonial Studies in Religion and Theology

Series Editor: Sheryl Kujawa-Holbrook, Claremont School of Theology

Series Editorial Board: Jon Berquist, Stephen Burns, Cláudio Carvalhaes, Jennifer Te Paa Daniel, Lynne St. Clair Darden, Christine J. Hong, Wonhee Anne Joh, HyeRan Kim-Cragg, Boyung Lee, Aprilfaye Tayag Manalang, Loida Yvette Martell, Stephanie Y. Mitchem, Jea Sophia Oh, Nicolas Esteban Panotto, Jeremy Punt, Patrick Reyes, Joerg Rieger, Fernando Segovia, Melinda McGarrah Sharp, Kay Higuera Smith, Jonathan Y. Tan, Mona West, and Amos Yong.

This series responds to the growing interest in postcolonial studies and re-examines the hegemonic, European-dominated religious systems of the old and new empires. It critically addresses the colonial biases of religions, the academy, and local faith communities, in an effort to make these institutions more polyvocal, receptive, and empowering to global cultures and epistemologies. The series will engage with a variety of hybrid, overlapping, and intersecting definitions of postcolonialism—as a critical discursive practice, as a political and ideological stance concerned with exposing patterns of dominance and hegemony, and as contexts shaped by ongoing colonization and decolonization. Books in the series will also explore the relationship between postcolonial values and religious practice, and the transformation of religious symbols and institutions in postcolonial contexts beyond the academy. The series aims to make high-quality and original research available to the scholarly community. The series welcomes monographs and edited volumes which forge new directions in contextual research across disciplines and explore key contemporary issues. Established scholars as well as new authors will be considered for publication, including scholars "on the margins" whose voices are under-represented in the academy and in religious discourse. Authors working in sub-disciplines of religious studies and/or theology are encouraged to submit proposals.

Titles in the Series

Postcolonial Preaching: Creating a Ripple Effect, by HyeRan Kim-Cragg
Decolonial Futures: Intercultural and Interreligious Intelligence for Theological Education, by Christine Hong
Unmasking White Preaching: Racial Hegemony, Resistance, and Possibilities in Homiletics, edited by Lis Valle-Ruiz and Andrew Wymer
Sámi Nature-centered Christianity in the European Arctic: Indigenous Theology beyond Hierarchical Worldmaking, by Tore Johnsen
Decolonizing Interreligious Education: Developing Theologies of Accountability, by Shannon Frediani
Re-membering the Reign of God: The Decolonial Witness of El Salvador's Church of the Poor, by Elizabeth O'Donnell Gandolfo and Laurel Marshall Potter

Re-membering the Reign of God

The Decolonial Witness of
El Salvador's Church of the Poor

Elizabeth O'Donnell Gandolfo
and Laurel Marshall Potter

LEXINGTON BOOKS
Lanham • Boulder • New York • London

Published by Lexington Books
An imprint of The Rowman & Littlefield Publishing Group, Inc.
4501 Forbes Boulevard, Suite 200, Lanham, Maryland 20706
www.rowman.com

86-90 Paul Street, London EC2A 4NE

Copyright © 2022 by The Rowman & Littlefield Publishing Group, Inc.

All rights reserved. No part of this book may be reproduced in any form or by any electronic or mechanical means, including information storage and retrieval systems, without written permission from the publisher, except by a reviewer who may quote passages in a review.

British Library Cataloguing in Publication Information Available

Library of Congress Cataloging-in-Publication Data

Names: Gandolfo, Elizabeth O'Donnell, author. | Potter, Laurel Marshall, 1989- author.
Title: Re-membering the reign of God : the decolonial witness of El Salvador's church of the poor / Elizabeth O'Donnell Gandolfo and Laurel Marshall Potter.
Description: Lanham : Lexington Books, [2022] | Series: Postcolonial and decolonial studies in religion and theology; vol. 6 | Includes bibliographical references and index.
Identifiers: LCCN 2022015371 (print) | LCCN 2022015372 (ebook) |
  ISBN 9781793618955 (cloth) | ISBN 9781793618979 (paperback) |
  ISBN 9781793618962 (epub)
Subjects: LCSH: Basic Christian communities—El Salvador—History. | Church work with the poor—El Salvador—History. | Church work with the poor—Catholic Church—History. | Decolonization—El Salvaor—History. | Postcolonialism—El Salvaor—History.
Classification: LCC BX2347.72.S2 G36 2022 (print) | LCC BX2347.72.S2 (ebook) |
  DDC 282/.728409051—dc23/eng/20220517
LC record available at https://lccn.loc.gov/2022015371
LC ebook record available at https://lccn.loc.gov/2022015372

To all remaining tecomate *seeds,
the community Nuevo Amanecer,
and the CEBs of Cacaopera
L.M.P.*

*To Rosa and Avelino,
the* canto popular *of the CEBs,
and my beloved raggedy family.
E.O.G.*

About the Cover Art

"La Mesa Común" (The Common Table) was created by the Salvadoran artist Alexander Serpas to accompany this book (Instagram: @alex_serpas). Alex creates images in keeping with traditional Salvadoran visual art that draw on the historical memory of the Salvadoran church of *lxs pobres*. This work is a dream of the eschatological banquet of the reign of God, surrounded by a "re-membered" community and society. Below the Tree of Life, different community dynamics are represented around the table. Emotions like surprise, joy, fear, sadness, anger, and worry are shown; this encounter is a place where our different feelings and emotions draw us together and are sources for our collective work. The pair arguing to the right represent the different opinions that always exist in community, and the figure in pink represents the contributions of those who participate even sporadically. The Jesus figure below carries a bowl of burning *ocote* to the banquet, recalling Luke 12:49, "I came to bring fire to the earth, and how I wish it were already kindled!" Two figures in the front of the table exchange coffee for chocolate, representing the solidarity economy, and different feminist, Indigenous, and cultural elements are depicted in the figures' clothes and accessories. This church is the destination and the journey, an encounter amid diversity. On the table is a meal, potluck-style, of everyday and locally grown foods: beans, plantains, tortilla, coffee. The cornfield and the coffee tree, ripe with fruit, represent the bread that becomes flesh and the wine that becomes blood from which human beings draw sustenance. Eucharist here is a natural and everyday occurrence (though not for that reason less treasured), rooted especially in the maize that has been the foundation of Mesoamerican existence for millennia.

The sun in the red sky represents God the Creator, who can be felt and seen by all in everyday life. The bird in the blue sky represents the Spirit of Jesus that descends and is made manifest in the prophets. The harvest in the bottom left reminds us how sugarcane must be cut back to grow anew, and the green circle pushing against burned earth testifies to the healing power of our planet. The group in the upper left, led by Monseñor Romero, Pedro Declercq, Prudencia Ayala, Farabundo Martí, and Anastasio Aquino, represents the church going outside of the building: an organized, conscious people whose energy is like the volcano that explodes above them. The celebration in the bottom right represents a spirituality fed by memory and music, and the children playing with a Salvadoran top represent the childlike spirit that trusts and befriends. The fish in the river along the bottom of the image recall the ancestral species of the Torola River; even extinct varieties of small fish are re-membered in the reign of God!

Contents

List of Abbreviations	xi
Introduction: *Otro mundo es posible*: Is An-Other Church Possible?	1
PART I: *UN LARGO CAMINAR*: SALVADORAN SALVATION HISTORY	**29**
Colonio-Genesis	31
Nuevo-Exodus	40
The *Librito* of the Prophet Anastasio Aquino	51
The *Librito* of the Prophet Prudencia Ayala	55
The *Librito* of the Prophet Farabundo Martí	57
The *Librito* of the Prophet Óscar Romero	61
The Gospel According to la Zacamil	67
The Gospel According to Suchitoto	75
The Gospel According to Morazán	82
Acts of the Repatriated	90
Letter from the Community "Pueblo de Dios en Camino"	100
Letter from the Community "Rutilio Grande"	105
Letter from the Community "Nuevo Amanecer"	108

Letter from the Hierarchy I 114

Letter from the Hierarchy II 118

Letter from the Hierarchy III 130

The *Librito* of the Prophet Reina Greisi Leiva 140

The *Librito* of the Prophet Miguel Zepeda Santos 144

The *Librito* of the Prophet María Ángela Domínguez Pérez 148

The *Librito* of the Prophet José Adonay Pérez 154

The *Librito* of the Prophet Berta Cáceres 159

Revelations after the Peace Accords 164

PART II: *EL REINO DE DIOS ES DE LXS POBRES*: DECOLONIAL THEOLOGICAL REFLECTION IN LIGHT OF THE ECCLESIAL BASE COMMUNITIES OF EL SALVADOR 185

1 *Sacramento histórico del reino de Dios*: Decoloniality and the Eschatological Horizons of El Salvador's Church of *lxs Pobres* 187

2 *Tomamos la palabra*: Decolonial Knowledge in the Salvadoran Church of *lxs Pobres* 213

3 *Celebramos la vida:* Decolonial Being in the Salvadoran Church of *lxs Pobres* 249

4 *Luchamos por la justicia*: Decolonial Power in the Salvadoran Church of *lxs Pobres* 285

5 *Si el grano de trigo no muere*: The Challenge of Decolonial Solidarity 321

Bibliography 359

Index 373

About the Authors 379

List of Abbreviations

ADESCO	Asociación de Desarrollo Comunal (Communal Development Association)
AG	*Ad Gentes Divinitus*, Vatican II Decree on the Church's Missionary Activity (1965)
ARENA	Alianza Republicana Nacionalista (Nationalist Republican Alliance)
CCC	Catechism of the Catholic Church (1993)
CCL	Code of Canon Law (1983)
CEB	Comunidad Eclesial de Base (Ecclesial Base Community)
CEBES	Comunidades Eclesiales de Base de El Salvador (Ecclesial Base Communities of El Salvador)
CEDES	Conferencia Episcopal de El Salvador (Bishops' Conference of El Salvador)
CEL	Comisión Ejecutiva Hidroeléctrica del Río Lempa (Executive Hydroelectric Commission of the Lempa River)
CELAM	Consejo Episcopal Latinoamericano (Latin American Bishops' Conference)
CONIP	Coordinación Nacional de la Iglesia Popular (National Coordination of the Popular Church)
COPINH	Consejo Cívico de Organizaciones Populares e Indígenas de Honduras (Civic Council of Popular and Indigenous Organizations of Honduras)
CRISPAZ	Christians for Peace in El Salvador
DV	*Dei Verbum*, Vatican II Dogmatic Constitution on Divine Revelation (1965)

	List of Abbreviations
EG	*Evangelii Gaudium*, Pope Francis, Apostolic Exhortation on the Proclamation of the Gospel in Today's World (2013)
EN	*Evangelii Nuntiandi*, Pope Paul VI, Apostolic Exhortation on Evangelization in the Modern World (1975)
FMLN	Frente Farabundo Martí para la Liberación Nacional (Farabundo Martí National Liberation Front)
FRTS	Federación Regional de Trabajadores de El Salvador (Regional Federation of Workers of El Salvador)
FT	*Fratelli Tutti: On Fraternity and Social Friendship*, Pope Francis, Encyclical Letter (2020)
FUNDAHMER	Fundación Hermano Mercedes Ruíz (Brother Mercedes Ruíz Foundation)
IFTJ	Ignatian Family Teach-In for Justice
IPLA	Instituto Pastoral de Latinoamérica (Pastoral Institute of Latin America)
ISN	Ignatian Solidarity Network
LG	*Lumen Gentium*, Vatican II Dogmatic Constitution on the Church (1964)
MM	*Misericordia et misera*, Pope Francis, Apostolic Letter at the Conclusion of the Jubilee Year of Mercy (2016)
MUPI	Museo de la Palabra y la Imagen (Museum of the Word and the Image)
NA	*Nostra Aetate*, Vatican II Declaration on the Relation of the Church to Non-Christian Religions (1965)
ONUSAL	United Nations Observer Mission in El Salvador
ORDEN	Organización Democrática Nacionalista (Nationalist Democratic Organization)
PCS	Partido Comunista Salvadoreño (Salvadoran Communist Party)
PNC	Policía Nacional Civil (National Civil Police)
QA	*Querida Amazonia*, Pope Francis, Post-Synodal Apostolic Exhortation (2020)
SC	*Sacrosanctum Concilium*, Vatican II Constitution on the Sacred Liturgy (1963)
SOA	School of the Americas
STM	Short Term Missions

UCA	Universidad Centroamericana "José Simeón Cañas" (Central American University)
UNDP	United Nations Development Program
UNHCR	United Nations High Commissioner for Refugees
WHINSEC	Western Hemisphere Institute for Security Cooperation
WMPM	World Meeting of Popular Movements

NB: All quotations from Vatican II documents are taken from the inclusive language translation by Austin Flannery, O.P., *Vatican Council II: Constitutions, Decrees, Declarations* (New York: Costello Publishing Company, 1996). Code of Canon Law quotations are taken from *Code of Canon Law: Latin-English Edition* (Washington, DC: Canon Law Society of America, 1998). Unless otherwise noted, all other quotations of Vatican documents are taken from the Vatican website at www.vatican.va.

Introduction

Otro mundo es posible:
Is An-Other Church Possible?

¡Cómo no me va a llenar el corazón de esperanza una Iglesia donde florecen las comunidades eclesiales de base!
—Mons. Óscar Arnulfo Romero[1]

The chapel floor is tamped-down dirt, and the walls are adobe bricks. Wooden beams hold up the red clay tile ceiling, from which a single dusty light bulb hangs. El Jocote is the last community on the road out of town that has electricity, so people walk down the mountain from San Sebastián and Garachilla and up from Pozo Seco, La Planta, and Jolotía to meet here, in the middle. The altar holds bright, glittery plastic flowers; half-melted white candles; a photo of Monseñor Romero shellacked onto a wooden frame; and an easel with poster paper and markers. Emilio, the catechist, strums the four functional strings of the communal guitar in a consistent, syncopated *corrido* downbeat in an out-of-tune A-minor, while María Santos, Laura, and Miguel fumble through a dog-eared song book, deciding on an opening hymn.[2]

Folks wait patiently. Polyester skirts from town fall between the knees of women sitting in a circle of plastic chairs as their toes slip in and out of their flip flops, pinching mosquitos from their ankles. Men sit on shadowy benches against the wall of the chapel, hats in hand, or linger in the doorway and windows, listening and keeping an eye on the road. Toddlers sit in mom's or grandma's lap, and older kids scroll between mp3 files and WhatsApp conversations on their phones, waiting for the meeting to begin. It's quiet, except for Emilio's guitar and the occasional rooster.

After a few more minutes, Miguel directs everyone to the song "Pueblo Mío, Tuyo, y Nuestro," a tune from the pamphlet of hymns that a group of ecclesial base communities (CEBs)[3] of El Salvador put together to learn at a music sharing workshop back in 2011. Protective plastic bags crinkle open as participants retrieve their worn copies from crocheted purses and *matatas* around the circle. Those who can't read know the lyrics by heart:

Llegó el momento de empezar,	The time has come to begin
nuevos caminos a buscar,	searching within ourselves
en medio de este pueblo nuestro,	for new ways forward as a people
que busca su libertad.	who desire our own freedom.
Sembraremos semillas de igualdad,	We will plant seeds of equality,
lucharemos por la fraternidad.	we will struggle for fraternity
Y en este pueblo	And among this people,
mío, tuyo, y nuestro,	mine and yours: ours,
nos encontraremos	we find each other
buscando la verdad.	searching for truth.
Y volveremos como la mañana	And we will return like the morning
que a la noche aclara en su despertar.	that brightens the night at dawn.[4]

With this song begins a meeting to finalize plans for commemorating the thirty-seventh anniversary of the massacre in El Chupadero on March 14, 1981. El Chupadero is a small hamlet near El Jocote, and members of the local Chicas Díaz family were among the seventy civilians in the region murdered that day by the Salvadoran army scouring the countryside for guerrilla combatants. For Christians in twenty-first-century ecclesial base communities, the "new ways forward" desired in the hymn begin by continually constructing the people's memory of the past. This year, 2018, the communities—including siblings, nieces, and nephews of the murdered Chicas Díaz family—plan to commemorate the massacre by finally building a small memorial at the site. For those who lived through the war years, this cement memorial will tell their stories to new generations of their *pueblo*.

Side conversations during the meeting include discussions of the recent mayoral elections, in which the communities' candidate, Pablo Amaya, of the left-leaning FLMN party established from guerrilla forces after the country's civil war, lost to the candidate from ARENA, the party formed by retired military generals. ARENA won elections across the country in March 2018, including the mayorship of the national capital, San Salvador, and the majority in the national legislative assembly. With presidential elections looming the following year, FMLN-*istas* accuse party leadership of not listening to the grassroots and bemoan the tendency of their fellow voters to choose a party intent on privatizing major public goods; enforcing policing strategies that have been proven to intensify social violence; and undermining movements for universal health care, education, and food sovereignty.[5] Just as the communities gathered in El Jocote this day remember the political violence of their traumatic past, they also seek to re-member and reimagine a new world in which freedom, equality, human dignity, peace, and justice reign. As Christian, these communities name that new world the reign of God, and they understand themselves as participants in the construction of that reign through their collective work of subversive memory and radical hope.

In recent years, the ministry of Pope Francis has been marked by his calls for the church to become a church of and for the poor. What does a church of the poor look like in practice, and what would it take for privileged churches to enter into solidarity with the church of the poor? The pope himself and those who have been enthused and empowered by the "Francis effect" have stressed the need for the clergy and church hierarchy, along with affluent believers, to imitate Christ by emptying themselves of power and privilege in order to encounter and serve the powerless. While this emphasis on self-emptying for the sake of solidarity with the poor is admirable and necessary, its prevalence in progressive theological discourse too often runs the risk of re-centering the privileged and powerful as the normative protagonists of Christian faith. Francis rightly impresses upon clergy the importance of living among the faithful, inviting them to be "shepherds with the smell of sheep,"[6] but does this metaphor not paint the faithful as a mindless herd of helpless animals in need of someone with greater knowledge and power to guide them? When Francis emphasizes the importance of healing the most basic and grave wounds of humanity by describing the church as a field hospital,[7] does this metaphor include the agency of suffering people themselves to be healers and liberators? Is it the rich church that becomes a field hospital for the poor? Or are the field hospital's healers made up of people living in poverty themselves? As Christians who benefit from coloniality attempt to discern our path forward in becoming a church of and for the poor, centering our own privileged agency runs the risk of reinscribing patterns of the "white savior complex" endemic to colonial Catholicism. Our introductory snapshot of El Salvador's church of the poor, like this book as a whole, seeks to decenter this normative role of the affluent and powerful in the church. In and through this decolonial process, we hope to recognize the rightful place of concrete communities of *lxs pobres* at the center of the church—and indeed at the forefront of the pilgrim church's journey toward the reign of God—as sacramental and incarnational agents of God's healing and liberating activity in history.

ANOTHER WORLD IS POSSIBLE: COLONIALITY AND DECOLONIALITY IN THE TWENTY-FIRST CENTURY

The 1981 massacre of El Chupadero, along with countless other acts of violent political repression in late twentieth-century El Salvador, fits broadly into the more than 500 years of conquest, colonization, neocolonialism, and persistent coloniality in Latin America and the Caribbean and in the world at large. Land-owning elites, largely descended from light-skinned Spanish and creole conquistadors and colonists, had enjoyed the backing of colonial regimes, military governments, the United States, and the institutional Roman Catholic church over the course of centuries. These oligarchs and their military strongmen would stop at nothing—not even killing innocent civilians, including children, in massacres like El Chupadero or the more widely known massacre of El Mozote—to maintain their ironclad grip on power. While the immediate violent repression of those years has thankfully passed, the coloniality of power in twenty-first-century El Salvador persists and can be felt in the entrenched material poverty of the Salvadoran people,[8] the social violence engendered by centuries of trauma and forced dislocation,[9] the subjugation of women and LGBTQ+ persons and widespread violence against their physical and psychological integrity,[10] the deforestation of the land and destruction of local ecosystems,[11] the displacement of rural lifeways and subsistence agriculture,[12] and the desperation of tens of thousands of Salvadorans forced by these conditions to migrate every year to *el Norte*.[13] Over a century of U.S. foreign and economic policy, the ravages of globalized neoliberal economics, the whims of transnational corporations, Western cultural hegemony, and the white supremacy undergirding both conservative and liberal religious sensibilities—all of these interrelated forces have contributed to the persistence of what many scholars and activists in Latin America, the Caribbean, and the Latinx diaspora are calling "coloniality." These scholars and activists are on the vanguard of the interdisciplinary field of decolonial studies, which involves critical reflection on (a) the enduring reality of coloniality in Western economics, politics, culture, and religion and (b) the praxis of decoloniality embedded in myriad forms of resistance to Western modernity that are embodied and enacted by historically marginalized groups and their allies.[14]

Prior to unpacking this field of study a bit more for introductory purposes, it is important to note that decolonial thinkers and activists are in conversation with but distinguish their movement from the related field of postcolonial theory in at least four ways: First, they see the "post" in postcolonial as a misnomer, given the enduring coloniality of knowledge, being, and power today—postcolonial theorists recognize this, of course, but the name itself remains somewhat misleading. Second, the genealogy of decolonial studies is distinctively Latin American and Caribbean, whereas postcolonial theory emerged primarily from the Middle East and South Asia. Third, decolonial scholars understand decoloniality to be primarily a praxis, not a theory. And finally, decolonial thinkers stress that the praxis of decoloniality has been taking place for over 500 years now since the first acts of resistance to European colonization by Indigenous peoples of the lands we now call Latin America and since the first acts of resistance by kidnapped and enslaved Africans.[15]

Most readers will be aware that colonialism refers to direct relations of political, social, economic, cultural, and religious domination that were established in modernity by European empires over the conquered peoples of all continents (e.g., Spain and Portugal over their respective colonies in the Americas). When direct political colonialism ended for many colonized peoples in the nineteenth- and twentieth-century wars for independence,[16] what followed was neocolonialism and Western imperialism, in which the unequal articulation of power continued, with greatest benefits accruing to Europe and to the dominant (i.e., predominantly white, or European-descendent) classes of the United States, along with the dominant local elites of Latin America, Africa, and Asia.[17] The power structure at work in the world today, therefore, is still determined by the power structure put into place under European colonialism. In the words of Peruvian social theorist Anibal Quijano,

> If we observe the main lines of world power today, and the distribution of resources and work among the world population, it is very clear that the large majority of the exploited, the dominated, the discriminated against, are precisely the members of the "races," "ethnicities," or "nations" into which the colonized populations were categorized in the formative process of that world power, from the conquest of America and onward.[18]

Capitalism is central to the operation of these power relations, for the logic of colonialism has always operated in and through what Walter Mignolo articulates as *"the implementation of capitalist appropriation of land, exploitation of labor and accumulation of wealth in fewer and fewer hands."*[19] However, Quijano, Mignolo, and other decolonial thinkers all insist that we understand historical and contemporary coloniality as far more complex and deeply embedded in contemporary power structures than critiques of economic and even political imperialism would allow us to admit.

To get at the depth and complexity of coloniality, Quijano lays out four interrelated domains of colonial dominance and control that coalesce to form what he calls the "colonial matrix of power." First, there is control of the economy, especially through the appropriation and exploitation of land, labor, and natural resources; second, control of authority, especially through political and military might; third, control of gender and sexuality, especially through the dichotomous gender norms of hetero-patriarchy; and fourth, control of subjectivity and knowledge, through Christian faith and theology along with modern rationality. More recently, decolonial scholars have added a fifth node of the matrix: control of nature and natural resources.[20] The fourth node of the colonial matrix of power (subjectivity and knowledge) is the prevailing focus of much decolonial scholarship today. The idea here is that we are not just living within the legacy of colonial politics and economics, but of colonial epistemology and ontology—that is, colonial ways of knowing and modes of existence in the world. As Quijano puts it, colonial repression

> fell, above all, over the modes of knowing, of producing knowledge, of producing perspectives, images and systems of images, symbols, modes of signification, over the resources, patterns, and instruments of formalized and objectivised expression, intellectual or visual. It was followed by the imposition of the use of the rulers' own patterns of expression, and of their beliefs and images with reference to the supernatural. These beliefs and images served not only to impede the cultural production of the dominated, but also as a very efficient means of social and cultural control, when the immediate repression ceased to be constant and systematic.[21]

It is in the realm of knowledge and being, then—of cosmovision, spirituality, imagination, identity, art, and culture—that coloniality sank its deepest roots, roots that continue to thrive and spread unseen today, even in liberal rhetoric of democracy and civil rights, and even in much progressive Christian rhetoric of social justice.

In the conquest and colonization of the Americas, the imposition of Christian doctrine and devotion on Indigenous peoples and enslaved Africans was at the heart of the coloniality of knowledge and being. In fact, Mignolo argues that authoritative "theo-logical" control of knowledge is baked into the glue that holds together the colonial matrix of power. In his words, *"The control of knowledge in Western Christendom belonged to Western Christian men, which meant the world would be conceived only from the perspective of Western Christian men."*[22] Christianity (or rather, Western Christian men), in turn, contributed to the invention and justification of the glue that binds together the colonial matrix of power: racialized and gendered hierarchies of being in which European men possess the exclusive right to ownership of land, labor, and production of knowledge. The Enlightenment offered emancipation from the religious authority of Christianity, but Mignolo points out that modernity's ego-logy and ego-politics of the disembodied rational subject simply replaced Christian theology and theo-politics. Modern Western rationality mirrored Christianity in its "exclusionary and totalitarian notion of [a] Totality . . . that negates, excludes, occludes the difference and possibilities of other totalities."[23] In other words, modernity (along with its constitutive colonial impulse) is grafted directly onto the totalizing tree of Christianity. One universalized source of truth, authority, and "salvation" is simply replaced with another. Sylvia Wynter also argues as much in her own extensive analysis of how the "true Christian self," as the subject redeemed by the Latin Christian Church, transmutes into Man1, as the rational subject of Renaissance humanism and the Enlightenment, which then further morphs into Man2, as the economic (bread)winner in the game of natural selection, according to the laws of economic scarcity.[24] In Mignolo's words again, "the rhetoric of modernity works through the imposition of 'salvation,' whether as Christianity, civilization, modernization and development after WWII, or market democracy after the fall of the Soviet Union."[25] We could spend the rest of this section discussing the coloniality of modern development, technocracy, and neoliberal economics. However, as Christian theologians, we see it as our task to confess and stress that, despite the dominant facade of (post)modern secular liberalism, Christian supremacy and epistemic control persist as a binding force among the nodes of the colonial matrix of power in our world, particularly in the Americas, today.[26]

If, in the words of Nelson Maldonado-Torres, "coloniality refers to a logic, metaphysics, ontology, and a matrix of power that can continue existing after formal independence and desegregation," then what is decoloniality? Maldonado-Torres describes decoloniality as efforts dedicated

> to rehumanizing the world, to breaking hierarchies of difference that dehumanize subjects and communities and that destroy nature, and to the production of counter-discourses, counter-knowledges, counter-creative acts, and counter-practices that seek to dismantle coloniality and to open up multiple other forms of being in the world.[27]

In decolonial praxis, epistemic "delinking" from the coloniality of knowledge opens up the space for multiple ways of knowing and being human. As Christian theologians, we understand this process through the lens of what Walter Brueggemann famously calls the "prophetic imagination"—decoloniality involves critical engagement in the dual prophetic tasks of unmasking and denouncing the dehumanizing "royal consciousness" of coloniality, on the one hand, and, on the other hand, offering hope and an energizing vision for another possible world.[28] The other possible world to which decolonial thinkers and activists aspire aligns with the vision of the Zapatistas—not another world under the control of yet another Totality, but an-other world in which many worlds are free and able to coexist.[29] Over the course of this book, it will become evident that the CEBs' theology of the reign of God offers a robust vision of precisely such an-other world of flourishing diversity and freedom. As historical sacrament of God's reign, the decolonial witness of the Salvadoran church of *lxs pobres* can help us to better understand the decolonial nature of that reign in history, as well as the nature and role of the church in the world.

IS AN-OTHER CHURCH POSSIBLE?
ECCLESIAL BASE COMMUNITIES DECOLONIZE THE CHURCH OF THE POOR

Like the Zapatistas and other popular movements throughout the world, the ecclesial base communities of El Salvador come together to proclaim and embody their conviction that *otro mundo es posible*—another world is possible. As communities of faith, they also proclaim and embody the possibility of another church—*la iglesia de lxs pobres*, the church of the poor. Though the CEBs themselves do not use academic language to categorize their way of being church as explicitly "decolonial" (they understand themselves first and foremost as *Christian* communities, disciples of Jesús of Nazareth), their ecclesial praxis is congruent with many characteristics of decolonial praxis in the secular sphere. The CEBs reject clericalism, sexism, racism, and other structural sins when they appear in the Catholic tradition and they perform alternative ways of being church that seek to overwrite these structural sins. They understand that these colonial trappings of Catholicism in Latin America oppose the coming of the reign of God, and they seek to understand and act to eradicate these enduring impediments so that God's way of building community may flourish.

The Salvadoran CEBs form part of a movement of small Christian communities that emerged throughout Latin America in the years leading up to and following the Second Vatican Council and the subsequent 1968 meeting of the Latin American Bishops' Conference in Medellín, Colombia. Originating in contexts of economic exploitation, political repression, and violent conflict, the CEBs were born as a means for economically impoverished communities of primarily Catholic lay persons to become ecclesial and historical subjects in the struggle for a more just and peaceful society. After centuries of religious justification for colonial and neocolonial oppression, these communities began to understand the God of the Bible as the God of *lxs pobres*, who desires that they have abundant life and liberation from all that hinders such life. With their focus on liberation and their social location on the underside of history, the CEBs have been both inspired by Latin American liberation theology and a *locus* of theological reflection for many liberation theologians.

Accompanied and empowered by radical priests and religious women, the CEBs began their communal and spiritual formation in simple *círculos bíblicos* or biblical circles. The ability to read, listen to, or act out the biblical narrative in the vernacular and in dialogue with the community was a first step toward decolonizing epistemology and social praxis in the CEBs. Urban workers and *campesinos/as* alike began to see themselves in the stories of the colonized peoples of the Bible and began to articulate a liberating faith in the God of *lxs pobres* who desires life and liberation, not oppression and injustice.

The CEBs proceeded to organize themselves for various communal activities oriented toward liberating faith, worship, and social action. Many members were motivated by their newfound understanding of Christian faith to become involved in popular organizing, radical politics, and even some of the armed revolutionary movements of the late twentieth century. The number of CEBs has diminished in the years since the waning of the revolutionary fervor of those decades. There are various reasons for this, including decades of violent repression, loss of key leaders, and diminished support and even antagonism from the clergy and hierarchy of the Roman Catholic church. Furthermore, the base communities that remain and the new ones that have been formed in the twenty-first century do not look exactly like their predecessors.

Nevertheless, a significant movement of base communities still exists across Latin America, and the Salvadoran CEBs are among the most organized and committed on the continent. Although the revolutionary fervor of the late twentieth century has waned and the CEBs have struggled to maintain an open and productive relationship with the Salvadoran institutional church, these communities have persisted in their mission as church of *lxs pobres*, heralds of the reign of God. As such, a new generation of CEBs has evolved to meet the new manifestations and challenges of coloniality in the twenty-first century, embodying decolonial resistance and grace-filled resilience in their praxis of decolonizing the church and society. Our theological reflection in this book draws on the practical theological wisdom of a contemporary network of a number of these communities that form part of a larger National Network of Ecclesial Base Communities. These communities are admittedly a small sampling of the progressive Christian experience in El Salvador.[30] They do not exhaust the experience of the Salvadoran church of the poor, nor are they the only CEBs active in El Salvador, and their experience as CEBs differs from the experience of CEBs in other parts of the country and the continent where clergy and/or the Catholic hierarchy are more supportive.[31] But their experience is a significant one that we believe can shed light on the coloniality of the world and church today, as well as point toward decolonial paths of resistance that build up social and ecclesial alternatives aligned more faithfully with the project of God's reign.

In February 2019, this new generation of Salvadoran base communities gathered together in Zacamil, the first Salvadoran CEB, to celebrate fifty years of existence as an organized and critically conscious *iglesia de los pobres*. One banner displayed at their celebration and shared widely on social media reads, "50 years of resistance and we are not ashamed to continue being the church of the Poor. 1969–2019. CEBs San Romero." In addition to their self-identification as *iglesia de lxs pobres*, the CEBs also refer to themselves as *la iglesia popular*, or the church of the people, and *el pueblo de Dios*, or the people of God. The ecclesiology behind the CEBs' identity is very much inspired by the Second Vatican Council, and the Latin American Bishops' Conference documents from their meetings at Medellín and Puebla. Indeed, these communities are a radical, grassroots embodiment of Pope Saint John XXIII's hope, now famously taken up by Pope Francis, that the church become a church of the poor. While the Second Vatican Council and Francis's reassertion of its pastoral theology have opened up decolonizing possibilities for such a church, we detect a dangerous dimension of coloniality in Roman Catholic church of the poor discourse, which too often centers the generosity and good intentions of the affluent and powerful in the church at the expense of the agency and dignity of the poor and oppressed. Not only is there an apparent lack of commitment to the poor among many of the power brokers of Roman Catholicism, including bishops and affluent parishes in both the Global North and the Global South. There is also, at times, a lingering dose of paternalism in even the most compassionate church of the poor discourse espoused by Pope Francis and progressive European and Euro-American Catholic theologians. We believe that paying attention to the base communities of El Salvador can help to decolonize the theory and praxis surrounding this important ecclesiological principle and the solidarity that it entails. The anti-imperial praxis of the reign of God is an essential element of the CEBs' decolonization of the church of the poor, and unless we as authors and we as a broader church join the CEBs in the project of re-membering the reign of God, our attempts at embodying an-other church will remain hopelessly colonial.

TOWARD A DECOLONIAL THEOLOGICAL METHOD

This book offers notes toward a decolonial ecclesiology informed by the witness and challenge of El Salvador's church of the poor as sacrament of the reign of God. In discerning a path toward this goal, we draw on the methodological foundations of Latin American liberation theology, which recognizes the world of the poor and marginalized as a *locus theologicus* and is committed to the sacramental nature of the pilgrim church. The contemporary CEBs should continue to be a *locus theologicus* for liberation theology and the church today, as their way of discerning, announcing, and preparing for the reign of God reveals something of God's self-gift in history. However, given the lingering coloniality of the church—even in its most modern, progressive, and liberation-oriented strands—we will also look to the theoretical and practical methodologies put forward by decolonial thinkers whose goal is to "delink" from the colonial matrix of power and move toward the creation of other possible worlds. Decolonial scholarship has helped us to understand and articulate the work of the Salvadoran CEBs as a form of decoloniality in practice and, in turn, the CEBs offer a positive, constructive response to decolonial critiques of both Christianity and modernity. Prior to further explication of our methodological approach, however, a decolonial method requires that we first name our own social locations, as well as the particular motivations that have led us to write this book.

Naming Our Own Positionality and Commitments

The reflections we put forward in this volume are necessarily informed by our own social and historical locations. All theological reflection emerges from a particular social context, whether that context is consciously acknowledged and explicitly stated or not. On an individual level, as authors of this project, we ourselves pursue theological questions from within the context of privileged, white U.S. citizenship in Empire. That is, we benefit materially from the enduring dynamics of coloniality that overvalue the color of our skin, our country of origin, and the kind of education we have received. Coloniality wants to convince us that these characteristics make us superior to other human beings and that we must perpetuate systems that reward these characteristics so as to secure stability and survival for ourselves; for our immediate loved ones; and for people who look, speak, and act like us. Such is the logic of whiteness, the ideology and practice on which colonial and contemporary empires are built.[32]

As authors, however, our theological reflection is not hermetically sealed by the bounds of our privilege. The questions that we bring to the study of theology emerge, at least in part, from our frustrations with the inability of white churches in the United States to understand, let alone embody, the radicality of Jesús's subversive proclamation of God's reign as the antithesis of Empire.[33] These questions and frustrations have emerged from our own experiences of marginality in the realms of gender and sexuality, as well as from our relationships, experiences, and conversations with marginalized communities and individuals—especially those who form part of the Salvadoran church of *lxs pobres*. Throughout church history, the world's faith communities have come together to share their testimony and theological questions. This is how theology works, or at least should work—in communal and dialogical pursuit of faith-filled understanding. However, the dialogue too often (nearly always) excludes the voices and experiences of those persons and communities who do not occupy seats of power or enjoy racial, class, gender, sexual, and/or ecclesial privilege. This too is the logic of whiteness, in tandem with the colonial logics of capitalism, patriarchy, and clericalism.

We are convinced, therefore, that Gospel-informed responses to our theological questions and the subversion of our knowledge base cannot come from powerful and privileged churches, which have historically allied themselves with Empire—the *anti-reino*, or the antithesis of God's reign.[34] These churches are complicit with the colonial matrix of power that perpetuates global white supremacy and local dislocations from ourselves, our neighbors, and the land itself.[35] To follow in the Way of Jesús, on pilgrimage to the reign of God, we believe that colonial Christian churches are called to be like Zacchaeus[36] and climb down from the towering tree of our coloniality to see, judge, and act with our proverbial feet on the ground of a concrete, decolonial location. For us, for Liz and Laurel, the CEBs of El Salvador have been that location. Liz spent two years living and working with the Salvadoran CEBs in the early 2000s. Laurel spent six years living and working with the CEBs in the 2010s, and her master's thesis involved community-based participatory research among the CEBs. Both of us continue to be in relationships of friendship and solidarity with members of the CEBs, and Laurel travels to El Salvador regularly to visit, study, and share life with them. While we are both citizens of Empire, with all the power and privilege that entails, we have been gifted with glimmers and glimpses of another way—the way of God's dream for Creation. This is the way of community, dialogue, and interdependence, and this way beckons us to work out of a theological method that is communal, dialogical, and interdependent—a method that is perhaps most aptly named by U.S. Hispanic/Latinx theologians as *"teología en conjunto."*[37] Our own decision to work together on this project is a reflection of our desire to do theology in this way, and so is our commitment to working, as best we can, *en conjunto* with the theological actors and expressions of the CEBs themselves.

Because of these experiences and commitments, the theological method of this book is grounded in the theological conviction that historical and contemporary expressions of ecclesial base communities in El Salvador are a legitimate and privileged *locus theologicus* for the church today, especially if the church seeks to be a "sacrament of salvation"[38] that is "poor and for the poor."[39] With the CEBs as our *locus theologicus*, we situate our methodological approach squarely within the legacy of Latin American liberation theology, but with the aim of uncovering new tools for analysis that are appropriate to our time and place as North American theologians seeking to decolonize Christian theology, Roman Catholic ecclesiology, and the colonial legacy of white Christianity in general. The field of decolonial studies provides these new tools, which we believe will help us to avoid falling into the colonial traps of paternalism and romanticism that can unfortunately undermine the good intentions of progressive theologians in North America and Europe, and perhaps even many liberation theologies and progressive Christians who benefit from coloniality within Latin America proper.

Inspired by the Legacy of Latin American Liberation Theology

The first generation of professional Latin American liberation theologians wrote under the inspiration of the activity of the Spirit at work in both the ecclesial base communities and in the larger movements for social transformation that were afoot during their epoch in Latin American history. In other words, liberation theology emerged not from abstract, ahistorical academic interests, but from the praxis (action *and reflection*) of the CEBs and other historical agents of liberation. Indeed, according to Gustavo Gutiérrez, "the historical womb from which liberation theology has emerged is the life of the poor and, in particular, of the Christian communities that have arisen within the bosom of the present-day Latin American church."[40] Theology is a second moment of reflection on an experience of God in history, and liberation theology is a reflection on the experiences of the poor and marginalized of a liberating God who is active in their own struggles to be free from oppression. This cycle of experience, reflection, and renewed action is typically described as the dialectical process of "see-judge-act." The CEBs use this model to read the signs of the times, to reflect on scripture, and to guide their involvement in their societies. We follow their lead in our own methodological approach—moving between (a) observation and description of both the enduring legacy of coloniality and the decolonial praxis of the historical and contemporary CEBs, (b) critical reflection on these realities in dialogue with scripture and the Christian faith tradition, and (c) critically informed suggestions for praxis.

We recognize that Latin American liberation theologians have been critiqued for their perceived deification of the poor and the situation of the poor as their starting point and *locus theologicus*.[41] Perhaps we will be critiqued similarly for our centering of *lxs pobres* in our reflections on the church of the poor as sacrament of God's reign. What these critiques overlook is the deeply theological—indeed, Christological—motivation for this methodological commitment. The preferential option for the poor in the liberationist method derives not from ideological principles. Rather, it derives from the biblical witness and Christian faith tradition in which the crucified Christ is present and re-crucified in the poor and oppressed—that is, in the "crucified people."[42] Moreover, the risen Body of Christ is present and active in the struggles of the poor and oppressed for dignity and liberation—that is, in the church of the poor as sacrament of liberation, as sign and efficacious manifestation of the reign of God.[43] As Jon Sobrino puts it, the *locus theologicus* is not only social but *theologal*, meaning that it is a place in which God's presence and saving power are experienced and embodied in history.[44] Therefore, the *locus* not only produces a particular reading of the traditional sources of theology, but also actualizes and makes present certain contents of those sources, thus becoming a source itself.[45]

Pedro Trigo similarly argues that it is not only the suffering of the crucified peoples that is a reliable theological place for encountering Christ in contemporary history, but that the everyday *living* of impoverished people reveals God at work in the world. Trigo emphasizes that wherever poor human beings *live* despite limited access to the basic conditions necessary to sustain life—adequate food, clean water, dignified housing, education, health care, and so on—and especially where poor people live *human* lives of mutual care—"by choosing what is human despite contextual incitement toward inhumanity"—there we can be sure of the presence of the Spirit of life.[46] Trigo points to globalization, to the commodification of human lives and labor, and to the totalitarianism of the market as the forces at work in contemporary Latin America that oppose God's desire for full and dignified life for all Creation.[47] These are forces that both descend from and contribute to the enduring reality of coloniality and stand against the reign of God that was announced by Jesús. This world of human life amid inhuman conditions—the world of *lxs pobres*—is a sign of God in history today and therefore a legitimate and necessary source for theology. In this book, it is the Salvadoran church of *lxs pobres* that is a sign of God's inbreaking reign in history today, and is thus a legitimate and necessary source for both eschatology and ecclesiology.

Out of these experiences of a God of Life in the world and church of the poor, theological reflection is made possible. More than concrete content, the world of the poor and the church of the poor offer us a light by which privileged Christians might see what would be difficult to see without such illumination.[48] Neither Trigo nor Sobrino intend to romanticize the world of the poor or suggest that poverty is necessary for Christian living. Nor do they reduce the mystery of God to God's presence in and among the poor. Rather, they identify that the world of the poor is a reliable source for encounter with the God of Jesucristo because in the world of the poor and marginalized there is life amid death, humanity amid inhumane conditions. For the church, then, the lives of the poor and marginalized masses of humanity—especially when these masses come together as a people and as the People of God[49]—should be a special authority for our reflections on how to follow Jesus as communities of faith in the contemporary world. This preferential option for the perspectives and experiences of the excluded and impoverished stands in direct contradiction to the claims of coloniality, which prefers the knowledge, bodies, and power of the dominant elites—of those at the center of world history. Thus, our theological method already begins to bleed into decolonial praxis: the CEBs' experience of God from within a context of life amid death is the *locus* for our theological reflection.

Toward a Decolonizing Theological Method

In his book, *Decolonial Love: Salvation in Colonial Modernity*, Joseph Drexler-Dreis argues that the liberationist method of first generation Latin American liberation theologians like Ellacuría, Sobrino, and Gutiérrez opens up the possibility of a decolonial theology insofar as they encounter the world of the poor and enter into dialogue with that world as "theologically pedagogic."[50] Encountering God in and theologizing from the world and church of the poor certainly unsettles the colonial epistemology and ecclesiology of Roman Catholicism. However, Drexler-Dreis points out that decolonial theological reflection must go a step further, "expanding sources of theological thought, de-centering the epistemologies that are pedagogic for theological reflection from a Eurocentered and 'continental' orientation, and ultimately decolonizing concrete theological images."[51] Drexler-Dreis's analysis here relies here on feminist, mujerista, and queer Latin American liberation theologians, most notably Marcella Althaus-Reid, who has asserted that her predecessors in the field have had a tendency to romanticize the Latin American poor, and therefore have simply reinscribed the "decent" theological narratives of Western, patriarchal Christianity.[52] In the language of decolonial studies, the first generation of Latin American liberation theologians only scratched the surface of the colonial matrix of power, thus leaving the complex, intersectional, and ontological depths of coloniality unscathed. What's more, Latin American liberation theology is known in the English-speaking world primarily, and at times even exclusively, for its first generation of iconic, male, ordained theologians, many (if not most) of whom are of predominantly European descent. The rich diversity and more thoroughly decolonial nature of contemporary Latin American theology—feminist, queer, Indigenous, Afro-descendent—is eclipsed by the problematic prominence of these emblematic men, however admirable they may be.

Even more pertinent for our study, we fear that the theological method of the first generation of Latin American liberation theologians has not made enough room for the theological insights of the CEBs themselves to directly and/or concretely inform and challenge their theological reflection. Latin American ecclesial base communities have been their own *locus* for socially conscious, liberating theological reflection since the very early days of their inception.[53] The people of the CEBs themselves have produced theological knowledge that could fill volumes in and through their own "critical reflection on praxis in light of the Word of God."[54] Biblical circles were a salient feature of the early CEBs, where members would reflect theologically on the Bible in relation to the realities of their social, economic, and political lives. For example, the famed community of Solentiname in Nicaragua gathered weekly in the 1970s to discuss how the Gospel offered insight for understanding and acting on the realities of wealth inequality, political violence, and social exclusion. And vice versa, discussion also centered around how the community's lived reality and Christian praxis shed light on the theological realities to which the biblical text bears witness.[55] Similarly, the base communities of El Salvador have been producers of theological knowledge, some of which we hope to convey in these pages. Over the course of more than five decades, the Salvadoran CEBs have published bits and pieces of their theological reflections in booklets, pastoral manuals, personal testimonies, communal histories, and so on. But they also engage in theological reflection in and through their oral traditions, songs and music, artwork, and other communal reflections that have been inscribed in the hearts and minds of the people. The fact that these reflections—published or not—are not accessible to the theological academy in North America and Europe does not mean that they are not significant and insightful contributions to the local and universal church's self-understanding as sacrament of salvation.

A decolonial theological method decenters the voices of male clerics and academic theologians, however admirable and trailblazing they may be. In turn, this method places at the center of its theological reflection the lived realities, struggles, hopes, joys, and insights of concrete communities of poor and oppressed peoples organized for their liberation. And yet this book is not a historical, sociological, anthropological, or ethnographic study of the CEBs. Rather, it is an attempt at decolonial theological reflection on the reign of God and the church of *lxs pobres* in conversation with the base communities as our principal source of theological wisdom. Therefore, we draw on written, oral, and artistic-creative resources generated by the CEBs themselves, including self-curated histories, personal testimonies, resources and curricula for pastoral work, songs, murals, protest banners and slogans, liturgical celebrations, press releases, social media posts, and their ecclesial "architecture"—the spaces where they celebrate liturgy, the altars they create, and the memorials, like the one at El Chupadero, that they build into their own environments. Other important sources for this book include participatory action research that Laurel conducted with the CEBs in 2015 for her graduate work at the Jesuit University of Central America,[56] as well as interviews that Laurel and her colleague José Gómez Martínez conducted with a cross-section of CEBs' membership in 2017 and published in the volume *Sigue porque la vida sigue: Voces de las comunidades eclesiales de base de El Salvador ayer y hoy*.[57] These sources often express conflicting or contradictory points of view, as even the CEBs in El Salvador—a small expression of the church universal—are not monolithic in their experiences of God or their theological reflection. We find these conflicts to be proof of real human expression, of persons in dialogue seeking communion. Indeed, holding space for such diversity is characteristic of a decolonial method, given the decolonial vision of a world in which many worlds are possible.

Sometimes these resources conflict with wider academic appraisal of the Latin American church. Indeed, the lack of recent scholarship on the CEBs may suggest that they no longer form a significant part of the church, that Latin American liberation theology was a failed initiative relegated to the annals of history, or even that their way of being church was misguided at best and heretical at worst. Additionally, the attention that the Latin American Catholic church does receive continues to center around the first Latin American pope, his rehabilitation of liberation theology, and the witness of recently canonized Archbishop Romero. These are all worthy topics for reflection, to be sure, but the centering of these male clerics creates the misperception that their witness to the mystery of divine liberation has the last word and is somehow more authoritative and significant than the witness of the people whom they have loved and served and learned from as pastors. In response to these misconceptions, we posit that the enduring epistemic violence of coloniality has produced the continued marginalization of contemporary Latin American theology and the work of the base communities in the global conversation. How many contemporary Latin American scholars have been translated into languages beyond Spanish and Portuguese? Does the practical and theoretical work of grassroots popular movements like the CEBs ever come to the attention of, let alone carry any weight within, theological academy? Just because this work is not being published in the English-speaking world does not mean that the church of the poor in the Majority World has stopped struggling to bring their experiences of the divine into their daily and communal lives in a meaningful way. By prioritizing the CEBs' own self-expression and by using resources they have had a hand in creating, we hope to re-member their ongoing history and to give reason to hope for the decolonial reign they announce.

A Brief Word about Words

It bears mentioning here that we have made some deliberate choices with regard to our use of language in this book. First, the base communities themselves, as communities of people living in varying degrees of poverty, have a strong sense of class consciousness as *las/los/lxs pobres*, which includes a critical consciousness of how their experiences of poverty stem from root causes of having been impoverished by an oppressive and exploitative global economic system. The CEBs critically and consciously claim this identity as their own and are "not ashamed" to proudly define themselves as *la iglesia de los/las/lxs pobres*.[58] We see the CEBs' use of the term *pobres* as akin to the decolonial use of the term *damnés* to indicate both the masses of colonized peoples damned to struggle for survival under the yoke of the colonial power matrix and movements of colonized peoples who act in history as critically conscious agents of decoloniality.[59] The CEBs' use of *las/los/lxs pobres* incorporates critical consciousness and orientation toward praxis, whereas common usage of the category of "the poor" in English often carries with it traces of paternalism and an assumption of passive victimhood. In contemporary times, the Latin American CEBs' use of *pobres* also includes poverties beyond the core experience of economic poverty, including women's experiences of sexism, Indigenous and Afro-descendent people's experiences of racism and colorism, ableism, classism, anthropocentrism, and hetero-patriarchy. The affirmation of *pobres* is a challenge to the entire matrix of colonial death. Therefore, henceforth we generally employ the Spanish *lxs pobres* where and whenever we are referring to the CEBs' self-understanding and, conversely, we generally use the English term "the poor" in contexts of statements about the poor made by the nonpoor (e.g., ecclesial documents). Finally, while the CEBs' oral usage of the term usually incorporates both the masculine and feminine articles, *los* and *las*, their written communication sometimes uses the gender-neutral *lxs*. Throughout the book we employ this written convention for both the purposes of efficiency and affirmation of the impulse in the CEBs toward gender-neutral language. The exception to this is when we are quoting directly from texts that use *los*, *las*, or both.

Second, we have also chosen to use the Spanish spelling of the name for Jesús and Jesucristo where and whenever we are referring to the way in which Jesus is understood by the CEBs—as *el pobre jornalero*, a laborer from Nazareth who announced and inaugurated the reign of God. We use the English spelling in references to Jesus outside of decolonial experiences and expressions of Jesús the liberator.[60]

Third, we use other Spanish words and phrases throughout the book, usually accompanied by translations, but sometimes not, depending on the context, readability, and/or translatability of a word, phrase, or sentence. Western Christian theology is often published in English with entire phrases, sentences, and paragraphs in Latin, Greek, German, or French, without the benefit of translation for the reader who is unfamiliar with those languages. Our strategic use of Spanish throughout the book is intended to break with the dominance of these "academic" languages and lift Spanish up as a legitimate scholarly language in the field of academic theology. This is a small step toward decolonizing theological studies, but it is an important one.

Fourth, we have made the decision to retain most of the real names of people, places, and organizations that inform our research where and whenever possible, particularly in the case of previously published personal and communal testimonies, as well as in reference to other sources that we have been granted express permission to use. In other cases, names and places are either changed or omitted entirely.

Finally, all translations from sources cited in Spanish are our own.

ROADMAP OF THE BOOK

Our overarching thesis in this book is that the Salvadoran CEBs, as a self-identified embodiment of the church of *lxs pobres* in El Salvador, are a decolonial sacrament of the reign of God in human history. As such, they can and should inform the way we think about and act upon what it means to be the church and journey toward God's reign in a world of enduring coloniality. The book is divided into two parts.

Part I takes an unconventional and creative approach to telling the story of the CEBs through the lens of what we dare to call "Salvadoran Salvation History." This section is patterned after books, genres, and themes of the biblical narrative, offering twenty-two *libritos*, or little books of sacred stories that are central to the Salvadoran base communities' self-understanding, historical memory, and theological outlook. The purpose of this section is not to present a scholarly historical or anthropological account of the CEBs' emergence and evolution over the past fifty years, but to creatively highlight the moments and movements in their historical memory that carry particular theological significance for their understanding of God's presence and action in and among the people of the land that is now known as El Salvador.

These narratives begin with an account of the deep roots of both coloniality and the church of *lxs pobres* in the *librito* of "Colonio-Genesis." We then proceed through narratives attesting to the church's initial steps toward a new exodus from coloniality in the twentieth century, prophetic *libritos* of twentieth-century heroes and martyrs, Gospel accounts of the first ecclesial base communities, acts of repatriated communities in the postwar era, epistles from new base communities formed in recent decades, epistles attesting to an evolving relationship with the institutional church, prophetic *libritos* from contemporary CEB leadership, and revelations of the new challenges and opportunities facing the CEBs in the twenty-first century. These *libritos* are each preceded by an introduction offering background information and a framework for understanding the place of each *librito* in the larger story of the Salvadoran church of *lxs pobres*.

In this section, we follow the CEBs' insistence on keeping historical memory alive, but the reader will do well to keep in mind that these sacred stories are more theological witness than historical record. While we as authors paraphrase and weave together the narrative in "Colonio-Genesis," most of these *libritos* simply contain excerpts from primary sources, the CEBs' archival materials, and other historical accounts that attest to the presence of the God of Life and the promise of God's reign in the midst of the death-dealing, *anti-reino* powers of coloniality. We see the placement of these stories and sources at the beginning of the book, rather than in an appendix, as a decolonial act of insistence on their immense value as theological witness. We invite our readers to immerse themselves in these sacred stories in order to re-center and re-member the base communities as ecclesial agents of God's reign in human history, prior to turning to theological reflection on them as such in part II.

Part II of the book draws on sources from part I and other primary sources from the CEBs to reflect theologically on the decolonial witness of the Salvadoran church of *lxs pobres* as a historical sacrament of God's reign. In chapter 1, "*Sacramento histórico del reino de Dios:* Decoloniality and the Eschatological Horizons of El Salvador's Church of *lxs Pobres*," we lay the theological foundations for the CEBs' decolonial witness in their understanding of the reign of God and what it means to be church of *lxs pobres*. We argue that, in the eschatology of the CEBs, the reign of God is a decolonial reality in which all people are free to exercise their subjectivity and live life in abundance. As pilgrim church, the CEBs' ecclesiology is founded on and oriented toward their eschatology, such that their identity and praxis as church of *lxs pobres* is determined by their relationship with God's reign. Their self-professed identity as the church of *lxs pobres* on pilgrimage to God's reign of abundant life represents a paradigmatic instance of the decolonial turn in which *lxs pobres* delink from coloniality and make a preferential option for *lxs pobres*.

Chapter 2, "*Tomamos la palabra:* Decolonial Knowledge in the Salvadoran Church of *lxs Pobres*," describes and analyzes the decolonization of knowledge production that has taken place in the base communities over the course of more than fifty years. This process has taken place in and through the CEBs' dialogical pastoral method, their commitment to historical memory, and their prophetic praxis of denouncing the forces of the *anti-reino* and announcing the good news of God's dream of abundant life for all Creation. We place the CEBs' decolonial epistemic praxis in critical conversation with Roman Catholic ecclesiology, pointing toward decolonial horizons in the CEBs' theological accounts of ecclesial tradition and teaching authority.

Chapter 3, "*Celebramos la vida*: Decolonial Being in the Salvadoran Church of *lxs Pobres*," describes and analyzes the CEBs' praxis of decolonial being in and through their aesthetic creations of personal/communal narrative and narrative theology, visual arts and *artesanía*, music and song, and liturgy and sacrament. Placed in critical conversation with Roman Catholic ecclesiology, these creative expressions and the CEBs' theological reflections on them point to decolonial horizons in the ontology of the ordained priesthood, sacramental theology, and liturgical inculturation.

Chapter 4, "*Luchamos por la justicia*: Decolonial Power in the Salvadoran Church of *lxs Pobres*" describes and analyzes the CEBs' praxis of decolonizing power in and through their organized commitment to mutual aid and action for social transformation. The CEBs' ecclesial ministry *ad extra*—for the sake of an-other world in which many worlds are free to exist—cannot be severed from their ecclesial ministry *ad intra*—for the sake of an-other church in which the structures of governing authority reflect the universally distributed subjectivity and abundant life of God's reign. Therefore, the CEBs pose a decolonial challenge to Roman Catholic structures of governance with their witness to the ecclesiological possibilities available in a model of organized, rather than hierarchical, communion.

Our fifth and final chapter considers the possibilities of decolonial solidarity for privileged Christians who benefit from the coloniality of power. In this chapter, entitled "*Si el grano de trigo no muere*: The Challenge of Decolonial Solidarity," we articulate how the CEBs' decolonial praxis challenges privileged churches that benefit from coloniality to enter into solidarity with the church of *lxs pobres* along with other marginalized communities in local and international contexts, and to thereby participate in the decolonial project of God's reign. We place the praxis of solidarity in and among the CEBs into dialogue with decolonial studies and the concept of solidarity in Catholic social thought in order to reimagine and re-member the possibility of decoloniality for the privileged.

CON LA HERMANDAD Y SOLIDARIDAD DE SIEMPRE

While we take full responsibility for any shortcomings in these pages as the result of our own limitations, we must also insist that it would not have been possible to complete this project without the witness and collaboration of the Salvadoran ecclesial base communities themselves. First and foremost, we owe a tremendous debt of gratitude to the members of these communities for forming and shaping and loving us as human beings and as people of faith at critical points in our lives. This book is our humble attempt to honor their *lucha* and their impact on us and so many others who have been transformed by their friendship and wisdom. We hope that, in turn, this book will expand that impact to others who have not had the blessed opportunity to travel to the land of *el divino Salvador*. When volunteers and delegations from the United States visit the Salvadoran CEBs to learn from the history of El Salvador and its *iglesia popular*, we almost invariably ask what we can do to practice solidarity with their struggles for justice and peace in their society. In response, the people of the CEBs often indicate that their guests should return home to the United States to share the stories we have heard with our own churches, communities, families, students, and elected officials. Whatever the limitations of this book may be, we hope that it serves as a means of fulfilling this purpose and expressing our gratitude for the honor of entrusting us with this task.

Given the centrality of the CEBs' own witness in this project, it seems fitting that we offer our particular words of acknowledgment and thanksgiving here in the Introduction, rather than in an easily bypassed Acknowledgments section. The Salvadoran base communities that contributed immensely to our own personal and theological development include Jardines de Colón, Tierra Nueva, Las Mesas, Los Naranjos, El Triunfo, El Limón, and Agua Escondida in La Libertad; Agua Blanca, Junquillo, La Hacienda, San Pedro, Guachipilín, El Rusio, El Salamo, Estancia, Colón, Jimilile, San Miguelito, and Yancolo in the municipality of Cacaopera, Morazán; El Ocotillo, Mons. Romero, Torola, and Segundo Montes in the municipalities surrounding Perquín, Morazán; Pueblo de Dios en Camino, San Romero, Nuevo Amanecer, Santa Cecilia, Zacamil, San Antonio Abad, and El Paraíso in greater San Salvador; Tierra Blanca and Nueva Esperanza in Usulután; and the CEBs of Nahuizalco in Sonsonate. The oral traditions we have been privileged to hear in these communities over the years, along with their artwork, music, memory practices, liturgies and more, are all foundational for the reflections in this book.

We offer special words of thanks to some of those whose own words grace these pages: the communities that participated in Laurel's research in 2015—San Romero, Pueblo de Dios en Camino, Nuevo Amanecer, and Segundo Montes—and the women and men whose testimonies make up the treasure that is *Sigue porque la vida sigue*: José Tomás Luna, Santiago Portillo, Rogelio Ponselle, Reina Greisi Leiva, Gustavo Ramos, Avelino Castro, Anita Ortiz Luna, Agustín Luna, Miguel Zepeda Santos, María Ángela Domínguez Pérez, Andrea Guadalupe Meléndez Moreno, and José Adonay Pérez. We also express our gratitude to FUNDAHMER, a Salvadoran NGO, that places its work at the service of the base communities and facilitates relationships of international solidarity with them. Without their unceasing commitment to the communities and their international counterparts, we might have never encountered the witness of El Salvador's church of *lxs pobres*. Finally, a research symposium on the church of the poor that we convened in 2019 yielded rich insights and further refinement for our research and writing process and we thank the following individuals for their participation: Ana Ortiz Luna, José Salvador Cornejo Ruíz, Teresa Moreno de Melendez, Armando Marquez Ochoa, and María Elena Sanabria de Cruz. We offer all of these individuals and communities not only our sincerest thanks for their witness and particular collaboration in this project, but the *compromiso* of our sisterhood and solidarity forever. ¡Que viva la iglesia de lxs pobres!

NOTES

1. "How could my heart not be filled with joy at a church where ecclesial base communities are flourishing!" Óscar Arnulfo Romero, Homily, September 10, 1978, *Homilías*, vol. 3, San Salvador: UCA Editores, 2005.
2. Names of people and cantons are changed in this vignette.
3. Throughout this book, we refer to ecclesial base communities by their Spanish acronym, CEBs, which stands for *comunidades eclesiales de base*.
4. Gilmer Torres, *Pueblo Mío, Tuyo, y Nuestro*, from lyrics accessed February 13, 2020 at http://siembracanciones.blogspot.com/2008/09/este-pueblo-mo-tuyo-y-nuestro.html.
5. Indeed, a third-party candidate, Nayib Bukele, won the 2019 presidential elections, with unprecedented support from disillusioned FMLN *militantes*. See Gene Palumbo and Elisabeth Malkin, "Nayib Bukele, an Outsider Candidate, Claims Victory in El Salvador Election," *New York Times*, February 3, 2019, https://www.nytimes.com/2019/02/03/world/americas/salvador-bukele-election.html.
6. Pope Francis, Chrism Mass Homily, March 28, 2013.
7. Antonio Spadaro, SJ, "A Big Heart Open to God: An Interview with Pope Francis," *America*, September 30, 2013. https://www.americamagazine.org/faith/2013/09/30/big-heart-open-god-interview-pope-francis.
8. See Guillermo Cruces et al., "The Growth-Employment-Poverty Nexus in Latin America in the 2000s: El Salvador Country Study," World Institute for Development Economics Research, United Nations University, September 2015, https://www.wider.unu.edu/sites/default/files/wp2015-077.pdf.
9. See Eduardo Sancho, "Causa de la Violencia en El Salvador: El Apartheid Social," *Realidad y Reflexión* 38 (2015): 101–113.
10. See Shannon Drysdale Walsh and Cecilia Menjívar, "Impunity and Multisided Violence in the Lives of Latin American Women: El Salvador in Comparative Perspective," *Current Sociology* 64, no. 4 (July 2016): 586–602. See also Amaral Palevi Gómez Arévalo, "Entre la Espada y la Pared: Movilidad Forzada de Personas Salvadoreñas LGBT," *Mediações* 22, no. 1 (2017): 130–155.
11. See Dahr Jamail, "El Salvador's Environmental Crisis," *Al Jazeera*, February 21, 2011, https://www.aljazeera.com/indepth/features/2011/02/201122017470922665.html. See also Heather Gies, "Once Lush, El Salvador Is Dangerously Close to Running Dry," *National Geographic*, November 2, 2018, https://www.nationalgeographic.com/environment/2018/11/el-salvador-water-crisis-drought-climate-change/#close.
12. See Heather Gies, "El Salvador's Disappearing Farmers," *Al Jazeera*, September 12, 2018, https://www.aljazeera.com/indepth/features/el-salvadors-disappearing-farmers-180911145112205.html.
13. Cecilia Menjívar and Andrea Gómez Cervantes, "El Salvador: Civil War, Natural Disasters, and Gang Violence Drive Migration," *Migration Information Source*, Online Journal of the Migration Policy Institute, August 29, 2018,
  https://www.migrationpolicy.org/article/el-salvador-civil-war-natural-disasters-and-gang-violence-drive-migration.

14. See, for example, Walter Mignolo, *The Darker Side of Western Modernity: Global Futures, Decolonial Options* (Durham, NC: Duke University Press, 2011); Walter Mignolo and Arturo Escobar, eds., *Globalization and the Decolonial Option* (London: Routledge, 2010); Nelson Maldonado-Torres, "On the Coloniality of Being: Contributions to the Development of a Concept," *Cultural Studies* 21, nos. 2–3 (2007): 240–70.

15. For a more in-depth exploration of the complex relationship between postcolonial thought and Latin America, see Mabel Morana, Enrique Dussel, and Carlos A. Jáuregui, eds., *Coloniality at Large: Latin America and the Postcolonial Debate* (Durham, NC: Duke University Press, 2008).

16. Of course, true political decolonization was not the result of independence for colonized Indigenous and Afrodescendent persons living within the nation-states of Europe and the Americas, nor was it the case for remaining protectorates and commonwealths of the United States, Britain, and France (e.g., Puerto Rico).

17. Aníbal Quijano, "Coloniality and Modernity/Rationality," *Cultural Studies* 21, nos. 2–3 (2007): 168.

18. Quijano, "Coloniality and Modernity/Rationality," 169.

19. Walter Mignolo, "Delinking," *Cultural Studies* 21, nos. 2–3 (2007): 477, https://doi.org/10.1080/09502380601162647. Emphasis in the author's original.

20. See Walter Mignolo, *Desobediencia Epistémica: Retórica de la Modernidad, Lógica de la Colonialidad, y Gramática de la Descolonialidad* (Buenos Aires: Ediciones del Signo, 2010), 12 and 79–80.

21. Quijano, "Coloniality and Modernity/Rationality," 169.

22. Mignolo, "Delinking," 478. Emphasis in the author's original.

23. Mignolo, "Delinking," 451.

24. Sylvia Wynter, "Unsettling the Coloniality of Being/Power/Truth/Freedom: Towards the Human, After Man, Its Overrepresentation—An Argument," *New Centennial Review* 3, no. 3 (2003): 257–337.

25. Mignolo, "Delinking," 463.

26. To cite just three examples:

1) The majority of white evangelicals supported the arguably racist and colonial policies of President Donald Trump in the United States, and administration officials have seen fit to use scripture to justify the separation of migrant families and detention of children at the U.S. southern border. See Gregory A. Smith, "Among White Evangelicals, Regular Churchgoers Are the Most Supportive of Trump," Pew Research Center, April 26, 2017. https://www.pewresearch.org/fact-tank/2017/04/26/among-white-evangelicals-regular-churchgoers-are-the-most-supportive-of-trump/. See also "Sessions Cites Bible Backing Immigration Policy," AP Archive, posted June 20, 2018, https://www.youtube.com/watch?v=ZxZRW-DAzPo.

2) Far-right president of Brazil, Jair Bolsonaro, came to power thanks to his evangelical base. Bolsonaro is notorious for licensing extractive business practices that are destroying the Amazon rainforests at unprecedented rates, and he has also appointed an evangelical ex-missionary to head the government agency that oversees isolated Indigenous tribes. See Chayenne Polimédio, "The Rise of the Brazilian Evangelicals," *Atlantic*, January 24, 2018, https://www.theatlantic.com/international

/archive/2018/01/the-evangelical-takeover-of-brazilian-politics/551423/; Marcelo Teixeira, "Brazil Amazon Deforestation Soars to 11-year High Under Bolsonaro," *Reuters*, November 18, 2019, https://www.reuters.com/article/us-brazil-deforestation/brazil-amazon-deforestation-soars-to-11-year-high-in-2019-idUSKBN1XS1PK; Dom Phillips, "'Genocide' Fears for Isolated Tribes as Ex-Missionary Named to Head Brazil Agency," *Guardian*, February 5, 2020, https://www.theguardian.com/world/2020/feb/05/brazil-indigenous-tribes-missionary-agency-ricardo-lopes-dias-christianity-disease.

3) Backers of the 2019 coup d'etat in Bolivia, which overthrew Indigenous president Evo Morales, employed Christian rhetoric to "cleanse" the government of "satanic" influences. See Tom Phillips, "'Satan, Be Gone!': Bolivian Christians Claim Credit for Ousting Evo Morales," https://www.theguardian.com/world/2020/jan/27/bolivian-christians-evo-morales-indigenous-catholic-protestant.

27. Nelson Maldonado-Torres, "Ten Theses on Coloniality and Decoloniality," 10, http://caribbeanstudiesassociation.org/docs/Maldonado-Torres_Outline_Ten_Theses-10.23.16.pdf.

28. See Walter Brueggemann, *The Prophetic Imagination*, 40th Anniversary Edition (Minneapolis, MN: Fortress Press, 2018).

29. See Mignolo, "Delinking," 463, and the Zapatista articulation of this motto: "The world that we desire is one in which many worlds fit. The Homeland that we are building is one in which all peoples and their languages fit, that is traversed by all paths, that all may enjoy, that is made to dawn by all." Comité Clandestino Revolucionario Indígena-Comandancia General del Ejército Zapatista de Liberación Nacional, "Cuarta Declaración de la Selva Lacandona," January 1, 1996, http://enlacezapatista.ezln.org.mx/1996/01/01/cuarta-declaracion-de-la-selva-lacandona/.

30. Anna L. Peterson has published two studies featuring the progressive Christian communities of Chalatenango based on fieldwork in that region of El Salvador during the 1990s. See *Martyrdom and the Politics of Religion: Progressive Catholicism in El Salvador's Civil War* (Albany, NY: State University of New York Press, 1997) and *Seeds of the Kingdom: Utopian Communities in the Americas* (New York: Oxford University Press, 2005).

31. Moreover, evangelical and Pentecostal forms of Christianity exert a tremendous attraction for people living in poverty in El Salvador, and across Latin America more broadly. For two significant studies of comparisons between CEBs and Pentecostalism, see Cecília Loreto Mariz, *Coping with Poverty: Pentecostals and Christian Base Communities in Brazil* (Philadelphia, PA: Temple University Press, 1994) and Philip D. Wingeier-Rayo, *Where Are the Poor? A Comparison of the Ecclesial Base Communities and Pentecostalism—A Case Study in Cuernavaca, Mexico* (Eugene, OR: Pickwick Publications, 2011).

32. For some preliminary literature on whiteness, see Stephen Middleton et al., eds., *The Construction of Whiteness: An Interdisciplinary Analysis of Race Formation and the Meaning of White Identity* (Jackson, MS: University Press of Mississippi, 2018); George Yancy, ed., *Whiteness and Christology: What Would Jesus Do?* (New York: Routledge, 2012); and Willie James Jennings, *After Whiteness: An Education in Belonging* (Grand Rapids, MI: Eerdmans, 2020).

33. See, for example, the following analyses of Jesus, the reign of God, and Empire: Antonio Gonzalez, *God's Reign and the End of Empires* (Miami, FL: Convivium, 2012); Jeorg Rieger, *Christ and Empire: From Paul to Postcolonial Times* (Minneapolis, MN: Fortress, 2007); and Richard A. Horsley, *Jesus and Empire: The Kingdom of God and the New World Disorder* (Minneapolis, MN: Fortress, 2003).

34. Jon Sobrino develops this concept in many of his writings. See, for example, *Jesus the Liberator: A Historical-Theological Reading of Jesus of Nazareth* (Maryknoll, NY: Orbis Books, 1993).

35. See Willie James Jennings's analysis of whiteness as a logic of dislocation in *The Christian Imagination: Theology and the Origins of Race* (New Haven, CT: Yale University Press, 2010).

36. Jennifer Harvey, "What Would Zacchaeus Do?" in *Whiteness and Christology: What Would Jesus Do?*, ed. George Yancy (New York: Routledge, 2012), 84–100.

37. See, for example, José David Rodríguez and Loida I. Martell-Otero, eds., *Teología en Conjunto: A Collaborative Hispanic Protestant Theology* (Louisville, KY: Westminster John Knox, 1997).

38. *LG* § 48.

39. *EG* § 198.

40. Gustavo Gutiérrez, *A Theology of Liberation, Revised Edition with a New Introduction* (Maryknoll, NY: Orbis, 1988), xxxiii.

41. See, for example, the Congregation for the Doctrine of the Faith, "Notification on the Works of Jon Sobrino, SJ," November 26, 2006.

42. For a detailed account of the identification of the oppressed masses as the "Crucified People" and the "Suffering Servant of Yahweh" and how it is that they are a "light for the nations," see the following: Ignacio Ellacuría, "The Crucified People," in *Mysterium Liberationis: Fundamental Concepts of Liberation Theology*, eds. Ignacio Ellacuría and Jon Sobrino (Maryknoll, NY: Orbis, 1993), 580–603; Sobrino, *Jesus the Liberator*, 254–271; Jon Sobrino, *Witnesses to the Kingdom: The Martyrs of El Salvador and the Crucified Peoples* (Maryknoll, NY: Orbis, 2003), 155–166; and Kevin Burke, "The Crucified People as 'Light for the Nations': A Reflection on Ignacio Ellacuría," in *Rethinking Martyrdom*, eds. Teresa Okure et al. (London: SCM Press, 2003), 120–130. See also Elizabeth O'Donnell Gandolfo's critical engagement with the concept in *The Power and Vulnerability of Love: A Theological Anthropology* (Minneapolis, MN: Fortress, 2015).

43. See Ignacio Ellacuría, "Church of the Poor, Historical Sacrament of Liberation," in *Ignacio Ellacuría: Essays on History, Liberation, and Salvation*, ed. Michael E. Lee (Maryknoll, NY: Orbis Books, 2013), 227–253.

44. See Ignacio Ellacuría's essays "The Historicity of Christian Salvation" and "Christian Spirituality," both of which are available in English translation in Michael E. Lee, ed., *Ignacio Ellacuría: Essays on History, Liberation, and Salvation* (Maryknoll, NY: Orbis Books, 2013). This neologism originates in the philosophy of Xavier Zubiri, Ellacuría's doctoral adviser, and is employed extensively in the liberation theology of Jon Sobrino.

45. For example, Jon Sobrino argues that any Christology that takes seriously the presence of Christ in history, thus avoiding a form of "christological deism," not only

operates out of a specific historical location, but also asks itself how Christ—crucified and risen—is actually present in the particular signs of the times that characterize that location. See Sobrino, *Jesucristo Liberador* (San Salvador: UCA Editores, 1991), 54–59.

46. Pedro Trigo, "Donde encontramos a Dios hoy en América Latina y lo que se le opone en esta época global," in *Desafíos de una teología iberoamericana inculturada en tiempos de globalización, interculturalidad y exclusión social: Actas del Primer Encuentro Iberoamericana de Teología*, eds. Luis Aranguren Gonzalo and Félix Palazzi (Miami, FL: Convivium Press, 2017), 53.

47. Trigo, 48 ff. See also Pedro Trigo, *Cómo relacionarnos humanizadoramente: relaciones humanas entre personas y en la sociedad* (Caracas: Centro Gumilla, 2014), Chapters 3–4.

48. See Sobrino, *Jesus the Liberator*, 33.

49. The martyred Salvadoran archbishop Óscar Romero encouraged this dynamic movement from masses to people to People of God throughout his ministry: "The mass apostolate ought to be a liberating response by the church, helping the masses to become a people, and helping the people to become the people of God." Romero's Fourth Pastoral Letter, "The Church's Mission amid the National Crisis" (August 6, 1979), in *Voice of the Voiceless: The Four Pastoral Letters and Other Statements* (Maryknoll, NY: Orbis Books, 2020), 167.

50. Joseph Drexler-Dreis, *Decolonial Love: Salvation in Colonial Modernity* (New York: Fordham University Press, 2019). It is important to note here that Drexler-Dreis distinguishes the incipiently decolonial methodology of Gutiérrez and Ellacuría from that of Clodovis Boff, whose method relies more heavily on Eurocentric social sciences as epistemologically foundational for socio-analytic mediation as the initial phase of theological reflection.

51. Drexler-Dreis, 69.

52. See Marcella Althaus-Reid, *Indecent Theology: Theological Perversions in Sex, Gender, and Politics* (New York: Routledge, 2000).

53. It is important to note here that lay apostolates like Catholic Action predate the CEBs in Latin America and were likely a *locus* of popular theological reflection as well. Furthermore, the laity have always engaged in theological reflection in their everyday lives. However, we aver that the CEBs seem to represent something new and different—a thoroughly conscious, concientized, and deliberate, intentional effort to theologize together in community.

54. Gutiérrez, *A Theology of Liberation*, 5 ff.

55. Ernesto Cardenal, *The Gospel in Solentiname* (Maryknoll, NY: Orbis, 2010).

56. See appendices in Laurel Anne Marshall, *Un gesto vale más que mil palabras: las comunidades eclesiales de base de El Salvador en la construcción de celebraciones eucarísticas y bautismales* (Actions Speak Louder than Words: Base Ecclesial Communities in El Salvador in the Construction of Eucharistic and Baptismal Celebrations) (Master's Thesis, San Salvador: Universidad Centroamericana "José Simeón Cañas," 2015).

57. José Gómez and Laurel Anne Marshall, eds., *Sigue porque la vida sigue: Voces de las comunidades eclesiales de base de El Salvador ayer y hoy* (Winston-Salem, NC: Library Partners Press, 2020).

58. *"No nos avergonzamos de ser la iglesia de los pobres"* ("We are not ashamed to be the church of *lxs pobres*") is a phrase invoked by the CEBs on banners and call-and-response chants to express their pride in both their ecclesial and their social/cultural identities. See chapter 1.

59. See Nelson Maldonado-Torres, "Outline of Ten Theses" and "On the Coloniality of Being," *Cultural Studies* 21, no. 2 (2007): 240–270. Maldonado-Torres draws on the work of Frantz Fanon to develop his account of the *damnés*.

60. This is the approach taken by Miguel De La Torre in *The Politics of Jesús: A Hispanic Political Theology* (Lanham, MD: Rowman & Littlefield, 2015), 76: "The linguistic sign *Jesus* provides coded access to the object it signifies, which masks a relationship of power. *Jesús* provides a very different coded access that masks a different relationship of power. Jesus is not Jesús, for Jesus means something different that masks certain power structures that justify the power and privilege of the dominant culture, while Jesús signifies liberation and resistance. Of course all languages fall short of fully describing the reality of deity. . . . Yet regardless of limitations of language, to the dominant culture, Jesús represents the ethnic stubbornness (or stupidity) that resists assimilation to what is perceived as an intellectually superior culture possessing a correct theological interpretation of divinity."

Part I

UN LARGO CAMINAR

SALVADORAN SALVATION HISTORY

Colonio-Genesis

This first *librito* of Salvadoran Salvation History tells of the origins of what is now known as the Republic of El Salvador. As such, it is also the story of the origins of the enduring matrix of coloniality on this land. Beginning with a brief, mythic re-membering of this corner of Creation before colonization, the story lapses into the arrival of Spanish conquerors brandishing the sword, the cross, and new diseases that wiped out a stunning percent of Indigenous life, changing Creation forever.

A major source for this account is the book *Historia de El Salvador: de cómo la gente guanaca no sucumbó ante los infames ultrajes de españoles, criollos, gringos, y otras plagas*,[1] a popular illustrated account of Salvadoran history published by Equipo Maíz, a cooperative, popular education press in El Salvador. Equipo Maíz produces accessible, informative resources for a general audience of various degrees of literacy and offers popular education workshops on a spectrum of topics ranging from Indigenous history or biographies of San Romero to illustrated guides for understanding legislative bills. Their *Historia de El Salvador* is a frequently referenced and widely accepted resource among the CEBs. Though contemporary historians complicate *Historia*'s claims and should be read alongside this popular account for a suitably complex understanding of Salvadoran history, *Historia de El Salvador* remains an important starting point for understanding popular Salvadoran consciousness as it manifests itself in the historical memory of the CEBs. We therefore draw on this book as a framework for tracing the broad strokes of Salvadoran salvation history, as understood and recounted by the Salvadoran church of *lxs pobres*.

This sacred story communicates how coloniality has shaped the Salvadoran narrative through the mid-twentieth century. As a sacred story of salvation history, it also suggests that God was not absent from the Salvadoran story throughout these long centuries, though neither we nor the CEBs consider the colonizing religion of the Spanish to be the theological *place* of this story. Rather, together with the CEBs, we sense the presence of the divine to be in the survival of the colonized and impoverished masses, despite continual oppression. If this account focuses primarily on the actions of the colonists and Salvadoran elites, it is only to reveal how miraculous the continued life of *lxs pobres* has been throughout this history. From the first Nahua-Pipil peoples who fought back against Pedro de Alvarado to the first dispossessed agitators for independence, to those who protested when communal lands were abolished, to the insurrectionists of 1932, to every *abuela* today who teaches Nawat to students from the National University, and to every ancient, endangered *tarro* seed planted with care on a terraced hillside, Latin American—here, Salvadoran—Christianity as it exists today was not the result of the imposed "evangelization" of the colonizers but rather the creative syncretic work of Afro-Indigenous communities and other *pobres* despite idolatry and heresy:

> Many colonized peoples perceived that the forced introduction of Christianity during colonial rule did not so much deliver the sacred as threaten to annihilate it. The arduous process of forging Latin American Christianity was therefore one of concentrated artistic, cultural, and spiritual production as indigenous, African, and mestizo peoples in Latin America worked on the imposed European Christianity to make it a usable, potent, and sacred religion.[2]

In the historical memory of the CEBs, the God of scripture was present to and active in this history through the struggle for life of those on the margins. It is for this reason that we present their historical roots not only as catastrophic destruction, but as salvation history.

BEFORE THE CONQUEST

1 In the beginning was the land. And it sloped from the sea up the mountains to a spine of volcanoes: Izalco, Ilamatepec, Quezaltepeque, Guazapa, Chinchontepec, and Chaparrastique. There were no borders or divisions on the land. All manner of plants and trees existed: *tarro, pasta, papaturro, ayote, huerta, ocote, guanacaste, pito, copinol,* and *ceiba*. And there were all kinds of animals, birds, and fish: *tigre y venado,*[3] *garrobo, cusuco, mono, cotusa, lechuza, perico, mojada, guabinas, tepemechín, filín, mojarra, chacalín, camarón,* and *golomina*.[4] The rains fell, and flowers bloomed. The rains dried up and fruits burst forth from every tree: *aguacate, cacao, marañón, jocote, guineo, mango, papaya,* and *nance*. The human beings who lived with the land lived also with a profound

sense of the sacred; they possessed "a certain awareness of a hidden power, which lies behind the course of nature and the events of human life . . . this awareness and recognition result[ed] in a way of life that is imbued with a deep religious sense."[5]

Many peoples inhabited the land. Their ancestors were the Maya.[6] They passed down the *Popol vuh* and knew human beings to be created from corn and water, as they themselves were. They built great temples and drank cacao when they met there. They developed their own calendar and writing system, and they were advanced in astronomy, architecture, and mathematics. The Maya grew their own beans, tomato, *yuca, jícama, ayotes,* and many varieties of maize they domesticated from wild *teosinte*. Their land was held in common, and they traded using cacao pods as currency. They lived for many years in this way until they migrated elsewhere, fleeing volcanoes, war, and tired earth.

The children of the Maya were the Lenca and the Kakawira. They lived east of the Lempa River in the mountains.

The Nahua peoples[7] lived west of the Lempa River in the *cacicazgos*[8] surrounding their capital, Cuscatlán.[9] The Nahua also lived in Izalco, Apanecatl,[10] Apastepetl,[11] and other territories. They had emigrated from the north and spoke Nawat. They used the human body as the basis for understanding the natural world: a hand had five fingers, so they counted by fives. Five were the extremities of the human body, and five were the points of a distant star. Seven were the orifices of the body, and so seven were the openings to the underworld, marked by *ceiba* trees.

The Nahua used *tarro, morro,* and *tecomate* gourds as dishes, for carrying and storing water, and for brewing *chicha*. They wove hammocks from *henequén* and *petates* from palm fronds for sleeping and resting. The Nahua used clay *comales* and *ollas* for cooking over fires, and they ground their food on sloping *molcajete* stone. They wove *matatas* from palm fronds and *canastos* from reeds.

The Nahua *cacique* was chosen by the warriors, and, together with the priests and nobles, lived off of what the merchants, artisans, plebeians, and slaves produced. They worshipped their own gods, Quetzalcoatl (the rising or birthing sun), Tlaloc (the goddess of the rain), Tonatiuh (the midday or adult sun), and Metzi (the moon). They put each human life under the protection of a *nahual*.

INVASION AND CONQUEST

2 When the King Ferdinand II of Aragon married Queen Isabella I of Castile, they formed the Catholic kingdom of Spain. To expand their political and religious reign, they sent their armies to the lands where the Maya, Nahua, and Inca peoples

and their descendants lived. When the Spaniards met the peoples who lived on the land, they did not ask, "Why are you?" They asked, "What are you?" and decided that the people were not beloved by the Spanish god as they themselves were.[12] The Spanish invaded lands to the north of Cuscatlán, and their priests claimed the land for the Spanish god.[13] As the Spanish empire expanded to the south, Pedro de Alvarado was ordered by Hernán Cortés to conquer Cuscatlán,[14] and he invaded in 1524 at La Hachadura.[15] The Nahua fought fiercely, and during the battle at Axacual,[16] they shot Pedro de Alvarado in the leg with an arrow. In a letter to Cortés, Alvarado wrote:

"Here, in this battle, they [the Nahua] hurt many of my Spaniards, and me along with them. They shot me with an arrow that went through my leg and right into my seat. I remain wounded from this injury, and one of my legs remains four fingers shorter than the other."[17]

The Nahua also fought the Spanish at Tacuxcalco[18] and in many other battles. They fought so fiercely against the Spaniard's horses, war dogs, armor, swords, and firearms that it took the Spanish fifteen years to conquer Cuscatlán. When they conquered it, they renamed it San Salvador.

The conquerors destroyed the Nahua holy places and made the Nahua people worship their god. They took Nahua land and made the Nahua work for them growing food and crops they could sell in Spain, like cacao and indigo. They also infected the Nahua peoples with new sicknesses like measles and smallpox. In 100 years, 90% of the conquered peoples in all the region were dead.

Fifty-four Spanish conquerors divided the land now called El Salvador among them, and still they complained because they did not have any gold.

SPANISH COLONIALISM

3 In those days, the Spanish enforced the *encomienda* system, which allowed the remaining Nahua to hold some land on which they grew corn and beans and paid heavy tributes to the Spanish:

"After conquering a territory, Indigenous men and their wives were distributed among the victors.

Indigenous men had to work for them [the Spanish] or pay them a tribute of products like corn, beans, cotton, honey, wax, salt, textiles, etc. The tribute was paid by the male head of house, so Indigenous men were pressured to marry at an early age.

Supposedly, the *encomienda* obligated the Spanish to 'protect' their Indigenous people and to educate them in the Catholic faith. But this was the least of their concerns, since the Spanish were more interested in exploiting them and gaining the highest profit possible.

Indigenous people were obligated to buy products brought by the

Spanish at a high price, even when the Indigenous people did not want to buy.

Indigenous women were given a certain quantity of cotton or thread that they were obligated to spin or weave for a very low price. Because they were given so much work, women often had to weave, even when they went to Mass."[19]

Spanish priests did not agree on how the conquerors should treat the Nahua people and their descendants. Some priests held land, taxed Nahua farmers, and forced the Nahua to take care of their horses, cattle, and enslaved Africans.[20] Juan Ginés de Sepúlveda, a court theologian, defended the conquerors to King Charles V, saying that the Nahua and other native peoples of the Americas were slaves by nature and that "the barbarians may be submitted to our domain by the same right that they can be compelled to hear the Gospel."[21] Other priests, like Bartolomé de las Casas, proclaimed, "I prefer an unbaptized but alive Indian than one who is dead but Christian."[22] He argued that enslavement of Nahua people should be illegal.[23] Las Casas's prophetic words persuaded the king to promulgate the New Laws of 1542, which outlawed slavery and the *encomienda* system and regulated further Spanish invasions. However, the New Laws angered the Spanish conquerors, and the viceroy of New Spain, Antonio de Mendoza, was not strict in applying them.[24] The abuses continued, and the cries of the people rose to the heavens.

INDIODEPENDENCE

After many years, the creole descendants of the Spanish conquerors stopped being loyal to the Spanish king and wanted to control the land and the people for themselves. The people, descendants of the Nahua of enslaved Africans, and of the Spanish, wanted to be free of oppression, induced labor, and poverty. They knew that the oppression they were suffering was wrong, and they let their oppressors know it.

The first "cry of independence" was in 1811 when popular protests broke out in San Salvador and surrounding colonial cities, including Santiago Nonualco, Chalatenango, Sensuntepeque, Metapán,[25] and Santa Ana.[26]

The provincial vicar of San Salvador, Fr. José Matías Delgado, initially supported the demonstrations, ringing church bells in encouragement, but later took a stance in opposition to the rebellions, saying, "Insolent men have dazzled [you] with false ideas of apparent goods and have driven you to the precipice ... thus, it is essential to abandon, for our part, these inopportune requests that only can be borne of the heat and flurry of this commotion."[27]

Popular uprisings continued to upset the social and political landscape until creole landholders throughout Central America declared independence from Spain in the Guatemalan capital on September 15, 1821, as a last attempt to secure control. The Central

American Act of Independence admits, "Since Independence from the Spanish Government is the general will of the people of Guatemala . . . the Lord Political Chief will publish it as such in order to prevent the consequences, which would be terrible, in the case that independence be declared in fact by the people."[28] Indeed, the Salvadoran priests and politicians who signed the Act of Independence, including Fr. Delgado, were large landholders; on average, they each held over 7,500 acres.[29] Salvadorans today often refer to Central American Independence as a "New Dependence" or as "Indio-dependence."[30]

THE SALVADORAN REPUBLIC

5 The Spirit of the God who liberates was at work among the people, who began to rise up against their new governors almost immediately. Remaining lands were seized by creole politicians, higher taxes were levied, men were forcibly recruited to the armed forces, and poverty continued to characterize everyday life. Communities in Tejutla, Chalatenango, San Vicente, and Zacatecoluca organized to oppose these policies, but examples were made of local leaders to terrorize the people into submission.[31]

The new creole rulers also wanted to have all the political power, so they worked to reduce the influence of their priests and the bishop of Rome. To achieve this goal, Francisco Morazán, one of the early Central American Heads of State, "expelled religious orders, abolished tithes and offerings and confiscated church lands, granted freedom of religion, and passed a divorce law. But these changes only favored the dominant classes. The situation of the people and, above all, of the Indigenous population, worsened by the day, since they had to pay taxes that did not exist before, and once wars began, they were forcibly recruited to fight for causes that they did not understand and which did not favor them."[32]

The new creole rulers accepted investment from a rising Northern empire to make coffee a lucrative export. Merchants and markets in the United States financed the construction of railroads throughout Central America so that the people of that far-off land could buy products like coffee and bananas.[33] Slowly, the United States began to replace Spain and other European countries as the Central Americans' main market partners. This meant that the United States also wanted to promote Central American politicians and laws that benefited their business interests in the region. The president of the United States, James Monroe, declared that the United States, not Europe, had rights to control Central American resources and politics.

6 Once they had enough riches from exporting coffee, some creole elites formally separated from the rest of Central America and established the Republic of El Salvador. This was in 1859, in the presidency of Gerardo Barrios, when James Buchanan was president of the United States, and Pius IX was bishop of Rome.

As Salvadoran elites cultivated more and more coffee, the Salvadoran people became more and more impoverished. When the Salvadoran government had sold all of the land that had been held by Spain and much of the land that had been held by the Catholic church, they seized land from *lxs pobres* to sell to large landowners who could plant coffee and generate more wealth for the country.

In order to take land from the people, President Rafael Zaldivar outlawed communal lands and *ejidos*. Most of the legislative representatives were large coffee growers, and they supported the president.

Without land to farm, the Salvadoran people had to work for wages on bigger *haciendas*. They would work in the landowner's coffee fields and plant their own *milpas*,[34] but they had to give the landowner a large part of their harvest as rent to use the land. Families would run out of corn before the next harvest and have to buy their own corn back from the large landowners with the wages they made from working on his *hacienda*.[35] Often, workers were paid in *fichas*[36] that could only be used to buy food from the same *hacienda*'s store.[37]

IMPERIALISM AND THE GREAT DEPRESSION

7 By the beginning of the 1900s, the U.S. empire had grown in power and exerted strong influence over Salvadoran economics and politics. U.S. businesses and government entities owned Salvadoran railroads and mines and loaned money to the Salvadoran government in exchange for a 70% share of all customs taxes.[38]

Some Salvadoran leaders, like Manuel Enrique Araujo, opposed U.S. imperial rule, but in 1913 the Quiñónez-Meléndez family took over the Salvadoran presidency. For fourteen years, they favored U.S. intervention and violently repressed political opposition. They prohibited political meetings and protests by instituting a long-standing curfew enforced by the National Guard.

By the end of the Quiñónez-Meléndez dynasty, workers were very unhappy and began to unionize, forming the Regional Federation of Workers of El Salvador (FRTS). This organization became the principal labor union for urban and rural workers, men and women, and they organized strikes and protests to demand labor laws that protected workers.

8 In the time of U.S. president Herbert Hoover and Salvadoran president Pío Romero Bosque, Pius XI being bishop of Rome, the crash of the U.S. stock market on Black Tuesday produced a global economic crisis known as the Great Depression.

The global price of coffee fell, and many government employees and peasants in El Salvador lost work. Those that remained were given receipts for collecting wages at a future date. Because the Depression lasted quite a long time, many workers sold their wage receipts for half their value in order to buy food. The large landowners and bankers who bought the receipts later cashed them in to the government for their full value.[39]

Before the Great Depression, a day laborer on a coffee farm earned fifty cents and two meals of beans and tortilla per day. After the crisis, that same labor was worth twenty-five cents and two meals.[40] Women workers were paid even less and given less food at mealtimes. The FRTS and its affiliates protested more and more frequently, and the Salvadoran Communist Party (PCS) was founded by unhappy workers in March 1930. Government security forces doubled down on their violent repression, especially in rural areas.[41]

The military wanted a president that would put an end to the peasant rebellions, so they staged a coup d'etat in December 1931 and installed General Maximiliano Hernández Martínez as president. The people called him "El Brujo."[42]

LA MATANZA OF 1932

9 In January 1932, *lxs pobres* in Santa Tecla, Colón, Izalco, Armenia, Nahuizalco, Juayúa, Tacuba, and Ahuachapán rose up against the government. Most of the people worked on coffee farms and were Indigenous. Hernández Martínez and his government repressed the insurrection cruelly; at least 10,000 campesinos were murdered and some count up to 30,000 dead. The leaders of the insurrection were killed by firing squad on February 1.[43] The cries of the people rose to the heavens and the God of *lxs pobres* cried out for justice and life along with them.

10 After the massacre, oligarchs donated large sums to the government and the military to patrol rural populations. The military founded the Civic Guard, civilians who collaborated with the army in spying on their neighbors. This pitted *lxs pobres* against *lxs pobres*, since members of the Civic Guard could accuse any person with whom they had a conflict as subversive.[44] During this time, Indigenous customs including dress, language, and religious observance became highly suspect. Christina Ramírez, a survivor of La Matanza, speaks about the pressure she felt to stop wearing a *refajo*:[45]

"I came back from Guatemala when it was all over and my friends told me to stop wearing a *refajo* because it could get me killed; one of them even offered to go with me to buy a dress, and I told her I would go buy one on my own. But in my own mind, I told myself that I didn't owe anybody anything . . . in those times, nobody went out in the streets, you never saw men outside, they killed everybody. Other people were captured and taken away. Another friend told me that her sons were at home one day, eating lunch, when soldiers arrived and 'bam, bam!' they were killed with no questions asked."[46]

The priests of the Catholic church in El Salvador openly supported Hernández Martínez because they were opposed to communism.[47] In a pastoral letter, Archbishop Belloso wrote, "a Catholic who is part of any socialist system runs the risk of contaminating himself with heresy. . . . Greater evils are accrued by socialist institutions founded on idealistic principles than by traditional [institutions] with all their deficiencies, scourges, and deformities."[48] After the massacre of 1932, many Catholic masses were celebrated in thanksgiving to their god for the repression.[49]

BETWEEN MASSACRE AND CIVIL WAR

11 For the next several decades, the Salvadoran military, backed by the increasingly powerful oligarchy, continued to control the government and repress popular opposition with increasing levels of violence. A "Police Law" penalized and imprisoned men who didn't have formal employment, and playing dice, cards, or sports was viewed as vagrancy, punishable by fines. Civilian spies called *orejas*[50] infiltrated community and union meetings, on high alert for any whiff of communism.[51] The Civic Guard and the *orejas* coalesced into the ironically named Nationalist Democratic Organization (ORDEN), which functioned as a terrorist organization during the Salvadoran Civil War.

The United States maintained high levels of interest and involvement in El Salvador during this time. After the triumph of the Cuban Revolution, the United States recruited El Salvador to the "Alliance for Progress," an attempt to quell popular discontent and avoid anti-capitalist rebellion. The gods of power and wealth were well pleased.

At the same time, the God of Life was at work in the Salvadoran people who continued to organize and struggle for their rights to land, dignified work, and peace. Professionals, factory workers, farmers, and students grew in knowledge and formed strong popular movements to protest injustice in the face of state repression.

Nuevo-Exodus

The ex-hodos (Gk., "a way out") stories of Salvadoran salvation history are stories of the forging of "a new way" for *lxs pobres* to think about their role in the church. Where Colonio-Genesis tells the story of how the land we now call El Salvador came to be colonized and how the foundations for enduring coloniality were established, the stories of this at least partial exodus from coloniality are some of the accounts of ecclesial epistemic, creative, and systemic liberation that opened the way for ecclesial base communities to take root and grow in the Salvadoran church. Though the stories of this ecclesial exodus are not complete without the accompanying stories of this people's struggle for political and civil liberation (vis-à-vis the growth of labor unions, farmworker's organizations, and professional and student movements, all of which worked hand in hand with ecclesial bodies and were comprised mostly of lay Catholics), this *librito* focuses on the specifically ecclesial transformation that was born of ecclesial reform movements ignited before the Second Vatican Council and the conciliar experience itself.

The main action of this *librito* takes place between 1965 and 1970, immediately before and concurrent with the formation of the country's first ecclesial base communities. These stories represent the ecclesial circumstances that, while informed by many pastors' work with rural lay women and men, also opened space for the faithful to strengthen their own participation in the church. They are by no means, however, the first or only accounts of resistance to coloniality. It would be unfaithful to the centuries of Indigenous and *campesino* struggle to characterize the lay faithful of El Salvador in the first half of the 1900s as entirely submissive to a natural view of history and a premodern Catholic imagination, as the truncated version of this story often does.[52] In the testimony of the following *libritos* of the Prophets Anastasio Aquino, Prudencia Ayala, and Farabundo Martí, the thread of resistance running throughout Salvadoran history suggests a shared subjective—albeit fractured and diffuse—consciousness among the colonized. Even the fact that Indigenous language, customs, food, and art have survived centuries of marginalization and violent repression challenges the assertion that lay Salvadorans fatalistically assumed the worldviews imposed by agents of colonial power. Rather, we see the events of the mid-1900s as a boiling over, as a tipping point of decolonial rage and love that had been present and growing among *lxs pobres* for centuries.

The *librito* opens with the *"Poema de amor"* by Salvadoran poet Roque Dalton, which has been interpreted musically by nearly every professional and amateur musician in the *pulgarcito*.[53] The idea of loving the rude, disparaged, uncultured image of a *guanaco*[54] that Dalton paints introduces the logic of loving *lxs pobres* in the flesh, the ideal of the efforts described in the rest of the book. The first formal section of this *librito* then presents three movements beyond the Salvadoran church that made its own exodus from empire possible: Vatican II (1962–1965), specifically the "Pact of the Catacombs"; the *Instituto Pastoral de Latinoamérica* (IPLA, first formed in 1967), a pastoral formation school formed by bishops who signed the Pact and backed by the CELAM; and the conclusions of the CELAM's meeting in Medellín, Colombia (1968), which brought Vatican II to bear on the Latin American reality. The second section of the *librito* highlights the diverse initiatives of the church of *lxs pobres* in El Salvador: local *"campesino* universities," new ministerial praxes that arose out of communities' needs, the National Week of a *"pastoral de conjunto"* (pastoral teamwork) in 1970, and the establishment of the first lay-led organizations that accompanied the church of *lxs pobres* when the clerics could or would not (CONIP and CEBES). The *librito* ends ambiguously, as those same seats of ecclesial authority that penned the documents quoted here—episcopal seats, parish priests, Rome itself (see §6)—felt their hearts hardened and called the people back. While the hierarchical "Nuevo-Exodus" was over before it began in El Salvador, the church of *lxs pobres* had changed irreversibly and would not go back.

LOVING THE DAMNED

1 Salvadoran poet Roque Dalton knew well how to love the damned:

"Those who widened the Panama Canal (and were classified 'silver roll' and not 'gold roll'),

the ones who repaired the Pacific fleet on the bases in California,
the ones who rotted in the jails of Guatemala, Mexico, Honduras, Nicaragua, for being thieves, smugglers, swindlers, for being hungry,
the ones who are always suspected of everything

('permit me to haul you in as a
   suspect for hanging out on corners
   suspiciously, and furthermore with the
   pretentious air of being Salvadoran'),
the ones who packed the bars and
   brothels of all the ports and capitals
   of the region
('The Blue Cave,' 'Hot Pants,'
   'Happyland'),
those planters of corn deep in foreign
   jungles,
the kings of cheap porn,
those who no one ever knows where
   they come from,
the best craftspeople in the world,
those who were stitched by bullets
   crossing the border,
the ones who died of malaria or from
   the sting of scorpions, or yellow fever
   in the hell of the banana plantations,
those drunkards who cried for the
   national anthem
under Pacific cyclones and northern
   snows,
the moochers, the beggars, the dope
   pushers,
guanaco sons of bitches,
the ones who hardly made it back,
the ones who had a little more luck,
those eternally undocumented,
those jacks-of-all-trades, those hustlers,
   those gluttons,
the first to flash a knife,
the sad, the saddest of all the world,
my people, my brothers."[55]

EXODUS OF THE PEOPLE OF GOD

2 The colonial church could never love the damned like this, but the God of *lxs pobres* was at work chipping away at hearts of stone. As the Second Vatican Council drew to a close, about forty bishops celebrated an evening eucharist in the Catacombs of Domitilla, where they professed their commitment to the poor and ratified the following commitments to evangelical poverty, known as the Pact of the Catacombs:

"We, bishops assembled in the Second Vatican Council, are conscious of the deficiencies of our lifestyle in terms of evangelical poverty. Motivated by one another in an initiative in which each of us has tried to avoid ambition and presumption . . . we will try to live according to the ordinary manner of our people in all that concerns housing, food, means of transport, and related matters. See Matthew 5:3; 6:3ff; 8:20.

We renounce forever the appearance and the substance of wealth, especially in clothing (rich vestments, loud colors) and symbols made of precious metals. See Mark 6:9; Matthew 10:9–10; Acts 3:6 (neither silver nor gold).

We will not possess in our own names any properties or other goods, nor will we have bank accounts or the like. If it is necessary to possess something, we will place everything in the name of the diocese or of social or charitable works. See Matthew 6:19–21; Luke 12:33–34.

As far as possible, we will entrust the financial and material running of our diocese to a commission of competent laypersons who are aware of their apostolic role, so that we can be less administrators and more pastors and apostles. See Matthew 10:8; Acts 6:1–7.

We do not want to be addressed verbally or in writing with names and titles that express prominence and power (such as Eminence, Excellency, Lordship). We prefer to be called by the evangelical name of 'Father.' See Matthew 20:25–28; 23:6–11; John 13:12–15.

In our communications and social relations we will avoid everything that may appear as a concession of privilege, prominence, or even preference to the wealthy and the powerful (for example, in religious services or by way of banquet invitations offered or accepted). See Luke 13:12–14; 1 Corinthians 9:14–19. . . .

Since the collegiality of the bishops finds its supreme evangelical realization in jointly serving the two-thirds of humanity who live in physical, cultural, and moral misery, we commit ourselves: a) to support as far as possible the most urgent projects of the episcopacies of the poor nations; and b) to request jointly, at the level of international organisms, the adoption of economic and cultural structures which, instead of producing poor nations in an ever richer world, make it possible for the poor majorities to free themselves of their wretchedness. We will do all this even as we bear witness to the gospel, after the example of Pope Paul VI at the United Nations. . . .

May God help us to be faithful."[56]

3 The Spirit at work in the Pact of the Catacombs was at work across the Americas in the Southern hemisphere and shaped the work of God's people in many ways and through many pastoral initiatives. The Pastoral Institute of Latin America (IPLA)[57] was one initiative that came to bear much fruit in the land of *el divino Liberador*. Indeed, it bore fruit in the witness of prophets and martyrs, such as Padre Rutilio (Tilo) Grande, SJ:

"In this way, Tilo arrived at one of the most important and creative sources of Latin American pastoral work. Truly, the IPLA had opened a path that many had traveled since before Medellín. In fact, the IPLA made Medellín possible, in part, by creating a channel for the exchange of pastoral and theological thought. There, for the first time, the need for a specifically Latin American theology was debated. It was out of the IPLA that the reality of Latin America and of the Latin American church was discovered. At the beginning, the IPLA was conceived as a traveling school, which traveled to almost all Latin American countries facilitating pastoral courses until 1967, when it became an institute with a fixed headquarters. After 1968, the IPLA worked out of Quito, by decision of the CELAM. Two exceptional men were linked to this enterprise and impressed upon it their character, Manuel Larraín, Bishop of Talca (Chile), and Leónidas Proaño, Bishop of Riobamba (Ecuador). . . .

On April 22, 1968, Proaño, in his inaugural speech, defined the objectives of the IPLA as an instrument with which all Latin America would discover a pastoral method appropriate for each need and circumstance. As a consequence, the primary and fundamental task of the IPLA would be a clear and objective uncovering and familiarity with the Latin American reality. From this knowledge of the reality would emerge theological reflection, and this would evolve into pastoral planning. The IPLA would strive to cultivate originality, dynamism, and a community spirit as specific characteristics. To do so, the pastoral courses would transmit a mysticism 'that brings [students] to the audacity and creativity of the Spirit.'"[58]

The pedagogical methodology of the IPLA was markedly different from the seminaries where Tilo and other clerics had received their priestly formation. Space was opened up for the God of Life to enter in and transform God's people for the sake of God's reign:

"The IPLA course was not reduced to academic activities, but rather involved the contributions of pastoral experiences shared by participants, intense community life, teamwork, and liturgical celebrations, which made for an intense ecclesial and Latin American experience. Upon finishing a first phase, the participants completed field research, directed by sociology and anthropology professors. The participants assumed direct responsibility for the direction of the course, and they organized complementary talks and seminars. To finish the course, they had to create, individually or in teams, a pastoral monograph."[59]

4 *Con-spirando* with the God of Life, new ways of being church began to emerge among *lxs pobres* in the form of *comunidades eclesiales de base*. Where the princes of the colonial church would have repressed these affirmations of God's Spirit at work on the underside of history, the hearts of the Latin American bishops continued to soften toward the people. At their meeting in Medellín, Colombia, in 1968, the bishops wrote:

"The Christian ought to find the living of the communion to which he has been called in his 'base community,' that is to say, in a community, local or environmental, which corresponds to the reality of a homogeneous group and whose size allows for personal fraternal contact among its members. Consequently, the Church's pastoral efforts must be oriented toward the transformation of these communities into a 'family of God,' beginning by making itself present in them as leaven by means of a nucleus, although it be small, which creates a community of faith, hope, and charity. Thus the Christian base community is the first and fundamental ecclesiastical nucleus, which on its own level must make itself responsible for the richness and expansion of the faith, as well as of the *culto* which is its expression. This community becomes then the initial cell of the ecclesiastical structures and the focus of evangelization, and it currently serves as the most important source of human advancement and development.

The essential element for the existence of Christian base communities is their leaders or directors. These can be priests, deacons, men or women religious, or laymen.[60] It is desirable that they belong to the community which they animate. The selection and formation of leaders ought to be a matter of highest priority for parish priests and bishops, who must always be mindful that moral and spiritual maturity depends in large measure on the assumption of responsibilities in a climate of autonomy.

The members of these communities, 'living in accord with the vocation to which they have been called, exercise the functions that God has confided to them, priestly, prophetic and royal,' and thus make of their community, 'a sign of the presence of God in the world.'"[61]

A NEW WAY FOR THE SALVADORAN CHURCH OF LXS POBRES

5 In imitation of the IPLA, pastoral and theological training centers were established in El Salvador to make way for the liberation promised by the God of *lxs pobres*:

"Probably the most popular element of the popular church in El Salvador was the *centros de formación campesina* (peasant training centers, also known as *universidades* *campesinas*, or peasant universities). These centers were not unique to El Salvador, since similar projects existed in Guatemala and Nicaragua, but the Salvadoran program was probably the most extensive. Each of El Salvador's five dioceses (San Vicente, San Miguel, Santa Ana, and Santiago de María, plus the archdiocese of San Salvador) sponsored a center, in addition to several specialized centers. The main *centros*, almost all established in the mid- to late 1960s, were *Escuela La Divina Providencia* in Santa Ana; *Centro Reino de la Paz* in El Castaño, San Miguel; *Escuela Los Naranjos* in Jiquilisco, Usulután (in the diocese of Santiago de María); and the *Centro Rural Itinerante*, based in San Salvador, an itinerant team that gave *cursillos* (courses) in rural parishes throughout the archdiocese. Smaller centers included the *Centro San Lucas* in San Miguel, which focused on health care training, and two centers run by and for women, the *Centro de Promoción Rural* (CEPROR) in Santa Tecla and the *Centro Guadalupe* in San Miguel."[62]

The author of this account interrupts her own rendering to note: "Ricardo Urioste, director of the *equipo itinerante*, recalls that there was also a *centro de formación* in San Vicente. I have found little information about this center, perhaps because the conservative bishop of San Vicente, Pedro Aparicio, limited both its work and publicity about it."[63]

The biography of one priest working in the diocese of San Vicente at this time, Padre David Rodríguez, corroborates Urioste's memory:

"The first small course set up by Rodriguez was held in the house of a wealthy landowner in Tecoluca, who later became minister of agriculture. Because he was seldom there, the landowner allowed Rodríguez to hold the course in his house. Once it was fully developed, the short course would begin on a Friday afternoon and end on a Sunday in the middle of the day, when a special mass was held for the trainees. The purpose of the course was to form young lay leaders by helping them to relate the Bible to the reality in Tecoluca 'at a deeper level.' The courses trained Delegates of the Word of God, who would be responsible for bringing people together in their communities for Bible discussion on at least a weekly basis. In general, lay leaders were either trained as catechists (those who taught catechism principally to children but also to adults) or as Delegates. Both of these types of lay leaders, however, would be 'awakened' by learning that the plight of the poor was not inevitable or sanctioned by God. The students, Rodríguez recalls, 'left the course very committed.' Rodríguez continued with the courses and broadened them to include men of the *Caballeros of Cristo Rey* [the Knights of Christ the King], women of the Parish Auxiliaries, and some peasants who would not necessarily become either catechists or Delegates. Rodríguez believes, however, that 'the greatest dynamism was with the young Delegates of the Word,' since they would serve as the acting priest when the priest was not available. In a country where one priest served roughly ten thousand believers, the Delegates took on substantial responsibility and 'gained a great deal of local respect.'"[64]

Indeed, when Bishop Aparicio found out about the courses, the protagonism of lay *campesinos*, and the displeasure of his diocese's wealthiest parishioners, he reassigned Padre David to the sub-parish of San Carlos Lempa.[65]

"The other *centros* also trained lay people for new ministries that responded to the pastoral needs of the People of God: Delegates or Celebrants of the Word led liturgies, *animadores* of communities functioned as community leaders and organizers without necessarily celebrating liturgy, and informal music ministries sprang up, composing songs and poems for worship. . . . The work of *centros* [*de formación*] and CEBs together comprised the base of the popular church in El Salvador. These programs had the greatest impact and reached the most people in the archdiocese of San Salvador (which in the 1970s included the departments of Chalatenango, Cuscatlán, and La Libertad, as well as San Salvador) and in the departments of Cabañas, Morazán, and San Vicente. The laypeople and pastoral workers in these areas articulated, in Bible studies, discussions, and ritual, the theology of the popular church, including ideas about martyrdom and persecution. Their ideas were not confined to their own communities, however, but were widely diffused in and through other social and political groups. By spreading the 'message' of Catholic reforms and recruiting more laypeople as active participants in the church's official structures, *centros* and CEBs broadened the social and political impact of progressive Catholicism throughout the country (as did similar programs elsewhere in Latin America)."[66]

God's Spirit of life and liberation continued to open up new ways of being God's people for the Salvadoran church of *lxs pobres*.

6 The reception of the Second Vatican Council at Medellín facilitated its further reception by the Central American bishops in Antigua, Guatemala, in early 1970.[67] Afterwards, the Salvadoran Bishops' Conference (CEDES) agreed to convene a week of pastoral reflection and planning that same year, to reflect on and incorporate into their own pastoral work the documents that had come out of the Antigua meeting. This specifically Salvadoran reception of Vatican II, the Pastoral Week for a *pastoral de conjunto*, was scheduled for June 22–26, 1970.

Pastoral workers, including priests who had studied at the IPLA or who were already working with ecclesial base communities, were enthusiastic about this opportunity to apply the conclusions of Vatican II and Medellín directly to the Salvadoran reality: "The general plan was very simple. First '*ver*,' that is, to analyze the reality of the Salvadoran man and the ecclesial reality. Then, to '*juzgar*' these dual realities by the light of Vatican II and Medellín, specifically asking about the vocation of man and the charism of the Church. The following two days would be about making pastoral decisions, that is, to influence reality to transform it according to God's plan."[68] Priests, seminarians, male and female members of religious orders, and lay people were invited to participate. However, the reception of Vatican II for the Salvadoran church was hindered by two signs of the ecclesial times.

First, although the meeting had been called by CEDES, representing the bishops of all five Salvadoran dioceses, only Archbishop Luis Chávez y González of San Salvador was present. The assembly worried that without the presence and full participation of the bishops, the week's conclusions and pastoral commitments would not be valid or implemented in the various dioceses. The following telegram was composed after the afternoon session of June 23: 'One hundred and twenty-three lay people, religious sisters, and religious and diocesan priests miss your Excellency here at the National Pastoral Meeting. Your presence would be of great help to discover and carry out a pastoral [plan] appropriate for our times. Respectfully, the participants of the National Pastoral

Week.' The telegram was sent to Mons. Barrera [of Santa Ana], Mons. Aparicio [of San Vicente], Mons. Alvarez [of Santiago de María], and Mons. Castro Ramírez [of San Miguel]. The invitation was not well-received by the bishops."[69]

The second way in which the Pastoral Week was weakened was by the edits that CEDES made, after the meeting in October 1970, to the final document that the participants had drafted. Whereas the participants' June draft begins, "The Bishops' Conference of El Salvador, after having heard from prudent priests, religious, and laypeople . . . ," the final document issued by the CEDES in October starts with, "We, the Church in El Salvador . . ." The CEDES document obscures "seeing" the country's social and ecclesial reality by eliminating references to the division and domination of some social classes over others. It refuses to connect that social reality with a theological judgment, for example, renaming a section of the document originally titled "The Church: Sacrament of Salvation for the Whole Human Being in His or Her Concrete Reality" as "Theological Reflection." The document avoids proposing concrete actions for Christians in an unjust society from a place of faith by eliminating references to itinerant pastoral teams that attended to the most rural areas, by diminishing an emphasis on lay pastoral and leadership formation, and by refusing to articulate the particular functions of lay delegates and ministers, which, in practice, included preaching, baptizing, distributing the Eucharist, and presiding at weddings. Rome applauded the CEDES edits.[70]

Ultimately, the Pastoral Week of 1970 proved the existence of the church of *lxs pobres* in El Salvador as the subject of a new model of church opposed to the CEDES model:

"Padre Edgard Beltrán was responsible for the analysis of the ecclesial reality; he questioned various dimensions of the Church and proposed two models. The first ecclesial model always found excuses to exonerate itself. It did not find this kind of examination pleasing because it felt satisfied, considering that it already knew everything and had already done everything. This model was about a Church interested in increasing the number of sacraments it dispensed. The second model corresponded to a searching Church, in a continual process of conversion. A Church that knew itself to be sinful and, by virtue of that, to recognize itself on a quest and in dialogue."[71]

The Spirit of Life is free to move and inspire God's people in the second model.

IN THE DESERT

7 Some say:
"Despite the social and political impact of these educational and pastoral programs, most of them struggled for support from the official church. Bishops in several dioceses, especially San Vicente and Santa Ana, were overly hostile to

progressive pastoral agents and their projects. The lack of support from the institutional church helped push progressive Catholics even closer to political groups, which offered moral and material support and sometimes physical protection. By the mid-1980s in El Salvador, some progressive Catholic programs had spilled beyond the confines of the institutional church. Most notable was the emergence of two left-leaning Catholic groups without official church recognition: the National Coordination of the Popular Church (CONIP) and Ecclesial Base Communities of El Salvador (CEBES). These developments resulted, at least in part, from the decline in official support for progressive Catholic initiatives, even from the Archdiocese of San Salvador, following the assassination of Archbishop Romero."[72]

But we say to you:

The decline in official support far preceded the assassination of San Romero or the formation of CONIP, CEBES, or any other para-ecclesial institution. The example of Bishop Aparicio relocating Padre David in San Vicente and the intra-ecclesial and intra-episcopal dynamics of the archdiocesan pastoral week of 1970 testify to this. Hard hearts were simply hardened even more.

The CEBs formed institutions outside of their parishes, not for ideological reasons, but rather for their survival, to communicate during the most difficult parts of the war and to coordinate the transfer of funds for the reconstruction of refugee communities in the late 1980s and early 1990s, which was "a time of redefinition for the CEBs. It is a context of war, of death, of suffering, of exile, or of diaspora. For this reason, at this time, the first coordination among the communities comes about. Without coordination, they were destined to disappear. It was from this need for unity that the National Coordination for the Popular Church in El Salvador (CONIP) was born, whose intention was to coordinate all Christians working along the pastoral lines that Monseñor Romero had opened:[73] it was a liberating pastoral effort for the masses, a symbolic pastoral effort from the communities and a pastoral effort that sought to accompany Christians who were committed [members of] grassroots [civil] organizations."[74]

And again we say to you: the Spirit at work in the church of *lxs pobres* was pushed out, locked out, and frozen out of the institutional church. But *lxs pobres* opted for fidelity to Jesús and the reign of abundant life that he announced:

"At the end of the years 2001–2010, given the marginalization and more on the part of some parishes and priests that do not share their way of being church, various CEBs decide to function no longer at the service of a parroquial project, but rather at the service of the project of the reign of God. This is why they begin to journey autonomously and among the base [of secular society]. . . .

[2011–2016] is an epoch increasingly marked by the celebrations of the martyrs, and participation in regional meetings, especially the one in Tecao, Honduras. At this meeting, El Salvador had the chance to assume a commitment to the connections between CEBs in the country and the re-launching of a national network. [At that point], El Salvador was the only country that didn't have a formal network. This is how, in August 2010, the National Network of CEBs in El Salvador was born and initiated the systematic and progressive journeying of this experience, representing different ecclesial base communities that one by one have connected themselves to this effort. The goal: to connect experiences of ecclesial base communities on a national level in order to announce and defend the Good News for *las y los pobres*, to promote exchange, to be more well-organized and to accompany the people in their struggles against death-dealing projects, continuing, in this way, the prophetic struggle of the martyrs to sustain life and hope in El Salvador."[75]

The Spirit of Life would not be buried and left for dead, but stubbornly rose again and again in God's people, *lxs pobres*.

The *Librito* of the Prophet Anastasio Aquino

Before the church of *lxs pobres* began to make a new way out of the colonial church in the late 1960s, the prophets and martyrs of Salvadoran history were secular and religious figures who resisted the colonial matrix of power and had the vision and the courage to imagine other possible worlds and social systems.

One such prophetic figure admired in the base communities is Anastasio Aquino, who, together with the Nonualco people, rebelled against creole governors shortly after Central American independence was declared in 1821. This sacred story comes from the period referred to in "Colonio-Genesis" §5, when Indigenous communities in the part of the new Central American Republic that would come to be called El Salvador rose up against the loss of land, higher taxes, and forced labor and military service they were suffering under the leadership of creole politicians. These large landowners, with the signatory support of landowning priests like Fr. José Matías Delgado, who had initially supported the popular cry for independence, had declared sovereignty over the region in order to reap the fruits of the land and the people's labor for themselves with as little conflict as possible. Without the minimal oversight that Spain and Rome had exerted over the colonists, *lxs pobres* were immediately vulnerable to harsher and more inhumane conditions. It is in this context that Anastasio Aquino and his collaborators stood in opposition to the hoarding of resources by the new Republic's self-appointed leaders.

Like much of the narrative in "Colonio-Genesis," this account of the Nonualco rebellion is taken from the Equipo Maíz popular education resource used in the base communities, *Historia de El Salvador*. Of note is how, once Aquino's armies defeated the creole governors and took back the Nonualco ancestral lands for themselves, they established their own laws, which they saw as a corrective to colonial rule. The final chapters of this story are the translated poems of Salvadoran poets Pedro Geoffrey Rivas and Roque Dalton.

1 "Francisco Morazán being president of the Federal Republic of Central America and Mariano Prado the Head of State of El Salvador, the Nonualco uprising occurred.

Neither independence nor Morazán's liberal reforms improved the people's situation. Lands were taken from Indigenous peoples, people had to pay new taxes, there was war, forced recruitment, and much misery.

This situation provoked the discontent of the people. There were Indigenous uprisings in Tejutla, Chalatenango, Zacatecoluca, and other places. The most important uprising was in the Nonualco region, in the department of La Paz, and it was led by Anastasio Aquino.

The Nonualco leader organized and armed the Nonualcos, defeating the army many times and taking the cities of San Vicente and Zacatecoluca. The Head of State, Mariano Prado, fled the country.

After his first victories, Aquino made some decrees:

'I, Anastasio Aquino, Commander General of the liberating armies of Santiago Nonualco, on this day have ordered the following: that you are free from obligation to pay all debtors that are to be found in the territory where the force of my government is felt.'"

The Tepetitán Declaration

2 "I, Anastasio Aquino, Commander General of the liberating armies of Santiago Nonualco, on this day agree to impose penalties for crimes that are committed, which are the following:

1. He who kills will pay for one life with another.
2. He who injures will have his hand cut off.
3. He who violates the [Indigenous] civil authorities and military chiefs will be punished with ten years of public service.
4. Those who violate married or partnered women will be punished according to the law.
5. He who steals will be punished by cutting off his hand, on first offense.
6. Those who produce liquor will suffer fines of five *pesos*, on first offense.

Given in Tepetitán on February 16, 1833."

3 "But Prado's government, supported by creoles, ladinos, and mestizos, was able to regain its strength and defeat the Nonualcos.

Anastasio Aquino was betrayed by one of his comrades, who was 'advised' by a priest. Aquino was captured and put on trial.

He was executed by firearm on July 24, 1833 and later beheaded. His head was put in a cage on so-called 'Hunter's Hill,' so that it would serve as an example to other Indigenous rebels."

4 "There are some who consider Aquino to be a revolutionary. His movement was a reaction against the changes that happened after independence and that had not favored the Indigenous population at all. It was a way of fighting against all of the abuse and of demanding respect for their rights and customs. In that sense, Aquino continues to be an example for our people.

But the most important thing is that the rebellion of Indigenous peoples did not disappear. Aquino's movement is only one of many that occurred during the 19th century. The Nonualco people, the Cojutepeque people, and other Indigenous peoples rose up on different occasions to put pressure on their governors. But this part of our history is only recently coming to be known."[76]

PEDRO GEOFFROY RIVAS REMEMBERS

5 "The land where you lay is still foreign,
Old grandfather of stone. Your indestructible race
Still toils under the yoke. Impossible
Is the cry that hard and hasty throats,
Under the bitter sign of the impassable tropics,
Clench like a lacerating branch of roses.
Their backs are curved, bloody and painful,
Furrowed by the footprints of the terrible whip.
Do not sleep anymore, Grandfather.
Vanquisher of death,
Lift your ancient voice, consoling and strong,
So that your great cry of war may once again be heard.
Standing tall always, with heads held high to the sun,
Your race will repeat from sunrise to sunset
The thousand-year echo of 'Land, Land, Land.'"[77]

ROQUE DALTON REMEMBERS

6 "A blow dealt for the land was your singular struggle:
A warrior's wing,
A rock wall of hopes rooted in the deepest cry of the *milpas*
Tlaloc,[78] with her humid voice,
made the ancestral veins of your sleeping people boil,
set the powerful storm on its vibrating route,
and crowned the fertile build of the machete with informative light.
Atonal,[79] the ancient, with his metallic food,
sang cornfields of fiery hope,
instituting the longing to raise one's head after a defeat.
After you, battle upon battle,
architect of bread, father of furrows,

Raising your tall chest as a shield
the struggle was born, the statute of the winds.
There was a naked cry, a sweaty clamor
of awakened ores of shame;
a loud and numerous voice
of pure, red blood that drove out tears;
a mistaken word
that defined the enormous criteria for future days.
But a violent toad,
A cunning crow,
and a dwarf lion,
after possessing each other mutually,
gave birth without effort, blue and bitter to the point of hatred;
a tangled, feudal laugh put its signature on the dagger.
It declared death, verbal malice, an obligatory insult.
It put you in a sack. It threw you to the sea closest to the densest undercurrent.
It dressed a hundred sharks in elegant togas of the Academy of History.
It poisoned the water,
it spit, it kicked, it bit.
It calmed its deaf throat with its broken memory.
An indian had died.
Anti-Christian, anti-cultural . . .
They could again, civilly,
build gallows, crack whips, award oppressors.
One had to laugh, and rightly so."[80]

The *Librito* of the Prophet Prudencia Ayala

Prudencia Ayala is another prophet of Salvadoran salvation history who is admired within the church of *lxs pobres*. Born to Indigenous parents and mostly self-taught, she was a tailor and wrote poetry, opinion pieces, and fortunes for local and regional newspapers. In 1931, at a time when women were not even allowed to vote in elections, she ran for president!

Prudencia Ayala is an important prophet of El Salvador's decolonial struggle because she was one of the first public figures that we know of who directly addressed the coloniality of gender and sexuality. Of course, this implied a struggle against the coloniality of the economy, of authority, and of subjectivity and knowledge; to assert that a woman is capable of being president is to assert that she is fit to lead the economy, exercise authority, and be her own free human being. Her candidacy was rejected by the Supreme Court. The events of this *librito* coincide with Colonio-Genesis §8.

1 "It is a stormy night. A pregnant woman gallops on horseback along clandestine paths that lead from Guatemala to Sonsonate.

In her womb, she carries Prudencia, who, a little while later, is born in a straw cabin in the town of Sonzacate, department of Sonsonate.

'When I was very little, with my mother I moved to the town of Santa Ana. When I was ten, I studied in a private school, run by a Colombian nun, María Luisa de Cristofini. However, I could not finish second grade due to my mother's poverty.'

When she was twelve, the girl Prudencia confessed to hearing mysterious voices that announced future events to her. In 1898, she started publishing her prophecies in the newspapers of the West, in Santa Ana. When some of her predictions came true, they began to call her 'The Sibyl of Santaneca.'

'I predict that the German Kaiser will fall, and the United States will get involved in the first World War.'

From that moment on, Prudencia began to publish her feminist proposals and her ideas about Central American unity, together with her poems, in different Guatemalan and Salvadoran newspapers.

In 1919, she was imprisoned for accusing the mayor of the city of Atiquizaya of corruption. That same year, she went to Guatemala, where she was imprisoned for several weeks based on accusations of participating in planning a coup against the dictator Estrada Cabrera. Later, she was exiled to El Salvador.

There are accounts that have Prudencia speaking at the Women's March that was violently repressed by the National Guard on the streets of San Salvador on December 25, 1922.

In the newspapers at the time, Prudencia wrote against Central American dictators and supported the struggle of Sandino [in Nicaragua]. In 1927, she condemned U.S. troops' military intervention in Nicaragua and demanded indemnization for the harm caused to that country."[81]

Prudencia soon sought access to the highest public office in the Republic of El Salvador: "In 1931, there were presidential elections. Unlike his predecessors, Romero Bosque did not impose a candidate and the people had freedom to choose. A woman, Prudencia Ayala, wanted to sign up to be a presidential candidate, but they did not let her. In those years, women still did not have the right to vote or be elected."[82]

2 Nevertheless, Prudencia persisted: "I will launch my candidacy for President of the Republic. My electoral platform will promote the rights of women, support for labor unions, honesty in public administration, limitations on the production and distribution of moonshine, respect for the freedom of religion and recognition for the so-called 'illegitimate' children. I launch my candidacy to the Presidency of El Salvador, proud of being a humble Salvadoran Indian!"[83]

3 Journalists and politicians ridiculed the attempts by a woman to exercise her civil rights. Many newspapers published caricatures making fun of Prudencia's candidacy. One of the newspapers of the time, *La Epoca*, interviewed Prudencia Ayala and published the story sarcastically.[84]

Inspired by Prudencia Ayala, suffragists struggled for women's right to vote until Salvadoran women were recognized as voting citizens in 1950. The country is still waiting to elect its first woman president.

The *Librito* of the Prophet Farabundo Martí

Farabundo Martí, active around the same time as Prudencia Ayala, was an important leader of the Indigenous peasant insurrection in early 1932. Under the oppressive dictatorial regime of military president General Maximiliano Hernández Martínez, Indigenous and other marginalized communities in San Salvador, Santa Tecla, Colón, Izalco, Armenia, Nahuizalco, Juayúa, Tacuba, and Ahuachapán coordinated popular protests to begin on January 22. The uprising was organized and coordinated locally, especially in the Western coffee-growing regions of the country, with some coordination with the recently founded Communist Party of El Salvador ("PCS," established 1930) and one of the country's earliest federation of labor unions, *la Regional*. However, the PCS cells in the capital were infiltrated days before the planned uprisings, and the police captured the principal organizers in San Salvador, including Farabundo Martí. With no way to receive news from their captured coconspirators, the provincial movements went ahead with their protests on the twenty-second and were violently repressed. It is estimated that upward of 10,000 *campesinos* and *campesinas* were killed over the course of the next several days. This repression is referred to as La Matanza, and while the replacement of indigeneity with *mestizaje* had long been the dominant trend in Salvadoran culture, the CEBs remember 1932 as a turning point after which indigeneity became explicitly suspect in El Salvador.

Farabundo Martí's role in Salvadoran history coincides with the events of Colonio-Genesis §9. Other leaders of the popular insurrections include Feliciano Ama, Francisco Sánchez, Mario Zapata, Alfonso Luna, and Miguel Mármol. These events are so significant to the collective memory and identity of *lxs pobres* in El Salvador and their struggles for justice that when disparate guerrilla forces united and began their armed conflict against the government in 1980, they named themselves "the Farabundo Martí National Liberation Front" (FMLN), marking their uprising in continuity with the fight of their *nanas* and *tatas* some fifty years prior. Today, the CEBs remember Martí and the uprising as both an inspiration for organized struggle against socioeconomic exploitation and a touchstone for recovering Indigenous identity.

The sources for this *librito* include an epic-style popular ballad about Martí's life, presented clandestinely, as a rumor: "They say that they say that they saw Farabundo Martí pass [through here]." Martí himself represents a sort of hero/spirit—of rebellion, of resistance—that passes through not only Izalco, Juayúa, and León, but history as well. The choice of the unified guerrilla forces (and later, political party) to sing of Martí's "reappearance" among their front is a re-membering of one who stood against coloniality and who continues to accompany *lxs pobres* in their decolonial turn.

1 "They say that they say that they
saw Farabundo Martí pass
Through Izalco, Juayúa and León,
Through Sonsonate and Quiché,
Through Nicaragua and El Salvador.
He passed through Guatemala.
With his light of liberation, Farabundo
    arrived.
In 1883 Farabundo Martí was born.
It was there in Teotepeque, department
    of La Libertad,
With freedom inside him, he grew up in
    El Salvador
Struggling for justice along the way and
    facing the sun.
It was in 1920, during the Meléndez
    dictatorship,
that because of his struggle and solidarity
    he was exiled from El Salvador.
Guatemala was his destination, and he
    lived there for a few years.
He was a day laborer, a mason, and a
    teacher, and he suffered exploitation
    with them.

He was a militant Central-Americanist,
    a propagandist and popular agitator.
He organized the struggles of the people
    and returned to El Salvador.
Nobody could imagine that he would
    return to his land and become involved
With the worker's fronts as José the
    Organizer.
In the year '28 he fought in Segovias
Comrade of Sandino, in that land he
    sowed
He sowed consciousness and a future,
    liberatory horizons.
He wrote with hope and fought with
    shrapnel.
His people grew with the morning and
    Farabundo returned.
He organized, then, his fight and
    together with them he fought.
He was imprisoned a thousand and one
    times and was exiled once more.
They say that he reappeared soon after,
    as Justo Francisco Juan.
With machetes and pistols, with
    revolvers and shotguns,

Laborers and farmworkers in the fields
and in the streets.
It was in January of '32 when the
people said, 'Enough!'
And his heart lit up against that house.
They say that then the earth roared an
immense cry,
The volcano shook with its infinite fury.
The enemy sowed the afternoon with
death.
With their cowardly shrapnel they killed
men and children.
Those who fell were 30,000, laborers
and farmworkers,
but none of them have died, and they
will return to the path
with Farabundo Martí. Our homeland,
killed by bullets,
will dawn again. Victory is near."[85]

2 Ana María Leddy reflects that "before the offensive of 1981, there was a call to record music to be transmitted on 'Liberation Radio' that began to operate clandestinely and which later became *Radio Venceremos* . . . so we had the opportunity to record, not just one song, but a whole cassette that included various songs dedicated to accompanying the struggle of the FMLN, among them the 'Song for the FMLN.' So we put together a group of different voices and we were accompanied musically by the group Igni-Tawanka.

It was a whole cassette of music, and we started recording in December of [1980], and I remember that we finished recording around dusk on December 24 of that same year. The offensive began on January 10, 1981, and we called it the 'final offensive,' [laughs], and turns out it was just the beginning. Just as they had said, the radio was launched, and the 'Song to the FMLN' began to be heard.

One time, a comrade, one of many who was on leave from the front to heal or to do other tasks, began to hum the song in front of me. It was a huge surprise that there were people who sang the song besides us. I asked where he knew it from, and he responded, 'Every day on the front of the war, when it's possible for us to stand in formation, we sing this song.'

That news filled me with joy, *¡púchica!*,[86] it was a wave of emotion to know that the song was playing its role to accompany and motivate the struggle of so many men and women that had decided to fight to end the dictatorship and build a new El Salvador":[87]

"We will overcome, either revolution or
death.
The FMLN, vanguard of a people who
struggle,
will be our guide to our final victory.
Brothers and sisters united in combat,
we push forward to revolution.
May we build a future of progress and
dignity.
We will overcome either revolution or
death.
Farabundo Martí has inspired us,
and today he reappears victorious
among our front.[88]
The red and white flag will protect us,
and the star will guide us on our path.
Farabundo forges new liberatory paths

on which the peace and justice of our people will travel.
Brothers and sisters united in combat, we push forward to revolution.
May we build a future of progress and dignity.

We will overcome, either revolution or death.
We will overcome, either revolution or death."[89]

The *Librito* of the Prophet Óscar Romero

Óscar Arnulfo Romero y Galdámez—archbishop of San Salvador from 1977 until his assassination on March 24, 1980, and, after many delays, canonized by the Catholic church on October 14, 2018—is a major prophet of the people of El Salvador. The full witness to his prophetic life is far from exhausted by the selections presented here; much of his testimony still lives in contemporary oral, visual, material, prayerful, and musical popular traditions and has been extensively documented in numerous books, documentaries, photo essays, and even plays and musicals about his life, martyrdom, and resurrection in the Salvadoran people.

This too-brief collection of stories highlights specific episodes of Romero's relationship with the church of *lxs pobres*, especially the ecclesial base communities. When he was chosen to be archbishop, ecclesial leaders in the *iglesia popular* protested his appointment. However, their ministry to their pastor contributed to the long process of conversion that led Romero to reshape his own ministry, a ministry that was the basis for his martyrdom and eventual canonization: "We see how Romero's neo-Scholastic theology encounters a new reality and a new theology, and how that encounter, which often put him in conflict with the progressive side of the church emerging in the CEBs and [pastoral formation] centers, would shape his positions, actions, and words."[90] After Romero's death, it was precisely this "progressive side of the church emerging in the CEBs" that would keep his memory and his witness to the Gospel alive, despite pushback and marginalization by his episcopal peers and hierarchical successors.

This *librito* begins with an account of Romero's own encounters with the church of *lxs pobres* before his tenure as archbishop, as told by members of the communities and related in *Fe de un pueblo*, a communally inspired account of the CEBs' early years written down by one of the priests who spent his life in service to their struggle. This is followed by the prophet Romero's meditation on the CEBs in one of his homilies. We also include his homily from March 23, 1980, the day before he was assassinated, and the words he was speaking as he turned to begin the offertory during his final mass, as he was shot. The lyrics to several songs are also included in this *librito* because popular hymns have been a primary vehicle for re-membering San Romero, keeping his memory alive, and reflecting on the significance of his life and death for the church of *lxs pobres*.

ROMERO WALKS WITH THE CHURCH OF *LXS POBRES*

1 "Before being the great prophet and martyr of El Salvador, Monseñor Romero had conflicts with our communities. Before his conversion, we were a stumbling block for him.

One of those stumbles went like this. When President Molina ordered the National University to close in 1972, the newspapers published an article from the bishops' conference signed by the then-secretary, Mons. Romero. It said that the closure was a good decision because the university was nothing but a center of communist activity. Our communities were indignant. With the closure, the displacement of the residents of the slum next to the University was also ordered: they demolished houses and arrested a few men. Many employees of the University, members of our communities, were beaten, and the academic authorities were kicked out in an incredible display of violence. How could the bishop praise that? We were sure that neither Monseñor Chávez[91] nor Monseñor Rivera[92] could applaud such barbarism.

This generated great conflict in the communities that became a flurry of meetings, reflections, and arguments. Should we stay silent and accept the word of the bishops, or should we use our own voice to condemn the interventions at the University?

We wrote a letter with our observations and critiques to Monseñor Romero and invited him to participate at a eucharist where we would reflect about the situation. Monseñor came to the parish. The conflict was so great that mass could not be concluded. After the readings and the homily, they began to ask about the bishops' position: 'Do the bishops know everything that happened? Who did they talk to before speaking out? Where is the gospel present in that document?'

With the Medellín document at hand, we rejected the episcopal press release. Monseñor Romero defended himself with a letter from a Chilean bishop of whom we had never heard. He accused us of disobedience to ecclesial authorities and of mixing politics and eucharist. We continued discussing with him, using the positions from Medellín, and we asked him why the church always took the side of the rich and why it couldn't draw near to the victims of the repression to make a more realistic judgment. The mood was very tense. At last, Monseñor said that the meeting was not a eucharist but a political rally. I was so indignant that I said, 'Friends, what Monseñor Romero says is true. Here in this atmosphere it is impossible to celebrate eucharist; it is impossible to thank the Lord for our call to faith when we are not permitted to dialogue with our superiors. Let us end our celebration here until dialogue and participation are possible.' I took off my alb and stole. The argument continued, heated and explosive.

The next day, we visited Monseñor Rivera to inform him of what had happened and to ask for his help. He promised to visit us and he did. When Monseñor Romero converted, when he was Archbishop of San Salvador, he returned to our communities. Like a prodigal son, it was the father who returned this time, and his return was a reconciliatory celebration."[93]

ROMERO'S HOMILIES

2 "Now, sisters and brothers, when I think about this community of the faithful and concretely about our beloved archdiocese, I feel it as something so divine that I experience in it God's initiative gathering us together. I experience the grace of Jesus Christ giving us faith and the communion of the Holy Spirit binding us together, lifting us up, and filling us with joy and consolation. I think of this present moment of our archdiocesan community on pilgrimage in the four departments; it is so beautiful, so enchanting in its base communities where men and women and young people come to know one another more intimately and feel in their hearts the love of the Father, the grace of the Son, and the communion of the Holy Spirit. That is why I insist so much, sisters and brothers, on there being more and more base communities. This is not some invention of recent times; it comes from the great need Christians have to know and love one another and to live together in full awareness of this divine energy."[94]

3 "I would like to appeal in a special way to the army's enlisted men, and in particular to the ranks of the National Guard and the police—those in the barracks. Brothers: you are of part of our own people. You kill your own campesino brothers and sisters. Before an order to kill that a man may give, God's law must prevail: Thou shalt not kill! No soldier is obliged to obey an order against the law of God. No one has to fulfill an immoral law. It is time to take back your consciences and to obey your consciences rather than the orders of sin. The Church, defender of the rights of God, of the law of God, of human dignity, of the person, cannot remain silent

before such abominations. We want the government to understand seriously that reforms are worth nothing if they are stained with so much blood. In the name of God, and in the name of this suffering people, whose laments rise to heaven each day more tumultuous, I beg you, I beseech you, I order you in the name of God: Stop the repression!"[95]

4 "By Christian faith we know that at this moment the host of wheat becomes the body of the Lord who offered himself for the redemption of the world, and that the wine in this chalice is transformed into the blood that was the price of salvation. May this body that was immolated and this flesh that was sacrificed for humankind also nourish us so that we can give our bodies and our blood to suffering and pain, as Christ did, not for our own sake but to bring justice and peace to our people. Let us therefore join closely together in faith and hope at this moment of prayer for Doña Sarita and ourselves."

(At that moment, a shot rang out.)[96]

RESURRECTION IN THE PEOPLE

5 "El 24 de marzo, the church will not forget.
Again, they bathe in blood the one who spoke the truth.
Today they took the bravest man of the church from us.
Because of his example and his courage, a true prophet.
Óscar Arnulfo Romero, you were our pastor.
You put your heart among simple and humble people.
 I remember when you used to come to our far-flung villages
To see the *campesinos*, to see your poor people.
The blood you spilled was for the cause of a people
that suffers great repression from the rich and the government.
The people are clear that your death was not an isolated incident.
It was caused by imperialism together with the Armed Forces.
Pilate has returned to earth; he is represented by the tyrant
because those who assassinated him wash their hands of it now.
Óscar Arnulfo Romero, you live in the struggles of the people
That's why we will never forget your heroic example."[97]

6 "Now he's no longer 'Monsignor' Today, he's 'Saint Romero'[98]
And from this holy place
he goes forth to accompany the worker.
The devil made a mistake
like the devil always makes mistakes
To want to shut the mouth of the man who gave himself entirely
because Óscar Arnulfo Romero lives with us
Now Saint Romero lights our path
That's why our peasant brother struggles harder
Hear what I am saying, pay me strict attention.
Let us never grow weary until we've achieved liberation.

On March 24th, an assassin's hand
   came forth
and in cowardly fashion took a life in
   exchange for pay.
But that foolish person didn't know
   what he was doing,
putting fire to the fuse of a people who
   continue to smolder."[99]

7 "I saw a traveler walking this land
   of hunger
Humble, gentle and sincere,
   courageously prophetic
Who confronted tyrants
   to accuse them of the crime
of assassinating their brothers to defend
   the rich
They can kill the prophet, but not his
   voice of justice.
They can impose silence on him,
   but history cannot be silenced.
With his gospel in hand,
   Monsignor Romero sought
to do justice, and he did it, but the tyrant
   wasn't pleased
because his voice was the breath
   that defended the peasant
illuminating the path, the freedom of
   this people.
His sin was to wish that the workers
   could eat,
That there truly be an Our Father
   so they can pray while eating.
Since the rich don't understand
   when God does justice
It's from *los pobres* that a shout comes,
   one they learned from their prophet.
His death is not a coincidence
   the tyrants should tremble.
They are the ones whose hands
   are stained by the crime.
And the whole oligarchy
is clouded by so much dementia.
They have signed their own sentence,
   their agony is already beginning."[100]

8 "You are risen in your people, as
   the voice of *los pobres*,
Óscar Arnulfo Romero, Salvadoran
   prophet
You were always united to Peter, true
   and faithful prophet.
The message of Medellin came to life in
   your people
Those rich townspeople thought they
   could silence your voice,
and they stained their hands
   with the blood of the prophet.
We are Latinos, of the Salvadoran earth
And great in dignity because of Saint
   Arnulfo Romero
It was Christ who consecrated you
   prophet and martyr of the people,
and you shall be saint for all the people
   throughout Latin America.
Your voice is the hope that calls us to
   conversion
because you see the sadness hunger and
   pain in *los pobres*,
those who have forgotten how to enact
   the gospels.
They must follow your lead
   and be the voice of the people.
Faith demands justice, a gospel brought
   to life.
When they marginalize *los pobres*, it's
   God who demands justice.
The day they killed you, the beast was
   thirsty
Killing many brothers and sisters,
   sons and daughters of the people.
The prophet never dies, so said Romero:
'If they happen to kill me, I will rise
   again in the people.'"[101]

9 "As a symbol of rebellion,
this was your way of loving.
You will always be a prophet,
A guide to freedom.
In those times of war,
You courage oriented [us].
In the hope of doing justice,
shouting, 'liberation!'
Monseñor, you live today
in the hearts
of the people that loved you so.

Monseñor, your truth
encourages us to march
to the *victoria final*.[102]
Today, your simple words
denounce our [social] reality.
They mark the tyrant with blood;
they call the people to [keep] struggling.
The Empire of Pain
cannot silence your example.
Your blood will be life,
the rebirth of love."[103]

The Gospel According to la Zacamil

The good news for El Salvador is the incarnation of Christ in history. The emergence of the CEBs and other ecclesial communities is good news; they represent a true instance of the ecclesial body of Jesucristo in El Salvador. Ignacio Ellacuría, a Jesuit priest who worked at the Universidad Centroamericana "José Simeón Cañas" (UCA) in Salvador and was martyred in 1989 for his commitment to peace, said of Óscar Romero, *"Con Monseñor Romero Dios pasó por El Salvador"* ("With Monseñor Romero, God passed through El Salvador").[104] Romero's people, *lxs pobres*, who were good news for his life and in whose lives he continues to be resurrected, share in this mystery. This new way of being church, taken up by the CEBs and other ecclesial communities of *lxs pobres* in the 1960s and 1970s and continuing to negotiate its pilgrimage in the world today, is a gospel of divine incarnation among *lxs pobres* for their own humanization and liberation. With the CEBs, God is still passing through El Salvador.

The Zacamil neighborhood near San Salvador in 1969 is one place where the nativity of this incarnation occurred. The accounts found here, in the first four subsections, were written by one of the Belgian missionary priests that accompanied the CEBs from their first meetings in La Zacamil until his passing in 2015. As the Zacamil experience grew, the lay-led pastoral team helped found other CEBs in the surrounding urban parishes, in marginal communities around San Salvador, near the National University. The second half of this Gospel account draws on those experiences, especially in the CEB belonging to the San Antonio Abad parish, where Padre Octavio Ortíz worked and was killed by Salvadoran armed forces on the morning of January 20, 1979, together with four young men who were participants in a youth retreat that Padre Octavio was leading.

These experiences of the Zacamil community and surrounding parishes are the foundations of the Salvadoran CEBs as they exist today. The voices that speak in these pages have taught the catechists who catechized the current pastoral leaders and ministers. These Gospel accounts as a whole represent the first generation of CEBs in El Salvador, characterized by clerical presence, coordination with local parishes, and recovery of scripture by the lay faithful.

PROLOGUE

1 "The communities began with the people. People who sought salvation. Salvation that we named happiness, friendship, love, justice, life, peace. Many people in El Salvador sought all this because they did not have it, and they had never had it. We also sought the people. We sought seekers to start something new with them."[105]

ZACAMIL

2 "The miracle was to see scattered folk meet together. We began to be a people. Everywhere, little groups popped up that were transformed into communities. The gospels were the books where the communities learned to become familiar with who they were and what the reality was where they lived.

In my parish, the first group formed during the preaching of a Sunday mass. The homily was a dialogue among everybody who was in attendance. In the gospel text, we looked for a way forward. We looked for answers and also questions. This collective dialogue bothered some people. I remember one man who stood up:

'Please, do not get into politics during mass!'

When mass was over, some stayed behind, talking about what had happened, and that's where the initiative was born: it was necessary to meet more frequently to form ourselves better, to know how to respond, to be able to give reason for our hope. Someone offered their house. That's how my first base group began."[106]

3 "Now we were a people. And we were also like a big family. We were friends. Each community meeting drew us closer. Doors were open; we greeted each other and visited each other. For the first time, the scattered people were united. Fear and shame disappeared. We shared everything; a cup of coffee, a glass of water, and our seeking.

This was because we learned to search together for solutions to our problems. There were so many people that didn't have time to reflect and try to search for a solution.

When the issue with Carlitos happened, we discovered among us all that illness does not come just from irresponsibility, but rather from lack of hygienic conditions. And that the lack of hygiene comes from poverty. We also discovered that children's illnesses were almost all due to malnutrition. And that malnourished children were not children of irresponsible mothers, but rather of mothers who were simply poor.

Carlitos was five. There wasn't a latrine in his house, and he took care of his needs a few meters behind his shack. His mom heard him bawling: his intestines had come out.

I took them to the hospital in a taxi. I had never seen such a bad state. What could it be? The doctor determined: second degree malnutrition. And how to heal it?

'Tell his mother to give him an egg and a little piece of meat every day. And his milk, too.'

And Berta didn't even have enough to pay for the taxi that brought us to the hospital. . . . She had five other children, her husband was a trash collector for the mayor's office . . .

A little later, the issue with Sandra happened. I came into her shack to visit her, and I found her crying.

'He's dying! Benjamin is dying on me!' It was true, the boy looked very bad. When we went to the doctor, the same word: malnutrition. The doctor asked Sandra how many children she had.

'Seven,' said Sandra.

'But madam,' he chastized her, 'we are people, not animals. You are culpable for the suffering of this child. And I'm sure that your other kids are sick, too!'

It was too much for Sandra. Bawling, she said to the doctor:

'You always tell me the same thing, that I have too many kids! But nobody asks me how much my husband makes! And you, how many children do you have? How much do you make? For you, I'm sure you make enough!'

The doctor was struck dumb. He gave her some medicine and told Sandra that she should come in the next day with her other children and that he would give them a free check-up."[107]

4 "That's what life is like for the majority of Salvadorans. It's a privilege to be healthy. To have medicine and access to a doctor is a luxury. When a poor person is between life and death, they have no option other than a money lender. They charge 10% or 20% per day, but there's no other option. People who are sick, the family members who cry when they are dead, abandoned women and the handicapped—are all victims of these loan sharks. What to do with all that?

And what to do with the young women who become prostitutes to save their little brother's life? Or with the children who never step into a school because there's no school in the neighborhood, or because there's not even money to buy them a pair of pants, or because they have to stay home caring for their smaller siblings while their moms go to sell at the market?

We discovered that *lxs pobres* pay more for light they don't have than those who have electricity in their homes. *Lxs pobres* use candles. Light from a candle is minimal, useful for not tripping on things. But with candlelight, nobody feels like reading, much less like studying. Four candles per night, 120 candles per month is four times as expensive than two light bulbs that stay on all night.

And the same was true with water. In the slums, you have to buy water because there are no faucets. Ten jugs full per day are enough to wash clothes, prepare food, and bathe everybody. Many women make a living washing clothes for others. The ten jugs of water that they buy costs four times more than if they had to pay for water running through faucets in their house.

That's how everything is. The misery of the Salvadoran people is unimaginable. And it was among them that God was choosing God's own people. To believe this was an act of faith. That was my experience, that was all of our experience. Like those shepherds who discovered the Messiah in the poorest child of Bethlehem.

How many times did the same thing happen to us as did to them? We invited each other to draw close to misery, to share in it, and to see God in it? One time it was Rosita, 'I have discovered a new slum over there. We should go!'

Or María, 'You know, behind those buildings, there are thousands of homes. Let's go!'

To go into a slum was not pretty in the least. People watched us with distrust, and the dogs barked at us aggressively. But, as at the first Christmas of the world, it was in this misery that *el Salvador*[108] was born; it was from these wretched people that the People of God in El Salvador was born and continues to grow."[109]

FROM ZACAMIL TO OTHER NEIGHBORHOODS

5 The Zacamil Pastoral Team began to visit their neighbors on adjacent streets.

Teresa, from El Paraíso, says, "I'm from San Esteban Catarina, department of San Vicente. I came to San Salvador with my mom when I was still a girl. Once I grew up, I rented a plot where I built my shack on Santa Teresa Street in the Libertad neighborhood. I lived there alone with my children. In 1973 people connected to the Zacamil parish began to visit us. A sister told me that they were meeting with Padre Pedro and talking about stuff from the Bible and everyday life. Later, Sister María Isabel, one of the religious sisters of the Zacamil community, started coming by my house. She spoke to me of the Christian community they were building. With her, I began to go to Zacamil to read and reflect on the Bible. Later, they came to meet with people in my house. At the beginning it was hard for us because we weren't used to having opinions about the Bible, just listening to it. There, we started forming our own ideas. Every conversation has a topic: injustice, evil, sin, God the Father, the Living Christ, the education of our children, marriage, alcoholism, etc."

Tilita, from the same community, adds, "We also lived in Santa Teresa Street in a shack that my husband, Macario built on a plot that we rented. Consuelo, our neighbor, started visiting Macario and invited him to a meeting in Zacamil. He went, he liked it, and he continued participating. Even though we were neighbors, we barely knew each other. When you live in a slum, you just say, 'Good morning' when you see people go by and nothing more. There really wasn't much communication.

These meetings didn't seem interesting to me. But after they visited me so many times, at last I said that I would go. I didn't like it much because I didn't understand what they were talking about, but I kept going. The fourth or fifth time, I figured out what was going on a little bit, I understood the Bible reading, and I would say a few words of my own opinion. After reading the text, they always asked us what we had understood from the reading and what it meant for our lives. That's what the initiation talks were like for me."[110]

6 María de Jesús, from the Tutunichapa CEB, says, "I drew close to the community when Sister Silvia began to come by. People trusted her more because she was a nun. She used a habit when she came because she was from the Guadalupan School.[111] With time, she began to wear regular clothes. She began to visit us and said that they were going to talk to us about learning interesting things for living better. She spoke kindly and of nice things to us, and what she said was true because we learned things we had no idea about. I had gone to mass since I was small. My mom, I guess, didn't prohibit me from going but didn't tell me to, either. Looking back, I laugh, because when we gave each other the sign of peace at the end, I didn't understand what was being said. I think I said, 'Happy New Year!' because I didn't know what was going on. In the community, we began to learn.

After a bunch of meetings, Silvia invited us to a retreat. This was a big deal for a woman. Men didn't like it much when their women left home for three days. At that time, I lived with a romantic partner, and it was difficult to be able to go. Once at the retreat, you wanted to stay there forever. Outside, things were so different."

Fredy, also from the Tutunichapa CEB, adds, "That moment is like when Jesús takes the disciples to the transfiguration. There, one of the apostles said to him:

'Lord, why don't we stay here forever? Let's make a house for you, one for Moses, and one for Elijah.'

That's how the retreats were. We all thought about how beautiful it would be to live like that all the time. We didn't understand that, like Jesús says, we have to take what we had seen there outside, to the rest of the world."[112]

7 Bersabé, from the San Antonio Abad CEB, says, "We were very active. Every time a new group

finished their initiation talks, we had a big party and everybody went; it didn't matter if it was here, in Tutunichapa, or in La Fosa. When a community celebrated something special, we all went to make the celebration more joyful. We even visited far away places like the department of Cabañas in this accompaniment of Christian communities that were working like us. This created among us a sense of being a family, of collaboration and of life. That's why our communities grew."

Adelita, also from the San Antonio Abad CEB, adds, "All of our children got involved and formed huge youth groups. The sense of happiness in the community attracted them, and their presence encouraged us even more, because young people are so dynamic. We organized eight different sectors in our parish: La Miranda, Mano de León, Molunca, El Centro, El Progreso, 15 de Septiembre, El Volcán, and El Roble. We formed a Central Team with two representatives from each sector. They were in charge of choosing our topics of study and facilitating meetings in each sector."

Fabio chimes in, "This all got so big that we came to be about five hundred people, and we didn't all fit in Segunda's house."

Tina completes the story: "Padre Guillermo[113] had some funding and bought a piece of land. There, among everybody, we built 'El Despertar' house: some donated nails, others brought their own tools, and even the kids helped carry sand with their buckets. We worked together with the other communities because El Despertar wasn't just for the priest, or just for the people in San Antonio Abad. It was for all the communities."[114]

PADRE OCTAVIO ORTÍZ

8 Mamá Tele says, "Octavio was humble, and he encouraged us. He danced and ate with us. It cheered us up in those sad days. The people on the parish council thought he was up to no good, but for us, it was very good."

Bersabé continues, "The parish council asked Octavio to celebrate mass for the feast day of San Antonio Abad in January.[115] Octavio asked us what we thought, and we accepted, on the condition that it wouldn't be mass just to fulfill an obligation, or just to have a party afterwards with moonshine and fireworks, but rather that we would reflect on the life of St. Anthony and our own lives. The council accepted our decision, but they weren't thrilled."

Mamá Tele adds, "On the day of the mass, Octavio was on a retreat with thirty-six young people who had finished their own initiation talks. It was two hours before mass when we began to hear fireworks. At first, we thought that it was celebratory, but they kept going on, and we thought that maybe something was happening in El Despertar."

Tina continues, "I lived right there, and I cooked for the retreats. That morning, I woke up at five in the morning to make breakfast. Crucita arrived and began to clean. As soon as she went out to the patio to sweep, we heard the great racket of the tank breaking through the entrance. Through the window on the second floor, I saw the tank full of men with their faces covered. They came in shooting everywhere. I turned off the fire in the kitchen, I took out the keys and the money for the refreshment later and put them in my bag. When there were no more shots fired, I thought that they had gone. I didn't think anybody had died, just that they were trying to scare us. I left by the side of the soccer field and headed to my room when one of the guards stopped me:

'Where are you going?'

'To check on my children who are sleeping in there.'

They searched me to make sure I didn't have any weapons and pushed me into the hallway, where they already had some people face-down on the floor. They forced me to lie down, too, and I heard my young daughter speaking to me. When I raised my head to answer her, a guard saw me and hit me in the neck. They took everybody out: old people, young people and children, to lie down in the street until a truck arrived to take us to the guards' cuartel. There, they asked me,

'Did you know that priest was armed?'

'Says who? Nobody here has weapons,' I answered.

'Yes, when we entered, that priest shot at us. You all were armed.'

They put pistols in the hands of some of the dead, took pictures, and put in the newspapers that there had been a confrontation in El Despertar."

Bersabe continues, "The family members of the young people who were at El Despertar went to the morgue to see who was dead. When we got there, it was full of people looking for their family members that had been killed or disappeared. Monseñor Romero was there, too. We saw five dead bodies there: David Caballero, Ángel Morales, Jorge Gómez, Roberto Orellana, and Padre Octavio. They were covered, but I saw that the soles of Jorge's feet were full of holes, like somebody had attacked him with a pickaxe. Octavio's face was destroyed."

Fabio concludes, "When the army sacked El Despertar, they destroyed everything that we had and robbed us of our money. We were back to zero, everything had disappeared: the store, the clinic, and a metalworking workshop."[116]

9 "Enough already, enough already, enough already of death and falsity. Enough already, enough already: That's the cry of San Antonio Abad. I bring you a shame of which to sing and not even bullets can stop me. Our blood fell again on January 20 in El Despertar.[117] Five bodies thrown to the ground raise up a people that begins to shout. The light that illuminated that early morning

was not the sun behind the mountain.
It was the example of one who valiantly
showed up for the oppressed
and gave his life for his friends
so that we, the blind,
could see clearly.
His ideal was liberty,
for everyone to live together in
   community.
He followed in the footsteps of
   Christ.
He was always ready
to take up his cross.
Now his light shines so brightly
in our own awakening.
Padre Octavio, you've left this earth
crushed by these beasts.
'Prophets go to heaven,'
sings the poet.
This is the hope of one who
reaches God's glory by shedding their
   blood,
opening up the history
of a new people.
Onward, with all our strength!
Let us erase all sadness.
Five brothers are calling us
to continue in the struggle.
We have to continue on
and never abandon our ideals,
this is what the martyrs of El Despertar
shout out to us."[118]

The Gospel According to Suchitoto

Like the Gospel accounts in scripture, the stories of the Good News of the church in El Salvador are multiple, at times contradictory, and written from a perspective of faith, in retrospect.

The story of the Gospel according to ecclesial communities in Suchitoto is, itself, dual. The first narrative attests to the leadership of Padre José Inocencio "Chencho" Alas, a diocesan priest who had studied at the IPLA[119] and was active in the 1970 Archdiocesan Pastoral Week for a *pastoral de conjunto*.[120] Padre Chencho had worked with upper middle class Catholics in San Salvador directing *cursillos de Cristiandad* ("little courses on Christianity"), but when he brought this work to the impoverished farmworker communities surrounding the town of Suchitoto, the fruits of the work became much juicier. The new ministries of Delegates/Celebrators of the Word and *animadores* of communities[121] flourished here, as they did in La Zacamil and in Morazán.

After Padre Chencho went into hiding, then exile, Padre Rutilio Grande was assigned to return to the land of his birth to be the parish priest in Aguilares, a small parish that had been split from Suchitoto in 1952. Padre "Tilo," as he was known, had also studied at the IPLA, and his first move as parish priest was to visit every local chapel in his sprawling rural parish to "see" the reality of the parish and create a pastoral plan based on the needs of the people. He reestablished theological formation courses with his parishioners and collaborated with local *campesino* organizers demanding access to land and fair working conditions for day laborers. As his friend Padre Octavio would be almost two years later, Padre Tilo was assassinated for his work on March 12, 1977.

It is no coincidence that the Gospel accounts of the first generation of Salvadoran CEBs, diverse as they may be, all end in passion and death. Like the original text of the Gospel of Mark, these experiences ended in terror, in fear; they end at the beginning of a civil war that would take approximately 75,000 lives and last for twelve years. Like the disciples of Jesús after the crucifixion, the members of these first communities went into hiding, faced persecution, and feared that their recent experiences of good news were over.

CAMPESINOS IN SUCHITOTO

1 Padre Chencho was assigned to the parish of Suchitoto in December 1968, the same year he completed his studies at the IPLA. Suchitoto was a municipality of just over 102 square miles, known for producing tobacco, cigars, and indigo. Of the 45,000 inhabitants of the parish/municipality, about 30% lived in the town center, and 70% lived in hamlets in the surrounding hills. Two large sugarcane plantations and a few "smaller" estates of up to 6,000 acres were owned by wealthy families and foreigners; the rest of the population worked primarily on small farms that rented land from large landholders or as landless day laborers. According to Padre Chencho,

"This concentration of land ownership, the lack of adequate and timely credit and technical assistance for small farmers, and a dependence on intermediaries, also known as 'coyotes,' at the markets have been some of the main causes of the injustices experienced in rural areas. These factors have engendered countless situations that have contributed to what the Latin American bishops have called the 'structures of violence.'

A ministry that does not, out of faith, confront these structures is out of step with history and becomes, as Marx said of religion, an 'opiate' of the masses. The truth is that religion in and of itself cannot be an opiate. We are the ones who make it an opiate or not, depending on our 'Christian' vision of the world and our commitment to our communities' existential reality."[122]

2 "The campesino man's cultural universe is concrete, not abstract. From childhood, he is used to working with materials, transforming them with his hands. His senses are highly developed. To understand the campesino's relationship with his environment, it is worth considering his relationship with corn. Before depositing the corn or bean seed in the furrow, he feels it in his hand, looks at it, admires it, and dreams of a lush corn and bean field in bloom. He uses his feet to cover the seeds. The plants have sprouted and are still very small when he clears them of weeds and fertilizes them. Once they have borne fruit, while the ear is tender, he makes atole from its grains, which is a family celebration, and later, once mature and the grains have dried, he transforms them into tortillas. The tortillas, patted out in the palms of the campesina women, are produced in alchemy with her body, which works, sweats, tires, and gives life; they are the culmination of a whole process. Therein lies corn's sacredness. It is work, food, life, the procreation of life, it is a gift from the gods or God. As a boy, I remember my mother forbidding me to cut a tortilla with a knife. I could not 'injure' it, because it is a divine gift."[123]

3 One day in early 1969, after administering the last rites to a rural man, surrounded by his wife and six children, Padre Chencho was riding his horse back to his house in the town center, reflecting on how much work was to be done in the parish and how helpless and alone he felt when faced with the task.

"Suddenly I was hit with an inspiration, a revelation that changed the course of my life. Clearly I could not do all the parish work on my own; it was impossible. Even if there were many fewer inhabitants, I would still not be able to do it. Instead, I needed to apply my theoretical knowledge learned at IPLA and other study centers. I must train people, leaders, who would then assume responsibility for many of the tasks for which I was non-essential . . .

I wondered, as I admired the fan of colors of the setting sun unfolding before my eyes, why I might not invite campesinos from all the cantons to attend courses on the Bible, leadership, social issues, and other subjects of interest to their lives."[124]

CELEBRANTS OF THE WORD

4 "The subject of the first course was the following: 'The formation of the community in the dynamics of divine revelation.' It dealt with achieving a clear idea of community, following step by step each book of scripture, from Genesis to Revelation. I had researched this subject in depth during my year of study at the Lumen Vitae International Institute in Brussels. 'Community' as a theme seemed very important to me for three reasons. First, the church is a community. Its founder, Jesús, conceived it this way, as a community of faith, hope, and love. Especially love, which is most needed. To believe is important, but we remember what the Apostle James says, 'Do not forget that the demons also believe, and tremble.'

. . . In the training we began to give in Suchitoto, we had courses in public speaking after dinner to end each day. This idea arose from a very interesting book written by Severo Martínez Peláez, a Guatemalan, titled *La patria del criollo* [*The fatherland of the creole*] . . . the part of the book that especially interested me was his reference to the pedagogy the conquistadores and their *criollo* descendants used with indigenous people to make them believe they could not think, and, therefore, could not speak, correctly. In my conversations with Salvadoran landowners and ranchers, I could see that they sustained the same assessment of campesinos, namely that they are lazy, immoral, and stupid, unable to express themselves; they are people without words. I therefore deemed it crucial to give them some public speaking techniques."[125]

5 "After two months of classes, of sleeping on the floor and eating beans and tortillas, we were wrapping up our first Celebrants of the Word course. Through their attendance, the nineteen campesino leaders had accepted the commitment of carrying out Celebrations of the Word every Sunday, giving Communion and working to organize their communities.

Before ending the course, we discussed the idea of having a celebration in one of the cantons. We planned to invite Monsignor Chávez[126] and the parishioners. It had to be something big to mark the launch of a new kind of ministry. I went to invite Monsignor Chávez and he gladly accepted. We chose the chapel of the Estanzuelas canton due to its easy access and location only four kilometers from Suchitoto. We selected two of the best speakers for the occasion.

It was an unforgettable day. The chapel was completely full, not a single person more could squeeze inside its four walls, and many had to participate from outside. Monsignor Chávez asked to attend without having an active role in the celebration, so I placed a chair close to the altar for him. It was the campesino's turn to preside over the liturgy and Communion. The homily, eloquent and poetic, was given by Antonio Valte, who years later was massacred by the National Guard in the Suchitoto marketplace.

After the service, I asked Monsignor Chávez to offer some words to the congregation, to tell us what he thought of the observance and to bless our work's continuation. Monsignor was visibly moved, tears of happiness streaming from his eyes. For the first time in the history of the Catholic Church in El Salvador, campesinos with calloused hands and sun-beaten faces gave out the sacred bread; they gave Communion to other campesinos who with faith and love approached the table of unity and love."[127]

6 "From then on, we had masses in each of the cantons. The leaders participated in the celebration of the Eucharist on Sundays at five in the morning in Suchitoto; afterwards, they returned to their chapels, and in the afternoon or evening the community congregated. The leaders of Zapote, Haciendita, and Mirandilla, neighboring cantons, decided to take turns with the services, one Sunday in one canton, the next in another. Their form of celebrating the Word was certainly the best, as it became a *fiesta*. Three or four hundred campesinos would come down Guazapa Hill. They would assemble on the roadside at about two in the afternoon.

When the leader who carried the hosts would arrive from Suchitoto, they would accompany him in a procession, singing psalms and songs of liberation. Songs with liberating lyrics have played an important role in the change processes of our countries; they have been an element that has gone hand in hand with our people's growing awareness.

As time passed, a new method of doing biblical readings in the services was introduced. Immediately after the readings, the congregation broke into groups of four or five persons and discussed the message among themselves. Then two or three small-group representatives were asked to present the opinions to the full group. Finally, the leader of the service summarized the exercise, motivating the participants to act. Sometimes the congregation decided upon a concrete action that the whole community would support. This way of discussing the biblical message gave rise to Christian Base Communities and their further development in Suchitoto. These were, to my knowledge, the first in the country."[128]

7 Before a eucharistic celebration in one of the communities, "several people approached me to confess, including a campesino about forty-five years old. As usual, he began in the traditional way, 'Forgive me, Father, for I have sinned.' I asked him what his sins were and he said, 'I have sinned against love.' To sin against love, in most cases, means the sexual abuse of a woman or a man, to be adulterous, and so on. I asked him to explain his sin and he said, 'I have sinned against love, because I am not organized.' His reply puzzled me. I did not expect it. I had not studied that kind of sin in morality coursework at the Gregorian Pontifical University of Rome, nor had I heard of it from the lips of the twentieth century's greatest professor of morality, Father Bernard Häring, at the Lumen Vitae Institute. My moral theology did not extend so far. I asked, 'And why do you say you have sinned by not being organized?' His answer was swift and sure. 'If I am not organized [as part of a farmworker association or labor union], it means I do not love my neighbor, that I do not care about my neighbor's life, that I am selfish.' For that campesino and for many others, to organize is an obligation that has its roots in the commandment to love. It is an obligation that goes beyond political, economic, or social reasons."[129]

The understanding that love of neighbor was connected to one's political and social commitments led the communities of Suchitoto to become very involved in the increasing social organizing around land reform, ultimately leading to Alas's participation in the 1969 congress on the topic called by the National Assembly. However, Fr. Alas, the new ministers of the Word, and the communities of the parish had begun to be targeted by the wealthy in Suchitoto and beyond. Spies had infiltrated the training courses and community liturgies. During the days of the congress, on January 8, 1970, Alas was kidnapped and later drugged and left alone near the town of Jayaque, only because of pressure from the archbishop. The parish of Suchitoto continued to suffer throughout the following decades; the Guazapa Volcano in rural Suchitoto was one of the most combative fronts of the war.

RUTILIO IN AGUILARES

8 After participating in the Archdiocesan Pastoral Week of 1970, Rutilio Grande traveled to Ecuador to study at the IPLA. When he returned, he was placed in the parish of Aguilares in September 1972. The parish of Aguilares had been formed in 1952, serving the municipalities of Aguilares and El Paisnal (which had previously belonged to the parish of Guazapa) and three communities from the municipality of Suchitoto. The pastoral plan Padre Tilo had worked on at the IPLA was ready to go, and he began his time in the parish with a "mission tour," visiting different neighborhoods of the town centers and different rural communities for two weeks at a time:

"The missions were intended to create communities of brothers and sisters, committed to the construction of a new world, without oppressors or oppressed, according to God's design.

'God is not in the clouds, reclining in a hammock, God is active and desires that you build the reign of God here on earth,' repeated Tilo untiringly. He also advised the most enthusiastic [parishioners] that they not be 'fireworks,' that is, that they not act like fireworks that shoot up to the sky, explode in a big show, and then fall as ash. The mission was to create a Christian commitment among the people."[130]

After the tour had completed its run, Padre Tilo organized *cursillos*, similar to Padre Chencho's earlier activity in neighboring Suchi. Instead of a public speaking focus, Tilo's courses included a general literacy campaign. New ways of celebrating liturgy emerged from these courses; "Delegates of the Word" were commissioned, and in addition to the traditional parish celebrations of patron saints, the first parroquial "corn festival" was celebrated on August 18, 1974.[131]

9 "Let us all go to the banquet, to the table of Creation.
Everyone who pulls us a seat
Has a place and a mission.
I wake up early today,
my community already awaits me.
I climb the hill happily,
I go in search of your friendship.
God invites all of *lxs pobres*,
To this common table of faith.
Where there are no hoarders,
and nobody is lacking for food.
God demands that we make of this world
a table of fraternity
working and struggling together
and sharing property."[132]

RUTILIO GRANDE, MARTYR[133]

10 "Passing the canton of Los Mangos, the children [who were in the car] testify that they saw a group of men along the edges of the sugarcane fields, 2 or 3 on each side of the highway. Then, all of a sudden, they saw Manuel [Solórzano, 72] and Nelson [Rutilio Lemus, 16] lean towards Tilo with tense faces. Nelson pushed his back against his seat with his hand on the door, as if an accident were about to happen. In the back, the kids looked at each other, afraid. Among the men posted on the sides of the highway they recognized Benito Estrada. Behind the Safari, another pickup drew near; it had apparently been following them from Aguilares. Without turning around, Tilo said in a low voice, 'We should do what God wants.' A friend of an informant in El Paisnal confirmed this affirmation of the surviving children . . .

Benito Estrada gave the signal and bullets began to rain down on the Safari and its occupants. When he was hit, Tilo lost control of the car, which was found with the bloody cadavers dumped over the left side, with the motor still running and the wheels spinning."[134]

The Gospel According to Morazán

The final selection of testimony about the first incarnations of the Gospel in the CEBs as the church of *lxs pobres* in El Salvador comes from Morazán, a mountainous, rural department in the northwest corner of the country, bordering Honduras. Faithful campesinos from this region testify to having participating in courses at Los Naranjos, the *centro de formación* run by the Passionists in Jiquilisco, Usulután, and at El Castaño, the *centro* run by the diocese of San Miguel.[135] In the testimony of this Gospel, Padre Rogelio refers to Padre Miguel Ventura's work forming delegates of the Word and ecclesial base communities in the early 1970s.

Most written testimony that has come out of these first experiences in Morazán was recorded in the mid-1980s. The majority of the first part of this account is taken from an undated booklet called *Luz de ocote* ("Light of Ocote Wood"),[136] a missive "from the church north of the Torola River in Morazán."[137] The booklet was likely written during the war and smuggled out to a refugee community in Nicaragua where it was published. This source material showcases the poetic imagery the CEBs use to describe their experience of this new way of being church, as different in tone from scholarly accounts as the Gospel of John is from the Synoptics. It also tells the story of the matriarchs of the church of *lxs pobres*, the "Congregations of Mothers" who formed during the war in Morazán to meet the vital needs of their children and communities.

The second half of this Gospel of the church of *lxs pobres* comes from a long-form interview with Belgian missionary priest Rogelio Ponselle. Padre Rogelio had been part of the early Zacamil experience and went to the front of the war when it began in early 1981. He ministered to guerrilla forces and civilian communities in FMLN-controlled territory.

As in other Gospel accounts of martyrdom, pastoral work in Morazán was interrupted in the late 1970s and early 1980s by the beginning of the war. Much of the civilian population in Morazán fled to refugee camps in Colomoncagua, Honduras, and elsewhere as government bombings and land incursions increased. Civilians who stayed sought refuge in town centers or lived mostly hidden in the woods. Others joined the guerrilla forces. It was to this remnant that Rogelio ministered, though the conflict made stable *centros de formación* and formal meetings and liturgy impossible.

HOW THE *OCOTE* CAUGHT FIRE

1 "Someone blows a couple times on the coals that seem to have died out, and they come alive again, and the breath moves the flame onto the *ocote*.

That's what happened in our life. The breath came, a new wind that brought a light that broke through the darkness. And our communities became a living church.

How did that breath arrive? In two ways: the Word of God came to us, and we, *los pobres*, began to have faith in other *pobres*.

We believed in God, it's true, but we did not know God's Word well. Perhaps the greatest fruit of the Second Vatican Council was to put in our hands, the hands of *los pobres* what was ours, though we didn't know it: our book, the Bible. The Council was an open window to the world and a fresh air that healed the Church. And it was how we came to read the Bible for the first time. Before, for all of history, the Bible was not familiar to us, nor read by us. It was even a prohibited book.

With the Council that changed. This book of God, subversive because it flips the tortilla, because it throws down the order of the kings and empires and lifts up *los pobres*, this book with its stories of liberation, with the messages of its prophets, with the life of Jesús that overcame death, with the stories of the first Christian communities, changed our lives. This book taught us that we, *los pobres*, are preferred by God, that God wants *los pobres* to stop being [poor], and that God wants us to work to change these things. Our encounter with the Bible was like an earthquake; it moved everything around, it changed our ways of thinking and of doing things. It was the first breath that turned the coals red. And in what seemed to be only ash, a fire was born.

After the Bible, which was brought to us by the Council, came the Medellín documents, which was the application of the Council to Latin America. The subversive wave of God arrived to our countries, so rife with injustice and oppression, and the bishops chose to be on the side of life for *los pobres*. The first document that they wrote spoke of justice. The second, of peace. Peace and justice: the two things that we, *los pobres*, most need and hope for, what we ask God for in our chapel on Sundays.

The coals became more red. It was only a question of a strong breath.

Priests, religious sisters, and new pastoral workers brought us the Bible and these documents. They opened catechetical centers where they prepared us to be catechists and Celebrants of the Word in our own communities. More and more breath.

Then Monseñor Romero came to us, and he preached the word of God in the midst of repression. His prophetic voice moved the flame to the *ocote*. The red coals became fire. He was the one who did this. Through him, we were able to understand what God was saying to us, we were able to understand that the Word of God spoke to our own lives. We began to see that Christian faith is a task and a commitment. And so we, men and women *pobres*, began to stop believing in the false promises of outsiders, of the great and powerful, and we turned to our fellow peasant, to our neighbor, to reflect with him and organize with him and to believe in him. 'When *el pobre* believes in *el pobre* / then we can sing of freedom ...' We began to believe and to sing. *Los pobres* turned to *los pobres*, the chosen of God. And our neighbor, who had nothing and could do nothing, became a brother in faith. And believing in God and believing in our brothers, we began to walk.

Our communities were born, the CEBs, the ecclesial base communities, communities of the church and of this base that we are poor Salvadoran Christians, thirsty for justice, hungry for bread and for dignified peace.

Many other Christian organizations were also born, which came from our pastoral leaders and our communal leaders. Our communities' organizing was born. We were no longer alone. The coals were on fire, and the flames came together. And in the fire, no one flame is alone, and they cannot be distinguished from each other. Where one ends, the other begins, and they are all light."[138]

2 "When the peasants returned to their villages [from courses at El Castaño in San Miguel], they began to organize CEBs that within a few years involved more or less one-third of the population. Reflecting on her experience, Altagracia, a middle peasant from a small village, a teenager in the early 1970s, says:

'We shared the difficulties.... Our first thoughts were always, "What can I do for my neighbor?" For us we went along as if we were like a flock; where the catechists went, we all went. And if something happened to someone all of us were ready to help. We protected each other.'

Gabriela Hernández, a poor peasant from a village near Torola, who was a teenager in the mid-1970s, discussed the origins of collective farming:

'When someone was unable to tend his or her fields, the organization helped. That's how it started.

Later, they made a collective, a large *milpa*. And Don Hernández who had fertile land... allowed for the people to cultivate there. When the harvest was ready they would divide it up. They divided it up among all those who worked and sometimes to those who didn't work as well. It was about improving the quality of life.'

Inspired by Acts 4:32, as Gabriela pointed out, some of the middle peasants donated land to the community: 'The people began to share their goods and properties... our sense of property changed.'

Regino, a poor peasant, from the Torola area, a young adult in the mid-1970s, conjured up the joyful quality of the experience: 'We finished weeding one *milpa* and went to another. We finished the other and continued to the next. We finished all the weeding in the whole valley. We didn't feel the burden of the labor.'

These practices were intimately involved in the process of individual and communal transformation, including to a degree, of gender relations. Although during the early 1970s, only males were chosen to attend the peasant training centre at El Castaño, San Miguel, female participation in the CEBs was extremely high. One salient effect of that participation was a significant decline in domestic abuse. Referring to her domestic abuse, Gabriela commented, 'It is a miracle that I am here,' ascribing the transformation of her husband to their participation in the CEB."[139]

SPARKS EVERYWHERE

3 "Once lit, the fire has its own story.

For example, we have the case of one of our new groups, the 'Congregation of Christian Mothers.' In 1985, the community of Carrizal, in Perquín, was forced by the Arce Battalion[140] to leave their homes, and all the families were forced to flee. When they got to Tejera, the Air Force[141] bombed them: there were two killed and many injured.

A group of people from Perquín went to see them. But they didn't even have a first aid kit to take care of those who were injured. Life was speaking there, in that pain, in that impotence of not being able to do anything. A group of women reflected about the gospel: 'I was hungry and you gave me to eat, I was naked and you clothed me.... Whenever you did this to the least of my brothers, you did it to me.... When you didn't do it to them, with my brothers, it was to me that you didn't do it.' So they felt interrogated by God, who spoke to them in this life event, so fresh and present.

From there, they decided to form a group committed to defending life: the Congregations of Christian Mothers. Soon, other women from other regions did the same. It was the first organization of women north of the Torola River. The Word of God and faith in my women neighbors, as poor as I myself was, lit the *ocote* fire.

So in that way, literacy groups and health brigades were born, and communal committees and cooperatives grew. More and more projects. They were all signs of life, signs of hope, while at the same time being signs of liberation.

Other women organized to find food for children. When they decided to do it, they didn't know that they would have to face the army, who gave them a hard no and didn't let them through.

These women, who had never traveled further than from the grinding stone to the well, found themselves all of a sudden fighting for their rights in the halls of power. They fought hard and returned victorious. They had to break through the fence, and the provisions arrived for the children and for everybody. From that victory others were born: raising chickens, baking bread, sewing, and guaranteeing bread and milk for the children. Every project was a sign of life, one more announcement that liberation was coming . . .

At last, a miracle. Any of us, man or woman, if we had gone before to the departmental capital, it was to fix a personal or family problem. And now we were going not just for ourselves but for the whole community. We had never before seen such marvels, never.

Prophetic actions were born, like the ones we had read about in the Bible. Because we, too, had to be prophets of the God in which we believed, the God of *los pobres*, the one who is with the least of these."[142]

4 "Before, we were like flies. We learned how to be wasps. This is another comparison we use. Before, it was like when there's a table full of flies and somebody kills one with a big slap of their hand. All the other flies are spooked and do not return. That's how we were. When they captured a brother, when they killed him, we were spooked. Everyone ran back into their houses, even thanking God that nothing had happened to me, that I was safe.

That's not how wasps are. When there's a hive and somebody comes to kill a wasp, all the wasps come out to sting the one who killed their sister. That's how we are now. We are all together, defending each other. We became wasps. We became a people. Or, as the gospel says: we became new women and new men. We were born from water and the Spirit. We were born again."[143]

MASS BEHIND ENEMY LINES

5 "Mass is a festive moment for everybody. We celebrate when we can, whether it's Sunday or not. People come from the villages, from the cantons, in their best dress. And however poor the community may be, it always seems like a festival, little vendors everywhere. They sell cookies, or bananas or watermelon, little things like that. Or they make *fresco*.[144]

When I have an alb, I put it on. Sometimes I don't have it because I've lost it. I always wear a stole. It helps make the mass feel more celebratory. And we can make any space into a sanctuary. A tree, a little table, a tablecloth, flowers ... what always makes an impression on me is that before mass, people come up to me to tell me the names of their fallen so that I can dedicate mass to them. I always bring a notebook.

'Write down the name of my dad, of my mom, of my three little brothers, of my grandma, my uncle ...'

Everybody like that. And those names are never of those who have died from sickness. They have been killed. They died in a massacre, or in a bombing. Sometimes in a page of my notebook I have just one or two names that are there for 'God's death.' That's what they call someone who died of sickness: that it was God's death. So many assassinated, so many ...

Mass is simple. Bible readings and then a reflection shared by everybody. A biblical text and then three simple little questions. From those three questions they start to make connections between the Bible and their own lives. They say:

'That's what's happening today! It's the same!'

It pleases them tremendously to discover that what is written in the Bible is what they are living, what they're doing. It gives them strength. The Bible is the most beautiful book that there is. Because we open a Bible to any page and:

'¡Púchica! Yeah, that's just like us!'

There's no better book to help the people understand their history, is there?

... There are many members [of the guerrilla] that come to mass and feel hesitant to come up to receive communion. Because they've participated in battle, they've shot and they've killed. And they carry this scruple. Although not everybody says it, they carry it. They come to mass, they participate, but they don't come up for communion. I always insist that they not feel squeamish, that the fact that they are fighting and willing to give their lives isn't just a job for them. Rather, it is a fact, and this is the greatest commitment, the most Christian commitment. Because they are willing to give their lives for the rest, they have the full right to draw near to communion. I tell them that and I am convinced of what I say.

So Mass is a festival, the community's party. When I've been in Europe, oh, those European masses are a crying shame! In Zacamil, too, mass was a festival, it was joy, it was participatory. One time I went back to Belgium and they had me celebrate mass in Louvain, in a very valuable church, centuries old. . . . They put me behind a giant altar, and I had to put on all the paraphernalia, the chasuble, everything. And I was fifty meters away from the people! I couldn't preach, I couldn't find the words to say anything. I had prepared beforehand, but I didn't know what to say. I just thought, 'What am I doing here? What does this mean?' I've never asked myself that when I celebrate mass under a tree here with the people."[145]

6 "We had to start doing community-based work. So I started giving courses for a few days at a time, like we had done before in San Salvador. I sat down with those who would be community animators, catechists, delegates of the Word. In Morazán I found many men who had been catechists years before. With them, we made a plan for our work, and we made some organizing decisions. In the whole region of Morazán, we had fifty catechists, but the really well-formed ones were very few. The catechists visit communities when we have to be far away for a while, going from one place to another because of the war. They are the ones who call the community to reflect as a group or for a celebration of the Word or for mass, when I cannot go to celebrate it.

The community meets with the delegate of the Word. They are campesinos who barely know how to read. To read a selection of the Bible, they take a long time, and I, who am so impatient, sometimes I get nervous. I start worrying about if the people understand them or not, if they're taking too long, if people are bored. Because after taking so long to read, they preach for a long time. But truly, the worry is all mine. The people understand each other and they like it. With their simple words, with little examples, they explain everything. Sometimes it's me whom they don't understand. Because there are always language deficiencies, cultural differences, so many differences."[146]

7 "Sometime about a year after I had been at the front another priest came to work here in Morazán: Padre Miguel Ventura, who is Salvadoran. At the beginning of the seventies, he had been very active in the area, working to raise consciousness, forming base ecclesial communities. A few years earlier, they had captured him and tortured him. He felt that he had no support from his bishop, nor from other priests who were around here then. And he left the country and went to the United States. There the danger is that one gets comfortable, little by little, right? He worked for solidarity, with refugees, he learned English, but he became comfortable.

In 1981 he realized that I was here in Morazán and he began to question himself. To get less comfortable, we could say. He passed through Nicaragua and saw some footage of the front of the war here, films that people have made about life here.... When he saw all his people, people that he had formed, now commanders of the FMLN, here working, they told me that he said:

'No more footage!'

And he went off to think. He began to think about returning. In 1982, he arrived here. He knew Morazán better than I did, he knew the map of every single footpath. We went to the cantons, and in every corner someone would come out:

'Bloody hell, Miguel, you're back!'

And hugs. His re-encounter with his people was so emotional. And he stayed. We are friends, peers.

I've learned to be patient from Miguel. I am very impatient, I always have been. He has helped me to be more calm with people. He is of campesino origins, a very deep and priestly man.

'No, Rogelio, it's good that the delegate of the Word be the one to do the reading, people will understand them. It's more important for him to do it than someone who knows how.'

I still have so much to learn from Salvadorans."[147]

Acts of the Repatriated

As the Gospel accounts indicate, the church of *lxs pobres* in El Salvador lived through their own experience of a Passion during the 1980s. Because of the war, many pastoral leaders and members of the CEBs were killed, disappeared, exiled, or traumatized because of their commitments to their Gospel. Whole communities were disbanded as people fled to internal refugee settlements, like at the major seminary, San José de la Montaña, or outside the country, to Mesa Grande or Colomoncagua in Honduras, to Nicaragua, to Mexico and Belize, or even to the United States, Europe, and Australia. If the communities that arose in the late 1960s and early 1970s were a true incarnation of the Gospel in El Salvador, the 1980s were a shroud and a stone rolled in front of the tomb.

However, after this death, the church of *lxs pobres* did not remain silenced. The CEBs were reborn as refugees came back to their homeland, even before the Peace Accords were signed. This *librito* tells a few of their stories. We conceive of these CEBs as a kind of "second generation," characterized by a postwar context; membership, both clerical and lay, who were formed during the 1960s and 1970s, and little accompaniment from the national hierarchy.

Lay and religious leaders of the church of *lxs pobres* who had gathered in San Salvador for protection and hiding during the war began to disperse back to accompany refugees returning to protected sites in rural municipalities: Padre Rogelio, Miguel Ventura, and Carmen Elena of the *Pequeña Comunidad*[148] accompanied the Segundo Montes resettlement as CEBES Perquín; Padre Pedro and others of the *Pequeña Comunidad* went to Usulután; still others of the *Pequeña Comunidad* stayed near San Salvador, in San Ramón and Mejicanos. A group of lay leaders continued to give life to CEBES,[149] the semi-institutional Pastoral Center in San Salvador that served as an informal point of communications and formation for pastoral agents in the late 1980s and 1990s. In 2000, CEBES became the FUNDAHMER, named for a lay catechist who worked tirelessly to form new CEBs after the war. Before he died, Mercedes, a father and husband, encouraged his fellow lay leaders to register CEBES as a formal nonprofit with the Salvadoran government so that they could receive funding from solidarity organizations and help people rebuild their communities. FUNDAHMER has since served as an important tool for the communities' continual formation and is the legal owner, on the CEBs' behalf, of a few parcels of land, trucks, and a meeting space in the capital. This proved to be an essential support as international missionary presence decreased and the Salvadoran clergy and hierarchy became increasingly intolerant of the CEBs. The tension between institutionalization and organic organization, however, has also been a challenge in this second generation of Salvadoran CEBs.

This *librito* hopes to describe, in community members' own words, some of the challenges and joys of the renascent CEBs at the very end of the 1980s and throughout the 1990s and early 2000s. Sources include didactic pamphlets and autobiographies of the CEBs from this period, a documentary about the Segundo Montes community, and testimony from individuals working pastorally among the CEBs during these years.

REFUGEE CEBS

1 "Persecution caused many refugees: Salvadorans that sought to save their lives had to emigrate to other countries. CEBES was also present among them, forming CEBs.

The initiation talks were the same. However, at the beginning, we added two talks about the reality [of refugee communities] and then continued with the same initiation topics we presented earlier.

The only way to begin this pastoral work of birthing CEBs, the church of *los pobres*, is to start from the lived reality of our brothers and sisters . . .

Topic B: We are refugees in 'X' place

1. Read Numbers 13:23–24
2. Do you believe that we can live with this same hope? Why or why not?
3. Since we left our country, have we been able to take advantage of opportunities to prepare ourselves to give something back when we return?
4. As a family, how are we doing in terms of education?
5. What have we learned about health and healthcare?
6. What have we learned about production?
7. How have we continued to support our people from here? What possibilities are there?
8. What tasks do we propose for ourselves in this sense?

9. Let's go back to the text to conclude: Numbers 13:23–24."[150]

SEGUNDO MONTES

2 "In Colomoncagua,[151] the 9,000 refugees began to organize little by little, thanks to the leadership that already existed among them and the support of NGOs and volunteers in solidarity with the victims. They organized teams for farming, sewing, shoemaking, welding, cooking, literacy campaigns, school, daycare, healthcare, a cafeteria for children, raising chickens, rabbits and goats, a radio team, and political and pastoral formation committees.

During a visit, the Jesuit priest and sociologist Segundo Montes saw this reality and his mind was illuminated and he prophesied: 'You all should organize yourselves to repatriate and live out this alternative economic system. This is an economic model for a participative democracy, of self-sustainability and mutual aid. You all can and should serve as a different kind of response to the conflict in El Salvador.'

From that point on, the work multiplied. They made contact with UNHCR,[152] they made plans and selected responsible leaders to coordinate all the different areas of life. They also had to confront the migration officials of El Salvador.

In response, the head migration official, Colonel Figueroa, came to say that a repatriation would not be possible: 'You all have come of your own will, through much danger, to this place and now you want to return of your own will to a highly conflictive zone. We don't want responsibility for that.'

But the multitude of 9,000 souls shouted in chorus: 'This Christmas we want to be in Meanguera, Morazán!'

That's how our true exodus began, with the footsteps of Salvadoran refugees back to their homeland. Wearing all their clothes and taking anything else they could carry. They were in the custody of the Honduran army, and the soldiers insisted to the journalists that accompanied the crowd, 'These are all communists.' But the People of God on their journey said, 'We are joyful.'

It was during the time of the insurgency's 'Until it's over' offensive of 1989. It was during the time when the Jesuit priests and their two collaborators were violently assassinated. Among them was that prophet who had inspired this great feat of returning, of repatriation: Segundo Montes. Because of this, their new settlement would be called 'Segundo Montes.' Juan José Rodríguez, of the leaders of the refugees clarified during the inauguration ceremony of the new city 'Segundo Montes' to the authorities and to the UNHCR that they demanded freedom of travel, of trade, and the free passage of people and the goods they produced. For this, it was necessary to build a bridge over the Torola River. It was a true Easter. The humble and crushed people had risen up, and with their heads held high and their hearts decided, they began to build houses and homes. They started primitively to give classes and administer healthcare. They began to cultivate the land and to raise animals. They were organized again, now in their own land. They made their own clothes and shoes. With the funds they had been given by the UNHCR for their journey, $50 per person, they founded their own bank: Bancomo.

Life began! Their own future had begun. The Lord was present among them. It was the Easter of the repatriated peoples."[153]

3 Segundo Montes proclaimed to the refugee community in Colomoncagua: "I think that your decision to live in community is the only right and possible choice. Only by creating community will you have your own means to work. Your own means of protection, your own energy to develop, to care for each other and to help those around you in El Salvador. Some people are going to try to prevent it because it is against the system. It's opposed to it. The current one is an individualistic system, a competitive system, a system where everyone goes for his or her own best interest. They will call you subversives, they will see you as a threat, they will try to break your unity in every way and your strength will be to remain united in community and to demand your rights collectively . . .

I believe that your decision to return now to El Salvador is a very important thing. You will have problems there and the situation will not be easy, but the challenges you face as a community and you can meet. You have proved that here in the camps. You can model for others a new way of living, especially for *los pobres*, a model that works, not just a theory. But don't let anyone else do your administration for you. Ask them to help you see where the mistakes might be and to teach you what you need to learn next. You can do it. You have already shown that. And if you're unable to run your own enterprises, your own production, you will have failed. You will always then be workers for a master, a patron or whatever, whether a foreigner or domestic and that's the trick behind it. If daddy does it for you, he will never release you, you have to take a risk, you have to make mistakes and correct them yourselves. I have thought many times that there really is no hope for the future of El Salvador, but when I came here for the first time, I changed my mind."[154]

CACAOPERA

4 The Segundo Montes settlement did not have the capacity to receive all 9,000 refugees from Colomoncagua; some folks decided to return to the land on which they had lived before. In particular, the municipality of Cacaopera, to the south of Segundo Montes, straddling the Torola River, received many repatriated families who brought their organized way of life with them.

The family of martyred priest Octavio Ortiz was among this group of refugees.[155] Before his assassination, Octavio's sisters had already fled the violence in their home, Cacaopera, to San Salvador, and after his assassination, Octavio's parents fled to Colomoncagua, where they remained for much of the war. His brothers were all killed. After the Peace Accords were signed, Octavio's parents, Don Alejandro and Niña Chon, reunited with their daughters and took up Octavio's work accompanying the CEBs that remained in San Salvador and forming new CEBs back home in Cacaopera. Octavio's youngest sister, Anita, started working with CEBES after she was reunited with her father:

"For me, this is the inheritance that my father left me. Because when he came back from the refugee camp, the first thing he did was to get involved in the communities where Octavio had been working, in Zacamil, San Ramón, San Antonio Abad. And when I started to live with them, he took me to all the liturgies; I think he still felt like I was a little girl to be dragged around everywhere. We walked from Mejicanos[156] to La Zacamil because there was no direct bus. We walked down 25th for about a half an hour, and we came to all of the Zacamil celebrations. And I got interested because, well, I had grown up with a different kind of religiosity when I was living with Fr. Roberto [during the war], it was totally different. He never talked about the Salvadoran reality, never . . .

I think that the most impactful experience for me was when my dad took me to Cacaopera to visit some communities. We would take long hikes, since he had started to visit the communities in Agua Blanca, meeting with people and families, because he wanted to help organize them again. So all of a sudden he was talking to Luis and me about the communities in Cacaopera, saying that people needed to be attended to, because nobody visited them and the parish priest never went to the communities and all that. So we thought it would be interesting to go with my dad, keeping him company and getting to know the area. One time we did a whole tour, starting from the town of Cacaopera, through Yancolo, passing through Junquillo, we went to Guachipilín, and down to El Rucio until we got to Estancia. We went with an Australian woman, Michelle Gierck, who had come as a volunteer. She said to me,

'Look, I don't know how your dad is so fit to be able to walk so much, and how he knows all these paths!'

Because yeah, he led us on so many trails and paths that I had never known. I remember very well that my dad knew everybody, even where each person lived, and we walked around visiting them, and seeing if they wanted to start meeting again, that the danger was over and that we should be organized. And he told them about the experience of the Zacamil community and others. He said,

'Folks over in San Salvador are really well-organized,' he told them. 'They meet and have celebrations, and here we have to be organized, too.'

I confess that for me, it wasn't just returning to the land we had left. This experience hit me hard, and it has stayed with me, recorded in my memory and my heart. I can still hear my dad saying that his wish was to live and work there. He would say,

'I will come here and we will be organized again and we will meet and we will celebrate.'

That was his dream, and he told so many people how he wanted to do it. I think that always stuck with me, and now I try to give it meaning in my own life. What I said to him was,

'Yeah, dad you can still walk this whole way, and my tongue is hanging out of my mouth!'

He was always so serene, climbing these mountains to get to Guachipilín without getting tired! So, for me, after walking through that whole region again, I think that's where my desire comes from, my desire to work like him. Later when we [CEBES, then FUNDAHMER] started to visit these communities, he always wanted to go to guide us and visit the families. We also started to go to the meetings with Padre Rogelio in Perquín, because that's where all the catechists went, like Cresencio from Yancolo. Victor went from Estancia, and Tomasito went from Calavera. They went from those three communities to Perquín to receive pastoral formation, and after those meetings, I went with them back to their communities . . .

When my dad died I made a commitment to continue working with and for these communities that my father loved so much. This long walk that I went on with my dad, it was like a second baptism that he gave me. The first was to bring me to church and introduce me to the Christian community, and the second was this, to reintroduce me to these communities where I was born, so that I would stay with them. My dad wanted to do so much, and he did a lot, and something that gave him so much satisfaction was to see one of his dreams become a reality: to build a chapel that was given the name of his son, Octavio. This was a milestone that he saw and experienced. But he also wanted to see untied and organized communities, and I think he sowed the seeds for that."[157]

5 "Brothers and sisters, let us walk!
The path is narrow,
but we should arrive.
The labors are difficult,
but there will be no tears at the end!
Sisters and brothers, let us walk!
Our pavilion is right up ahead.
It doesn't matter if we fall.
At last, we will overcome the
  mediocrity
of this society."[158]

BAJO LEMPA

6 "The first pastoral team that was beginning to do its evangelizing work in the Bajo Lempa region[159] had met to start planning the Ash Wednesday and Lenten celebrations. There were still very few communities in the area. It was 1992.

But new communities were coming from Morazán. There were so many repatriated people in the community of Segundo Montes. Many families had decided that it was better to migrate towards the Bajo Lempa region where there were two new communities, Ciudad Romero and Nueva Esperanza. A little further south was the Lempamar Hacienda where they thought it would be possible to squat and begin a new life. Silently, clandestinely, the families traveled with a little bit of corn, a little bit of beans and one change of clothing to take up residence among the trees and start to build their shacks to live in. Solidarity was built among us, *los pobres*, and the refugees of Ciudad Romero and Nueva Esperanza were feeding the new occupants hidden [in the woods].

The pastoral team had some knowledge of this migration. They reflected that these people were good, religious people. Maybe they would like to celebrate Ash Wednesday. But on Wednesday, there wasn't any time because of the schedule of celebrations in the other communities. We proposed doing something on Tuesday afternoon before Ash Wednesday. The pastoral team was sure that they would like it, and it was an opportunity to initiate contact with these new residents. It was the new Galilee of the repatriated. It was called Lempamar.

The Pastoral team set out. They got to the place and looked to speak with someone to tell them about our decision and to ask them to let people know to gather in a place that was a little clear but still had shade. We saw some movement in the trees. They were telling each other, and from what we could tell, it was hurried. We began to look for a plank of wood to improvise an altar. The priest brought the chalice and the paten and everything that was necessary for mass. While we waited for the priest, we thought about possible readings for the event. Isaiah 58:2–7 seemed good. It seemed right to explain, together with Isaiah, that the fasting that God wants is to break unjust chains and to untie the knots of the yokes. They would understand this well because they had suffered for years and years."[160]

7 "All of a sudden, the new occupants came out at a gallop. The men had machetes in their hands, the women had sticks and branches, and young people had rocks. They did not run toward our improvised altar, but rather towards the road and up the hill. What was going on? Nobody said anything. The priest gathered up his ritual instruments and followed the crowd in a big cloud of dust generated by the pace of a people on their way, in his pickup that became full of grandmothers and children armed with sticks and stones.

The people arrived at a place on the road where their neighbor, Santos, was giving a speech, encouraged by the arrival of a whole group of folks. Some strange visitors had arrived who were claiming their land. The supposed owner of the land, with his bodyguards well-armed with pistols, was demanding the displacement of the people. Santos, full of the Holy Spirit, in defense of the people, explained that this demand would never be fulfilled and that these poor folks, these *pobres*, were in negotiation with the government and that the visitors please put down their weapons to avoid a full battle. The visitors, clearly surprised by the certainty with which Santos spoke and intimidated by the arrival of so many people, put their weapons down, and let Santos arrest them in front of everybody. It was already dark. The prisoners spent all night on the shores of the Lempa River, watched and cared for by the people. The next morning, Santos called the police force of the UN peace process observers (ONUSAL) who came to pick up the visitors without a scratch. The land had been saved.

After that incident, the pastoral team went back to where they had come from meditating on what had happened. The priest hadn't preached a word. Rather, the people had given a great sermon on Isaiah 58:2–7. With all these events, the homily for the next day was ready. The pastoral team had learned so much!"[161]

PENTECOST

8 "In the formation of our CEBs together with the [formation of a political] people struggling for their lives, we had many chats and talks about topics from our lives. For many weeks, and on many of our neighbors' patios we met to dialogue, to reflect, and to debate about real life. This taught us to speak again. For three years, Monseñor Romero had been our voice, the voice of the voiceless. Now we learned to speak. And afterwards, we were invited by the pastoral team to participate in a two day Christian retreat.

The retreat with Jesús transformed people. Common, everyday people suddenly were transformed into extraordinary people. They committed, body and soul, and headed back towards their homes full of purpose and excellent proposals. The Spirit present in them said that they could change, that they could change their lives, their families, and to convince others with the examples of their new lives and to proclaim that there was still hope for a future. They wanted to talk about all that when they got back.

But there was one more surprise. When they got back to their communities, at the chapel or the community space, there was a crowd of family members, their children and their neighbors, waiting for them with flowers and songs. They hadn't expected this. They were forgiven before asking for forgiveness. They were awaited before arriving. They were celebrated before giving their testimony. Emotions and joy mixed together. They had thought to speak upon their arrival, but first, they had to hear how their families, friends, and neighbors awaited them as new kind of people. This time, the songs bore their full weight.

Nobody understood what was happening. Their faces shone from emotions and hope. They began to talk about their retreat with Jesús. And they talked about commitment and self-gift, about reconciliation and new life. The people who had gathered there were somewhat disconcerted because they saw the true image of their family member or neighbor. Some who had come by to see what all the noise was about said, 'Maybe they are drunk.'

So they stood up again to give testimony about how their lives were going to change because they had discovered their mission. It was the Spirit that allowed them to speak.

They had had the experience of a new kind of life. It wasn't just knowledge. It wasn't a doctrine. It was the very stuff of new life that was born in them that they expressed.

It was time to finish the retreat. It was necessary for each one, after their public testimony, to go home to start the first fulfillment of their promises. But not without first agreeing on a time and place for the next meeting, because we had to make plans for this dynamic group.

It was the first Pentecost in the experience of our CEBs."[162]

9 "It was in 1999 when the bishop proposed that a new pastoral plan be made to begin the new millennium and the jubilee year with a new pastoral attitude . . .

The CEBs' method was used: see, judge or illuminate, and act.

The result of more than a year of work was expressed through a primary objective and four specific objectives. The primary or general objective went like this:

'To consolidate our diocesan church in communion and participation, as a witness and ferment of the reign of God, to accompany processes towards a society of justice, fraternity, and solidarity.'

The four specific objectives were:

- Ecclesial Base Communities
- The formation of pastoral agents
- Family Ministry
- Social Ministry . . .

The first specific objective stated: 'To empower the process of the CEBs, which, living the triple ministries of Christ,[163] would be a ferment of the reign of God in history.'

Criteria for action:

1. That in the parishes, all decisions, debates, and actions are taken with the criteria of the reign of God as the goal and the Church as a sign and an instrument of the reign of God.
2. That in the parishes, all decisions, debates, and actions take into account that the CEBs are church, in communion with the hierarchy.
3. That 'participation' be the most important criterion for the parish: in liturgy, in reflection, in formation, in prophetic and social ministries, in the form of suggestions, decision-making,

and even the execution of these pastoral goals.
4. That all reflection and action be open to the 'signs of the times,' the surprise factor of the Holy Spirit.
5. That for all reflections and actions, the Bible and magisterial documents, especially those documents of the Latin American magisterium, illuminate us. That the first [early Christian] communities be our model and that the travelers to Emmaus (Luke 24) model for us our method: see, judge, act . . .

Then, a team was formed to share and promote this plan. The existing CEBs were on the front lines of this mission, and four two-day retreats were held in four of the five vicariates of the diocese, with the presence of an average of seventy-five lay people per retreat.

We have also been able to carry out three follow-up sessions with a large part of those attendees. We even held some workshops to produce materials for the pastoral agents, which resulted in the book 'Accompanying the CEBs' *animadores*.'"[164]

10 "The Bible is the word of life, the Bible is the word of God, and it is the word of the people who seek and create their own liberation.
It is the word of the people who seek and construct their own liberation.
The Bible is a candle that shines in the midst of darkness, and it is the word that guides the whole community.
The Bible is like our *cuma*[165]—
We have to use it to weed out every bitterness
that exists in our reality.
The Bible is like the rain
that makes our *milpas* grow,
and that sprouts the seeds
of love and joy.
The Bible is like the tortillas
that we make in the *comal*[166]
because it is for sharing
in order to cultivate fraternity."[167]

Letter from the Community "Pueblo de Dios en Camino"

The following series of letters in the salvation history of the CEBs of El Salvador is drawn from the contemporary testimony of communities that represent a third "generation" of CEBs. This third stage of the church of *lxs pobres* is marked by a post-reconstruction context (i.e., from the 2000s to the present), a marked separation from the parish, and (thus) an increased interest in and concern for sacramental and liturgical celebration. The letters respond to the signs of the times of our contemporary era, including migration, violence, and the destruction of the natural world. One of the first communities to experience a separation from their home parish is the CEB Pueblo de Dios en Camino (People of God on the Way), in the neighborhood of San Ramón, near San Salvador.

The words of this account come almost exclusively from the community members themselves, as recorded in different interviews over the span of two to three years. The people of Pueblo de Dios en Camino cover many topics in these conversations, published elsewhere, but here we have selected particular events from their history and some of the topics they find most compelling as a community, including Indigenous heritage and the sacraments.

1 "Maybe I should begin by saying that the way we are now, and have been for fifteen years, is a small fruit of other experiences that began forty-six years ago. We ecclesial base communities have just celebrated forty-six years of existence. And on that banner over there, is a man, and he is the one who was the first missionary who came to San Salvador, motivated by Medellín, by the practice of Medellín, came to call the baptized to be church. Because before, the idea was that the church

was the temple, the building. But very early on, we discovered that we, the baptized, are the church. And I think our greatest motivation comes from having known people who gave great testimony with their lives, people who really gave of themselves, so generously, who felt so much responsibility to be citizens and to make changes. And along the way, many gave their lives. And so, yes, we are the inheritors of that generation.

I, personally, am so grateful to God that I have encountered this way of being church. And I had this encounter because of one of our martyrs, Silvia. Silvia was a religious sister of the people. That is, she spent all of her time with the people, she took her three vows, and she consecrated her life in service. And with her, we learned together, forming youth groups and sharing our talents, putting what we knew at the service of the people. She was assassinated in this massacre [of Cutumay Camones in Santa Ana]. She died there with ninety-seven others, assassinated by the army. And her life is what motivated me and other young people; we didn't want her to be forgotten. So she is a source of energy and life for my own life and for other young people, for people now who want to learn about our martyrs.

To tell you a little more about us, before our community looked like we do now, we were part of a parish. We were organized into a parish, and our commitments were there. It was a parish run by a team of priests from the Maryknoll Association that worked in this area for many years. The work in the parish was very dynamic, very participative, very horizontal, where lay people, women and men, made decisions.

But once that team left, a different story began. Then, we were working with a very verticalist and powerful ecclesial vision, where we lay people had no voice and made no decisions. We just had to get on board and say, 'Yes, Father. Yes, Father.' But since we had learned from our past, we could not be subdued. And we knew we had dignity, too. We couldn't let ourselves be disrespected by them. So we began to question the priest. And he said it was better for us to be out than in. And well, he, too, had his own problems. He was a pedophile priest. He abused children. So the official church, to avoid the scandal, just moved him and stayed silent.

And then another priest came. And so, again, we sought communication with him, but just the same, he said, 'You can come to Mass.' But we don't need only to go and listen to Mass! We want to manifest our faith and our Christian way of living. But we do not fit in the institution. So, 'We have a challenge,' we said to ourselves fifteen years ago. 'We will continue to meet, and if this is of God, it will continue.' And now it has been fifteen years!"[168]

2 "We began meeting in a house that a young Maryknoll missionary was renting, and that's where the name of the Christian community that I belong to today was born:

Pueblo de Dios en Camino. Even though I had received a little formation and had grown up in the church, I didn't know anything about the ecclesial base communities. One of the women who met with us had been born before me and had belonged to these Christian communities since her adolescence. And so we began to do our own celebrations, going from one place to another. Little by little, we began to understand what an ecclesial base community was. According to my humble opinion, an ecclesial base community is a Christian experience where you learn and unlearn about the life of Jesús and try to understand human beings/being human from one's own wisdom and mistakes, in reflection with the group, in community, while making contributions, even in the smallest way, to create a new society.

I believe that we are where we are because history has moved us to this place. Something made us search for another way, and as a believer, I would say that it was the Spirit of Jesús, or of the Creator and Former.[169] In our ancestors' way of thinking, nothing was a coincidence because everything was a coincidence. Things happen because they have to happen for a specific reason.

We are in another stage in history where we are obligated to reflect on Jesús from outside of the temple. This has caused me to deepen in restlessness, and I wonder about the following questions:

Why call ourselves *ecclesial* base communities if this new reality contrasts with the canons and norms of the church where I grew up?

Why be Christian, if this is a name that is too big for us, compared to the ideal of Jesús and the reality we see every day of injustice, of death, of rape, of abuse, of discrimination, and the religious representatives of Christian churches do not say anything, so approving of injustice and war?

How are we to transform this reality that destroys our being, and [causes] the slow death of the natural world from our small Christian community?

Why should we follow a Hebraic religious culture that comes from other very different ways of thinking, if we, too, come from cultures that are rich in a philosophy that loves all living things?

Why won't the Catholic church stop conquering other aboriginal cultures to inculcate them about the Hebrew God and all of the canons and norms?

. . . As Christians, we speak of God, we exalt him, we worship him, we make him omnipresent, omniscient, all-powerful, invincible, we applaud him, we have him saved away in the temple, we take him flowers, we bow down, we celebrate his *fiestas*, but what do we do for the common good of all?"[170]

3 "Now is the moment for our language, Nawat, and as CEBs we join this movement. If we are to speak of our identity as CEBs, of course, we have Jesús as our reference point, and we have other martyrs, men and women, but we also have to study, as CEBs, who we are in this country called America. We have to analyze all that. Who was I in 1932, or in 1883 with Anastasio Aquino, or in 1932, in the war, who am I, where do I come from? That stuff, all that. This makes us reflect, why are we building so many roads these days? Why is that beautiful old mango tree no longer here? Why don't we hear birdsong in this area anymore? As CEBs, we should analyze all this, too, without leaving behind our participation in the manifestation of the gospels."[171]

4 "We are at a breaking point, we've been reflecting. For the sacrament of baptism, you need that documented in the church. And that means that when we have a baptism in our community, we have to go register it in the parish. Even though we have done the formation and catechesis. And I say that we are at a breaking point because we wonder: Jesús, when he was baptized, where did he register? Who were his godparents? So for us, that's a big question . . .

And I think that [registering baptism with the parish] is something the church invented because they want to know how many members the Catholic church has. Because you need your *fe de bautismo*, a document that proves that you were baptized, to get into private or religious schools, because that's the first sacrament. And then they want to know if you continue in the Catholic church, and they put you through a second sacrament, which is confirmation. And they want to know how many Catholic families there are, so that's why marriage [is a sacrament]. So in these religious institutions, when parents go sign up their children for Catholic schools, they ask for a document. And this document is also valid to prove that you are established as a person in the mayor's office! So yeah, looking at it with a Jesús lens, we ask, what was the sacrament of baptism *really* for? It was to commit yourself to the people. After his baptism, Jesús carried out his mission. What should interrogate us is rather, for those of us who are baptized, what are we doing for our people? And I mean baptism of any kind, Catholic or non-Catholic, we are all baptized.

. . . When we were with the Maryknoll priests, that group invited people who wanted to be baptized to receive formation. They never asked for any money. But as soon as the other priests came, all of a sudden we had to pay five dollars per baptism. So. And that's in a lot of churches, not just El Salvador. This is the business of the sacraments. It's not about a commitment. Like I say, we're at a point of asking, 'Well, so do we even need to be baptized [to be Christian]? Or can we do it ourselves?'"[172]

5 "And more CEBs are emerging. The most recent one has arisen from a group of families three or four months ago.[173] Because the priest said to them, 'Leave, if you want to.' This is what's happening in our country. But we believe that this phenomenon is of Jesús, that it is of the Spirit. The Catholic church is not

the official sponsor of the Spirit. As if it were Coca-Cola. No way. That's why we also believe that the Spirit is in the evangelical churches, too. Not just in the Catholic church. And in people who are atheists. We believe that Jesús is there. And often, with much more presence than in those who raise hosts.

It's interesting to know that in the CEBs now, there are many young people. That is hopeful. The new communities that arise are young people who want to renew the church. They want to rethink the CEBs. On the 15th, we are going to a community where the majority are young people, and it's in a region that has been very hard-hit in the past. And now it's coming back, with open-minded young people. It's in Nahuizalco."[174]

Letter from the Community "Rutilio Grande"

In this second letter from a contemporary Salvadoran base ecclesial community, the community Rutilio Grande in Nahuizalco tells of how they came together out of a concern, motivated by their faith, to protect the natural world in the municipality where they live. Water scarcity is increasingly a problem for rural communities in El Salvador; houses that *do* have plumbing are at the mercy of the prices set by ANDA, the Administración Nacional de Acueductos y Alcantarillados (National Administration of Aqueducts and Sewage Systems), the public-private governmental group that administrates water distribution in the country. Families who live in houses without plumbing either run tubes from a water tank built on a hill or carry water from a nearby well or river. Water has been a vital issue for *lxs pobres* and, as such, has been a central concern for the church of *lxs pobres*.[175] Community elders in rural areas throughout the country testify that many local wells or natural water springs are drying up, and that water has become more difficult to find, especially during the dry season.

Many CEBs, including the Rutilio Grande community in Nahuizalco, have studied the national water problem, analyzed the unjust distribution of available water, and reflected during their meetings and liturgies that water is an essential source of life for all Creation. It is our human and Christian responsibility to protect water and work to make it available to all creatures in need. Out of these convictions, in recent years the CEBs have become involved in the political struggle to pass a law in the National Assembly that would define water as a common resource in order to prevent the total privatization of national water management. However, in Nahuizalco, the diocese closed the parish down in order to quell the CEBs' organizing activity.

The short testimony of this *librito* was recorded by Argentine theologian Francisco Bosch during a popular theology workshop among the CEBs in El Salvador. The words belong to Eustaquio, a pastoral leader from the Rutilio Grande CEB in Nahuizalco.

1 "My name is Eustaquio Isidro. I am 38 years old, and I am from Tajcuiluijlan, in the municipality of Nahuizalco, Sonsonate, in the western part of El Salvador.

I want to tell a story that is now over ten years old, from 2009.

In the municipality of Nahuizalco, as ecclesial base communities, we began to work, to be organized, to plan coordinated efforts, together with the diocese of Sonsonate. At that time, our bishop was Adolfo Morales, and he was the one who gave us guidelines and checked in on our pastoral work.

And we really held ourselves to working according to the diocesan plan. At that time, we were just a few small communities that were organized. And then, there was some growth in our communities, and we began to work in catechesis, in formation, in consciousness-raising, especially working to protect and defend life.[176]

At that time, a new priest named Reinaldo Libra arrived to the municipality of Nahuizalco and he accompanied the people in our struggles defending water, defending life, that is, incarnating the Gospel in the reality where we live. And this is why we had serious problems, because one night, a Sunday evening, September 26, 2009, new priests arrived who went into the parish church. A legal representative from the archdiocese, who was a lawyer, arrived, and the police. They told us,

'Well, the temple will be uninhabitable for three months, and nobody can meet here.'

And the community had to leave because they locked it up, and they told us that anybody who entered would incur legal proceedings because we would be on diocesan land.

And so that's when we were born as CEBs, and we have been working without a link to the hierarchy because they excommunicated us. They excommunicated the priest, they excommunicated our communities, and we were left out.[177]

So since then, we have worked very closely with the religious order in our community to protect water as a resource, a vital resource for each inhabitant of this place.

I want to mention that the Sensuntepán River, the one we defend, already has nine dams along its course; it is the most exploited river in the west. And that is what drives us. I think that Jesús passes through our community, just like when he passed through Israel. He had conflicts with religion, and he had conflicts with political power.

Our community, too, has these same conflicts, religious persecution, and persecution from the businesses who want to hoard all of the resources of our community. But we are here to keep defending life, you know? It is a pleasure to share this information, and I hope to make it understood that Jesúcristo is present in each moment, in each community."[178]

Letter from the Community "Nuevo Amanecer"

This letter, from the community Nuevo Amanecer (New Dawn) in San Bartolo, Ilopango, represents yet another contemporary experience of CEBs in El Salvador, forced to choose between their commitment to discipleship in service of the reign of God and communion with their parish priest. To be clear, #not all CEBs in El Salvador have separated from their home parish, and #not all priests deny the CEBs and other groups of lay people their own questioning and discernment of discipleship in the everyday political commitments of their lives. However, this kind of situation has become increasingly common in the last fifteen to twenty years and is characteristic especially of new CEBs that have formed in that period. This is also a phenomenon relatively particular to El Salvador. In neighboring Guatemala and Honduras, for example, the CEBs often have a supportive relationship with their local and national hierarchy. Though there are signs of a shift in this trend in El Salvador, particularly surrounding the events of San Romero's canonization,[179] the hierarchical ignoring of—and active opposition to—the CEBs, which the Latin American bishops themselves characterized as "initial cell of the ecclesiastical structures,"[180] is an essential piece of the CEBs' history and struggle as the church of *lxs pobres*.

The primary source for the first three sections of this *librito* is the community's autobiography, an ongoing account of their history that they generously shared with us in 2015. Section 4 tells the experience of Andrea, a young woman in the community, and the final section is a meditation on the reign of God, that one community member, Tere, shared at our research symposium at Wake Forest University in 2019.

1 "Ecclesial base communities are all different from each other, even though we might be very close geographically. We are different in the way we reflect and how we live out our spirituality. Many communities that call themselves 'ecclesial base communities' are groups that meet to pray the rosary, or, or put it another way, they are really prayer groups without the slightest understanding of what it really means to belong to a community. And some reflect on the Bible according to the spirituality of the CEBs. It's important to note that, at some point, the sense was lost of the need for critical analysis of structures that generate death and poverty for the people. Truly, it was very palpable, when, all of a sudden, in opposition to the CEBs, those committed to the Charismatic Renewal appeared in our parishes and were accepted by the institutional church. They had a vertical kind of spirituality that only looked up at heaven without looking at what's happening around them, thinking that this is the way to please the Lord they praise. So anything that had to do with justice was 'talking about politics,' and the church should not be involved in that; we should render to God what is God's, and God isn't about politics, according to the spirituality of the Charismatic Renewal. This was the best way to put the people to sleep, making them think that this was the right way to praise God, and it was the best way to finish off the ecclesial base communities . . . and from that time on, our communities were very weakened. It was also because priests weren't receiving the same kind of liberating formation that their predecessors had. And if they did get it, they had their arms twisted because of their precious vow of obedience to the institutional church. And that's offensive, because it goes against the criteria of obedience to the Gospel!

THE PARISH OF SAN BARTOLO

2 San Bartolo belongs to the jurisdiction of [the municipality of] Ilopango, and even though we're legally a canton, in the last few years we've had a population boom and rapid economic growth, so we're even larger than the city of Ilopango itself, as of now, 2014. There are banks, grocery stores and malls, like Unicentro AltaVista, which has many chain stores and two locations of the *Despensa de Don Juan*.[181] There are also private and public health clinics, a *zona franca*[182] that produces for many well known national and international brands, and a hospital run by the Ministry of Health. Unfortunately, there is only one soccer field, though there are many alleys and back streets where our youth play their favorite sport, soccer.

. . . The Franciscans always made sure that all pastoral decisions, at least the majority, were taken by consensus, and sometimes decisions were submitted to each council that represented the different zones of the parish for approval. We had a pastoral plan that was designed in a circular way where everyone had a say and a vote, at least as far as pastoral concerns went. And if they [the Franciscans] had any authority at all, it wasn't in our faces, since they were very involved with the people, familiar with our needs and often helping us to meet them. They took care to spend time with people, and another important thing is that they never made us feel like they were more than we were. At parish events, the priests and friars never took the most important positions or made us treat them in a privileged way. The parish was a welcoming place, and there was a real accompaniment of the communities. . . .

Many things began to change with time, and new priests started to arrive with different ways of thinking in line with the instructions for parishes coming from the Archbishop's office. This all depended on the theological formation they received in seminary and, why not say it, the fact that it's inconvenient for the clergy to have critically conscious lay people committed to the Gospel without personal interests. Much later we understood, just like the apostles understood many words and sayings after Jesús was killed. We understood why some priests had insisted that we form/educate ourselves well, and that a moment would come, they said, when we would have to defend our communities. At the time, we didn't understand, or we didn't think that it was so important."[183]

A NEW PARISH ADMINISTRATION

3 The archbishop split the parish in 2011, and half was assigned to the Comboni Missionary Brotherhood: "We had been fundraising and planning to build our own chapel, but they took that project over so it was no longer a chapel but a temple to the brotherhood of St. Daniele Comboni.[184]

. . . [T]he first effect that we saw was that the [pastoral] teams in each zone, which were already weakened under the Franciscans that obeyed all the orders from the Archbishop of San Salvador, were totally devastated with this new administration. For example, in our chapel of the Holy Family, the number of people on the team was at least thirty, and each person represented the communities of their sector. With the new priests, these teams were reduced to twelve members, and this only when every member attended the meetings. It was surprising that nobody thought to ask themselves what was going on, and that's because we thought that they were the ones who knew everything and because they were priests we had to respect what they said . . .

An assault against the communities was unleashed, especially against the CEBs commission. They used people who, in quotes, 'were part of the communities' but who were really more Charismatics than part of the

CEBs. These people work to change all the members of the commission to be more Charismatic, and whenever we had to report something that was going on to the parish council, it was clear that the priest condoned their actions, which empowered them even more. They said that they were in charge of the communities, and they showed up to our meetings speaking of new rules, rules that nobody knew where they came from. Many people thought that they were in charge of the parish because they made such random decisions, all with the consent of the priest. He seemed to enjoy the situation."[185]

4 Andrea's story illustrates the fraught relationship with the parish priest well: "I'm going to tell you about the *alfombra*[186] that we made [when I belonged to the youth group in the parish]; this was maybe four years ago. It was during Holy Week. We always made *alfombras* on Good Friday. The whole week before, we would prepare the salt, get the design ready, everything. This was the first *alfombra* that [the group] put me in charge of. We made the face of a baby with prison bars. And we gave it a serial number. And our reflection on that section of the *alfombra* was that for society, we are just a number, a number that consumes, a number that's good for nothing else, a number that does not have rights and is not respected in an endless number of ways. And that sometimes we have to defend rights that seem impossible or unreachable.

We also put a scale right in the middle of the *alfombra*. On the left side of the scale was money and a Pope, and on the other side there was a *campesino*, crucified on the scale itself. So there we tried to represent how religious power is so far from the people, from *campesinos*, how far it is from its true vocation, to put it one way, to struggle and to support.

And in the final section, because we always had three different parts, we put the hand of a woman. And on each finger we wrote, for example, 'rape,' 'abuse,' 'violent circumstances,' and we reflected about how there should be rights, not just for women, but an equality of rights for both [men and women]. And we put the symbol of woman and the symbol of man, but united, to demonstrate that they should work together for equal rights.

And when it was our turn at night to describe it as the procession came by, my brother started to share our reflections about the baby, about the serial number, and then he jumped right to the part about the woman. So he left the part about the scale, the Pope, and the crucified *campesino* to me. And I was just starting to explain this part, beginning with the Pope, when the priest, our parish priest, grabbed the microphone right out of my hands. And everybody was like, 'Whoa, what's up with him?'

And from that time on, they decided that they weren't going to let us make *alfombras* anymore, and the processions changed their route. And it was like, so disappointing, because really, we were younger then, and it was maybe the only opportunity we had in the parish to express ourselves ...

Just a little bit ago, I said to my dad,

'Thank God they kicked you guys out.'

And my mom looked at me, kind of angrily, and I told her,

'I never liked the parish, and you guys always fought.' Because yeah, they had to fight with us to get up and go on Sundays. And in the first celebration of the CEB where we are now, my dad said to my brother and me,

'Let's go. If you guys like it, we'll keep going. And if not, it's up to you guys. You're old enough.'

So we went, and we liked it, and we never left."[187]

THE REIGN OF GOD

5 "The reign of God is what Jesús of Nazareth spoke about when he got together with *los pobres*, the marginalized, women, and everyone who was 'suspicious' in the eyes of others.

The reign of God is what we can make present, when we are able to help those who need it most, when we are able to accompany those who have nothing and when we can support them in the hard reality of their daily lives—hard for lack of resources, health care, or dignified employment. The reign of God is when we are able to accompany young people, who are always seen as dangerous and are also in danger. The reign of God is not located in any other place or any other dimension; it is here today among us, when we are in solidarity, when we are just, when we treat each other as equals.

Jesús preached the reign of God and the CEBs that live into their identity are faithful to the project of Jesús. These days, the church does not talk about the project of Jesús, they don't talk about the reign of God, and when they do, they talk about a realm after death, a realm that has nothing to do with our lives. And to try to confuse people, they preach the Reign of Heaven, a realm that does not commit itself to the people or to the things that oppress the people because they think it's enough to try to be good people and get into heaven.

The ecclesial base communities want to be faithful to the project of Jesús, and we keep trying to make the reign of God and the justice of God a reality in our midst because we believe that if we don't do that, then we are not followers of Jesús and we are not disciples of Jesús. And there will always be other hidden interests, camouflaged as Christianity, that try to fool us. Today we see a lot of spirituality, a lot of songs, a lot of vigils, a lot of prayers, but not a bit of commitment to the defense of life, in defense of those who nobody listens to, who are just numbers in political campaign seasons.

The ecclesial base communities want to be faithful to that project [of Jesús] and therefore we have been marginalized by the institutional church, and the majority of us have been expelled. The majority of the CEBs are persevering outside of the institutional church, because we want to live in synthesis with that great project. We are small groups, poor people, doing great things for the project of God.

Unfortunately, the reign of God is sometimes a forgotten reality by most Christians. Many people have not even heard of this project of God; they don't know that it is the only task of the church and of Christians. They are ignorant of the fact that, to see life through the eyes of Jesús, you have to see it from the perspective of the reign of God; to live like him you have to live with his passion for the reign of God.

To love God is to have hunger and thirst for justice like God does; to follow Jesús is to live for the reign of God like him; to belong to the church is to commit yourself to a more just world."[188]

Letter from the Hierarchy I

This first Letter from the Hierarchy represents an effort to clarify the attitude of the Salvadoran bishops and Roman Curia as the first CEBs became established in El Salvador in the late 1960s and early 1970s. Although both Archbishop Chavez y González and his successor Archbishop Óscar Romero were receptive to the CEBs' and other pastoral leaders' push for ecclesial reform following Vatican II and Medellín, the other Salvadoran bishops were not. This ambiguity and diversity of opinion and approach within the Salvadoran episcopate greatly compromised the reception of the council by the Salvadoran church and weakened the church of *lxs pobres* as it was emerging in its own right. We include these ecclesial *sombras* within the narrative of the CEBs' salvation history because they represent the shadow side of the sacred stories that the CEBs tell of their struggles to be church in the face of not only state-sponsored violence, but also the institutional violence of a church that rejects their witness to God's reign. Even in the *sombras*, and especially in the struggle, God accompanies the church of *lxs pobres*, and the reign of God is their guiding light.

The contents of this letter coincide with the events of "Nuevo-Exodus" §6, specifically the National Week of a *pastoral de conjunto*, and demonstrate how reticent the majority of Salvadoran bishops were to enter into sincere and genuine dialogue with their church. Interestingly, the events of this week are presented in "Nuevo-Exodus" §6 as a source of *support* for the birth and growth of the CEBs in El Salvador. While this remains true, the week was also a referendum of sorts on the reception of Vatican II in the Salvadoran church in which the council was not resoundingly received by the Salvadoran bishops. This is significant for the history of the CEBs in El Salvador in particular because while in other countries, like Brazil, the CEBs were established over a decade earlier and grew with the full support of their national bishops' council, the Salvadoran CEBs have *always* existed in the tension of needing to negotiate their ecclesial belonging. Their contemporary struggles are nothing new; the Salvadoran church of *lxs pobres* has only ever existed as persecuted, liminal, *de lucha*.

The letter opens with a genealogy of the current seat of the archbishop of San Salvador, which is important context for these three letters. Since the postwar reconstruction period, the archbishops of San Salvador, and thus the leaders of the National Bishops' Conference, have been appointed by popes suspicious of progressive Latin American theologies, including the CEBs' praxis and liberation theologians' reflections on their experiences. The second section is a short quote from Ronaldo Muñoz, a contemporary Latin American theologian, who ratifies Padre Edgard Beltrán's proposal of a dual-church model in El Salvador.[189]

The rest of the letter is a selection of the dissenting bishops' opinions on the 1970 Pastoral Week, supported by the Roman curia, especially the Congregation for the Clergy, drawn from an extensively researched account by Nicaraguan Rodolfo Cardenal of the life of Rutilio Grande. The letter ends with the prophetic voice of Padre Tilo himself, speaking firmly against the recalcitrant attitude of the bishops.

1 These have been the archbishops of San Salvador:[190]

Monseñor Luis Cárcamo y Rodríguez was succeeded by Monseñor José Alfonso Belloso by authority of Pope Pius XI in 1927.

Monseñor José Alfonso Belloso was succeeded by Servant of God Luis Chávez y González by authority of Pope Pius XI in 1938.

Servant of God Luis Chávez y González was succeeded by Saint Óscar Arnulfo Romero y Galdámez by authority of Pope Saint Paul VI in 1977.

Saint Óscar Arnulfo Romero y Galdámez was martyred by authority of Roberto D'Aubuisson on March 24, 1980.[191]

Monseñor Arturo Rivera y Damas was named apostolic administrator of San Salvador by authority Pope Saint John Paul II in 1980. By that same authority, he did not succeed Saint Óscar Arnulfo Romero y Galdámez as archbishop until 1983.

Monseñor Arturo Rivera y Damas was succeeded by Monseñor Fernando Sáenz Lacalle by authority of Pope Saint John Paul II in 1995.

Monseñor Fernando Sáenz Lacalle was succeeded by Monseñor José Luis Escobar Alas by authority of Pope Benedict XVI in 2009.

2 The reception of Vatican II in Latin America has always reflected the two ecclesiologies present in the council documents: "In *Lumen Gentium*, two models or paradigms of Church are juxtaposed without resolution: one, in the forefront, that recuperates the tradition more firmly rooted in history, biblical studies, and patristics, of the Church as people of God

and fraternal communion; another, in the background, that maintains (with binding force) the more recent counter-reform and anti-modern tradition of the Church as 'perfect society' and as hierarchy."[192]

THE NATIONAL WEEK OF A *PASTORAL DE CONJUNTO*

3 These two models came to a head in El Salvador during the National Week of a *pastoral de conjunto*, sponsored by the Bishops' Council of El Salvador in 1970. Besides Archbishop Chávez y González, none of the bishops contributed the "fully conscious and active participation" that the people of God asked of them.[193] Each bishop had their own goals for the church, many of which emphasized a continued spiritualization of Christian life, in following with the second model of church listed above. Monseñor Barrera of the diocese of Santa Ana criticized a perceived lack of faith and too much social activity among priests. He clamored for a "campaign of spiritualization" and argued for more prayer during the CEDES meetings. Monseñor Aparicio of San Vicente lamented the lack of adequate spiritual formation for priests and wanted to establish a retreat center for clergy. The bishop of San Miguel agreed that priests were malformed in the major seminary—run at that time by the Jesuits—and Monseñor Castro y Ramirez of the diocese of Santiago de María criticized priests for not using their cassocks, for alcoholism, for participating in popular religious feast days, and for a general lack of ecclesiastical discipline.[194] CEDES declared its official discontent with the "First Week of a *Pastoral de Conjunto*" in July 1970 and didn't publish their exceedingly watered-down version of the final document until October of the same year:

"[The bishops] avoided mentioning either the *centros* for campesino formation or the itinerant pastoral teams, true forces of change for rural evangelization. They repressed the need for different groups, each in its own context, to support denouncements of injustices. They avoided mentioning that it was important to change the capitalist system and to work against individualism; instead, they preferred to ask for changes in the deficiencies of the dominant system in the country. They repressed the decision to accelerate the consciousness-raising process of campesino populations. They recognized the need to work for holistic campesino liberation, but specifically did not mention the decision [made by participants in the Week] to work toward achieving a total and radical change to the socio-economic, cultural, religious, and educational system and all its rationale that impeded campesino liberation. While the Week had asked for [explicit ecclesial support for] the right of campesinos to unionize freely, the bishops nuanced, 'insofar as it lies within the limits of the competencies of the Church to do so.' In summary, it is clear that the bishops did not want to commit themselves directly to the promotion and liberation of campesinos."[195]

ROME'S RESPONSE

4 Rome too, merely five years after the council, was willing to support CEDES' repression of the church as people of God in favor of the more "anti-modern tradition":

"The assessment of the political and social situation of the country [made in the document composed by the Week's participants] was offensive to the Congregation for the Clergy, as was the assessment of the religious situation. They also considered the document's conclusions about the sacraments and sacramental pastoral work to be too ambiguous. Their most serious reservations were shown with respect to the ministerial figure of the Delegate [or Celebrator of the Word] and their possible functions. To regularly delegate the functions of sacred ministry to lay people seemed to them to be a theological contradiction and a source of juridically invalid and illegitimate acts because it would lead to the confusion of the hierarchical priesthood with the common priesthood.

The national commission for a *pastoral de conjunto* seemed to be a theological and pastoral deviation because it was made up of both religious and secular priests with pastoral jurisdiction over other priests and religious superiors. The fact that they signaled concrete long- and short-term goals would be equivalent to directing all pastoral activity, which was intolerable, according to the above-mentioned Congregation for the Clergy."[196]

PADRE TILO'S PROPHECY

5 "Padre Tilo made a public pronouncement against the episcopal position, which he found to be neither sincere nor realistic. 'A tumor full of pus is not healed simply by anointing it with oil. To say this is to fool oneself. It is to hide one's head like an ostrich in danger and in difficulty. A crisis remains, like a tumor, and we have to deal with it and heal it to overcome it.' The Week and its conclusions had generated a collective crisis that could not be overcome simply by pushing it aside, masking the conflictive elements. Effectively, this is what CEDES had done with its intervention; they covered their eyes so as not to see reality. The church had to accept the crisis as a sign of the times, as an indication that God was demanding something else, 'because no incident is outside of this history of salvation, and God is always in these events, even when it is difficult to recognize.' For the moment, the crisis of the Week's conclusions had served to awaken. 'It was time for us to awaken from this painful reality. We tarried too long! Five long years have passed since the closure of Vatican II,' and still, nothing practical had been done in the country to put it into practice [by the hierarchy]."[197]

Letter from the Hierarchy II

This second Letter from the Hierarchy is a collection of texts that reflect the Roman Catholic hierarchy's attitude toward both Romero and Romero's people, the church of *lxs pobres*, after it became clear that early reflections on the conclusions of Medellín and Vatican II in El Salvador were not received faithfully by the Salvadoran church as a whole. Specifically, just as members of the curia in Rome and Salvadoran bishops were suspicious of Monseñor Romero's work as archbishop from 1977 to 1980, so too the Salvadoran hierarchy was suspicious of, and worked to subvert, Romero's people as the church and society began to rebuild after the war (1992 and on). It is during this period that the CEBs fade from wider ecclesial and international view. This "disappearance" of the CEBs, however, was not the neutral stabilizing of a radical position over time. As the contents of this letter show, there was a concerted effort by different elements of the ecclesial hierarchy to weaken and marginalize *lxs pobres*' way of being church—an ecclesial way that was in continuity with Medellín and the 1970 National Week of a *pastoral de conjunto*.

As a result of this deliberate marginalization, many CEBs' bonds of communion with their parishes have been broken, as attested to in the previous Letters from Pueblo de Dios en Camino, the Rutilio Grande community in Nahuizalco, and Nuevo Amanecer. Is it from this experience of pastoral abandonment and, in some cases, persecution, that many CEBs today have assumed the necessary work of priesthood for the continuation of their own ecclesial communities. To be clear: the CEBs do not seek their own formation, preside at their own liturgies, or govern their own communities as a thought experiment. It is out of an existential need for theological formation, sacramental worship, and servant leadership that these CEBs have taken up these responsibilities. They were prepared for this work in the first decades of their existence, accompanied by priests who exercised pastoral leadership "*al lado de lxs pobres,*" on the side of the poor.

The letter opens with Pope Francis's recognition of the hierarchy's persecution of Romero. It follows with accounts of the opposition to Romero expressed by both the Roman and Salvadoran hierarchy during his life. Section 4 in particular describes specific actions taken by archbishop of San Salvador, Fernando Saenz Lacalle (1995–2009), to transform structures of the Salvadoran church away from Vatican II and Medellín, which had resounding effects for the church of *lxs pobres* in the years that followed. Sections 5–6 detail a recent conflict between contemporary CEBs in the Bajo Lempa region and their bishop, William Iraheta, over the resources of the communities technically owned by the diocese; this conflict demonstrates that the differences between the hierarchy and the church of *lxs pobres* in El Salvador are not merely ideological but concrete and practical as well. The sources for these sections are archival documents that were provided by FUNDAHMER with the express consent of the National Network of Salvadoran CEBs; we are grateful to have access to these texts. Finally, the Letter closes with the reality of a totally divided Salvadoran church at the beatification of Romero.

PROLOGUE

1 With these words, Pope Francis spoke of a truth that the church of *lxs pobres* already knew: "The martyrdom of Monseñor Romero was not only his death: it began earlier, with the suffering that resulted from persecution before his death and continued afterwards, because it wasn't enough that he die. They defamed him, they slandered him, they slung mud at him. His martyrdom continued at the hands of his brother priests and bishops. . . . Only God knows the [full] story of the person [of Monseñor Romero]. God saw that they were stoning him with the heaviest stone that exists in the world: the tongue."[198]

THE STONING OF ROMERO

2 Some of the heaviest stones were cast by Rome itself:

"He came like a true inquisitor with his entire bag of tricks. At the end of 1978, the Holy See sent him to San Salvador with the title of 'Apostolic Visitor' so that he could investigate what Monseñor Romero was doing. He was Antonio Quarracino, an Argentinian bishop who later became a cardinal.

'He's already talked with everyone in the right wing of the Church,' Monseñor Romero told me. 'I'd like you to spend some time with him and give him your point of view.'

I agreed. Monseñor had already taken him a big pile of written homilies, newspaper clippings, letters and minutes from the meetings of the Bishops' Conference. In other words, Quarracino had plenty of information at his disposal.

I talked with him for about two and a half hours at the nuncio's office. The 'visitor' had his head full of every prejudice you could imagine and then some. And he was not at all favorably disposed to people in the grassroots organizations. He just couldn't let go of it.

'They're violent, and they're Marxists!' he kept insisting.

'They say that hunger justifies the means,' I said, smiling, but he didn't understand where I was coming from.

'And the worst thing is that they've infiltrated the Church because Monseñor Romero has allowed them to!'

'Why don't you look at it another way? They're in the Church because they're the sheep of his flock, and Monseñor Romero knows them by name . . .'

He didn't go for that, either. It was hard for him to understand. He wanted a simple explanation of the Salvadoran reality. And he didn't understand where I was coming from because I was neither poor, nor a member of a grassroots organization, nor an atheist. Rather, I was from a working-class Catholic family that had managed to earn a lot of money.

'They've brainwashed you, too!'

His visit ended after three or four days. I didn't think he had come to understand much of anything by the time he left. Monseñor Romero came to one conclusion:

'If they don't want me here, they can fire me as archbishop and send me back to being a parish priest. But I'm not going to change what I say simply to keep that from happening. I'm going to speak according to my conscience,' he told us.

Quarracino came to a conclusion of his own. As he was leaving to go to the airport and was going down the stairs at the seminary, suitcase in hand, he said:

'I can't say anything negative about Monseñor Romero. If I say anything against him, and they find out here, these Salvadorans will have my hide!'

Well, maybe he'd learned something after all."[199]

3 Other stones were thrown by Romero's brother bishops from El Salvador:

"I went to Puebla as a journalist. I had a good relationship with the team of liberation theologians that had been denied entry to the meeting by the Latin American Bishops' Conference (CELAM). They were working 'outside the walls' in connection with many of the bishops who were inside. I made it my job to be a bridge between the two groups.

Monseñor Romero arrived in Puebla as a celebrity of sorts, and even though he wasn't the kind to make a lot of noise, he was one of the bishops that the journalists and the curious onlookers were most eager to talk with.

Monseñor Aparicio, on the other hand, did make a lot of noise. He was the one the Salvadoran bishops had sent as their representative. I went with a friend of mine to interview him and see what kind of position he was taking. That man said the most outrageous things! Among other things, he blamed Romero for everything that was happening in El Salvador: for planting bombs, for kidnapping people, for training children as guerrillas. He even said that the disappeared were just people who were hiding so they could make the government look bad . . .

When Aparicio's comments got around, everyone was anxiously waiting to hear how Romero would respond. A press conference was organized . . .

When they asked him about the divisions among the bishops of El Salvador, he answered:

'Unfortunately, there is division. But I think there's a verse in the Gospel that speaks of such things. It's when Christ says that he has not come to bring peace, but a sword. When he goes on to explain this, he talks about divisions in the family. That's because true unity is not romanticism. It's not appearances. The kind of unity that Christ calls for is unity in truth. And that truth is hard sometimes. It means giving up things we like. True unity means that kind of sacrifice. So it's not hard to understand that even within the Church there might be division.'

He never fell into the trap of being a 'political' bishop. It wasn't hard for him. He didn't look like one because he wasn't."[200]

4 Romero was not the only target of the vitriol and persecution. During Pope St. John Paul II's visit to Central America in 1996, division within the Salvadoran church continued to be in the spotlight:

"Another major theme stressed on the trip was church unity, long weakened in much of Central America by divisions within the national hierarchies over questions of social policy and in particular over liberation theology. In remarks aboard his airplane, the pontiff said,

'With the fall of communism, liberation theology, with its Marxist inspiration, also fell. Today, the real problems are social.'

The comment elicited an immediate response from Jon Sobrino, a Jesuit theologian and director of the Óscar Arnulfo Romero Pastoral Center in San Salvador.

'As long as there is oppression, liberation theology will exist,' Sobrino said.

Sobrino suggested that the pope remember Romero and the other adherents of liberation theology who were victims of repression, and that he get more in touch with the poor. Sobrino's comment reflects the lingering conflict in the Salvadoran church—and throughout much of Latin America—between conservatives and the socially committed clergy who have chosen the 'preferential option for the poor.' Last year, the pope bypassed the socially committed Gregorio Rosa y Chavez, then acting archbishop of San Salvador, to name conservative Fernando Saenz Lacalle as archbishop. Saenz is a member of the ultraconservative Catholic organization Opus Dei and was the Vatican liaison with the Salvadoran military.

When asked if Saenz's appointment meant a change in the political or social views of the Salvadoran church, the pontiff said he knew of no such change but saw the appointment as an example of continuity in the church's official pastoral line. Nevertheless, soon after his appointment, Saenz—along with the nine-member Bishops' Conference (Conferencia Episcopal de El Salvador, CEDES), which is dominated by six conservative bishops—began replacing progressive priests from key archdiocesan posts.

Just days before the papal visit, Saenz removed rector Luis Coto and his teaching staff at the archdiocesan seminary. The seminary has had a progressive orientation for several years, and Coto is a leading exponent of Romero's social views. Saenz also removed Fabian Amaya, director of *Orientación*, the archdiocesan newspaper, and closed the local office of Caritas, an organization that distributed food and other aid to the poor. Coto's firing received extensive press coverage and criticism. However, Saenz treated Coto's removal as a simple personnel shift and insisted that the church stood united. Nevertheless, both the president of the Bishops' Conference, Marco Rene Revelo, and Rosa y Chavez [*sic*] said that the church is deeply divided between conservative and progressive elements. Some priests, described as proponents of liberation theology, say that they are being persecuted by the hierarchy for their social activism.

Miguel Cavada, professor of theology at the Universidad Centroamericana (UCA), told the press that the Salvadoran church has 'entered a process of regression . . . with the appointment of Saenz,' whom he described as more conservative than the pope.

'Far from ending the option for the poor, what he will do is revive it,' said Cavada.

Despite the split over liberation theology, the pope paid homage at the tomb of its best known martyr, Óscar Arnulfo Romero, whose cause for canonization is now in process."[201]

The process would be stalled for another nineteen years at the hands of ecclesial and social opposition in Rome and in El Salvador.[202] In the meantime, the division in the Salvadoran church would continue to be evident: "For any Sunday visitor to the San Salvador metropolitan cathedral in the postwar '90s, the symbolism was powerful: Mass in the elegant, freshly renovated nave upstairs (completed in 1999), contrasted with the 'Romero' Mass held downstairs in the crypt where he was buried. Communities of people, many who carried on the work of liberation theology, would come from miles away to celebrate the Eucharist in the presence of their beloved Monseñor."[203] The hierarchy's suppression of Romero extended to Romero's people; the church of *lxs pobres* was pushed to the margins, literally underground, in the years after the war and into the new millennium.

THE STONING OF THE CHURCH OF *LXS POBRES*

5 With time, the CEBs' association with Romero and with a theology toward which many members of the hierarchy demonstrated disdain and avoidance meant that the communities did not receive adequate accompaniment from their pastors. The protagonism and leadership of the laity, which had begun in the late 1960s for both theological and practical reasons, took on a new urgency. As priests increasingly refused to teach, worship with, and serve the church of *lxs pobres*, community members continued to find it necessary to teach, minister to, and govern themselves.[204]

In 2016, soon after the 2015 death of Padre Pedro,[205] William Iraheta, bishop of the diocese of Santiago de María, including the Bajo Lempa region, attempted to repossess the buildings and vehicles that the CEBs had accumulated as resources for their pastoral work since their repatriation and establishment in the early 1990s. These resources were legally held in the name of the archdiocese, and without a priest among the communities, the bishop felt justified in reclaiming the vehicles and buildings "for the church." The National Network of CEBs in El Salvador describes the situation in this way: "Facts:

1. In the canton of Tierra Blanca, municipality of Jiquilisco, department of Usulután, at 11:50 [a.m] on January 14, 2016, there arrived at the Monseñor Romero Cultural Center the Lic. Diana Samantha Zelaya Zelaya, accompanied by two agents of the PNC and a person of the masculine sex who did not want to identify himself and who we believe to be a priest. They presented us with an order from the Bishop which demanded the gray four-wheel-drive truck that used to belong to Fr. Dominique, who accompanied the Ecclesial Base Communities for over ten years and who, due to family health concerns, returned to Belgium. The truck stayed at the Romero Center to be of service to the Ecclesial Base Communities. We mention that this car was purchased with the help of Adveniat, and with a part that was given by Padre Pedro Declercq, a founder of our Ecclesial Base Communities. The argument was that we do not belong to the diocese, since we do not obey the guidelines of the Bishop or of the Parish.

2. There exists, in these moments, an internal rupture among the communities. Today, two pastoral approaches are clearly defined, the traditional Roman model imposed by the current parish priest of Tierra Blanca and the Latin American model of the Ecclesial Base Communities out of which we have been working for the last twenty-five years in the Bajo Lempa region. We highlight that the Roman model is currently using all kinds of strategies to attack the CEBs' very nature, for example, using the communities' ADESCOs[206] to remove the CEBs from those places that are the center of life in our communities, like street plazas and places for meetings and liturgy. We offer as an example the case of the San Hilario community, where ADESCO leaders have insulted and denigrated members of the Christian community with incredibly grotesque words, with the goal of handing space over to the priest. On May 25, the San Hilario community celebrated the 24th anniversary of its foundation, in which *memoria histórica*, our heroes and martyrs, and the community's own process of liberation were to play a central role. Two blocks away, in the same community at the same time, the other model held a traditional Mass whose goal was to work against unity and kick the CEBs out because women were leading the celebration, and according to the priest, women are not authorized to do so.

    This same strategy of having Mass at the same time was also implemented in the La Noria community. The CEB there always celebrates at 4:00 p.m. every Sunday, and all of a sudden in recent weeks, he is arriving at the same time some 300 meters away from the CEBs' celebration with speakers, inviting people to attend Mass, arguing that it is the original Mass.

3. On June 8 at 8:30 a.m., there arrived at the 'The 72' Pastoral Center in the community of Nueva Esperanza, Usulután, two legal representatives of the Catholic Diocese of Santiago de María in the name of Bishop William Ernesto Iraheta Rivera and two agents of the PNC with the goal of removing two vehicles that are registered in the name of the Diocese of Santiago de María and which have always been used by the Missionary Sisters of the *Pequeña Comunidad* for pastoral work in the area.

    That same day, at 10:30 a.m., the same representatives arrived at the house of Sister Elena Jaramillo, of the Congregation of the Sisters of St. Joseph in Orange, CA, USA to communicate with her and to leave her a note from the Bishop, asking her to leave the residence since the Diocese wishes to remodel the house, giving her a month to move.

4. Confronted with these situations, Sister Nohemí Ortíz scheduled a meeting with Bishop Iraheta, who agreed to meet her that same day at the diocesan offices at 4:30 p.m. Nohemí asked the pastoral team to accompany her to said meeting, with the goal of meeting the Bishop and telling him about the pastoral work that the Ecclesial Base Communities have been doing in the area for more than 25 years.

The surprise was, upon arriving, that the following were all there: the Bishop, the Vicar General, the Parochial Vicar of the Diocese and the Parish Priest of Tierra Blanca, Nilton Ademir García and his collaborator, Padre Ángel Arnaiz.

At said meeting, the [Pastoral] Team introduced themselves and the work they do and opened the space for comments, at which time the Bishop expressed his desire for 'order and communion' and that in this case, 'communion in the Parish is based on the Parish Priest, around whom all organization must turn.' In addition, Padre Arnaiz, when speaking to Nohemí throughout the meeting, said that she has 'the tongue of a viper because her heart is full of venom' and that she is 'cynical,' among other insults. This was all said in the presence of the Bishop, who said nothing."[207]

6 After the CEBs talked about these incidents on their radio program, *La Verdad al Aire*,[208] the Diocese issued a press release:

"The Diocese of Santiago de María, given the declaration made during the YSUCA radio program of the Ecclesial Base Communities this past July 10 at 5 p.m.:
CLARIFIES:
The goods managed in different Parishes in collaboration with international Catholic institutions are managed in the name of the Church, and the donors give them to the Diocese to serve the Church in its evangelizing activity.

On the morning of July 8 of this year, two vehicles from the Bajo Lempa were requested and transferred to the Curia in Santiago de María in order to redistribute them to parishes that do not have a car, in order to fulfill the end for which they were acquired. Additionally, the parish house of Tierra Blanca Parish was requested so that it may be used by the Parish Priest and his parroquial vicars.
DEFINES:
According to the documents of the Church, the Ecclesial Base Community 'is the living cell of the Parish,' understood as an organic and missionary community.

The CEB in itself, usually made up of a few families, is called to live as a community of faith, of worship, and of love. It can be animated by lay people, men and women adequately prepared in the same processes of the community. These *animadores* should be in communion with their respective Parish Priest and the Bishop (John 15:1–17). . . .

DECLARES:

That we value the contribution of the CEBs to the evangelizing work of the Catholic Church, but we are conscious that 'when there exists no clear ecclesiological foundation and the sincere quest for *communion*, they are no longer ecclesial and may be victims of ideological or political manipulation' (Santo Domingo 62).

In the Bajo Lempa, there is a group who calls themselves 'the Missionary Sisters of the *Pequeña Comunidad*,' who claim to give continuity to an advanced church founded by Father Pedro Declercq, affirming that they have their own way of being church, even celebrating eucharist with one of them presiding. In their meeting with the Bishop of the Diocese on the afternoon of July 8, they asked that this practice be respected. This position is contrary to what the Magisterium of the Catholic Church defines for us, and so they are not in full communion with [the Church]. To avoid confusion among the faithful, it is opportune that they not use the goods of the Catholic Church.

Assuming the 'Feeling with the Church' of Blessed Óscar Arnulfo Romero y Galdámez, Bishop and Martyr, as a Diocese we live through this moment with sadness, and we trust that the Holy Spirit shows us the path to follow. We remember that the Church is mother and teacher, and she always awaits her sons and daughters who have voluntarily distanced themselves from her.

[Signed,] Monseñor William Ernesto Iraheta Rivera, Bishop of Santiago de María"[209]

THE BEATIFICATION OF ROMERO

7 Just over a year previous to these events among the CEBs in the Bajo Lempa, Monseñor Romero had been beatified in San Salvador with no coordination between the CEBs and the Archdiocese. Having been left out of the planning process, the CEBs and other marginalized groups held their own overnight vigil at a roundabout in the capital and marched to the beatification Mass in the morning to participate among the masses. The reflections swirling around at this time were poignant laments, full of questions. One pastoral leader wrote:

"The celebration on May 23 is a religious act prepared and organized in a coordinated way between the hierarchy of the Roman [Catholic] church and the State. They will speak of great joy, of the feast of the most famous Salvadoran in the whole world, on account of being the first Salvadoran to be officially beatified, and of the 'religious fervor' in the style of the processions during Holy Week. It will be the maximum eucharistic expression, presided with much religious solemnity. Hundreds of priests will have received penitents that wish to confess, and they will give them communion (in the stadium, too!).

But I wonder: will there be conversion? Will the rich convert to sharing their wealth to be distributed among all? Will *los pobres* believe in *los pobres* and organize in solidarity for the conquest of justice? Will the politicians and leaders present begin to serve the people instead of serving themselves by way of the people? Will the judges and public prosecutors who are present be converted into administrators of justice without corruption? Will the owners of the communications media and their employees be converted to be sentinels of truth instead of ideological instruments of the neoliberal system? Will *los pobres* be converted into microphones of God? Will the priests, bishops and cardinals present be converted to live their ministry as Monseñor Romero did? I suspect, in fact, that there will be much religious euphoria but little true conversion! I suspect that it will be like the string lights we hang as Christmas approaches: 'Ooooh, how beautiful!' For a little while, and then they turn off and everything is dark again. Will Monseñor Romero be present?"[210]

8 Pronouncement of the National Network of Base Ecclesial Communities of El Salvador for the Beatification of Monseñor Romero:

"The official notice of Monseñor Romero's beatification is a recognition of the declaration of the people that have made Romero a saint since the day of his assassination. His passage through this world was no coincidence; he was sent by God to inspire Latin America as part of God's mission to be light and hope for the world and to sow God's reign during new moments for humanity.

With the passage of Monseñor Romero through El Salvador, a 'before' and 'after' is marked in Latin American history. His voice and his prophetic word summon *los y las pobres* to be the subjects of their own history, true authors of society; he also calls to the hierarchical figures of the churches to conversion and to assume their role, which is the formation of the people of God.

Because of the inheritance of Monseñor Romero, impoverished people have better understood the message of Jesús, and we are convinced that it is the only way to construct this new heaven and new earth.

For these reasons, we declare:

1. To declare Monseñor Romero a saint is to break with the traditional vision and practice of the hierarchy of the church on this topic, and we hope that this openness constitutes a historic step towards resuming the teachings of the Second Vatican Council, Medellín, and Puebla, which so fed Romero in his own fidelity to God and to the human person. Also, the call remains to build the church of Jesús from the exemplary vision of Monseñor, which is based on the preferential option for *los pobres*.

2. Monseñor Romero pleases God because he unmasked the historic lie of his moment that made people believe that the poverty and misery of the majorities was the will of God. And he courageously spoke the truth about the God of Jesús, the God who sent God's Son, Jesúcristo, to make an unambiguously preferential option for *los pobres*.
3. Monseñor Romero renewed the key to salvation, which is the people of God. 'God wants us to be saved as a people' (Homily of January 5, 1978). 'The people are my prophet,' 'With this people it is not difficult to be a good shepherd/pastor,' 'I will be resurrected in the Salvadoran people': these are some of his transcendent statements. Because without a people, without community, there cannot be salvation. This implies the reestablishment of the church as a PEOPLE.
4. To recognize Romero as beatified or as a saint is to promote and revitalize both liberation theology and the ecclesial base communities, realities that have been threatened with burial but that for Monseñor Romero were inspiration for his liberating practice. As such, it is a recognition of the struggle of the Salvadoran people to define their own destiny and of the memory of our heroes and martyrs who, together with Romero, marked the new direction of our history.
5. For the Salvadoran people, Monseñor Romero is a gift from God, which means that God has fixed upon us and has tasked us with a historic mission in this new moment for humanity. This incident should GENERATE a renewed encounter with the people. That is, to renew our own encounter with our great popular values of truth, justice, and freedom.

For the above reasons, we call upon the people of El Salvador:

- To create and strengthen ecclesial base communities in their own places, as the model for the church proclaimed by Romero on May 21, 1978.
- To the traditional faithful of the Catholic church, to study Monseñor Romero's vision and practice of his faith in the construction of the true people of God.
- To the Bishops' Conference of El Salvador, to change priestly formation, to put them in contact with reality so that the true pastors that the people need may arise.
- To the Ministry of Education, that the thought of Monseñor Romero be incorporated HOLISTICALLY into the formation and building-up of our citizenry, as he himself expressed: 'The first thing that an education should seek is to incarnate man in his reality, be able to analyze it, and to be critical of it' (Homily, April 30, 1978).
- An urgent call to the Salvadoran state (executive, legislative, and

judicial branches) and the Attorney General of the Republic, that they enforce, with no further delay, the three recommendations given by the International Commission on Human Rights in report #37/00 of April 15, 2000, about state responsibility for the assassination of Romero and the denial of justice."[211]

EPILOGUE

9 One member of the CEBs summarizes her opinion of the relationship between the hierarchy and the church of *lxs pobres*:

"The ecclesial base communities have been isolated from the structure [of the church]. Three years ago, the Apostolic *nuncio* to El Salvador, that is, one who represents Rome, that great economic, political, and religious structure, said, upon leaving the country, 'I'm glad that there are no more base ecclesial communities, because they are a cancer for the Church.'

He did not know us. He didn't know, because of his ignorance, that we are here, we are still alive, all over the country. And new ecclesial base communities continue to emerge."[212]

Letter from the Hierarchy III

At the end of the events of the second Letter from the Hierarchy, it would appear that hope for reconciliation between the hierarchy and the church of *lxs pobres* was rather far-fetched. Division seemed to become more and more entrenched as time went on, and the more radical responsibilities the CEBs were forced to take on for their own ecclesial survival seemed to burn the bridges of ecclesial communion. The dual celebration of the beatification of Romero reflected a truly divided Salvadoran church.

However, the relationship between the hierarchy and the church of *lxs pobres* has begun to change in recent years. The current archbishop, José Luis Escobar Alas (2009 to present), has been a key figure in this shift. At the beginning of his tenure, many of his decisions, like removing a popular mosaic on the outside of the Metropolitan Cathedral and closing Tutela Legal, the archdiocesan office for human rights, seemed to reflect a continuation of pastoral leadership in the style of Saenz Lacalle. However, after the beatification of Romero, Escobar Alas began to speak out on social issues in public and released pastoral letters that surprised the CEBs in their level of analysis and commitment to justice. The contents of this letter detail how Escobar Alas and the CEBs began to meet, to get to know each other, and how they planned the celebration for Romero's canonization together.

The content of this letter may seem trivial; sources include meeting minutes of the National Network of Salvadoran CEBs, a letter from the CEBs to Escobar Alas, and the archbishop's homily during the canonization celebration in October 2018. However, they signal an emerging paradigm shift for the better in the relationship between the church of *lxs pobres* and church hierarchy. Again, we are grateful to the National Network of Salvadoran CEBs and specifically to their secretary, María Elena Sanabria, for providing us with these documents and for allowing us to reflect on them in this work.

THE FIRST MEETINGS WITH THE ARCHBISHOP

1 From the minutes of the meeting of the National Network of CEBs on August 19, 2017:
"Maria Elena says there is a possibility for a meeting with the Archbishop of San Salvador. This is the result of a meeting he had with a delegation of CEBs from the Sierra Tarahumara, Mexico, which she attended, and [where she] told the archbishop that some months ago, the CEBs in El Salvador had written a letter to him, but for various reasons had not been able to deliver it personally at a meeting. The Archbishop manifested that he would be very interested in speaking with the CEBs and that he would speak with his secretary to set a date. Given this possibility and openness, we make the following comments:

- It is important that he recognize the CEBs
- We should continue to demand justice for our martyrs. What kind of follow up [do we expect]?
- We do not feel disdain for the hierarchy; rather, we simply do not share their model.
- We should see the signs that the Archbishop has given with Christian eyes. They are signs that give hope.
- We consider ourselves to be church.
- We should tell him about our experiences and what we do and our crisis.
- It would be opportune to meet with him.
- We shouldn't lose sight of the fact that this would be a first meeting: we should speak about the reality we live in and how we do not think he has a pastoral plan '*de conjunto.*'[213] We should also ask what he thinks about us and what we do.
- We must be present.
- We should read our letter to him and give it to him . . .

After these comments, we agreed that we would meet with the Archbishop."[214]

2 The letter from the CEBs to the archbishop, dated September 17, 2017:
"Dear Archbishop José Luis Escobar Alas,

Receive from the Ecclesial Base Communities (CEBs) of El Salvador a fraternal greeting and a strong hug, in the spirit of Jesús of Nazareth and our Saint Romero, and know that our communities wish you much fruit in your own struggle towards the reign of God, which is Justice, Life, Solidarious Love, and Freedom, as we have been taught by Padre Pedro Declercq.

Our motive for writing to you, Monseñor, is to thank you, as the people of God and as the people of Monseñor Romero, for your position in favor of a law that would prohibit metallic mining in our country. We are grateful that you understand how serious it would have been for all of us and for future generations if Ocean Gold and other businesses had been allowed to plan and execute mining projects in our country, which is already suffering a great deal environmentally...

Additionally, we want to congratulate you for your defense of working men and women, when you demanded that each person should be paid at least minimum wage. We share your posture on this topic because we believe it is just to demand a dignified salary for each person, especially for the most *pobres*, who do not often have enough money to buy basic foods for our families.

We also believe that it is important to continue speaking the truth on the topic of pensions, because we think that it's important to effect a reform that benefits the pensioners and not the owners of the business responsible for the administration of pensions.

Given all this, we know that some sectors of economic power in our country are not comfortable with your way of thinking and acting, as we have seen in some national newspapers like *El Diario de Hoy* and spokespersons for private businesses who have criticized you on these issues. We have also seen that *La Prensa Gráfica* [another national newspaper] has given coverage to so-called 'Green Mining,' which makes it clear to us that these groups defend their own economic interests and not those of the majority.

We also recognize your expression in favor of a Water Law that could guarantee the human right to water for all, instead of a law that would seek to privatize this vital liquid, treating it as merchandise, as is expressed in the recent Integral Water Law, recently presented in the Legislative Assembly by the right-wing parties and supported by business leaders in the country.

Similarly, we thank you for the two pastoral letters you have written: the first, *I see violence and discord in the city*,[215] and the second, *You, too will give testimony because you have been with me*.[216] We have studied this most recent letter together in our communities because it takes up what we have historically considered to be part of our martyrial and historical memory.

For all of these reasons, Monseñor Escobar Alas, we thank you from the bottom of our hearts for raising your voice and for walking together in these just struggles, for defending the most *pobres* in our country. Please know that this encourages us greatly in our faith, and we feel united in the same Spirit because we have begun to speak the same language (Acts 2:7–9). Know that you are not alone, that the Ecclesial Base Communities, by way of this national network, give you our support and encourage you to continue in this same Spirit.

Certainly, at different moments in our journey, we have not agreed with certain decisions you have made (like the closing of Tutela Legal),[217] and at that time we raised our voices. But also, as responsible Christians, we must recognize and accompany the decisions you have made and the positions you have taken that today allow you to stand next to the communities and the people in our struggle for a world that is more human, more equitable, more solidarious, and in harmony with the environment.

Monseñor Romero, in his homily on January 22, 1978, said, 'Preaching that does not denounce sin, is not the preaching of the gospel. Preaching that gladdens the sinner and makes him secure in his situation of sin is treason to the call of the gospel. To preach in a way that does not disrupt the sinner but rather puts him to sleep in his sin is to leave Zebulun and Naphtali in their darkness of sin. Preaching that awakens, preaching that illuminates, as when a light is turned on when someone is sleeping, naturally disrupts them because it has awakened them. This is the preaching of Christ: awaken, be converted. This is the authentic preaching of the church. Naturally, brothers, this kind of preaching will find conflict, it will lose prestige and be misunderstood, it will disrupt, it will be persecuted. It cannot be on good terms with the powers of darkness and of sin.'

As CEBs, we encourage [you] to continue being a 'microphone of God,' as Monseñor Óscar Arnulfo Romero said. This is also a call that the communities and we who make them up take on in our pastoral and community work, inspired by Jesús of Nazareth and in our martyrs, heroes, and those who continue today constructing a church as the service of those who most need it.

As siblings,
The National Network of CEBs in El Salvador"[218]

3 From the minutes of the meeting of the National Network of CEBs on October 21, 2017:

"Those of us who participated in the meeting with Mons. Escobar Alas this past September 21 at the Archbishop's office share the following impressions:

This was a different kind of meeting, compared to the experience that we had with the Bishop of Santiago de María. The Archbishop had a good attitude when he was deciding where to sit, because the secretary had already told us that there was a seat where only he was allowed to sit, but he changed his mind and sat next to Chamba. We thought he was very interested in getting to know us and understanding our experience. When we were introducing ourselves personally and explaining where we were from, he wanted to know more. He was open and non-judgmental. He was empathetic, and he wanted to treat us well. It was a good discussion and a good meeting. He expressed his opinion, and we got to know him a little bit.

He was interested, too, in continuing to get to know us and expressed a desire to continue meeting. I didn't get the impression that he held all the power. It was more like a chat, even though we didn't get to everything. It's important now to figure out what's next.

He was interested in us. He told us of a meeting he had with the clergy in which they had received a letter from Bolivia asking how the CEBs were doing. For him, we do not seem to be a problem, because our issue is with the bishop of our diocese. Our letter was read, and he said that the only thing he didn't agree with was our position on the closure of Tutela Legal, which [he said] was closed because of a series of internal irregularities. He told us that information about the cases held in Tutela Legal is accessible. He expressed his support of us and indicated that we should not feel outside of the church. We will have to discuss among ourselves to see how to continue and what our goals are. He treated us well, and now we have to figure out our goals in continuing to meet with him.

We shared with him what we do and how we live as communities, including how they have offended us. But he asked for forgiveness in the name of those who committed those offenses. This all could turn into some sort of process; we will have to continue to analyze it.

There has to be a reason to continue. Our first objective is fulfilled: to give him our letter and to encourage him to continue with this same Spirit and attitude. He continues to take a side, and we have to be open; he said, 'Whoever doesn't vote for the Water Law doesn't deserve a vote.' And he is going to be alone in that position. On this issue, the church and society are very conservative. But there are points which for the communities are inalienable, for example, our way of being church, not having to return to the parish, our expression of faith, our identity, etc. We are clear that on doctrinal issues, we have differences.

It was a good meeting to get to know each other and to read him the letter. As a person and as an Archbishop, he expressed his opinion, but it would be another thing for him to say 'this is what the clergy think.' I think that he is getting rather personally involved in these struggles. He seemed very clear on his position on the justice that we desire for the cases in Tutela and the backing and protection he can offer. He said, 'I am with you,' 'I am very saddened by what's happening,' 'We reach out our hands to you, I ask for your forgiveness,' 'Sometimes we are misinformed.' And speaking of another meeting, he said it wouldn't be just one but many times. His openness was sincere. Now we have to figure out the correct path to follow . . .

After those who were present in the meeting shared, the following came up:

We are not trying to belong to a parish. If he wants to meet with us, he has to respect us as CEBs.

We CEBs have to be about action. There is a danger that we might turn into propaganda. We have to be well-prepared when we go to reflect on the gospel.

They are strategic. If for a time the communities have been disconnected from the hierarchy, why now are they drawing close? At least in Nahuizalco, we would not agree to reconnecting with hierarchical figures. In some social actions, we agree to acting together. If we reconnect with him, we could lose our identity.

We have to see this as a prophetic and gospel mission. We should say what we think... we will not submit to a religious system. If they want to talk and be united in the work, great! Learning and teaching. They do not come down to become familiar with the reality of the people. We have to use the gospel to clarify the path we are to take...

In the beginning we worked with priests who had clear ideals about the gospel and the struggle. We were not submissive then. By talking things out we clarify things as a community, with maturity for arguments, from our Christian praxis, getting into the issues we want to keep discussing. It's not about rejecting all priests and bishops. We come from a tradition of faith that was imposed on us with a sword. We won't make any headway on doctrinal issues.

This has been our experience—eight communities expelled and pushed out. Coming to a consensus on this point is not easy. It is difficult for all of us to come to consensus among everybody there to define what to do. We should take up the prophetic Spirit with courage. The CEBs have been invisibilized because of our positions. The great majorities of the hierarchical church are with the system, not with *el pobre*. You can't be on the side of both. The great majority of bishops and priests preach from their desks. The proposal could be that we invite everybody and from there talk about how to define a path forward.

On social issues maybe, but on doctrinal issues, this will be difficult. We have to discuss out of a concern for the common good, without losing sight of either the gospel or of human beings.

The first step is to come down to the suffering, to the crucified. We have to teach with our own testimony. This is what Jesús of Nazareth was about.

It is important to have theological arguments and foundations for who we are and what we do. We don't have to see everything as so much gray area. We, the CEBs, were born out of a meeting of bishops, at the Second Vatican Council. Our motivation is that this church be promoted. We have to work out a good proposal for our way of being church. I think we have to start thinking about a meeting with topics for debate: sacraments, etc., and try to talk about this all together. That is, to have a national meeting. We also have our own Guidelines for our work, which is the path we take in this way of being church. We have to have a point in common and to define how we are going to be in order to reach consensus on some points that are up for debate; what are our obstacles and on what are we backwards, and write it out as a document. We should be constructive in forwarding our model of church; 'personally, I try to see the light in people. How are we to strengthen that which gives us hope?' Let's make some proposals, and at our next meeting, this can be the focal point."[219]

THE CANONIZATION OF MONSEÑOR ROMERO

4 As October 14, 2018 approached, the day of Romero's canonization in Rome, various collectives began to meet to plan the celebration in El Salvador. The CEBs met with Equipo Maiz, representatives of non-Catholic churches, faith-based organizations, historic grassroots musicians and leaders at the UCA to brainstorm, as they had done for the beatification when they were not included in the archdiocesan plan. However, this time would prove to be different. On July 14, 2018, these groups met with representatives from the Archdiocese, who were open to and interested in planning the event together. Two proposals for October 14 were set forth in common, one from the CEBs and affiliated groups and another from the Archdiocese. Given the two proposals, a third proposal was negotiated between the groups, which involved a procession down the main boulevard in the capital city, the same route that Romero memorial marches had trod for the last thirty-eight years, followed by Mass outside of the Cathedral, followed by an overnight celebration of grassroots music, dancing, and other cultural presentations. The time had come for the two groups to decide a way forward, to decide if they were going to work together. Dialogue ensued:

"We should be centered by our visions and our convictions. It is a grassroots event, and should have many popular dimensions. We do not want a Saint for our altars, but rather a celebration that is a dynamic expression of our people.

The third option, working together, is preferable. We can coordinate who leads different spaces and times. It is important that the people not just be there as spectators.

It will be important to be careful about our message and our speech. If we work together with the Catholic church, we start at a disadvantage because they already have the path set. So will we really have the freedom to express ourselves? Will we be able to negotiate and reframe our Monseñor Romero of the people? We must not allow ourselves to feel dazzled. We should be united without getting turned around.

This canonization is not the beatification [all over again]. We have to focus on what is most important. We can talk to Padre Chema[220] about the liturgy.

We don't want them to make Romero into a devotional saint!

We have to follow Romero's example of unity without stopping out denouncements. He spoke to the army, to the oligarchy. He did not renounce speaking prophetically. He converted together with the people. There are still parish priests who have no love for Romero.

We should highlight the conversion of the Monseñor Romero of history. He is linked to so many decisive and deciding moments: conflicts, massacres . . . he even spoke to Empire itself![221] Romero is a saint of our people. We should call the institutional church to conversion, so that they take up the legacy of Romero.

We should provide the content for the vigil—combining music, testimonies . . .

Even if we are prohibited from singing some songs or if we are forced to change some lyrics, we cannot stop singing them.

The church has caught up with the people who have already declared Romero to be a saint. We should walk together in this canonization without losing sight of the vision of the people.

It's a long agenda, but we have to present our acts. We can provide dance, music, and other content in those spaces. We have to plan it out concretely. We have to be yeast in the dough, so it's important to be in the procession and take with us our colorfulness, our banners, our sayings and slogans . . .

Even if we do this together, they are not going to change us. To the contrary, if we display our own dynamics we can even help other cases like Romero's to be known. We should be open to the different expressions from all of us who will participate.

We can let some of the accessories go, but nothing fundamental.

It's up to us. We have to make our message stand out and communicate the depth of our reflection.

If we vote to do this together, we ought to know beforehand that the institution will have final say.

It is an opportunity to be known by our people.

Okay, we have decided. We have an identity we will not lose, and we will be present with this identity.

This process is an ongoing journey."[222]

5 With the collaboration of the CEBs and the Archdiocese, the third proposal was the blueprint for the celebration. What follows is a homily that Archbishop Escobar Alas gave in gratitude for this event:

"Eminent Cardinals, Honorable Apostolic Nuncio, Bishops, dear brother priests, religious sisters, religious brothers, seminarians, beloved brothers and sisters in Jesus Christ,

We celebrate this act of thanksgiving to God for the canonization of our beloved Monseñor Romero. We also thank Pope Francis for his great love for [Romero] and for canonizing him. Thank you to the bishops, priests and laypeople who have come from other countries to celebrate this great event with us. Thank you to you, beloved brothers and sisters, for being with us in this celebration. 'The Lord has done great things for us,' we just proclaimed together with the Psalmist. A saying that has been fulfilled in this people. The Lord truly has done great things for us in conceding us the canonization of our Pastor, Bishop, and Martyr, and now Saint, Óscar Arnulfo Romero.

In the midst of this jubilee, I want to fulfil an act of justice: I publicly ask forgiveness in the name of that part of the Church that mistreated and defamed Monseñor Romero: among those his brother bishops, priests, and lay people who abandoned and attacked him with an anti-gospel attitude. And not only during his life, but even after his martyrial death. We ask for forgiveness from the holy people of God for the scandal that this unjustified attitude has caused them.

Additionally, I want to publicly acknowledge and express sincere gratitude for all those who did know how to respond to that historic moment of salvation, giving faithful testimony to their faith at Monseñor Romero's side. They knew to stand with the saintly, as did the Apostle St. John. This is directed, in the first place, to our martyrs, priests, religious sisters, and lay people who offered their lives for their faith. We also recognize and thank all those who, even if they did not shed blood, have given steadfast testimony of their faith. They are true confessors of the faith, as we have stated in our Second Pastoral Letter. At the same time, I also want to thank the Carmelite sisters of St. Teresa, our dear Monseñor Arturo Rivera Damas (of fond memory), our dear Cardinal Gregorio Rosa, and all of the priests, members of the Jesuit order, Ecclesial Base Communities, and all of the religious sisters, religious brothers and the holy people of God, all the churches and diverse creeds of the whole world that have given testimony to the holiness of Romero. We are immensely grateful to you all. Now our dreams have been fulfilled in seeing our Saint on the altar. Thanks be to God.

It is our joint task to know more about Monseñor Romero and to imitate him. I take this occasion to respectfully ask the Government of our country to include the topic 'The person and the teaching of Monseñor Romero' in the curricula for middle and high school. I invite us all to truly be united around our saint Monseñor Romero and to put his doctrines into practice. Like the blind man from Jericho, we also ask that Jesús give us the grace to be able to see Him in *lxs pobres*, to see him in each of our brothers and sisters, and to see him with the vision of Romero. In the footsteps of our saint, I invite us all to struggle for justice.

I wonder, beloved brothers and sisters, what Saint Óscar Romero would say to us Salvadorans in this historic time we are living in. His decisive, prophetic voice appears in my imagination condemning:

- the great zeal to privatize water, a homicidal zeal that sadly exists and persists in some. May we make use of our rights as citizens, may we all fight for respect for the human right to water for all Salvadorans.

- I also seem to be able to hear Monseñor Romero's strong denouncement of the grave injustice of our pension system, which is perversely designed so that retired workers live in misery and that the administrative agents of the workers' funds have profits in the millions. This is a grave injustice that cries out to God. This unjust system should be replaced by one that truly favors workers.
- It also seems to me that the voice of Monseñor Romero denounces the great quantity of taxes in our country and how they all are a burden for our poor people in this regressive tributary system that obliges *los pobres* to pay more, without exception, leaving those with more money free from paying some taxes and allowing them to evade or elude paying others. This form [of taxation] condemns the *pobre* to become more and more *pobre*.
- It is easy for our imaginations to 'hear' the voice of Monseñor Romero at this moment, courageously defending the right of migrants from Central America and all over the world. Our migrant brothers and sisters are noble, honest, and hardworking people. Their only 'crime,' if we can call it that, is being *pobre*, but *los pobres* are the favored of God. They migrate because they are obligated to do so because of injustices like the ones we have mentioned and others. The mobility of persons is an invulnerable human right. They have the right to migrate, they have the right to refuge, and they have the right to asylum. It is a human task to protect and help migrants. We thank those who are helping the Central American migrant caravans and ask other states that they not be criminalized and that their rights not be violated, but rather that their rights be respected and that they be helped.

As the people of God, today we raise our prayer to the Lord for the intercession of Our Lady Queen of Peace, Patroness of El Salvador, and for the intercession of our beloved Saint Monseñor Romero. May God grant us the grace to work together for the cessation of social exclusion, of inequity, impunity and violence, and in this way grant us the social peace that we so desire.

May it be so."[223]

The *Librito* of the Prophet Reina Greisi Leiva

Reina Greisi Leiva was born near Acajutla in Sonsonate and for many years formed part of the ecclesial base community "Monseñor Romero" in Jardines de Colón, La Libertad. This community was formed mostly by families that were internally displaced during the persecution of the 1970s and armed conflict of 1980–1992. Some of these families had experienced a new way of being the church of *lxs pobres* in places like Suchitoto and Chalatenango, others were formed by experiences with the Archdiocese and Monseñor Romero, and still others were ex-combatants with the FMLN who came to the community after they were demobilized. Jardines de Colón has a particularly strong organizational structure and has been a leading community for others in the region. Reina now works for FUNDAHMER, the nonprofit that grew out of CEBES in 2000 and accompanies organized groups of women in Morazán and La Libertad, inheritors of the wartime Congregations of Mothers[224] and other forms of grassroots organizing in internal and external refugee camps. These groups include women who were alive during the war, women born during the conflict, and their daughters and granddaughters who are part of a new generation of CEB membership. They are interested in deepening their understanding and experience with traditional and contemporary trades, recovering some of the most ancient hammock-weaving and natural medicine practices while also crocheting *matatas* with synthetic fibers and setting up sewing machines in lean-to workshops built on the side of their community chapels. Reina helps coordinate instructors, often leaders of different women's groups who travel to teach others, and accompanies the groups in their learning. She herself is a skilled craftsperson, especially in the areas of natural medicine, reflexology, and crocheting, and she is constantly setting up workshops for beginners to start to learn these and other trades.

Reina is one person among many committed members of the contemporary CEBs, but her prophetic words about being a woman in the church reflect sentiments expressed by many others. Like Anastasio Aquino, Prudencia Ayala, Farabundo Martí, and Monseñor Romero in their own contexts, Reina's life in community witnesses to a saving decolonial praxis in the present day.

1 "At the beginning in our community, it was just the pastoral team, but as the community grew, there were more and more of us women, and there were more and more young people, and we felt like every Sunday we were just sitting there, filling the benches, listening to the same 'blah, blah, blah,' every Sunday. So we decided that it would be nice for the young people to do the celebration one day with their own youthful way of thinking, because they are in school, in high school, wherever they went. But the idea was that they would, from their own lived experience, reflect on the Gospel out of their own way of thinking, and that's how the young people started. And they loved it! They said, 'Yes, we are going to do it.' And if they messed up, nobody said anything to them.

'Hey, you really stuck your foot in your mouth there!' No, nobody. It was a beautiful thing. It was respectful. Same thing with the women. We women celebrated, and when we celebrated, the men were right there: Pedro Pérez, our head catechist, in the first row, and Salvador Hernández, another principal catechist there. And they were there to support us, you know, to support and not to criticize. I'm telling you, that was what encouraged me to experience my faith, a stronger faith, a more rooted faith, a much more secure faith. And I'll tell you what, I think that motivates me here or wherever I go, to be a group, to establish oneself as a community, not an individual, because that's how I've learned to study the Bible, communally, and it's been a great benefit and satisfaction to me."[225]

2 "Projects are short. They begin and they end, but there are always more projects. They go on because life goes on. My life isn't over because some project is over, like somebody came and started a project and then it runs out of steam and then my inspiration to struggle is gone? No! Because life goes on. Because I am alive and because I have this spirit that wants to keep going. So a project ends—oh well! We've gotta figure out another, we have to begin again. They are formative processes.

For example, here. The first round of our women's project was over—this part that I was telling you about—our women's group was formed, and then we looked around and said, 'What now? What are we going to do?'

Ah well. We had to make a diagnostic tool for our community and go see what was happening, because if I'm just sitting here locked in my house, I don't know what people need on my block, on my street, or in my community. I have to go walk, to ask, to make a diagnostic assessment. It's as simple as that. It's about going. So we did a first diagnostic assessment with the women, and with the young people, but in this case the women, and we decided to focus on single women, single mothers, to try to get to know their reality.

Because there were many single mothers. And the group of us who met were, they called us, like puritan women. We were married, we had husbands who gave us money for the house's food, that's who was in the group. But what about the other women in our community who are out there and who aren't in here with us? They weren't there because they were working in a sweatshop. But how do they live? What do they do? How can we get to know them? So we went to go visit them and talk to them. And it wasn't just a one-day thing. It was many outings. Little groups that would go visit and chat. And in this way, we visited over fifty women.

And when we all returned, we talked about it all! They told me such-and-such a thing, gossip, you know, we sat down and we would say,

'What did they tell you?'

'Oh that Susie so-and-so did such-and-such . . .' We put it all out there. And damn, I'm telling you, I was surprised. That's when I realized that we women that have partners, a husband, somebody, anyone who gives you some money, we think that because I have food three times a day, or that I get some money every payday, we take it for granted that other women are in the same boat! But no! The reality of these women was different. It's like having three jobs. Why? Because they have to work. Then they come home and take care of their children and their parents who are elderly. And if they have a boyfriend, which they do, sometimes, on the side, they have to be available for him when he says!"

3 "And you know, for the hierarchical church, women, single women, are like sinners. The priest doesn't pick them to come read the Gospel. That's a sin. It would make anyone tremble. So that won't happen. The priest in Colón doesn't do it, and neither does the one in Lourdes. Certainly not. This only happens in Jardines. That's, on the one hand.

On the other hand, is that women are so exploited by businesses! I'm telling you, women who are single mothers sacrifice themselves. Because they don't have any other income, they always want to do extra, to earn a little more. They scoop up extra shifts and sometimes even turn to prostitution, we found many such cases. Some single mothers said to us,

'Look, my salary at the sweatshop isn't enough, so if a John or two come around and they pay enough, I do it.'

And we aren't going to judge her for it. We don't have an alternative for her. We can't say,

'Look, no, here we have another salary for you.'

How? Where would it come from? We simply do not judge her, and with this, we help her. By accepting her to be part of our collective. We do not reject her. And I can tell you that many women from back then liked that whole experience, and for me, it was like a three-step diagnostic because it was about gathering information, coming here, and then going back out to try to offer some solutions, and then searching, applying, gathering resources the best we could.

And what came out of all that was: a daycare. With somebody who would care for their kids and their elderly mom or dad, knowing that someone was caring for them while you were at work, we helped with maybe half of the worries that a single mother has."[226]

The *Librito* of the Prophet Miguel Zepeda Santos

In this *librito*, Miguel speaks as a thirty-something father-to-be about his experience growing up in the CEBs. At the time these words were recorded in 2017, he was finishing a degree in social work from the Lutheran University in San Salvador and growing in leadership in the CEB "Padre Mauricio Merino" in Sacacoyo, where he lived with his partner and stepdaughter. What is striking in Miguel's story is his account of becoming aware of the sexism in his environment growing up and his own, ongoing process of delinking from *machismo*.

Miguel also thinks deeply about how to involve other young people in the life of the church. He is incredibly biblically literate and is a talented weaver of connections between biblical stories and the realities of young people in his neighborhood and country. He is one example of other young adults who are taking on leadership positions in the Salvadoran church of *lxs pobres* and prophetically facing the challenges of the signs of our times.

1 "I was about fifteen years old when I began to be involved because of my sister's influence: she encouraged me and took me with her on a trip to Guatemala with some Paulist seminarians. That's where my whole story began, my closeness [to the church of *lxs pobres*]. But I think that my first personal formation process, of course, was within my family, though a lot of it had to do with the community. It was a very strong community, very respected, very active in those times. It has been a great school for me, a great university, the community has . . .

Look, I have this great memory from my youth—a bit of a sad example—but it's about the death of my father and how that impacted me.

It hurt me, it changed me, shit, it changed my life. But the community was there. I was a young kid, very young. This was ten years ago, about. I was in the prime of my youth, twenty-six years old. And with my mother. My brothers and sisters were in very difficult situations, so everything became my responsibility. I had to figure out how to keep life going with my mom and my younger siblings. But there was something that gave me life, that made me feel strong, something that helped me step up, and that was the community. My dad was a rural man his whole life, a campesino, a farmer, always working in the *milpa*. When he died, he left four fields of *milpa*, a luxury cornfield! Huge ears of corn. The bean plants were tall, and each vine was full of beans, already turning red! It was a marvel of a *milpa*. A luxury *milpa*. Huge squash in and among the beans and corn—they were huge! Going to this *milpa* was a point of pride. And my dad left it when he died. I was working in Sello de Oro (a business that slaughters and distributes chicken in El Salvador), and I had younger siblings, right, and who was going to harvest this *milpa*? We were going to lose it. But then the community stepped in.

I was organizing my father's overnight vigil, running around, getting the death certificate from the mayor's office, trying to figure out who could dig the grave. I had to figure everything out. And right outside my house, the whole community had gathered. I went out to apologize that I couldn't give them a better welcome because I was running around, but around three in the morning they said to me,

'Miguel we want to speak with you for a second.'

'Okay, give me a second,' I said. And I'll never forget what they said to me, such a beautiful gesture. They said,

'Miguel, your dad had a *milpa*, right?'

'Yes.'

'Have you thought about what you're going to do, how you're going to harvest it?'

'Well, not really, I don't really know yet.' And they said,

'Okay, well, you can count on us. We are going to harvest your *milpa*. We are going to take turns, and we'll start tomorrow. Tomorrow, my dad and Oscar are going to go, and then whoever . . .'

Damn! I mean, that really gave me life. That filled me with strength and for that moment on, I made a decision. From that moment on, I decided that I would never leave the community. So yeah, even though it's a sad example, it's a great testimony to life."[227]

2 "My dad used to tell how my grandfather used to like to drink liquor on the weekends. And that was so normal in El Salvador in those times, you know. He says that my grandfather would come home on Sundays and call all his sons,

'Come, sons, we are going to drink because moonshine is for men!'

To see a woman drinking a beer, oh no! That was the worst. They would treat her like the worst trash. But for a man, come, sons, moonshine is for men. Pure *machismo*!

... My mother doesn't know how to read or write. Nevertheless, her awareness of the problems women face is well-defined. For example, in my house, she always had me wash dishes, cook, wash clothes, clean, we all did that at home. I mean, I did it because she made me, I didn't like it. And I would say,

'Why do I have to cook and wash clothes and dishes and clean and all this and nobody else does?' Because I was the exception. My other brothers didn't. And they would whisper among themselves ... but my mom made me do it. So it was my same sister, the one who influenced me a lot, I remember she would tell my other sisters,

'Girls, wash your plate only, they have to wash their plates, too! You don't have to wash your brother's plates!'

And so, for us, my sister was one of those terrible bad influences on the rest of my sisters, you know? Now I understand why, but I didn't at that time. It seemed illogical to me, it seemed selfish, and she seemed like a bad woman. That's how a *machista* society paints people. Now I understand why and I have no problem washing dishes at home, but that was how I learned how deeply-rooted our *machismo* is."

3 "We used to go to the river to bring water back to the house. Not drinking water, water for washing. We would bathe in the river and wash clothes there, and I remember really well how one time I saw two men arguing. One of them had bathed and put his dirty underwear in his bag and started heading home. The other one, however, bathed and then in front of everybody began to wash his underwear. And the first one said to him,

'Damn? You really are a dumbass, washing your underwear is a woman's job!'

'And why?' the other said to him.

'Well, here you are, washing your underwear, and your woman, what is she doing, huh? That's why you have a woman, so she can wash it for you!'

And the other man said to him, 'Okay, but I have hands, and this is hardly anything! This isn't a mountain of clothes, I'm not even washing her clothes! It's my own clothing, and I can do it.'

'I can do it, too, but I have a woman, and my woman does what I say, and that's how it should be!' the first man said to him.

And it was this whole argument there in the river in front of everybody. One man who washed his underwear and another who didn't. But how much *machismo* there is in something so simple, so basic, and so good for us, too."[228]

4 "Look, the problem with God is that God never does anything. God does not solve our problems. God always sends someone to solve our problems. This is the big mess and the big challenge, and this is something I want to talk about in my community and with other young people, so that we understand that God never does anything. Not even miracles! For example, you have the people enslaved in Egypt, and God appears there on the mountain,

'Moses, Moses, I have heard the cry of my people, and I have come to liberate them!'

'Ah, shoot, thanks, God, for coming to liberate the people!'

Is that what happened? No! God doesn't take a human form and come walking down on a camel to liberate the people. He sends Moses to do it!

'Moses, go. You are going to do it.' And Moses is shocked, because he stutters.

'And how am I going to do it?'

'You've got your brother, don't you? Get your brother to help you!'

God didn't do anything! God sent someone. But the people were liberated, right? So that happened, many more years passed, and then the people are enslaved again. This time, in the book of Judges, it tells how Gideon is hiding the harvest because other armies are coming to steal it. And good ole God appears again. Thanking himself that he appears again, huh?

'Gideon, with your courage you will save Israel!'

Damn! With YOUR courage! I bet Gideon hoped for an angel who would say to him,

'I'm here to liberate again!' At least to Moses, God said,

'I have heard and I have come to liberate.' At least that! Not to *pobre* Gideon! Right away, God says, with your courage you will save Israel. It's another really illogical story because Gideon is a young man. He is not a warrior, he's a farmer, he's gathering the harvest and he was from the smallest family, which was very important in the times of Israel.

'And how exactly am I going to save my people?'

And God always looks for the least dignified person, the least worthy, the one who isn't worth anything, that's where God always is.

But God never does anything himself! Never! So with this crisis we have about water, maybe God has already spoken to our Moses, but Moses hasn't stepped up yet. Maybe God already spoke to Gideon,

'With your courage you will save Las Mesas, with your courage you will save rural communities,' and maybe Gideon hasn't stepped up yet. He hasn't found his 300 people yet to make noise with their empty water jugs. I guess not. But that's God's message. We hope that some Moses or some Gideon steps up and shows strength. Maybe Gideon is waiting for a sign from God that guarantees that he's really being called to this. That's God's message for me in our struggle for water. Our people are suffering this calamity because there are others who live in the hills with their golf courses and their pools, while we don't even have a well to get drinking water. But I see God's message at work."[229]

The *Librito* of the Prophet María Ángela Domínguez Pérez

Ángela—born in 1986, in the middle of the war—is a social worker who can often be seen visiting rural communities in Cacaopera on her motorcycle. She grew up mostly in Segundo Montes[230] and now lives in her mother's homeland of Junquillo, Cacaopera. At the time of the 2017 interview from which these selections are taken, she was finishing her own social work degree and working with FUNDAHMER, accompanying students and youth groups from the CEBs in Morazán. Upon her graduation at the end of 2017, she was the first woman from the CEBs in her region to graduate from university. She now continues her work with young people at a different local nonprofit while she finishes a master's degree in university teaching. The best word to describe Ángela is "badass."

In Ángela's own assessment of the CEBs and her own worldview, she reflects on how young people are discriminated against and treated by police in contemporary El Salvador. Much like the history of policing in the United States, policing in El Salvador has roots in the defense of wealthy, European descendants' claims to land and the surveillance of *lxs pobres*.[231] The National Civil Police (PNC) was created as part of the 1992 Peace Accords in order to demilitarize policing among the civilian population. However, in recent years the PNC has disregarded this separation of civilian and military armed forces, allowing the military to become involved with domestic policing and national security, to the point of both forces jointly occupying the Legislative Assembly in early 2020[232] and both forces regularly profiling groups of young people and unjustly arresting and detaining them.[233]

Ángela also reflects on her own vocation as a social worker and what vocation means for her in a context where economic scarcity forces many workers to migrate North in search of work or to do backbreaking labor in *maquiladoras* or as day laborers on farms. She also thinks about gender, as a mother of two sons, and about what it means to struggle against systemic oppression. Ultimately, though Ángela's christology reflects the classic image in liberation theology of a human Jesús struggling against injustice, an example for his followers, her reflections also hint at the crushing impossibility of human struggle on its own. The growing awareness that "I cannot do it alone" echoes in many other reflections among young people in the CEBs after over fifty years of struggle, and a more nuanced commitment to "building" the reign of God emerges.

1 "So look, I was born on November 30, 1986, in a place called Colomoncagua, which is in Honduras because my mother at that time had fled the war. She went to Honduras and was there for a few years before I was born.

We returned on November 18, 1989, and I was almost three.

I don't remember absolutely anything about leaving, but when we were on our way, maybe passing by San Fernando, which I didn't even know where that was at the time, I remember that I woke up. I had been laying down, like, in the truck, not a pickup truck, but one of those big trucks. And I was in a little hammock, I was little, and I was sleeping, and I woke up because the road was really bad, and there was a big hole and boom, I fell out of the hammock. I hit my head on the truck, I remember that.

I remember that my mom picked me up and tried to console me. I fell asleep again and I woke up when we were by Perquín, in the town. And then I don't remember anything until we were in Segundo Montes. And I remember that it was crazy because it was like, imagine, you're in an isolated place, like a desert practically, where there's nothing, nothing!

It was a forest, but it wasn't, like, a thick forest, either, because it was at the end of the war and everything was burned. So we got to a place where there was nothing, nothing, no food, no houses. We had to build everything. We had unbuilt our houses in Colomoncagua and brought the materials to make houses here in Segundo Montes.

So I remember that, there was nowhere to sleep. We slept in the open field, only with something under us to keep us warmer; it was November . . .

My mother was on the shoemaking commission. She knew how to make shoes. And she was also on the *jarcia* commission, for artisan work, making hammocks out of mezcal fibers. And she was a leader, organizing the people. So she was a leader on three commissions: the shoemaking workshops, the organizing team, and the artisan work team. It wasn't so hard to make houses after all because we all worked in groups and got a lot done."

2 "And I was maybe four when we went to Usulután, and I remember well. A member of the Guard grabbed me by the arm and threw me up on his truck like I was any old object. And I was on top of the car and I didn't understand why I was up there, with a bunch of other kids. And I saw that all the others were crying, so I cried, too, because I saw that my mom was fighting with the Guardsmen down below. My mom fought with the soldiers. I saw that they were hitting her, but ultimately, I don't know, I didn't understand what was going on. And I don't know how, but they got me down. I don't know what happened, but they pushed me down, that's all I remember. When I think about it now, I think, damn! If my mom hadn't fought, maybe, who knows where I would be right now . . .

It was because we were guerrilla soldiers' kids. Yeah, they took kids and the kids disappeared. So yeah, I feel like that affected me a lot because . . . yeah, I can't forget it."[234]

3 "Maybe it's because I lived through all that that I have a way of thinking that is really against repression, and against military bodies. Because when I see a soldier, I never say anything, and I never act in any way against them, but the color of the uniform really sticks with me. And just seeing somebody with a rifle or any long weapon, I feel that same way—I don't know if it's hate or maybe resentment, but it's something that doesn't sit right with me, something that I don't like. And yeah, truly, I am not in favor of repression from the military, which is something that still happens.

Now, perhaps, *perhaps*, [police repression] not against all civilians, but rather certain groups, for example, young people. The thing is, supposedly, the military bodies and the police are supposed to offer us security. But many times, they use this power that they have in a different way. Sometimes they take advantage of it because they want something, because they have power and because they are dressed in their uniform. Many times they take advantage of people that are not doing anything wrong.

Yesterday, for example. We got in trouble yesterday with Anita in the school in town. Now there's a soldier at the entrance to the school, supposedly providing security. And right when we were leaving, after our visit to the school [for work], he had two young boys. He had grabbed them and put his hands on their shoulders and hit them so they would look at him. And so when we saw that, Anita shouted. She told him that this was no way to behave and no way to treat a student. The students had their uniforms on, and at least he should respect their uniform and the education they were trying to get. If he was going to demand respect for his uniform, the students should get respect, too.

And he told us to shut up and to go do our work somewhere else and not to get involved because we were interrupting his work. And yeah, we were indignant, and I felt like he was treating me the way he was treating the boys. And maybe that's why we shouted at him with Anita, for him to leave them alone and let them go to class.

The deal with young people is that you have to do a lot of preventative work, not only paying attention when the problem is already upon you. Maybe [the police] should use some other method, or another tactic, to try to reduce violence and insecurity, but at the same time, they just don't know how to do it. Because they just know how to repress, and sometimes they have the wrong person. And that's exactly why we got involved yesterday, because one of those boys was that boy who was offering music classes to our scholarship students. . . . When I saw him [with the police], I felt that feeling inside me because I know who he is. I know that I can't just stick my hand in the fire for everybody, and I don't want to be making excuses for delinquent kids, either. But I knew that kid because he was the one offering guitar classes."[235]

4 "I think that ever since the moment I started studying social work—look, I am often resentful, and I've even said, if God exists, why are so many terrible things permitted? But there are moments where, they say, even the strongest person has to believe in God, and I believe that God acts. In everything, I think, God has a plan for each one of us, and I believe that God had a plan for me.

After I finished high school, I lost six years. And maybe if I had started studying [at university] right when I finished high school, I wouldn't have studied the same thing. I was in the exact right place in my life, after six years, to study social work, because everything was so different for me. I had a different way of thinking. The way life hits you, makes you think, and maybe because of everything life has thrown at me, maybe because of all my struggles, maybe that's how I knew that social work was about working with people, to be hand-in-hand with people, struggling together with people, living with people, giving yourself to people, in order to be able to understand people. Other degrees don't allow you to do that. Yeah, there are other careers that are nice, that help people, and serve people, but from a different kind of perspective.

For example, nursing. You study nursing, and you serve people, and you have to have a human side, yes, good, that's fine. But someone shows up with a wound, and the nurse doesn't know why they are hurt, what gave rise to this, or what really happened that injured this person? Why did this happen to them? What is this person's life like?

And social work sees all that. It studies the whole person. Completely. We are not psychologists, but we do therapy. We are not nurses, but we do serve people. We are not judges, but we struggle for justice and for real, enforceable rights. And sometimes, we make huge mistakes. That's true. As a social work student,

I'm telling you, I have made many mistakes, but these mistakes are what make me reflect. And I hope, I hope, that if one day I graduate and am able to execute the profession of social work, I hope, maybe, to think differently than many other social workers and to see reality from a different point of view . . .

Vocation isn't something that to do because you said you would, or because it's your job, and it's not something you do because they pay you, no. I think that vocation is about what you do from your heart, what you give with your heart. To give of yourself, not in the sense of 'oh, because I am going to receive a salary,' or 'because I am going to receive a check for however much on whatever day every month.' I believe that vocation is to give of yourself without worrying about being hungry or just to be doing something, for the sake of another. Without worrying about if you have money or not, you share what little you have, even if it is very little. And it doesn't matter if it's raining or if the sun is shining. You do this thing because you never had it. And I think that—I know I'm crazy, but I believe this, and that's why I say it—if God one day allowed me to die and gave me a new opportunity to live and said, 'Ángela, choose, what do you want to study?' I would not doubt choosing social work again."[236]

5 "I don't want all of this to keep reproducing itself. *Machismo*. We are in the twenty-first century, and *machismo* is so latent in our communities, in our homes, in our lives, in our every-day goings-on. And many times, we women commit the greatest error of reproducing that *machismo*. Because they raised us in a *machista* way, that women have to be submissive, and women have to be obedient, and women have to be everything that is opposite men. And so when we raise our children, many times we commit the error of saying, 'Behave like a young man.'

But then later, you realize that you are studying social work and struggling in your own trenches and so what the hell was that about? What the hell?

Many times, I have bought my son pink shirts. Pink! He has three pink shirts! And I take my kids with me everywhere, when I have the chance. And many times I've brought him to school with me, and he's wearing his pink shirt. And the people here scare me, saying, 'Hey, what's with your kid?' Here at university. Among all these professionals there is *machismo* . . .

[If you try to stop *machismo* . . .] oh, boy. You are standing against a whole system that, shit, you're fighting against something that just doesn't budge. Many times, I've gone through this, when I have struggled against it within my own family, or in my community, or at work. The consequences: you will be repressed, you will have limits put on you, you will be restricted in certain things, they try to get on your nerves, they will try to tie your hands, cover your mouth, so that you can't speak or do anything. And it's this way because it's a *machista* system that we live in and everything in our system is powered by *machismo*, and that's why we don't see the efforts that so many women have made, just like me. I haven't done anything really great, but from the very moment that I start thinking differently or start being conscious that I have to think differently and act differently and start treating my son differently, I think I'm doing something. Of course! I know that I've won no Nobel Peace Prize, and I'm not sitting around waiting for that to happen. But at least I will have the satisfaction of knowing that I struggled against a whole system, and that I could do something, even if only with my own son. That is my hope."[237]

6 "Jesús also struggled against injustice. Jesús struggled against the violence of his times. It was in a different way; they fought with swords and today we fight with firearms and bullets, but he had great struggles. He fought against a series of injustices that, well, damn! I think that that was Jesús's work, to struggle against all that and to open many people's eyes. And now I think that Jesús is someone who gives us a great example, a great example, because he denounced injustice; he denounced so much oppression and so much evil. And now we have the same struggle but in a different way, yeah, but those of us who are here, I think that this is our challenge and our struggle. If we want to build a better world, we have to struggle against it all.

Look, I know that many times I've almost hung up my gloves and said, 'Okay, world, here I am, do with me what seems right, here I am, Ángela Domínguez, do with me what you will.' There are moments when I lose hope. I think that we are struggling against something that is not going to change. People's way of thinking that isn't going to change, people who don't want to see the world in a different way, who take it upon themselves to make life impossible for others. And I don't blame them, because they have let themselves be carried away by all this, maybe because of trauma, the wounds and scars that life leaves you with. But what a shame that they try to get even with someone else who is not at fault.

Imagine it—me, sometimes, I put myself against all that, and I fight in my own little corner, making my own barricades, in my own place striking, struggling, wanting to combat an invisible giant in front of me, and I know that I cannot do it alone. I don't know where the hell I get the strength, but I do!"[238]

The *Librito* of the Prophet José Adonay Pérez

Adonay speaks prophetically from his rural community Flor del Muerto in Cacaopera, Morazán. This librito contains selections from his musings on his experiences in the CEBs, recorded in February 2017, when he was a fourteen-year-old starting ninth grade. Adonay's grandmother, Pilar, has been like a mother to him, and she has introduced him to the work of the CEB in their community. Pilar is a member of the Mother's Congregation in Flor Muerto that formed when the community repatriated back to El Salvador after the war and settled in Cacaopera after living in Segundo Montes for a few years.

Adonay has been very involved in the CEB in his community and with other CEBs in the region, even nationally. He regularly attends the monthly "*escuelita de teología*" (school of theology) facilitated by FUNDAHMER. The escuelita is one of the ways the CEBs continue to sharpen their theological skills without the pastoral formation centers run by the Archdiocese and religious orders that existed in the 1970s. He also represents El Salvador in "Bendita Mezcla," a popular education style theological formation curriculum designed by other young leaders from CEBs throughout Latin America and the Caribbean and facilitated by the Continental Network of CEBs based in Mexico, the popular theology network Amerindia, and CLACSO, the Latin American Council for the Social Sciences.

The celebration of Octavio Ortiz in the plaza of Cacaopera to which Adonay refers in the first section was the thirty-seventh anniversary celebration of Octavio's martyrdom.[239] The CEBs of Cacaopera decided to celebrate this anniversary in the main plaza in front of the parish church in town because weeks before, the new parish priest had removed Octavio's photo from inside the church. The priest claimed that no photos of anyone who is not a canonized saint are allowed in a church, and CEBs members who were at Mass that day brought the photo back home with them to their chapel in Agua Blanca. The day of his anniversary, they marched with the photo from the chapel in Agua Blanca to the plaza in front of the parish church, about a two-hour march, to celebrate Octavio's witness to the Gospel in their lives. The parish priest concelebrated Mass with Fr. Rogelio Ponselle, who knew Octavio personally and preached the homily. Different youth groups presented songs and skits about Octavio's life and martyrdom, and Adonay spoke publicly, representing the youth of his community.

1 "My name is José Adonay Pérez. I was born here in Flor Muerto. Right now, I am fourteen years old. I study in the ninth grade at the Flor Muerto school, and my family supports my work in the CEBs. It's not something that many young people choose to do.

I remember that, in second grade, my classmates told me that I was very quiet and asked why I didn't like to talk too much. I told them that, really, I didn't know why I felt the way I felt, but I did get good grades. I remember my report cards fondly, and I got good grades. I'm happy to have that memory.

I stopped being so quiet when, one time, in a CEBs meeting, when Mercedes was here still, they asked me for my opinion. I gave them my opinion, but still, I felt really nervous. When I stopped feeling nervous was in Cacaopera, for the anniversary of Fr. Octavio Ortiz, the year we celebrated it there in the plaza. Because I went to the front, Mercedes had picked me to do it, and yeah, I felt really nervous, but then everything was okay. My knees were shaking at the beginning, but then everything was okay. That was the first time I stopped being nervous, and it was a beautiful feeling, because not being nervous is a big challenge for me."

2 "[It was my grandmother] who talked to me a lot about the CEBs. Really, she used to take my sister, Marta Patricia, to meetings with her, but when she stopped going, I started going because my grandmother couldn't write very quickly. And I could write a little bit already, not very well, but yeah. My grandma took me and had me write down what was going on.

Sometimes, I remember, we would go as far as Naranjera, and I have another very beautiful memory that one time with Edgardo, we ate watermelon and I got stains all over my shirt.

Before, our formation workshops were two days long. I went with my grandmother, who was really like my mother, and she took me so I could write everything down in a notebook. That's when I began to go. Then, maybe three years ago now, I started being involved in the CEBs of my own account."

3 "Now, I feel like I've honed my skills quite a bit, and I've organized a group of young people in the community . . . because I wasn't shy anymore, I assumed leadership of the youth group.

Last year, we hosted a few activities, and this year we have more activities planned, and I'm still the leader. Last year, we hosted a Christmas dinner, just us, the youth group, and this year we started a trash pick up campaign, and yeah, we've collected a lot of trash. We've had to work with the mayor's office so that they come to collect the trash so we don't just burn it here.

And I'm so, so happy because we've been able to unite two groups, the youth group and the scholarship group, as we call them. So the whole group together is called the Father Octavio Ortiz Luna Youth Group. There are twenty-six or twenty-seven members, and I feel very happy that young people want to work together in this organized way.

It's hard to work with youth sometimes because when they start joking around and don't want to stop, it's a little difficult to keep things interesting. Normally, what I do is ask for a little bit of quiet, and in the time they're quiet, I talk really fast . . . but I feel like since we've united the two groups, they've been a little more focused. They really want to know more about the CEBs, and so we've started picking topics to talk about as a CEB. Our first topic was family disintegration."[240]

4 "[What happens at a meeting is that] I greet everybody at the beginning and welcome them. Then I ask someone else to say a prayer, so that they can participate. I always have a little agenda, and, following the plan, we talk about a certain topic and reflect as a group, thinking about what solutions there might be. We usually take between an hour and a half or two hours. I try to help them understand how to talk directly, to identify a core problem, so that we don't just talk around an issue.

Once everybody understands the issue, everyone says their piece. And I think that there are other young people in the community who are really interested, but they haven't come to a meeting because there are others in the community who discourage them.

But I don't know, really, I don't know why they trust me and pay attention to what I say. And yeah, it's a little more difficult to work with adults because they have greater knowledge. With everything they've lived through, they have so much experience.

But I learn from them, and they learn from me, too, because there are always new topics that we talk about. For example, this Saturday, we were talking about our martyrs, and what are some ideas we might have to recover our historical memory here in our community. Going to other communities to do interviews, asking who all the fallen are, for example, in all the communities [around here]. That would be, we might say, a

The Librito *of the Prophet José Adonay Pérez* 157

solution I might propose as an example. And if they understand me and support the idea, then each person contributes . . .

And in every meeting, I always bring the picture of Monseñor Romero, I put it in the center, and people who bring flowers put them there, and we'll put out a light, a candle, and I'll put something else appropriate, a little plant or something, a glass of water, that's a very typical CEBs altar, too. It's what's practical. It's what I see in the escuelita,[241] and that's what I then do in my community. And people bring their small symbols, too. I'll put, for example, the calendar 'Faces Not To Forget'[242] or a song book, you know, important things."[243]

5 "I feel the responsibility I feel because the CEBs have awakened something in me that nobody else had awakened, not even the Catholic church, which is the traditional church. But really, yeah, I feel like it's something that motivates me and that interests me because I like to see the people organized. So it's something that I feel like, yeah, really, I can do it, or I'm capable, or maybe because God asks it of me. Because that's how the CEBs are, it's all volunteer work leading a group or accompanying other groups and all that. And I feel like a leader, and I'm interested because yeah, I want to see the community organized. The four communities here in Agua Blanca, totally organized in this sector, since we have the chapel here . . .

I had, we could say, a gift that was very deep inside of me, and that nobody had ever been able to show to me that, yes, I was capable of doing this. And so now I have realized that I am capable of many things, and I feel like the CEBs have helped me in that way. When I was with my grandmother, who was really like my mother, many years ago, I would sometimes just come to play, but not anymore. Now I've decided to take this seriously, as of three years ago, and I feel motivated when members of CEBs in other communities support me, too."[244]

6 "I see Jesús as a teacher for me because I learn from him, since in his teachings he gives us so much. He was a great prophet, and it's incredible how people have betrayed him. But I see Jesús as someone who really loved humanity and who wasn't afraid to lose his life. And we sometimes commit errors and are afraid of many things, but not Jesús. And I feel like I see Jesús calling me to not stop and to not be afraid because the more afraid we are, the more imperialism can dominate us, that is, the temptations of Satan and all that. I see Jesús as someone who always supports me because his teachings and morals and parables have already helped me so much . . .

A dream I have is that we are able to decrease environmental pollution, since that is something that really worries me. But to achieve that, there is a great challenge, like, I can't do anything up against a big monster, but I can start with my little communities. So from there, just keep going little by little until we achieve many things. My dream is that we could really reduce environmental pollution in El Salvador.

For the whole world, [my dream is] that there not be so much inequality among each other. So much violence. So much *machismo*. Among other things that we see a lot in the world. And that there be no more war. Yes, that would be a great dream I have for the entire world."[245]

The *Librito* of the Prophet Berta Cáceres

Berta Isabel Cáceres Flores is a martyr of the church of *lxs pobres*, killed on March 2, 2016. She was of Lenca ancestry and cofounded the Civic Council of Popular and Indigenous Organizations of Honduras (COPINH).

The Lenca are an Indigenous people who have lived in a region bisected by the Honduras-El Salvador border and who are ancestral river custodians. In particular, Berta protected the Gualcarque River in Honduras. Together with members of the community of Río Blanco, Berta mounted a campaign against the Agua Zarca dam, a joint project of a Honduran energy company and Sinohydro—a Chinese state-owned company, the largest dam developer in the world. Berta's campaign included community-based democratic practices, peaceful demonstrations in the Honduran capital, and international work with the Inter-American Human Rights Commission lodging appeals against the International Finance Corporation, the private sector arm of the World Bank and one of the Agua Zarca project funders.

Berta herself identified more with the Lencan cosmovision than the Catholicism of her upbringing. But as with other prophets, Berta's life and work is interpreted by the Salvadoran church of *lxs pobres* to be true evangelization—the work of the Gospel—and her assassination is interpreted as the ultimate witness to her commitment to and faith in other possible worlds. Her case is not an isolated one, as section 4 of this *librito* testifies; environmental activists are vulnerable to disappearance and assassination by economic and political actors, in the same way that martyrs were made of activists and defenders of human rights in the 1970s and 1980s.

The first four sections of this *librito* draw on Berta Cáceres's own prophetic words and her daughter's account of her assassination. The final section is a hymn sung by the Salvadoran CEBs in honor of this contemporary prophet and martyr, guardian of rivers.

WAKE UP, HUMANITY!

1 "I came into political activism when I was very young, about seven years old. My mother was a midwife and activist. I accompanied her on many of her activities around the community. She attended to Indigenous women, assisted refugees and worked closely with students. It was dangerous work. She was kidnapped by an army colonel because of her activism. My brother has also been kidnapped and tortured. Our house was monitored and watched for more than ten years by government death squads.

The mountain range where the Gualcarque River begins is the point where the Lenca myth of the female spirit originates. Spiritually, the site is one of the most important cultural sites for the Lenca. They believe rivers should be able to run free and clean. The Gualcarque supplies water for the Lenca people's livelihood, including beans and other fresh fruits and vegetables, and traditional medicinal plants. The river is the Lenca people's key to food sovereignty. They fish and drink from the Gualcarque.

In 2006, the community of Rio Blanco came to COPINH (National Council of Popular and Indigenous Organizations of Honduras) asking for our help. The community mentioned witnessing an influx of machinery—for an unknown project—into their town. In 2011, construction on the dam started in full form.

The existence of the river is important both spiritually and territorially to the people who live in the Rio Blanco region. Any act of aggression against the river is, in itself, an act against the community, its free will and autonomy. If the project were to go ahead, control of the rivers would be put into private hands. This would mean the denial of the existence of indigenous communities—an act equivalent to assassinating these communities.

The first step organizing against the development was to strengthen the COPINH organization itself. We then set up a system of alerts, using different methods of communication (i.e., house visits) to keep everyone in the loop of what was happening. The Lenca intensified their spiritual practice of giving thanks to the river, which was very effective in illustrating the importance of the river to the government. Through solidarity efforts, we were able to reduce fear amongst the community and other marginalized groups, including blacks and urban children.

The road blockade has been in place for twenty-one months, intensely for fifteen months. I stayed at the blockade for weeks at a time while other community members stayed for up to a week and rotated. In order to facilitate the roadblock, the Lenca split responsibilities within the community. If someone couldn't make it, someone from their family would take their place. There is a specific committee that helps organize and allocate these responsibilities around the community.

In our fight to protect the Gualcarque River, the most powerful element has been the Lenca people's spirituality, and an impressive tenacity in the struggle that continues to this day. This has been the most effective in getting us heard. Also our solidarity has been very powerful. They haven't been able to stop us despite the threats, the fear, the persecution, the deaths."[246]

2 Berta was recognized with the Goldman Environmental Prize in 2015 for her work with COPINH defending the Gualcarque River. Upon accepting the award, she proclaimed,

"In our worldviews, we are beings that arise from the Earth, from water, and from corn. The Lenca people are ancestral custodians of rivers, in turn protected by the spirits of young girls, who teach us that giving our lives in various ways for the defense of rivers is to give our lives for the good of all humanity and of this planet.

COPINH, walking alongside peoples struggling for their emancipation, validates this commitment to continue protecting water, rivers, our shared resources and all nature, as well as our rights as a people.

Wake up! Wake up, humanity! We are out of time!

Our conscience will take a beating because we are simply contemplating the self-destruction based in capitalist, racist, and patriarchal depravity.

The Gualcarque River has called upon us, as have other gravely threatened rivers throughout the world. We must answer their call. Mother Earth—militarized, fenced-in, poisoned, a place where basic rights are systematically violated—demands that we take action.

Let us build, then, societies that are able to coexist in a just, dignified, and life-giving way. Let us come together and remain hopeful in our defense and care for the blood of the Earth and of its spirits.

I dedicate this prize to all the rebels out there: my mother, the Lenca people, to Río Blanco, to COPINH, and to the martyrs who gave their lives in the struggle to defend our natural resources."[247]

THE MURDER OF BERTA CÁCERES

3 "Just before 9:30 p.m., a black double-cabin Toyota Hilux with polarized windows and no number plates was seen by a neighbor outside her mother's house. Soon after, Berta and Gustavo arrived back at her place . . .

Gustavo retired to the guest bedroom nearest the lounge. Berta's room was at the other end of the narrow hallway. After changing into an olive-green T-shirt and black shorts, she sat on her bed and kept working. At 11:25 she sent a message to Juan Carlos Juárez, a police liaison officer charged with overseeing her protection. 'Wherever you are, I wish you well. Please be careful. Besos [kisses].'

At around 11:35, Gustavo heard a noise. Tap! Tap! Tap! He thought it was Berta cleaning or fetching something from the kitchen, and barely looked up from his laptop. A minute or less later there was a louder, duller sound. Thud! Gustavo assumed Berta had dropped something in the kitchen. Then he heard her call out: 'Who's there?'

'It was then I realized that someone was in the house and something bad was going to happen,' Gustavo recalled. Seconds later, a tall, dark-skinned youth with cropped hair, wearing a black top and white scarf, kicked open the bedroom door and aimed a gun at his head from about two meters away. He heard the fuzzy sound of a walkie-talkie. Seated on the bed, Gustavo was looking straight at the gunman, when he heard Berta's bedroom door being forced open. It sounded as if she was struggling to push someone away. Then he heard three shots. Bang! Bang! Bang! Berta's legs gave way and she fell backwards. She tried to defend herself and scratched at the gunman as he bent over her. But she was weak, and the killer stamped on her bleeding body until she could no longer resist.

Gustavo jumped up off the bed and in a split second lifted his left hand to protect his face as the gunman fired a single shot. Bang! The bullet grazed the back of his left hand and the top of his left ear. Gustavo lay completely still on the floor as blood oozed from the wounds. The gunman was convinced and left, but still Gustavo dared not move. Moments later he heard Berta's voice. 'Gustavo! Gustavo!'

He ran to her and saw his friend sprawled on her back between the bedroom door and the wooden closet, struggling to breathe. Her curly black hair was sticky with the blood from three bullet wounds, spreading across her shorts and T-shirt.

Gustavo squeezed through the small gap between the door and her shivering body. He knelt down and wrapped his arms around her, trying to keep her warm and alive. 'Don't go, Berta! Don't die! Stay with me,' he begged. But Berta Cáceres was bleeding to death.

'Get my phone,' she murmured. 'On the table.' At around a quarter to midnight Berta uttered her last words. 'Call Salvador! Call Salvador!'

Then she was gone.

Berta Cáceres had been murdered. Killed in her bedroom less than a year after winning the foremost prize for environmental defenders."[248]

4 "Another indigenous environmentalist has been murdered in Honduras, less than two weeks after the assassination of renowned activist Berta Cáceres. Nelson García was shot to death Tuesday after returning home from helping indigenous people who had been displaced in a mass eviction by Honduran security forces. García was a member of COPINH, the Civic Council of Popular and Indigenous Organizations of Honduras, co-founded by Berta Cáceres, who won the prestigious Goldman Environmental Prize last year for her decade-long fight against the Agua Zarca Dam, a project planned along a river sacred to the indigenous Lenca people. She was shot to death at her home on March 3. On Thursday, thousands converged in Tegucigalpa for the start of a mobilization to demand justice for Berta Cáceres and an end to what they say is a culture of repression and impunity linked to the Honduran government's support for corporate interests."[249]

At the protest, Berta's daughter, Laura, says, "My mother has not been killed. My mother has been planted, and she is born and reborn. And this, which they tried to put out today, this fire that is the struggle of the people, the only thing they did was ignite it more, because they tried to put out the fire with gasoline!"[250]

GUARDIAN OF THE RIVER

5 "Your midwife mother
Caught my people
As they were born, fleeing from war.
They crossed the Torola and the Sumpul [rivers] toward Honduras
We became sisters again.
You are born, I am born, consciousness.
You are born, I am born, resistance.
Our Lenca veins,
The course/flow of our race
Flow down our arms and legs,
flowing with your blood to the ocean;
we are the river guardians.
To defend them is our destiny.
Giving our lives is part of the journey.
We were born and we were alone
We grew and we were hundreds
We resisted and we were thousands
You will return and we will be millions.
The monsters from outside,
hoarders, dyed the rivers with money.
With bullets, they took our sanctuary
And our guardian.
But Berta left us her words,
And words live on when they are
  repeated.
Edith, a Kakawira girl eleven years old,
bathes in the river in the early morning.
Her mother, grandmother, and sister go
  with her;
it's less dangerous together.
But the river is not their enemy.
Among us all, let's take back our river!
We were born and we were alone
We grew and we were hundreds
We resisted and we were thousands
You will return and we will be
  millions!"[251]

Revelations after the Peace Accords

As with Colonio-Genesis and Nuevo-Exodos, this *librito* witnesses to the CEBs' sociopolitical context and their relentless commitment to "keep walking" on the long journey out from coloniality to the abundant life of God's reign. This book picks up after the war, after the passion of the first generation of CEBs, in the midst of the Pentecost of the repatriated communities, with the failure to implement the Peace Accords over the long months of 1992 through to the present day.

The prologue of this *librito* is a hymn that characterizes the CEBs' arduous journey through the postwar decades and the spirituality that has come to define their movement. Beset by an antagonistic Salvadoran hierarchy, an increasingly globalized neoliberal economy, social violence, mass migration, rising militarization, the climate crisis, and now a global pandemic, *lxs pobres* lament the aftermath of armed conflict: "It's worse than the war."[252] In the face of such expanding and seemingly all-powerful forces of *anti-reino*, they sing, "we just have to keep walking."

The following sections consist of excerpts pulled from Jon Sobrino's annual letters to Ignacio Ellacuria and the seven other martyrs at the UCA, Sobrino's housemates and coworkers, who were killed on November 16, 1989. The excerpts correspond to different eras of Salvadoran postwar history, as follows:

- Section 2 (1992): Sobrino writes as the promises of the Peace Accords fall short. Repatriated communities are rebuilding in remote rural areas, and the right-wing ARENA government is on the cusp of borrowing millions of dollars from the World Bank and the International Monetary Fund for reconstruction. These funds come with strings attached, in the form of neoliberal structural adjustment programs. On July 23, 1992, the government imposes a 10% sales tax on consumer goods for the first time in the country's history, which disproportionately affected *lxs pobres* (taxes that mostly affect the wealthy, like property taxes, have yet to be levied in El Salvador).[253] The CEBs launch a weekly radio program, *La Verdad al Aire*, which runs Sunday evenings on the UCA's radio station through the present day. The UN Truth Commission will begin working in a few months.

- Section 3 (1998): Sobrino writes as Hurricane Mitch devastates Central America. 240 die and 84,000 are left without a home.[254] Conservative Archbishop Fernando Saenz LaCalle, a member of Opus Dei, is in the third year of his tenure. The third ARENA president in a row will win elections in a few months, and grassroots social movements remain in postwar paralysis.
- Section 4 (2003): Sobrino writes as the ARENA government implements the first round of *"mano dura"* [iron fist] policies against increasing gang activity in the country. So begins the progressive escalation between the extortion, youth violence, and eventual drug trafficking of the gangs answered by horrific levels of militarization, incarceration, and elimination of due process by the State. The CEBs begin to write their own stories and histories. In 2005, they have their first national congress.[255]
- Section 5 (2011): Sobrino writes under the first ever FMLN government which, in order to cover a grossly unbalanced budget inherited from their ARENA predecessors, borrows even more money from international lenders. The price of basic necessities rises. Under free trade laws signed in 2006, foreign mining companies sue the FMLN government for not granting them drilling rights, and Monsanto attempts to sue the FMLN government for buying seeds produced by national agricultural cooperatives instead of their own. Grassroots bills are submitted to the Legislative Assembly, petitioning for the protection of clean water, the protection of Indigenous identity, food security laws, pension laws. For the first time ever, students at public schools through grade nine are guaranteed a uniform and a glass of milk during the school day.

This *librito* closes with two short snippets from two members of contemporary CEBs, Tomasito (age eighty-seven) and Adonay (age fourteen). Tomasito speaks to God being in everything, from the crucifixion of Jesús to the joy of one's neighbor while Adonay affirms that the glory of God is the human being fully alive on our planet, in God's own belly. These mystical visions, together with Sobrino's epistolary appeals to his friend Ellacu and the omnipresent songs of the CEBs, are gathered in this final *librito* as an attempt to describe the CEBs' ongoing challenges beyond the war, beyond their own emergence and Pentecost, and to highlight their enduring yearning for the reign of God.

PROLOGUE

1 "Friends, we are hurt to the bone, and our entrails are in a knot because of so much injustice and cowardice.
Hypocrisy begins to invade us.
So many accumulated quarrels, so much hidden treason.
Even our arms are crossed, and disenchantment quiets us.
But we have to keep walking, that's all.
We just have to keep walking.
Many are not here, my brother, and my heart feels the emptiness.
Tears run down our faces, and they are here with us.
The voice silenced by pain that hits us hard, it crushes us.
The man who is caged resists, the people, riddled with wounds, resist.
And we have to keep walking, that's all.
We just have to keep walking.
Let's not let our views be blinded, becuase our history is not over.
[Those who are absent] are our cry, our joy,
open seeds, of new life.
God continues to create the new man, out of our clay he is born.
Jesús walks at our side, do not be afraid, raise your fist, too.
We have to keep walking, that's all.
We just have to keep walking.
His Spirit keeps pushing this crucified people.
It will be possible for us to be a free people,
many witnesses tell us today.
Angelelli, Óscar Romero, Carlos Mujica, a thousand companions, Their blood sings on our strings,
This is the time of the new man.
We have to keep walking, that's all.
We just have to keep walking."[256]

LETTERS TO ELLACU

2 "Dear Ellacu,
Today is October 31—here among us—and it is the day on which the Peace Accords should have reached their fulfillment. That's why we chose to remember you this Saturday, because although all of the martyrs fought and gave their lives for peace, perhaps you (this gift has been given to you by God) may symbolize them. But this has not come to be, the accords have not been fulfilled, and since you know this country very well, you will not be surprised. Once more, things have gotten complicated, and the forces of evil—the extreme right—have tried to destabilize the process . . .

But that's not all that's happening in this country, Ellacu. Even with all the problems, we have changed a little, but I have begun by telling you how things are because liberation theology always starts with the reality, and also because at these times, we need your example at a critical point: to keep walking and to keep looking for solutions. I will explain this first tongue-in-cheek and then more seriously.

You will remember in our community how Montes always used to repeat that you had embarked us many times on unsuccessful journeys: in '72 and certainly in '76 you wanted to get the UCA on board with Molina's agrarian reform, and later you got us involved in the coup in '79, then the political-military [*junta*] solution, then in more negotiating . . . and on and on. The consequences of these processes were always the same: the failure of the attempts at a solution and bombs for the UCA. Nevertheless, you did not seem to get discouraged, and you insisted that there were small steps forward, and with exceptional creativity, you found the course for working in each new situation. The extreme right did not like the paths you opened, and our brothers on the left sometimes criticized you. And Montes, every time there was a new idea, said sharply, 'Here he goes, embarking us all on some new thing again.'

And, well, I have thought about these messes of yours, and I relate them to a passage from the prophet Micah, whom we have often cited in this chapel: 'It has been declared to you, O mortal, what is good; and what does the Lord require of you but to practice justice, to love tenderly, and to walk humbly with your God?' The bit about tenderness, Ellacu, didn't seem to be your thing—because of your personality, more than anything—but you did love the crucified people, and you did work for justice in order to take them down from the cross.

However, I want to focus on this about 'walking humbly with God.'

What Montes called 'messes' were truly nothing more than this humble way of walking, because it is not easy to find the definitive path, and the objectivity of history, not only the form of our subjectivity, is what makes the walking humble. And I believe that is the inheritance you left us: that we must continue walking, as persons, as the UCA, as church, as a people, and that we always must be ready—'humbly'—to remake the path, without sterile laments, without anchoring ourselves in any form of dogmatism. What you taught us is that the only thing we cannot do is to stop walking or to stop searching.

And to close, I believe, Ellacu, that this walking was a walking with God. You were not very given, in your public presentations, to mellifluous religious language, and perhaps it only occurred to very few to think of God when they saw you arguing on television with politicians or intellectuals, but I saw you putting the text of Micah to work. This constant speaking and writing about solutions for the country, this undoing of paths taken when they no longer work and taking others, this was a walking through this world to transform it into the reign of God, and this was a humble walking of someone who doesn't have a solution.

So that's what I think, that you walked with God until that November 16th—with Julia Elba and Celina, and with your brothers—when you arrived to God. This walking without discouragement, without paralysis, with hope and humility, is what we ask of you for us, Ellacu. And hopefully next year, we can tell you that the Peace Accords have been fulfilled and that there is Peace in El Salvador."[257]

3 "Dear Ellacu,
I write to you, one more year, about what inspires and afflicts us. I feel like writing to you all is like writing to our God. Although many times, there is no answer, even the silence is a powerful invitation to continue trying to do good in history. Today, I write to you about two things, of two battles that we are fighting today: the battle of compassion and the battle of truth.

Our afflictions are great, Ellacu. The skies have opened in Central America and here on earth we have been unable to stop the rains; sometimes we don't even try. We wait for the rainbow which will again show us the benign face of God, and we hope for an even greater miracle: that the great compassion that many have shown in these days become 'sustainable compassion.'

The scenes have been horrific. People up in trees for days until they, too, are overcome by water. People who are half-buried in mud—they are alive—but the ones who haven't been rescued. . . . The numbers are staggering. The dead and the disappeared are counted by the tens of thousands, the damned by millions. The headlines are terrifying, but they are closer to truth than lies: '75% of Honduras has disappeared.' I could go on.

All this brings indignation and silence. Indignation because something could have been done to to palliate the magnitude of the disaster. Here in El Salvador, the government knew by the 28th that the storm was drawing near, and the experts say that if they had opened the levies of the dams the water wouldn't have destroyed bridges. . . . And the worst is what it always is: that it's been worse for *los pobres* than for the rich. Before the heavens are opened or the earth trembles, natural catastrophes have already occurred with the poverty of millions of people, 'predestined'—like the damned of the old theology—to historical condemnation. And having said that about human beings, I'd like to say this about God: 'Where are you in these moments?' Like Jesús on the cross, we let slip: 'My God, my God, why have you abandoned us?'

. . . despite the inequality of these forces, nevertheless, we continue betting on compassion and truth, with hope and hard work. This is what you left us. Are we naive? Are we obsessed? Are we just foolish Salvadorans? '*A saber*,' [Who knows?] as we say here. But what we do know is that we will build the country with compassion and truth, and without them, the country will keep belonging to some more than others, and to some over and against others.

I tell you because you are the ones who best understand. At the end of it all, you lived for compassion and truth until the very end. That is why you were martyrs and they killed you. That is why you are still alive. And that is why we do not forget you. Help us."[258]

4 "Dear Ellacu,
In 1980 you gave a class on ecclesiology. With your characteristic rigor, you spoke of the Church of *los pobres*, of its identity and mission, and you underscored how persecuted that church was, from within and without. Indeed, a few months later you had to cancel that class after that assassination of a student, who was a priest, and because of threats against others. You yourself had to leave the country because you were at the top of the list of who was to be killed. But anyway, speaking of the church of *los pobres* and its problems, one of those lapidary phrases of yours came out: 'the ultimate weapon of the church of *los pobres* is its holiness.'

I do not know if the benevolent reader of this letter will feel surprised by these words, but that's what you said, and you said it with no airs. By 'holiness' you didn't mean, of course, flight from the world or piety. Nor were you encouraging an individualist 'self-dedication to holiness,' which, as Anouilh wrote, 'is also a temptation'; you didn't even give a definition. By 'holiness,' I think you simply meant that the church of *los pobres* was a church in accord with the Gospels. And that's not evident at all.

. . . The holiness that you talked about that day, Ellacu, I think that it goes beyond virtues, as heroic as they may be. It is something deeper. It is like a reflection of the celestial Father, the 'all-good,' as Matthew says, 'good even with the ungrateful,' completes Luke. It is the keenness and quality of goodness. It is what you desired and saw in the church of *los pobres*. In the midst of persecution and suffering, of limitations and failures, you saw there the reflection of Jesús and of his God. And that, accompanied by liberating praxis, is what you thought was their ultimate weapon as church.

. . . Dear Ellacu, we have much need of holiness and kindness. The UNDP does good things and can measure how we are doing in terms of development and poverty, but it doesn't usually measure how much of the spirit of kindness we possess, if it's increasing or decreasing. And nevertheless we continue to live off of the goodness that has accumulated in history, that is, yours. Amando and Lolo, Juan Ramón and Nacho, Elba and Celina, Segundo Montes and you, Ellacu, and that of many others. You all gave some—a lot—of kindness and holiness to our world and our church. Upon this we build our hope and we continue working for the reign [of God]. For that we thank you and we remember you.[259]

5 "Dear Ellacu,
It is a fiction to write to you, but maybe this is how we tell ourselves things that might be important. In that spirit, I would like to

set the stage for the anniversary of your martyrdom. I'm going to tell you about three things that are going on which, as I see them, have to do with what you were and what you said.

The first is the 'always' of the crucified people. They don't talk about the crucified peoples anymore like you and Monseñor Romero did, arriving at that brilliant formulation independently of each other, I think, and guided by the same Salvadoran and Christian spirit. And even less do they insist that the crucified people is 'always' the sign of the times, as you wrote in exile in Madrid. The reason for this silence is that the utopian thinking of philosopher Ernst Bloch or theologian Teilhard de Chardin is back in vogue. And the world is not getting better, but rather is gravely ill, as you said in your last speech. What has gotten worse is our ability to be honest with what is real [*honradez con lo real*], and the 'always' is not politically correct. But we shouldn't avoid the issue. [The crucified peoples] continue to exist in Haiti, in Somalia, and in our new homicide epidemic, twelve to fifteen per day in the last years, the leading cause of death in our country. But the 'diet' version has developed in our way of thinking, and 'political correctness' has enslaved our language: 'vulnerability,' 'disadvantaged,' 'developing countries.' Nothing sounds bad . . .".²³⁰

DRAWING GOD

6 "'Tomasito, if you were to draw God, what would you draw? If someone gave you a sheet of paper and a pen and said "Draw God for me," what would you draw?'

'Maybe the death of Jesús on the cross. Maybe I would draw a child, too, because Jesús was born just like all the children here who are born small and grow up little by little. That's how we might see God, right, because God is in everything, in nature, in any thing, in water, in the heavens. Yesterday, I was thinking about that a little bit, that we see God on high, in many things, perhaps in the smile of others, in the joy of others.'"²⁶¹

7 "'Adonay, if you had to draw God, what would you draw?'

'If I had to draw God, I would draw a face and then a big round body, but with arms. The round part would be the planet with people inside, and we would be the ones who are destroying the planet and God. I would draw God with glasses, which means that God sees reality and sees our hearts and the whole world. And the round part would also mean the planet that God could destroy just like that, with a few words. And I feel that humanity is eating God's body, just like we are destroying our planet.'

'Do you think you could draw God without humanity or are humanity and God too linked together?'

'Both things are very linked together because God created us, and I think that it's truly important to God that we be able to live in our world.'"²⁶²

NOTES

1. Ninth edition (San Salvador: Equipo Maiz, 2012).
2. Jennifer Scheper Hughes, "The Sacred Art of Counter-Conquest: Material Christianity in Latin America," in *The Oxford Handbook of Latin American Christianity*, eds. Manuel A. Vasquez, Susan Fitzpatrick Behrens, and David Orique (New York: Oxford University Press, 2015), 58.
3. *El tigre y el venado* ("The tiger/mountain lion and the deer") is a 2013 documentary by director Sergio Sibrián and named for a Nahua ceremonial dance. The documentary recovers Indigenous history, language, and customs from the perspective of Don Marcelino Galicia of the town of Tacuba, one of the last living witnesses to pre-1932 Indigenous life: https://www.youtube.com/watch?v=J4V5v5t2aHs&t=4s.
4. The list of fish (from *mojadas* on) is from the testimony of José Tomás Luna in José Gómez Martínez and Laurel Anne Marshall, *Sigue porque la vida sigue: Voces de las comunidades eclesiales de base de El Salvador ayer y hoy* (Winston-Salem: Library Partners Press, 2020), 25.
5. *NA*, § 2.
6. This poetic interpretation of the Maya peoples is drawn from *Historia de El Salvador: de cómo la gente guanaca no sucumbó ante los infames ultrajes de españoles, criollos, gringos y otras plagas*, ninth edition (San Salvador: Equipo Maiz, 2012), 14–18.
7. This section on the Nahua peoples is drawn from *Historia de El Salvador*, 23–28, and from Rafael Lara-Martínez, *Mitos en la lengua materna de los pipiles de Izalco en El Salvador: versión poética* (San Salvador: El Monstruo Editorial, 2012).
8. Area of land ruled by a chief, a *cacique*.
9. Meaning "jewel by the sea," located in the present day Salvadoran municipality of Antiguo Cuscatlán as in Scott Wright, Minor Sinclair, Margaret Lyle, and David Scott (eds.), *El Salvador: A Spring Whose Waters Never Run Dry* (Washington DC: EPICA, 1990), 10.
10. Present-day Apaneca.
11. Present-day Apastepeque.
12. This is how decolonial scholar Aníbal Quijano imagines the first encounter between the Spanish invaders and the Indigenous inhabitants of the land in Anibal Quijano's keynote address at the III Latin American and Caribbean Congress for the Social Sciences, FLASCO Ecuador (August 25, 2015), https://www.youtube.com/watch?v=OxL5KwZGvdY.
13. In papal bull *Inter Caetera* of 1493, Pope Alexander VI declared, "By the authority of Almighty God conferred upon us in blessed Peter and of the vicarship of Jesus Christ, which we hold on earth, do by tenor of these presents, should any of said islands have been found by your envoys and captains, give, grant, and assign to you and your heirs and successors, kings of Castile and Leon, forever, together with all their dominions, cities, camps, places, and villages, and all rights, jurisdictions, and appurtenances, all islands and mainlands found and to be found, discovered and to be discovered towards the west and south, by drawing and establishing a line from the Arctic pole, namely the north, to the Antarctic pole, namely the south, no matter whether the said mainlands and islands are found and to be found in the direction of

India or towards any other quarter, the said line to be distant one hundred leagues towards the west and south from any of the islands commonly known as the Azores and Cape Verde." Accessed at papalencyclicals.net/Alex06/alex06inter.htm.

14. For the invasion of Cuscatlán, we draw on *Historia de El Salvador*, 46–50.

15. Today, La Hachadura is still the legal point of entry on the Western border between El Salvador and Guatemala.

16. Present-day Acajutla.

17. *Historia de El Salvador*, 47.

18. Near present-day Sonsonate.

19. These descriptions of colonial life draw on *Historia de El Salvador*, 56–57.

20. Jorge Lardé y Larín, *El Salvador: descubrimiento, conquista, y colonización*, 2nd ed. (San Salvador: Consejo Nacional para la Cultura y el Arte, 2000), 292.

21. Juan Ginés de Sepúlveda, *Demócrates segundo, o, Tratado sobre las justas causas de la guerra contra los indios*, 2nd ed. (Madrid: Consejo Superior de Investigaciones Científicas, Instituto Francisco de Vitoria, 1984), 65, our translation.

22. Cited in *Historia de El Salvador*, 64.

23. For more on Las Casas, see his writings, *A Short Account of the Destruction of the Indies* (1542), which was essential for Spain's adoption of the New Laws in 1542, and *History of the Indies* (begun in 1527), in which Las Casas repents of his previous advocacy for African American enslavement.

24. Mark A. Burkholder, "New Laws of 1542," in *Encyclopedia of Latin American History and Culture*, vol. 4, ed. Barbara A. Tenenbaum and Georgette M. Dorn (New York: Charles Scribner's and Sons, 1996), 177.

25. *Historia de El Salvador*, 72.

26. José Antonio Fernández, *La huella colonial* (San Salvador: Banco Agrícola Comercial, 1996), 175.

27. Gilberto Aguilar Avilés, "El Surgimiento de la Nación (1808–1823)," in *El Salvador, la República* (San Salvador: Banco Agrícola, 2000), 24–25, cited in *Historia de El Salvador*, 74.

28. "Acta de Independencia," in *Documentos de la Unión Centroamericana* (Organization of American States, July 1956), Article 1, page 4, translation our own. Accessed at http://www.sice.oas.org/sica/Studies/DocUnionCentroamericana.pdf.

29. *Historia de El Salvador*, 81.

30. *Historia de El Salvador*, 81.

31. See "The *Librito* of the Prophet Anastasio Aquino."

32. *Historia de El Salvador*, 89.

33. United Fruit (Chiquita) was one of the big U.S. investors that built railroads in Central America to facilitate the import of bananas. These railroads also helped coffee become a viable product. For more detail, see "El Ferrocarril, sus orígenes y su historia," Website of FENADESAL and the Salvadoran Port Authority (2009), https://web.archive.org/web/20100308022920/http://www.fenadesal.gob.sv/contenido.php?cont=52&id=87.

34. *Milpa* is the ancestral way of growing corn, beans, squash, and other food crops together in a plot.

35. This is still, in large part, the dynamic of subsistence agriculture in El Salvador today.

36. Informal, hyperlocal currency, closer to a token. El Salvador did not have a standard national currency until the end of the nineteenth century, after the establishment of a national bank. The national currency was called the "colón," named for Cristobal Colón (Christopher Columbus) (*Historia de El Salvador*, 110).
37. *Historia de El Salvador*, 108.
38. The material for Chapter 7 is drawn from *Historia de El Salvador*, 112–118.
39. *Historia de El Salvador*, 120–124.
40. *Historia de El Salvador*, 122.
41. This time period includes the events of "The *Librito* of the Prophet Prudencia Ayala."
42. Sorcerer, warlock, magician, witch-man. This was in reference to Hernández Martínez's reported interest in the occult. He was reported as saying things like, "It's good for children to be barefoot. That's how they receive the vibrations of the earth. Plants and animals don't use shoes," and "It is a bigger crime to kill an ant than a man because men are reincarnated, while ants die definitively" (*Historia de El Salvador*, 139).
43. The material for Chapter 9 is drawn from *Historia de El Salvador*, 126–130. For more on this period, see "The *Librito* of the Prophet Farabundo Martí."
44. *Historia de El Salvador*, 131.
45. A skirt worn every day by Indigenous women.
46. Lauri García Dueñas, "El Salvador: Ancianos de Izalco recuerdan masacre de miles de indígenas 1932," *Indymedia Argentina*, January 23, 2005, https://archivo.argentina.indymedia.org/news/2005/01/258611.php, translation our own.
47. *Historia de El Salvador*, 132.
48. Archbishop José Alfonso Belloso y Sánchez, Pastoral Letter (October 31, 1927), cited in *Historia de El Salvador*, 140.
49. *Historia de El Salvador*, 140.
50. Literally, "ears."
51. Information in this paragraph is pulled from *Historia de El Salvador*, 137.
52. Even rather long accounts, like Rodolfo Cardenal's 400-plus page account of the life of Rutilio Grande, ascribe to Catholic laypeople a "magical consciousness," a "culture of silence." While these descriptions are helpful in showing how much of a departure the changes of the 1960s were, we believe it to be an unfair characterization of pre-Vatican II *campesinos* if taken as a universal or totalizing description. For more of this kind of description, see Cardenal, *Historia de una esperanza: vida de Rutilio Grande* (San Salvador: UCA Editores, 1985), 235–241.
53. Nickname for El Salvador, the "little thumb" or "Tom Thumb" of the Americas.
54. Slang term for a Salvadoran, originating from the Potón-Lenca word for "brotherhood."
55. The original Spanish poem can be found at https://republicalibertad.com/2013/06/13/el-poema-de-amor-de-roque-dalton/. The musical version—composed by Saúl López, first recorded by Yolocamba Ita, and sung by heart in the CEBs—is performed by Guillermo Cuellar here: https://youtu.be/vopoy_JJiPk.
56. "The Pact of the Catacombs," cited in Maria Clara Lucchetti Bingemer, *Latin American Theology: Roots and Branches* (Maryknoll: Orbis, 2016), 51–53. The majority of signatories were Latin American bishops, including Bishop Manuel

Larraín of Chile, Bishop Marcos McGrath of Panama, and Bishop Leonidas Proaño of Ecuador. The only North American bishop to sign was Bishop Gerard-Marie Coderre of Quebec. See also Cindy Wooden, "Back to the Catacombs: New Emphasis Placed on Bishops' Simplicity Pact," *Catholic News Service* (November 13, 2015).

57. The IPLA was founded by two of the Latin American bishops who had signed the Pact of the Catacombs, Manuel Larraín and Leonidas Proaño, as a center for pastoral training for ministers in Latin America, sponsored by the CELAM.

58. Cardenal, *Historia de una esperanza,* 192–193.

59. Cardenal, *Historial de una esperanza,* 194.

60. It is unclear, due to the sexist language of the text in both Spanish and English, if lay women are included in this list.

61. Latin American Bishops' Council (CELAM), "15. Joint Pastoral Planning," *The Church in the Present-Day Transformation of Latin America in the Light of the Council* (Medellín Conclusions), ed. Louis Michael Colonnese (Bogotá: CELAM, 1970), 226–227.

62. Anna L. Peterson, *Martyrdom and the Politics of Religion: Progressive Catholicism in El Salvador's Civil War* (Albany: State University of New York Press, 1997), 55–56.

63. Peterson, 70, footnote 26.

64. Peter M. Sánchez, *Priest Under Fire: Padre David Rodríguez, the Catholic Church, and El Salvador's Revolutionary Movement* (Gainesville: University Press of Florida, 2015), 72–73.

65. Sánchez, 82.

66. Peterson, *Martyrdom,* 57–58.

67. Cardenal, *Historia de una esperanza,* 143.

68. Cardenal, *Historia de una esperanza,* 145.

69. Cardenal, *Historia de una esperanza,* 147.

70. Cardenal, *Historia de una esperanza,* 149–153. See "Letter from the Salvadoran Hierarchy I" for more on this dynamic.

71. Cardenal, *Historia de una esperanza,* 148.

72. Peterson, *Martyrdom,* 58.

73. This was an *explicitly* ecumenical effort. Non-Catholic participants include the Emmanuel Baptist Church, the Salvadoran Lutheran Church, and the Anglican Church of El Salvador.

74. From Luis Coto, "Una Historia de las Comunidades Eclesiales de Base en El Salvador," Keynote address given during the fiftieth anniversary celebration of the Salvadoran Base Ecclesial Communities in San Salvador, February 8, 2019, 12. The essential subtext here is that this coordination, support, and pastoral accompaniment was *not* being provided by the pastors of the Roman Catholic church.

75. Coto, 13.

76. *Historia de El Salvador,* 92–98.

77. Pedro Geoffroy Rivas, "Anastasio Aquino," in "Poemas a Anastasio Aquino," *Diario CoLatino* (October, 8 2016), https://www.diariocolatino.com/poemas-a-anastasio-aquino/.

78. The goddess of rain.

79. The Nahua *cacique* said to have fought against the invasion of Pedro de Alvarado.
80. Roque Dalton, "Anastasio Aquino, tu lucha . . . ," *La ventana en el rostro* (Mexico City: Ocean Sur, 2015), page number unavailable.
81. Museo de la Palabra y la Imagen (MUPI), "Prudencia Ayala (animación)," March 9, 2017, https://www.youtube.com/watch?v=7Zqap0omZVA.
82. *Historia de El Salvador*, 123.
83. MUPI, "Prudencia Ayala (animación)."
84. MUPI, "Humor Machista," *Prudencia Ayala: Presidenta*, museum exhibit, San Salvador, 2016, https://issuu.com/mupi/docs/exposicio__n_sobre_prudencia_ayala.
85. Adrián Goizueta y el Experimental, "Farabundo Martí," *Antología 80–83*, compact disc, 2016. This song has been recorded on a number of Goizueta's albums over the years, but he wrote and recorded the original version for the 1982 film, *El Salvador, el pueblo vencerá*, directed by Diego de la Texera.
86. Here, "hot damn!"
87. From "An Interview with Ana María Leddy, Author of the Hymn of the *Frente*," official website of the FMLN, February 23, 2010, https://fmln.org.sv/index.php/nuestro-partido/himno-del-fmln.
88. Here, the recurring theme from Martí's life of being exiled from El Salvador and reappearing with a new name among popular organizations is applied to his death and the resurgence of his name among popular movements in the 1970s.
89. Lyrics of the "Hymn of the *Frente*," official website of the FMLN, https://fmln.org.sv/index.php/nuestro-partido/himno-del-fmln.
90. Michael Lee, *Revolutionary Saint: The Theological Legacy of Óscar Romero* (Maryknoll: Orbis, 2018), 30.
91. Monseñor Luis Chávez y González, the archbishop at the time, largely sympathetic to the emerging church of *lxs pobres*.
92. Monseñor Arturo Rivera y Damas, then the auxiliary bishop of San Salvador. The communities hoped that he would be appointed archbishop when Monseñor Chávez stepped down and were disappointed when Romero was appointed in February 1977.
93. N.a., *La fe de un pueblo, historia de una comunidad cristiana en el salvador (1970–1980)* (San Salvador: UCA Editores, 1983), 80–82.
94. St. Óscar Romero, "The God of our Faith," *Homily* (May 21, 1978), http://www.romerotrust.org.uk/homilies-and-writings/homilies/god-our-faith.
95. These are the final words of Romero's homily during Sunday Mass in the Metropolitan Cathedral the day before he was killed. Many believe that this "order" violated the unspoken stalemate between the ecclesial hierarchy and the military. St. Óscar Romero, "The Church in the Service of Personal, Community, and Transcendent Liberation," *Homily* (March 23, 1980), http://www.romerotrust.org.uk/homilies-and-writings/homilies/church-service-personal-community-and-transcendent-liberation.
96. These are the final words of the homily Romero was preaching as he was shot, in St. Óscar Romero, "The Final Homily of Archbishop Romero," *Homily*

(March 24, 1980), http://www.romerotrust.org.uk/homilies-and-writings/homilies/final-homily-archbishop-romero. Audio of this moment can be heard at the same web address.

97. José Roberto Gómez Menjívar y Ovidio Escobar, "Corrido a Monseñor Romero," lyrics in *El Pueblo Canta: Libro de Cantos* (San Salvador: Talleres de Imprenta Criterio, 1998), #161.

98. It should be noted that this song was commonly sung long before Romero's canonization process was "unblocked" by Pope Francis in 2013. The Salvadoran people prophetically announced his canonization before Rome was ready to do so.

99. Anonymous, "Cumbia de Monseñor Romero," accessed October 12, 2020 at https://www.youtube.com/watch?v=CCosBo7CjV0.

100. Jorge Palencia, "Monseñor Romero," lyrics in *El Pueblo Canta*, #490. Jorge Palencia's own recording of this song can be found at https://youtu.be/WUTMNl_G_-c (accessed December 12, 2021).

101. Grupo Horizontes, "Profeta Salvadoreño," https://www.youtube.com/watch?v=QPtobAQzz9k, accessed October 12, 2020.

102. Final victory. In the context of the Salvadoran Civil War, this was the hope of victory for the popular movements and revolutionary forces in their collective struggle against the repressive political and economic status quo and for a better society.

103. Álvar Castillo, "Símbolo de rebeldía," lyrics in *El Pueblo Canta*, #491.

104. These words are memorialized at the entrance to the "Room of the Martyrs" at the UCA today, a small, living museum dedicated to the Christian martyrs, named and anonymous, of the Salvadoran Civil War.

105. *La fe de un pueblo: historia de una comunidad cristiana en El Salvador (1970–1980)* (San Salvador: UCA Editores, 1983), 17.

106. *La fe de un pueblo*, 23–24.

107. *La fe de un pueblo*, 41–42.

108. The Savior.

109. *La fe de un pueblo*, 42–45.

110. Teresa and Tilita, members of the El Paraíso community in *La semilla que cayó en tierra fértil: testimonio de miembros de las comunidades cristianas* (San Salvador: Consejo de Mujeres Misioneras por la Paz, 1996), 93–95.

111. A Catholic school run by the Sisters of Guadalupe.

112. María de Jesús and Fredy, members of the Tutunichapa community in *La semilla que cayó en tierra fértil*, 70–71.

113. Guillermo DeNaux, part of the Belgian missionary team.

114. Bersabé, Adelita, Fabio, and Tina from the San Antonio Abad community, in *La semilla que cayó en tierra fértil*, 133–134.

115. St. Anthony the Great, the patron saint of the parish.

116. Mamá Tele, Tina, Bersabé, and Fabio, of the San Antonio Abad community, in *La semilla que cayó en tierra fértil*, 139–141.

117. The word "despertar" can mean "awakening," "dawn," or even "beginning," so the many references to light, the people awakening, and seeing anew in this song all invoke the name of Octavio's place of martyrdom.

118. Guillermo Cuéllar, "Canción a Octavio Ortiz," lyrics as written and titled "Basta Ya" in *La semilla que cayó en tierra fértil*, 157.
119. "Nuevo-Exodus," §3.
120. "Nuevo-Exodus," §6.
121. "Nuevo-Exodus," §5.
122. José Inocencio Alas, *Land, Liberation and Death Squads: A Priest's Story, Suchitoto, El Salvador, 1968–1977*, trans. Robin Fazio and Emily Wade Will (Eugene, OR: RESOURCE, 2016), 37.
123. Alas, 47.
124. Alas, 40.
125. Alas, 44–46.
126. Luis Chávez y González, archbishop of San Salvador from 1938 to 1977.
127. Alas, 48.
128. Alas, 48–49.
129. Alas, 50.
130. Rodolfo Cardenal, *Historia de una esperanza: vida de Rutilio Grande* (San Salvador: UCA Editores, 1985), 251–252.
131. Cardenal, 335.
132. Guillermo Cuéllar, "Vamos Todos al Banquete," entrance hymn of the "Salvadoran Popular Mass." This song, especially the final verse, is based on the work of Padre Tilo in Aguilares and the words he preached there. The lyrics here are taken from *El Pueblo Canta*, # 821.
133. The church of *lxs pobres* has consistently re-membered Rutilio Grande as a martyr since his death. He was officially recognized as a martyr by the Catholic church in February 2020.
134. Cuéllar, "Vamos Todos al Banquete," 573.
135. "Nuevo-Exodus," §5.
136. Ocote is a kind of high-resin pine, used for easy fire starting in rural kitchens.
137. Comunidades Eclesiales de Base de El Salvador (CEBES), "Luz de Ocote" (Managua, Nicaragua: no date or publisher), 2. Thank you to the FUNDAHMER for sharing this historic pamphlet with us.
138. "Luz de Ocote," 7–10.
139. Jeffrey L. Gould, "Ignacio Ellacuría and the Salvadorean Revolution," *Journal of Latin American Studies* 47 (2015): 294–295.
140. A battalion of the FMLN. The guerrilla controlled the area of Morazán north of the Torola River and was headquartered in Perquín.
141. Salvadoran government forces.
142. "Luz de Ocote," 10–11.
143. "Luz de Ocote," 12–13.
144. A drink made from seasonal fruit blended with water, strained, and mixed with sugar.
145. Testimony of Rogelio Ponselle, Belgian missionary priest who still serves the communities north of the Torola River. In María López Vigil, *Muerte y vida en Morazán: testimonio de un sacerdote* (San Salvador: UCA Editores, 1987), 57–60.
146. Vigil, *Muerte y vida*, 63–64.
147. Vigil, *Muerte y vida*, 64–65.

148. The "Pequeña Comunidad" was a small group of women who made a commitment to live a life dedicated to the Gospel and the church of *lxs pobres*. See Pat Marrin, "Pequeña Comunidad: The Road to New Hope in El Salvador," *National Catholic Reporter* (June 15, 2010), https://www.ncronline.org/news/peque-comunidad-road-new-hope-el-salvador.

149. CEBES was an association of Salvadoran CEBs, made up of the sisters of the Pequeña Comunidad, priests who served the communities, and many lay pastoral agents and collaborators. A hallmark of this second wave of CEBs that arose during the refugee and repatriation period (roughly from the mid-1980s to 2000) is the existence of some informal institutions that served to coordinate CEBs' work as support from Catholic hierarchy began to wane.

150. Comunidades Eclesiales de Base de El Salvador, *Una Experiencia de Iglesia: Mística y Metodología* (San Salvador, El Salvador: CEBES, n.d.), 63–64. From clues in the text, we can date this workbook to around 1990. We are grateful to the FUNDAHMER for access to this historic document.

151. A UN-monitored refugee settlement right over the border in Honduras that received Salvadorans from the eastern part of the country, especially Morazán. Many who sought refuge there arrived on foot, fleeing the war.

152. UN Refugee Agency.

153. Pablo Galdámez, *Esperanza de un pueblo* (San Salvador: Equipo Maíz, 2012), 24–25.

154. Words of Padre Segundo Montes to the refugees in Colomoncagua in *El Salvador: Portraits in a Revolution*, produced by Laura Jackson and Betsy Morgan and directed by Laura Jackson (New York: Filmakers Library, 1994), DVD, retrieved from https://video.alexanderstreet.com/watch/el-salvador-portraits-in-a-revolution.

155. See "The Gospel according to Zacamil," §8–9.

156. Another neighborhood in San Salvador.

157. Words of Anita Ortiz Luna in Gómez and Marshall, *Sigue porque la vida sigue*, 120–122.

158. CEBES, "Nuestro Centro Pastoral 'Hermano Mercedes Ruiz'" (San Salvador, undated), 7. This poem is by Mercedes Ruiz, a catechist in Cacaopera and other communities after the war, who died of cancer in 1995. The CEBES office in San Salvador renamed itself the FUNDAHMER when it became a registered nonprofit in 2000.

159. The "Bajo Lempa region" refers to the communities that surround the Lempa River delta that empties into the Pacific Ocean on El Salvador's southern coast, in the department of Usulután.

160. *Esperanza de un pueblo*, 33–34.

161. *Esperanza de un pueblo*, 34–35.

162. *Esperanza de un pueblo*, 69–71.

163. This is an explicit reference to the *tria munera*, the teaching, sanctifying, and governing offices of both the ordained priesthood and the priesthood of all the faithful. At baptism, all Christians are anointed prophet, priest, and king.

164. *Esperanza de un pueblo*, 227–229.

165. A curved machete used for weeding fields.

Notes 179

166. A slightly concave clay or metal plate used to toast tortillas over a fire.

167. Miguel Cavada Díaz, "La Biblia," inter-lectionary hymn of the Mesoamerican Mass. Included in the collection *Canciones de lucha y esperanza: Cancionero histórico de las comunidades eclesiales de base de El Salvador*, disc II, performed by Guillermo Cuéllar, CM Recording Arts [2012], audio CD. Miguel Cavada was a priest dedicated to the CEBs, especially in their resurgence among repatriated communities and land cooperatives in La Libertad after the war. He died of cancer in 2011.

168. Marshall, *Un gesto vale más*, Appendix 2, ii–iii.

169. The "Creator and Former" [of heaven and earth] is a widely accepted way that the Indigenous people who lived in El Salvador before in colonial invasion referred to their Creator. Some people in the CEBs use this as another name for the first person of the Holy Trinity.

170. Gómez and Marshall, "Gustavo Ramos," in *Sigue porque la vida sigue*, 81–82.

171. Marshall, *Un gesto vale más*, Appendix 3, xi–xii.

172. Marshall, *Un gesto vale más*, Appendix 2, iii–iv.

173. See Letter from the Community "Nuevo Amanecer."

174. Marshall, *Un gesto vale más*, Appendix 2, vi–vii.

175. In "The Gospel according to the Zacamil," §4, the community laments that people living in marginal slums in San Salvador with no plumbing in the late 1960s paid high prices for water to be delivered to their neighborhoods in jugs. They paid more than people with plumbing!

176. We understand this to mean environmental advocacy. In the town where this CEB lives, many private businesses and housing developments threaten to eliminate much of the forest, rivers, and wildlife in the area. They are particularly active in defending their local river, which is vulnerable to the construction of hydroelectric dams, which disrupt the river's ecosystem, reduce local water availability, and displace local communities.

177. We are unsure whether a canonical excommunication took place here, or whether the priest's threat of excommunication effectively, for all intents and purposes, excommunicated them from the parish community.

178. Fransico Bosch, *Bendita Mezcla: Hermanxs escuchadorxs, comunidades palabreras* (Montevideo: Fundación Amerindia, 2020), 42–43.

179. See especially "Letter from the Salvadoran Hierarchy III."

180. "Nuevo-Exodus," §4 (see Medellín conclusions, Document #15 on "Joint Pastoral Planning," §10).

181. La Despensa de Don Juan is a discount grocery store owned by Walmart.

182. *Zonas francas* are economic zones where import taxes are waived so that products can be processed and reexported at no cost to the manufacturer. Many employees of *zonas francas* also report that labor laws and environmental regulations are ignored or violated by the companies that operate in these areas. In El Salvador, many businesses that operate in the *zonas francas* are textile sweatshops (*maquiladoras*). They were established during the postwar neoliberal reforms of the 1990s and ratified by free trade agreements like CAFTA (2006).

183. Nuevo Amanecer, "Historia de la comunidad Nuevo Amanecer," email (2015). We are grateful to the community for sharing this document with us.

184. This missionary order was given responsibility for half of the parroquial territory when the parish was split in 2011.

185. Nuevo Amanecer, "Historia."

186. *Alfombras* are images made by families or community groups out of dyed sawdust or salt on the road or path where Holy Week processions tread. They are brightly colored, creative expressions of the religious sensibility of the people, usually depicting both folkloric and explicitly Christian imagery.

187. Gómez and Marshall, eds., *Sigue porque la vida sigue*, 200–201.

188. Teresa Inmaculada Moreno de Melendez, "La Iglesia de los pobres—Reino de Dios," presentation given at the Wake Forest University research symposium, "Does Church of the Poor Discourse Matter to the Marginalized?" Marietta, South Carolina, October 2019. This selection was cited directly from the transcript of Tere's presentation.

189. Padre Beltrán's opinión can be found in "Nuevo-Exodus," §6; Cardenal, *Historia de una esperanza*, 148.

190. The succession described in this section is based on "Reseña Histórica," on the official website of the Archdiocese of San Salvador, http://www.arzobispadosansalvador.org/sobre-nosotros/resena-historica/, accessed August 28, 2020.

191. United Nations' Commission on the Truth, "De la locura a la esperanza: la guerra de 12 años en El Salvador" (San José: DEI, 1993), 188.

192. Ronaldo Muñoz, "La Recepción de la Lumen Gentium en América Latina: a los cuarenta años de su promulgación," *Revista Latinoamericana de Teología* 21, no. 62 (2004): 268. This assessment coincides with the assertions of Edgard Beltrán recorded in Exodus §6 of the present work.

193. See "Nuevo-Exodus," §6 for the text of the telegram sent to the bishops on day two of the meetings, inviting them once again to full participation.

194. See Cardenal, *Historia de una esperanza*, 154–155.

195. Cardenal, 152.

196. Cardenal, 154.

197. Cardenal, 159.

198. Words of Pope Francis to a delegation of Salvadoran faithful at the Vatican, in "El papa acusa al episcopado salvadoreño de 'difamar y calumniar' a monseñor Romero," *Prensa Libre* (Guatemala, October 30, 2015), https://www.prensalibre.com/internacional/el-papa-acusa-al-episcopado-de-el-salvador-de-difamar-y-calumniar-a-monseor-romero/.

199. As told by Jose Simán/Rogelio Pedraz in María López Vigil, *Óscar Romero: Memories in Mosaic*, trans. Kathy Ogle (Washington, DC: EPICA, 2000), 236–237.

200. As told by Julian Filochowski in López Vigil, *Óscar Romero: Memories in Mosaic*, 241–242.

201. "Pope Stresses Church Unity & Completion of the Central American Peace Process during Latin American Trip," *NotiSur—Latin American Political Affairs* 6, no. 7 (February 16, 1996).

202. For more on Romero's halting journey toward recognition by the Roman Catholic hierarchy, see Michael Lee, *Revolutionary Saint: The Theological Legacy of Oscar Romero* (Maryknoll: Orbis, 2018), especially 180–188.

203. Lee, 185.

204. For the experiences of particular communities, see the Letters from "Pueblo de Dios en Camino," from the community in Nahuizalco, and from "Nuevo Amanecer." For personal reflections on these and other experiences, see the *libritos* of contemporary prophets.

205. Padre Pedro Declercq has not come up by name often in these sacred stories, but he is present in many of them. He lived with the CEBs as a pastoral agent from their beginning in the Zacamil in 1969 to his death in the Bajo Lempa in 2015 and has written extensively about their *caminar* under a pen name, even in many works cited in the present volume.

206. *Asociaciones de Desarrollo Comunal.* Communal Development Associations are hyperlocal community councils that coordinate with the local mayor's office.

207. National Network of CEBs in El Salvador, "Pastoral Letter by the CEBs in El Salvador," July 2016.

208. Sunday evenings at 5 p.m. local time on YSUCA, 91.7 FM, available to stream at http://ysuca.org.sv/.

209. Press release from the Diocese of Santiago de María, July 2016, emphasis original. Citation of CELAM Santo Domingo document in the original.

210. Luis Van de Velde, "¿Estará presente Monseñor Romero el 23 de mayo?" email newsletter (San Salvador, May 17, 2015). These reflections are drawn from the weekly email newsletter of Luis Van de Velde, one of the Belgian priests active in the early days of the first CEBs in the Zacamil neighborhood. Until recently, he continued to live in El Salvador and serve as a minister to the church of *lxs pobres*.

211. Joint public letter written by the National Network of Ecclesial Base Communities of El Salvador, FUNDAHMER, and Voices on the Border, May 23, 2015.

212. Marshall, *Un gesto vale más*, Appendix 2, vi.

213. A *pastoral de conjunto* is the kind of collaborative pastoral work envisioned by Medellín and the Salvadoran Pastoral Week of 1970.

214. National Network of CEBs of El Salvador, "Meeting #82," meeting minutes from September 30, 2017.

215. The archbishop's first pastoral letter, which is about a Christian response to the violent realities of the country. Its title is taken from Psalm 55:9, and it was released in 2016 on the anniversary of Romero's assassination.

216. The archbishop's second pastoral letter, which is about martyrdom, specifically naming many popularly canonized martyrs of the Salvadoran church of *lxs pobres*. The title is taken from John 15:27, and it was released in 2017 on the fortieth anniversary of the assassination of Padre Rutilio Grande.

217. Tutela Legal was the archbishop's office for human rights, where many denouncements of wartime and postwar human rights violations were recorded in hope of justice. In 2013, it was closed by the archbishop with no explanation. See Tracy Wilkinson, "Catholic Church in El Salvador Shuts Down Rights and Legal

Office," *Los Angeles Times* (October 2, 2020), https://www.latimes.com/world/la-xpm-2013-oct-02-la-fg-salvador-rights-20131003-story.html.

218. Letter to Monseñor José Luis Escobar Alas from the National Network of Ecclesial Base Communities of El Salvador, September 21, 2017.

219. National Network of CEBs of El Salvador, "Meeting #83," meeting minutes from October 21, 2017. Individual names of participants have been omitted.

220. Fr. José María Tojeira, a prominent and outspoken Jesuit, former rector of the UCA.

221. The meeting summary indicates that this is a reference to Romero's letter to U.S. president Jimmy Carter a month before his assassination, asking Carter to stop sending military aid and weapons to the Salvadoran government.

222. National Network of CEBs, summary of meetings in late July 2018 between the CEBs, a representative of the archdiocese, and other organizations to coordinate the joint planning of the celebration of Romero's canonization. August 11, 2018.

223. Monseñor José Luis Escobar Alas, "Invito a todos que, siguiendo las huellas de nuestro Santo, luchemos por la justicia," homily two weeks following St. Óscar Romero's canonization celebration, delivered on October 28, 2018.

224. See "The Gospel according to Morazán," §3.

225. "Reina Greisi Leiva," in Gómez y Marshall, *Sigue porque la vida sigue*, 70.

226. "Reina Greisi Leiva," 71–72.

227. "Miguel Zepeda Santos" in Gómez and Marshall, *Sigue porque la vida sigue*, 147–149.

228. "Miguel Zepeda Santos," 156–158.

229. "Miguel Zepeda Santos," 166–167.

230. See "Acts of the Repatriated," §2–3.

231. See "Colonio-Genesis," §6 and §11.

232. "Heavily-Armed Police and Soldiers Enter El Salvador Parliament," *British Broadcasting Service*, February 10, 2020, https://www.bbc.com/news/world-latin-america-51439020.

233. Heather Gies, "The Kids Aren't Alright—When Being Young Is a Crime in El Salvador," *The World* (November 6, 2018), https://www.pri.org/stories/2018-11-06/kids-arent-alright-when-being-young-crime-el-salvador.

234. "María Ángela Domínguez Pérez," in Gómez y Marshall, *Sigue porque la vida sigue*, 179–181.

235. "María Ángela Domínguez Pérez," 184–185.

236. "María Ángela Domínguez Pérez," 187–188.

237. "María Ángela Domínguez Pérez," 190–191.

238. "María Ángela Domínguez Pérez," 189–190.

239. See "The Gospel according to Zacami," §8–9.

240. "José Adonay Pérez Pérez," in Gómez and Marshall, *Sigue porque la vida sigue*, 207–209.

241. A monthly theological formation workshop facilitated by FUNDAHMER, together with regional CEBs leaders.

242. This is a calendar produced every year by Equipo Maíz of photos of peoples' family members, neighbors, and friends who were disappeared during the war and have not been found, or killed without justice being served for their deaths.

243. "José Adonay Pérez Pérez," 210–211.
244. "José Adonay Pérez Pérez," 213.
245. "José Adonay Pérez Pérez," 214–215.
246. "Q & A with Berta Cáceres," The Goldman Environmental Prize website, May 12, 2015, https://www.goldmanprize.org/blog/qa-with-berta-caceres/.
247. Berta Cáceres, "Berta Caceres Acceptance Speech, 2015 Goldman Prize Ceremony," YouTube, Goldman Environmental Prize, channel, April 22, 2015, https://www.youtube.com/watch?v=AR1kwx8b0ms&t=12s.
248. "Slain Activist Berta Cáceres' Daughter: US Military Aid Has Fueled Repression & Violence in Honduras," *Democracy NOW!* (March 18, 2016), https://www.democracynow.org/2016/3/18/slain_activist_berta_caceras_daughter_us.
249. "Slain Activist."
250. "Slain Activist."
251. CEBs Nuevo Amanecer, FUNDAHMER, Memena y Laurel, "Guardiana del río," *Las CEBs Cantamos*, San Salvador, compact disc, 2018. This song has also been popularized in El Salvador by the all-women band, *Las Musas Desconectadas* and appears on their album *Reconexión*, 2019, San Salvador.
252. Ellen Moodie explores reasons for this assertion in her chapter "Democracy, Disenchantment, and the Future in El Salvador," in *Central America in the New Millennium: Living Transition and Reimagining Democracy*, ed. Jennifer L. Burell and Ellen Moodie (New York: Berghahn Books, 2013), 96–112. Moodie parses the phrase, suggesting that "it" refers to Salvadorans' perceptions about crime and violence or the possibility of democracy. Though the situation may seem worse now, Moodie cites the 2011–2012 protests of *"indignado"* youth as evidence that "some Salvadorans may be moving beyond disenchantment" (110–111). This is consistent with our observations in the CEBs and with a more recent resurgence of popular protest against the mounting authoritarianism of the government of President Nayib Bukele. See "Thousands Defy Bukele on El Salvador's 200th Birthday," *El Faro* (September 16, 2021), https://elfaro.net/en/202109/el_salvador/25728/Thousands-Defy-Bukele-on-El-Salvador, accessed December 10, 2021. See also Carlos Barrera, "The Day Bukele Lost the Streets," *El Faro* (September 16, 2021), https://elfaro.net/en/202109/ef_photo/25727/The-Day-Bukele-Lost-the-Streets.htm, accessed December 10, 2021.
253. CEBs Continental, "Camino Histórico de las CEBs, Región Centroamericana: Nicaragua, Panamá, Guatemala, El Salvador, Honduras" (Mexico City: August 11, 2017), 15, http://www.cebcontinental.org/index.php/en/quienes-somos/historia-de-las-ceb/region-centroamerica.
254. CEBs Continental, 16.
255. CEBs Continental, 21.
256. "Hay que seguir andando nomás" is a popular hymn sung in the contemporary CEBs that was originally composed by the Argentine singer-songwriter Father Carlos Saracini as a meditation on Latin American martyrdom and the CEBs' manner of being church. His account of the inspiration for writing this song, along with an embedded video of León Gieco's rendition of the song can be found here: https://eltalacomunicacionpopular.com/angelellivive-como-nacio-la-cancion-hay-que-seguir-andando-nomas/. A video montage featuring the voices of León Gieco and other

popular singers can be found here: https://youtu.be/dcx04JM-PsY. And Saracini's own rendition can be found here: https://youtu.be/ejWrnUby0Zw.

257. Jon Sobrino, "Carta a Ellacu," *Homily* (October 31, 1992), in *Carta a las iglesias*, November 1-15, 1992, http://www.uca.edu.sv/martires/new/memorias/cart3.htm.

258. Jon Sobrino, "Carta a Ignacio Ellacuría," *Carta a las Iglesias* #413, November 1998, http://www.uca.edu.sv/publica/cartas/ci413.html.

259. Jon Sobrino, "Carta a Ellacuría: fineza y santidad," *Carta a las Iglesias* # 523, November 2003, http://www.uca.edu.sv/publica/cartas/ci523.html#ELLACURIA.

260. Jon Sobrino, "Carta a Ellacuría," *Carta a las Iglesias* 2011.

261. Gómez and Marshall, eds., *Sigue porque la vida sigue*, 31.

262. Gómez and Marshall, 214.

Part II

EL REINO DE DIOS ES DE LXS POBRES

DECOLONIAL THEOLOGICAL REFLECTION IN LIGHT OF THE ECCLESIAL BASE COMMUNITIES OF EL SALVADOR

Chapter 1

Sacramento histórico del reino de Dios

Decoloniality and the Eschatological Horizons of El Salvador's Church of lxs Pobres

Ana Ortiz Luna is the youngest of twelve siblings in a Salvadoran family that lost all five of its male children during the armed conflict of the 1970s and 1980s. Her oldest brother was the martyred diocesan priest, Father Octavio Ortiz, whose pastoral ministry was dedicated to accompaniment of CEBs on the outskirts of San Salvador.[1] In a presentation on historical memory that Anita gave to a research symposium on the church of *lxs pobres* in October 2019, she reminded her audience that the etymology of the Spanish word "*recordar*" implies returning to the past to live through an experience again with one's heart, "*re-cordar.*" In English, the word "remember" has a different etymology, which connotes calling to mind the past, but which can also break down into the hyphenated "re-member," expressing an embodied process of bringing together that which has been dis-membered, or torn asunder.[2] When the Spanish and English meanings of this verb are both invoked, *re-cordar/*re-member harkens hearts, minds, and bodies back to history and points with hope toward a future of re-membered, or reconciled, creation. We have chosen to title this book *Re-membering the Reign of God* not only because of the pivotal role that historical memory plays in the CEBs' ecclesial praxis, but because the CEBs embody precisely this eschatological task of *re-cordando* and re-membering a fractured past and present on the way to a future of abundant life, wholeness, and right relationship in God's reign.

For 500 years, the impoverished majorities of the land that is now called El Salvador have been governed by the dis-membering forces of colonial domination. Everyday life for contemporary Salvadorans is dominated by structures and systems of oppression that coalesce in the varied, but interrelated domains of what decolonial scholars call a "colonial matrix of power."[3]

These domains, from which colonial power was born and through which contemporary coloniality exerts its continued domination, include control of

1. the economy, especially through colonial and capitalist appropriation and exploitation of land and labor;
2. authority, especially through monopolization of political power and military might;
3. gender and sexuality, through strict enforcement of patriarchal gender roles and heteronormativity;
4. subjectivity and knowledge, through Christian faith and theology, along with modern rationality; and
5. the natural world and natural resources, through a hierarchical dichotomy between culture and nature, along with the neoliberal capitalist paradigm of unlimited growth.[4]

According to Walter Mignolo, each of these realms is interrelated with the others, and all of them are bound together by the Eurocentric glue of racialized hierarchies, global capital, and epistemic hegemony. Through the workings of this colonial power matrix, the domination of Salvadoran church and society has been naturalized as God's will, the way of the free market, and an inherent marker of racial and sexual inferiority. Decolonial scholars have called the destructive domination and dis-memberment of being wrought by coloniality a "metaphysical catastrophe." As the first part of this book attests, varied modes of resistance to this catastrophe of nonbeing have been ongoing since the arrival of Spanish conquerors in the early sixteenth century, and the Salvadoran CEBs stand in a long line of decolonial movements for liberation. The emergence of the CEBs in El Salvador represents what decolonial scholars call a decided and deliberate "decolonial turn" away from forms of religion, rationality, economics, politics, gender relations, and relations with the earth that dis-member and negate the very being of the colonized—whether their physical, cultural, spiritual, and/or psychological being—through perpetual violence.[5]

Drawing on Frantz Fanon and Steve Biko, Nelson Maldonado-Torres describes the decolonial turn at its most basic level as an attitude whereby the *damné* is able to "shift away from the imperatives and norms that are imposed over it and keep it split with itself." This attitude is the "dimension of the subject by virtue of which the subject can seek to challenge knowledge, power, and being" and thereby struggle against the negation of the *damné*'s own being. This struggle, this *lucha*, is "pursued with love, as the positive attitude of the *damné*, and rage, as a form of negation that is inspired and oriented by the positive attitude of love."[6] The decolonial turn involves both of these positive and negative orientations—the yes to abundant life and community,

Sacramento histórico del reino de Dios   189

as well as the no to all that which dis-members and destroys such life. In and through the decolonial turn, Maldonado-Torres argues, the *damnés*

> transition from isolated self-hating subjects to decolonizing agents and bridges who serve as connectors between themselves and many others. It is in this process that true love and understanding—philosophy in the most abstract but also the most concrete of senses—can flourish.[7]

The CEBs of El Salvador have made and continue to make this decolonial turn with every step they take toward re-membering themselves as ecclesial subjects of the divine dream of abundant life for creation.

As Christian communities striving to re-member and incarnate the reign of God in human history, the CEBs understand themselves to be the church of *lxs pobres*—the people of God organized at the base of the church and society for the sake of and on the move toward the reign of God. Unlike the triumphalist visions of the "Kingdom of God" held by imperial and colonizing powers throughout much of Christian history, the CEBs envision the reign of God as *de lxs pobres*—a reality in which the agency and full humanity of *lxs pobres* is central to God's dream for re-membering creation into right relationships of justice, equality, and abundant life for all. This chapter therefore identifies and unpacks the reign of God as the eschatological foundation and ultimate horizon of both the Salvadoran base communities' ecclesial praxis and their concomitant understanding of what it means to be church, particularly the church of *lxs pobres*. Here we place the CEBs' theology of the reign of God and its role in their ecclesiology in critical conversation with decolonial scholarship, arguing that the reign of God, at least as the CEBs envision it at work in human history, is a decolonial reality that resists and subverts the coloniality of the world as know it. The reign of God is that already-but-not-yet dimension within the CEBs that empowers them to challenge colonial knowledge, being, and power. In more positive and cosmic terms, the reign of God is an-other world in which many worlds are free to flourish, a world in which all peoples are free to exercise subjectivity in relationship to one another and the rest of creation.[8]

Furthermore, we argue that, as the church of *lxs pobres*, the CEBs' historical turning, or *metanoia*, toward God's reign and toward one another, *lxs pobres*, as historical subjects of God's reign, is a paradigmatic experience and embodiment of the decolonial turn. We conclude that, insofar as the CEBs reach for, participate in, and incarnate God's reign in their historical context, these communities are a decolonial sacrament of God's reign in the midst of an enduringly colonial church and world. The ecclesiological chapters that follow all flow from this foundational decolonial understanding of the CEBs' eschatological horizon.

Chapter 1

THE DECOLONIALITY OF GOD'S REIGN: ESCHATOLOGY IN THE ECCLESIAL BASE COMMUNITIES

The Centrality of the Reign of God in the CEBs

A defining feature of ecclesial identity in the base communities of Latin America as a whole is their commitment to collaboration with Jesús of Nazareth in the historical project of building the reign of God. From 2016 to 2020, Argentine theologian Francisco Bosch traveled throughout Latin America to document the stories and theology of the CEBs as a *"bendita mezcla"* of "diverse rhythms, desires, struggles, ages, cultures, languages, experiences, preoccupations, and many other characteristics." He notes that all of this beautiful, blessed diversity

> comes together and is strengthened in [the CEBs'] determination and commitment to living out a different way of being church, similar to the primitive communities in the Acts of the Apostles, and to be collaborators with Jesús so that the reign that he announced will come about.[9]

Bosch echoes the CEBs' laments over the *gritos* (cries) and *bestias* (beasts) that beset the Latin American continent due to the enduring legacies of coloniality, but he also lifts up the *grietas* (cracks) in the coloniality of power where the reign of God breaks through in the ecclesial life of the CEBs. The continental network of Latin American CEBs corroborates this centrality of the reign of God as the commitment that defines their shared identity in a document on five common features of the CEBs today. Their first identity marker includes this affirmation of the reign of God as central to the mission of Jesús and thus, of the CEBs: "The center of the mission of Jesucristo lies in the announcement of the Reign of God. Jesús indicates that the Reign of God is among us and leads to abundance."[10] The Latin American CEBs' commitment to following Jesús necessarily involves their commitment to his vision and praxis of God's reign.

The CEBs in El Salvador, also quite diverse in their makeup, share with their continental counterparts this defining and unifying feature of commitment to the reign of God. While it does not appear that the language of the reign of God was as developed in the early years of the CEBs' formation and persecution during the 1970s–1980s, a manual for pastoral formation published in the early 1990s includes the reign of God as a foundational element of the CEBs' self-definition and identity. This manual defines the CEBs as "a pastoral praxis, both prophetic and ecumenical, that announces the reign of God and denounces the powers of death and the idols that try to turn the people of God away from its path."[11] More recent pastoral pamphlets and formation booklets published and utilized by the CEBs have included a statement of purpose indicating the desire "to be more and more ecclesial base communities, the church of Jesús, that announces and commits itself to the construction of the reign of God."[12] The Brother Mercedes Ruíz Foundation (FUNDAHMER), a Salvadoran NGO that serves as a legally recognized entity carrying on the work of the CEBs, also includes the reign of God in their self-definition, declaring their commitment "to contributing to God's reign of peace and justice here on earth."[13]

In accordance with Bosch's assertion that the CEBs of *NuestrAmérica* "do away with the monologue of reason," we would be remiss to highlight only straightforward, discursive instances of the CEBs' self-definition in terms of the reign of God. Members of the CEBs also speak in aesthetic, parabolic, musical, and sacramental terms about their identity as historical collaborators in Jesús's project of God's reign. For example, a music group from the remote rural region of Morazán named *Grupo Libre* recently composed a song entitled "Las CEBES," which begins with a verse that repeats twice:

Las CEBES vienen trabajando por construir el reino de Dios.	The CEBs come along working to construct the reign of God.
Somos una red que nadie la puede reventar (¿por qué?)	We are a network that no one can break (why?)
porque está construida con base social.	because we are constructed on a social foundation.[14]

In other instances, the CEBs sing even more poetically of themselves as a simple church and a pilgrim church, a seed of God's reign, and as a missionary church, a burning fire that illuminates the coming of that reign. Furthermore, the sacramental life of the CEBs is suffused with and often interpreted in terms of the reign of God. Baptism and eucharistic celebrations, as they are practiced within the CEBs, are understood to be signs of individual and communal commitment to God's reign, along with embodied manifestations of and contributions to the *compartir* that God's reign entails. In a series of workshops in 2014 studying the sacraments, especially baptism and eucharist, baptism was understood as important for Christian life "because it's from that moment on that your faith deepens in order to construct the reign of God in the community."[15] Regarding eucharist, one community member in particular expressed how the eucharistic celebration speaks to her of the community's commitment to build the reign of God.[16] These aesthetic, sacramental, and embodied dimensions of the CEBs' commitment to the reign of God will become clearer as we work our way through the eschatology and ecclesiology of these communities in the rest of this chapter and the three that follow.

The Reign of God, Coloniality, and Decoloniality

Before we flesh out our argument for the decoloniality of the CEBs' commitment to and praxis of the reign of God, it is important to remember that the reign of God is a religious symbol that has been used and abused to justify, rather than challenge the European colonial project in Latin America and the continued coloniality of existence on the continent today. Iberian Catholic colonizers, backed by the Roman Catholic church, saw their invasion and conquest of the Americas as justified and even necessitated by the Christian imperative to spread the Christian faith and the reign of theocratic Christendom to the ends of the earth.[17] Postcolonial, feminist, womanist, and mujerista theologians have all critiqued the language of "God's Reign" or "God's Kingdom" for its patriarchal, monarchial, and imperial overtones. Mujerista theologian Ada María Isasi-Díaz argues that there are two reasons for not using the English words "kingdom" or "reign" for the divine gift that Jesús called *basileia tou theou* (and these critiques would also apply to the word *reino* in Spanish as well): "First, it is obviously a sexist word that presumes that God is male. Second, the concept of the kingdom in our world today is both hierarchical and elitist—which is why I do not use the word reign." She proposes the word "kin-dom" as an English alternative to the traditional language that she finds problematic: "The word kin-dom makes it clear that when the fullness of God becomes a day-to-day reality in the world at large, we will all be sisters and brothers—kin to each other."[18] Many anti-imperial, anti-patriarchal theologians and preachers have followed Isasi-Díaz's example here in their reimagined English language and imagery for what the CEBs continue to name in Spanish as the reign of God.

For decolonial scholars, the problem with Christian eschatology runs even deeper than Isasi-Díaz's critique and, in general, they would be exceedingly wary of correlating the religious symbol of the reign of God with decolonial struggles to delink from racialized and patriarchal Western Christian hegemony. Walter Mignolo's work is especially critical of any form of theo- or ego-politics undergirded by a missionary impulse to impart "salvation" to others, even in the form of kinship, emancipation, or material liberation. In his view, the decolonial option rejects "any option that claims universality, or that has not yet clearly rejected the legacies of universalism in their own trajectory."[19] Such presumptions of universality often buy into the modern idea of a singular history and tend to have "an imperial bent to 'save the world' by making of the world an extended Euro-America," a goal which Mignolo deems as "unacceptable."[20] Decoloniality dispels these soteriological and eschatological myths of universality. The CEBs' self-proclaimed mission of participation in the construction of God's reign might appear, at first glance, to fall prey to these presumptions of universality, if not Eurocentrism, that Mignolo's decolonial option rejects. Not only is the reign of God a religious symbol that carries with it the colonial baggage of violent conquest, enslavement, and Christianization, its eschatological nature presumes a totalizing *telos* for all human life, the planet, and the cosmos as a whole. Could any religious symbol possibly be less decolonial?

The decolonial option is necessarily limited to a local or regional scope that is linked to specific bodies in specific places at specific times. The body-politics of decolonial subjects, "who do not want to be managed by the state and want to delink from the technologies of power to which they are being summated,"[21] stands in direct opposition to the theo- and ego-politics of projects like the reign of God, as it is envisioned in traditional Christian soteriology and eschatology. However, Mignolo and other decolonial scholars and activists do not lack a soteriological and eschatological vision of their own. For Mignolo, the decolonial option not only unveils, delinks from, and resists the logic of totalizing coloniality. It also positively proposes the universal project of *pluriversality*, contributing to the construction of a world in which many worlds coexist,[22] in which "no human being has the right to dominate and be imposed over other human beings."[23] The horizon (eschatological vision?) of the decolonial option is "the flourishing of creativity and fullness (in the sense of Sumak Kawsay), and not the imperial management of authority, economy, subjectivity, knowledge, and gender/sexuality."[24] As the following pages will demonstrate, this vision of human and planetary flourishing aligns with the understanding of the historical project of God's reign that is generally held in the base communities. Far from a world-conquering project of universal salvation that erases human differences and imposes yet another form of empire, the CEBs' vision of the reign of God sets them on a trajectory that values diversity and aligns more closely with the traditional cosmovisions of non-Western cultures in which, Anibal Quijano argues,

> the perspective of totality in knowledge includes the acknowledgement of the heterogeneity of all reality, of the irreducible, contradictory character of the latter; of the legitimacy, i.e., the desirability, of the diverse character of the components of all reality—and therefore, of the social.[25]

It is important to note here that the Salvadoran CEBs have also critiqued how the traditional, colonial symbol of the reign of God has served the interests of the powerful by projecting God's promise of redemption to a future, supra-terrestrial realm, equating eschatological salvation with the Kingdom of Heaven, where *lxs pobres* who suffer now would one day enjoy "*calles de oro, mares de cristal*" ("streets of gold, crystal seas").[26] Such visions of otherworldly solace fed into what Salvadoran priest Luis Coto calls the institutional church's

> collusion . . . with the privileged classes, and [its] lack of evangelical commitment to denouncing the injustices in their concrete forms due to fear of losing privileges or suffering persecution. It was a church that was not incarnate in reality, which by emphasizing the supra-terrestrial aspect alienated Christians from their task of making real the Christian message of liberation for the whole person.[27]

Members of the CEBs go so far as to critique this purely spiritualistic understanding of the reign of God as a manifestation of the *anti-reino*, the antithesis of God's will and liberating action in human history. In the same aforementioned sacramental workshops, community members contrast the *anti-reino* emptiness and egoism of their experiences of eucharistic celebration in the institutional church with the experience of communion in the CEBs, which expresses and embodies the CEBs' commitment to God's reign.[28] In this very critique of traditional Christian Kingdom theology as *anti-reino*, the CEBs are making the decolonial turn away from imperatives and norms that "split them from themselves."[29] This decolonial turn away from the political and otherworldly universalisms of the *anti-reino* sets the base communities on a pilgrim's path of participation in the historical construction of the pluriversality of God's reign. When Jesús and his own community of disciples proclaimed and practiced the reign of God, they engaged in the subversion of the imperial myth of Roman dominion.[30] When the CEBs of El Salvador proclaim and practice the reign of God today, they subvert the colonial myths of European/U.S. supremacy, capitalist accumulation, and Roman Catholic triumphalism.

The Reign of God in the Theology of the CEBs: A Decolonial Horizon

The reign of God, as the CEBs understand it, is most fundamentally a social and relational reality—a *koinonia*,[31] or communion, in which human beings and nonhuman creation are able to live with dignity and enjoy life together in abundance. While the armed struggle of Salvadoran revolutionaries in the twentieth century did not pretend to promise the coming of God's reign once and for all, the struggle did have utopian underpinnings, and the utopic hope of many Christians who incorporated themselves into the struggle was simply that the people could have dignified work, good salaries, that the rich wouldn't mistreat the workers and *campesinos*, that the land would be for all, so that when farmers would plant they would have land to plant on because the haciendas of the rich were hoarding everything.[32]

Many older members of the contemporary CEBs joined or supported this revolutionary struggle, and the fulfillment of these most fundamental human needs and desires for life and dignity are the baseline for the CEBs' vision of the reign of God. Without structural access to the basic needs of human life, the world of the vast majority of Salvadoran people was hardly free to exist at all. Today the CEBs add to these basic criteria food sovereignty, protection of waterways, ecological sustainability, and cultural autonomy, along with access to education, health care, potable water, housing, and recreation.[33]

In broader terms, the reign of God encompasses a whole host of historical human values and social goods, all of which contradict the realities of the *anti-reino* (coloniality) at work in the church and world:

- justice that stands against all injustice;
- truth that stands against all deception;
- life that stands against the forces of death;
- "solidarious" love against all selfishness, individualism, and monopolizing of resources; and
- freedom that stands against all forms of oppression.[34]

The same sentiment is expressed in song: "There is one place / where God cannot be. / Where there is injustice / God is not there."[35] The CEBs are firm that God is existentially opposed to injustice, deception, death, and oppression and apply this logic to the reign of God, God's dream for creation. In short, the reign of God is a social and political reality that stands against all forms of empire.[36]

While these visions of the reign of God call for structural transformation of oppressive social, economic, and ecological systems, the CEBs also understand the reign of God to be a reality that is lived, experienced, and embodied in the microstructures and experience of *lo cotidiano*, or everyday life.[37] Teresa ("Tere") Moreno de Melendez, a founding member of the CEB Nuevo Amanecer in San Bartolo, Ilopango, articulates this everydayness of the reign of God as follows:

> The reign of God is what Jesús of Nazareth spoke about when he got together with *los pobres*, the marginalized, women, and everyone who was "suspicious" in the eyes of others. The reign of God is what we can make present, when we are able to help those who need it most, when we are able to accompany those

who have nothing, and when we can support them in the hard reality of their daily lives—hard for lack of resources, health care, or dignified employment. The reign of God is when we are able to accompany young people, who are always seen as dangerous and are also in danger. The reign of God is not located in any other place or any other dimension; it is here today among us, when we are in solidarity, when we are just, when we treat each other as equals. Jesús preached the reign of God and the CEBs that live into their identity are faithful to the project of Jesús.[38]

Many members of the CEBs relate that they experience a sense of fulfillment and divine presence in their participation in the life of the community, especially in their daily *compartir* and their practices of mutual aid: caring for the sick, burying the dead, providing nourishment for the hungry, and simply coming together in community to support one another in the daily struggle to survive. The *koinonia* that emerges from these communal practices is reflective of the radical solidarity that characterizes God's reign.

Gustavo, a member of the Pueblo de Dios en Camino community, specifically identifies these daily experiences of walking through life together as communal experiences of the reign of God. When asked what he thought the reign of God should look like, he responds:

> *Híjole*, that's a complicated question! Look, I feel like it's complicated when Jesús says that the reign of God is here. That the reign of God has arrived. That the reign of God is among you. Lots of people speak of the reign of God. I have learned that, well, if I speak about the reign of God, of justice, of truth, of love, of life. . . . I think the reign of God is something you do/make [*hacer*]. In your family, in community, in your profession, in life. Whenever we are making experiences, whenever we are walking, we are making the reign of God. I think that's it. . . . To speak of the reign of God is about going through life by way of experience, it's that which is born little by little, developing itself within a particular society and that by nature is transcendent. Therefore, it's something that surges up from an ideal with its own philosophy of life. In this case, the philosophy of Jesús. The challenge for me is what role do I have to play in this society in order to go about creating the reign of God in my own life—a reign of justice, of truth, of peace, of solidarity, of equity, of communion, of struggle. If I don't do that, then what the devil am I doing in this world?[39]

Going on to quote Luke 4:18 here, Gustavo highlights both the daily, lived experience of God's reign and its transcendence, which we will return to momentarily.

The daily experience of God's reign in community life—or at least the dream of living this experience—is expressed concretely in the song "Sueño Comunidad," written by the Monseñor Romero network of CEBs in La Libertad:[40]

Sueño que un día despertemos convencidos bien adentro y realizamos, de que vale más la vida vivir con los demás y en comunidad que una vida preocupada cada quien con sus problemas, que una vida destinada a más dinero, más poder, y más razón.	I dream that one day we'll wake up convinced deep down and we'll realize that life lived with others and in community is worth more than a life preoccupied each of us with our own problems, than a life destined for more money, more power, and more verdicts.[41]

This dream for communal living also includes a vision of gender equality and therefore an implicit critique of sexism and patriarchy:

Sueño que se levanta la muchacha con firmeza en sus pasos y se convence, que sus derechos no son menos a pesar que así le dicen los demás. Que su libertad es pa' vivirla sin dejarse dominar. Y seguir luchando por sus sueños de una vida con dignidad. Sueño que se levanta el muchacho, el fuerte y cachimbón y realiza, que no tiene más sentido de ser siempre quien gana e impresiona. Sino simplemente el compañero con su forma de ser, y sencillamente el amigo con sus dones, uno más.	I dream that the young woman gets up with firmness in her steps and is convinced, that her rights are not any less even though that's what others tell her. That her freedom is for living without allowing herself to be dominated. And she continues to fight for her dreams of a life with dignity. I dream that the young man gets up, the strong and cool guy, and he realizes that it doesn't make much sense to be the one who always wins and makes an impression. But rather simply a companion with his own way of being, and sincerely a friend with his gifts, just one more.

And finally, the dream offers a vision of relational equality and inclusion in the leadership, structure, and culture of the community as a whole:

Sueño que se levante nuestro líder de la comunidad y practica con ganas escuchar al distante, al complicado y al que jode. Y nunca más excluir a nadie solo por su opinión. Sino buscar la fuerza colectiva que está en la unidad.	I dream that the leader of our community wakes up and practices eager listening to the distant one, the complicated one, and the one who is just screwing around. And never excludes anyone just because of their opinion. but rather strives for the collective strength that can be found in unity.

Here the dream reimagines community and unity in such a way that diversity is not frowned upon or excised from community life but is listened to and learned from. The collective strength that comes from a united community does not depend on everyone looking, thinking, and acting alike. Rather, it celebrates difference and seeks our wisdom in unlikely places, even in those who seem like they are just fooling around! While these lyrics do not explicitly mention the reign of God or any other theological concept, they do offer a compelling vision of the collective strength and equality needed for a community to reflect what the CEBs understand to be God's reign in their daily experiences of sociality, relationships, solidarity, and communal organization. María Elena Sanabria de Cruz, executive director of FUNDAHMER, argues that the reign of God is constructed from these smallest and most basic things, which add up to the most important thing: saving human lives, saving the natural world, and saving the community.[42]

One other song, based on the homilies of Rutilio Grande and intoned with such frequency in the CEBs that it naturally forms part of "The Gospel According to Suchitoto" in part I.[43] The song is entitled "Vamos Todos al Banquete" and it was written for the Salvadoran Popular Mass by Salvadoran singer-songwriter, Guillermo Cuéllar. It offers such a powerful vision of the communal life typical of God's reign that it merits repeating here in full:

Vamos todos al banquete,	Let us all go to the banquet,
A la mesa de la creación,	to the table of Creation.
Cada cual con su taburete,	Everyone who pulls us a seat
Tiene un puesto y una misión.	Has a place and a mission.
Hoy me levanto muy temprano,	I wake up early today,
Ya me espera la comunidad,	my community already awaits me.
Voy subiendo alegre la cuesta,	I climb the hill happily,
Voy en busca de tu amistad.	I go in search of your friendship.
Dios invita a todos los pobres,	God invites all of lxs pobres,
A esta mesa común por la fe,	To this common table of faith.
Donde no hay acaparadores,	Where there are no hoarders,
Y a nadie le falta el con que.	and nobody is lacking for food.
Dios nos manda hacer de este mundo,	God demands that we make of this world
Una mesa de fraternidad,	a table of fraternity
Trabajando y luchando juntos,	working and struggling together
Compartiendo la propiedad.	and sharing property.

Once again, the common themes of community, solidarity, equality, equity, justice, and shared struggle define the CEBs' vision of God's dream for creation, and their overall understanding and historical praxis of God's reign. This vision is antithetical to the coloniality of power, in which Western values of individualism, hierarchy, domination, and wealth accumulation reign. The reign of God, which breaks through in fragments of human history in the CEBs, resists these *anti-reino* values and thus decolonizes the church and society for the sake of constructing a world in which many worlds are welcome.

There are three other characteristics of the CEBs' understanding of the reign of God that are significant for understanding this theological concept and praxis, along with its decoloniality, in their communal life. First, the reign of God is understood by the CEBs to be *"de lxs pobres."* This understanding of the reign of God has deep biblical roots in God's preferential option for *lxs pobres* throughout salvation history, from the Exodus story to the prophets of ancient Israel, and from the choice of a humble peasant girl as the mother of the promised liberator to the proclamation and praxis of that liberator, Jesús of Nazareth, who blessed *lxs pobres* and sent the rich away empty:[44]

> Blessed are you who are poor,
> for yours is the kingdom of God.
> Blessed are you who are hungry now,
> for you will be filled.
> Blessed are you who weep now,
> for you will laugh.
> . . .
> But woe to you who are rich,
> for you have received your consolation.
> Woe to you who are full now,
> for you will be hungry.
> Woe to you who are laughing now,
> for you will mourn and weep. (Luke 6:20–21, 24–25)

The primary recipients of God's promised justice are those who have been denied justice in human history—*lxs pobres*, the marginalized, the oppressed, and excluded. But not only do the CEBs know the reign of God to be of *lxs pobres*, it is made manifest and carried forth in human history by *lxs pobres*. The second part of this chapter, along with ecclesiological chapters that follow, explores at greater length this protagonism of *lxs pobres*, particularly the church of *lxs pobres*, in the service of and as sacrament of God's reign. For now, it suffices to say that the decoloniality of God's reign in human history becomes all the more evident in this reactivated and re-membered subjectivity of the colonized, which subverts colonial hierarchies of knowledge, being, and power that deny *lxs pobres* their very existence, let alone their subjectivity.

Second, the reign of God is a gift of grace, not a reward for those who strive to merit its blessings. María Elena points this out, arguing that it is not as if the organized struggles of the CEBs and of other grassroots movements for justice are carried out for the sake of themselves or their families and communities alone. To the contrary, the CEBs take their cues from their martyrs, who struggled for the sake of justice and peace for the whole Salvadoran people and for future generations. Chamba, a grassroots musician and community leader from the Bajo Lempa, stresses this point with an example, indicating that if the CEBs win in their collective struggles against the privatization of water, or for food sovereignty, the results would be for the good of the whole community and the whole country—for everyone![45] This approach to the age-old grace vs. merit debate offers a transcendent, yet immanently practical resolution to what turns out to be a false dichotomy. The reign of God is a gratuitous offering of God's good gifts of created abundance, right relationship, community, solidarity, love, and so forth. Human beings are invited to partner with God in the work of bringing these gifts to fruition. And yet those who do choose the lifegiving path of active partnership in the project of God's reign are no more deserving of the gifts of that reign than anyone else. In fact, justice, equality, and peace are only fully enjoyed by these collaborators in the divine project if they can be enjoyed by everyone. The reign of God is a world in which many worlds and all peoples are free to enjoy these gifts. How very different from the colonial "meritocracies" of Western modernity, neoliberal capitalism, and Christian soteriology! Even in the "grace alone, faith alone" varieties of the latter, only certain bodies are "graced" and only certain faith traditions suffice for "salvation." The CEBs subvert the coloniality of these soteriological categories with an eschatological vision of God's desire for all peoples to enjoy the good gifts of creation in relationships of justice and equity with one another as human beings, and in sustainable relationships of respect and mutual care with the more-than-human world.

Third, and finally, the CEBs understand their participation in the construction of the reign of God to be provisional and ongoing, a process that is in constant dynamism within human history and that ultimately has a mysterious and transcendent *telos* of life together in God's presence. Not only do the CEBs faithfully speak and sing of themselves as an *iglesia peregrina*, they also articulate life together in Christian community as a journey, or an ongoing process that must always be critically engaged and examined lest we think we have arrived at our destination when we are really only resting by the wayside. One community member, Avelino, observes that "the struggle is not just one moment. It's your whole life." Another, Reina, similarly remarks that "the system isn't something that one changes overnight."[46] Given the persistence and insidiousness of empire and coloniality in human history, Maldonado-Torres echoes these sentiments in explicitly decolonial terms:

> Decoloniality is never pure nor perfect, and it does not count with a full picture of what a decolonized institution, society, or world can be. Asking for purity or perfection, for a complete plan of action, or for a complete design of the new decolonized reality are forms of decadence and bad faith.[47]

In human history, the reign of God is neither pure nor perfect. The CEBs do not have a full picture of what it can be, nor do they possess a blueprint for how to get there. For us to pretend that they are pure or perfect in their understanding and praxis of God's reign would indeed be a form of bad faith.

The CEBs are a pilgrim people continually *en camino hacia el reino de Dios*, on a journey to the reign of God. Where and whenever these communities embody decolonial ways of knowing and being in the midst of coloniality, that reign breaks into history and inspires decolonial hope for a world in which many worlds are free to exist and enjoy life in abundance. Where and when that world breaks into human history through the proclamation and praxis of the CEBs, they fulfill their ecclesial mission as the body of Christ, the church of *lxs pobres*, historical sacrament of liberation, historical sacrament of God's reign.[48]

DECOLONIALITY AND THE CHURCH OF *LXS POBRES* AS HISTORICAL SACRAMENT OF THE REIGN OF GOD

"*¡NO NOS AVERGONZAMOS DE SER . . . LA IGLESIA DE LXS POBRES!*" This call-and-response cheer rings through the streets of downtown San Salvador when marches dance toward the Metropolitan Cathedral or the Legislative Assembly. Whether it is March 24—the anniversary of Archbishop Oscar Romero's martyrdom—or a day the national legislative body is set to vote on the privatization of water or a food sovereignty law, the ecclesial base communities of El Salvador are yeast in the dough of El Salvador's marginalized secular and ecclesial populations. "It doesn't embarrass us to be the church of *lxs pobres*!" They chant in singsong from their block in the environmental march, parading past Metrocentro, one of a chain of malls owned by the *Grupo Roble*, a real estate conglomerate whose residential and commercial projects have devastated the ecology of the capital city. The church of *lxs pobres* shows up for International Workers' Day, for International Women's Day, and on the anniversaries of massacres and martyrdoms, protesting metallic mining, and celebrating the beatification and canonization of their beloved San Romero. And they show up for the everyday needs and well-being of their own particular communities—whether it be in liturgical celebrations, artistic presentations, or pastoral projects aimed at survival and quality of life. The decolonial vision and praxis of the reign of God detailed above call the CEBs to embody the fullness of their ecclesial identity as church of *lxs pobres*—in the words of Ignacio Ellacuría, "a church in which *los pobres* are its principal subject and its principle of internal structuring."[49] Indeed, any church that commits itself to following Jesús and participating in his mission of proclaiming the reign of God, which is of *lxs pobres*, must be a church of *lxs pobres*.

One month prior to the opening of the Second Vatican Council, Pope John XXIII declared in a radio message that "Today the Church is above all the Church of the poor."[50] While the council failed to implement this statement as a major theme of its deliberations and documents, it did provide some ecclesial openings that would permit and even inspire the development of a pastoral commitment to nurturing and defending a church of *lxs pobres* in Latin America. The Latin American Bishops' Conference (CELAM) made this commitment clear in its meetings at Medellín (1968) and Puebla (1979) and in the witness of those bishops and other clerics who embodied solidarity with the church of *lxs pobres* in their everyday pastoral ministry with their suffering people. Included in these bishops' commitment to the church of *lxs pobres* were encouraging words and provision of pastoral support for the formation, flourishing, and prophetic defense of ecclesial base communities during some of the most conflict-ridden years of political violence and repression. These bishops embraced the centrality of the people of God in the ecclesiology of *Lumen Gentium*, immersing and incarnating themselves in the reality of the great majority of Latin American peoples and thus making great strides toward becoming a church of and for *lxs pobres*, committed to God's reign. New possibilities for decolonizing Latin American Catholicism were emerging, even within the institutional church.

However, many Latin American bishops continued to stress the primacy of hierarchical communion in their interpretation of *Lumen Gentium*, in contradistinction to a communion ecclesiology of the whole people of God. These men therefore distanced themselves from the people and either ignored or directly opposed the church of *lxs pobres* altogether. These bishops garnered support for their reassertion of hierarchical communion from Pope Paul VI's 1975 Apostolic Exhortation, *Evangelii Nuntiandi*, in which a distinction is made between CEBs that develop "within the Church, having solidarity with her life, being nourished by her teaching and united with her pastors" from those that come together in a spirit of bitter criticism of the Church, which they are quick to stigmatize as "institutional" . . . their obvious characteristic is an attitude of fault-finding and rejection with regard to the Church's outward manifestations: her hierarchy, her signs.[51]

Even CELAM's Puebla documents caution against political manipulation of the CEBs that might "separate them from authentic communion with their bishops."[52] Indeed, as the examples provided in the "Letters from the Hierarchy" in part I attest, the overriding attitude of the hierarchy toward the church of *lxs pobres* in El Salvador has increasingly been one of suspicion and neglect, and in some cases outright marginalization and exclusion. Here we can see that the coloniality of knowledge, being, and power still hold sway in the Latin American church.

Unlike many of his brother bishops, Pope Francis has emphasized the evangelizing mission of the entire people of God, and has embodied an ecclesial desire to become a church of and for *lxs pobres*, emptied of clerical privilege and alliances with the powerful.[53] His papacy has been marked by symbolic and concrete gestures of solidarity with the vulnerable and marginalized; his preaching and teaching have offered prophetic denunciations of an economy of exclusion; and he has been an advocate for the struggles of popular and ecological movements throughout the world.[54] With the full weight of scripture and the Catholic social tradition in his corner, as well as the experience of the church in late twentieth-century Latin America, Pope Francis has struggled against the forces of coloniality in the realms of economics, ecology, and culture, calling for a "church which is poor and for the poor."[55] The 2019 Synod of Bishops for the Pan-Amazon Region and the pope's subsequent apostolic exhortation, *Querida Amazonia*, embody this decolonial impulse of his papacy. His attitude of humble listening and following the lead of *lxs pobres* and marginalized in their struggles for social, economic, and ecological liberation are modes of decolonizing the relationship between the church *ad extra*, in its relationship with the world. However, as the following three chapters will attest, it seems that Pope Francis is only willing (or able) to go so far in decolonizing the church *ad intra*.[56] Our final chapter will also return to the traces of coloniality that remain even in Pope Francis's understanding of solidarity in and with the church of *lxs pobres*.

As a constitutive, though not exhaustive, dimension of the church of *lxs pobres* in El Salvador,[57] the CEBs' "new way of being church" decolonizes not only the church's mission toward the world, but also in its internal workings and organizational structure. In the CEBs' ecclesiology, the church of *lxs pobres* is guided by its commitment to the reign of God. It is a seed of that reign, which does not burst forth in its full eschatological flowering, to be sure, but which bears all the potency and divine DNA of that reign within its internal structures. Leaving the metaphor of the seed behind, the church of *lxs pobres* is a historical sacrament of the reign of God: it is a visible sign of God's reign that makes that reign present and active in the church of *lxs pobres* itself and, through the church of *lxs pobres*, in human history. Ellacuría words once again illuminate the CEBs' ecclesiology here:

> The church makes real its historic, salvific sacramentality by announcing and fulfilling the reign of God in history. Its fundamental praxis consists in the fulfillment of the reign of God in history, in action that leads to the fulfillment of the reign of God in history.[58]

The church of *lxs pobres*, as historical sacrament of the liberation that ushers in God's reign, not only strives for the manifestation and construction of the reign of God in sociopolitical or economic affairs; it strives to incarnate the justice and radical egalitarianism of God's reign in the internal structures of its ecclesial life—in both the institutional and communal dimensions of that life. Therefore, *lxs pobres* are not only protagonists of God's reign in their external struggles for an-other world, they are also protagonists of God's reign within the church itself, announcing and re-membering an-other way of being church. While the ecclesiological chapters that follow will flesh this out in greater detail, the words of Tere and her community about the reign of God once again offer some general contours of this protagonism from below in the church of *lxs pobres*:

> To speak of the church of *los pobres* is to speak of a church without structures of power; it is to speak from the place of the last and the least, of those who don't count, of the marginalized and excluded by the market system. To speak of the church of *los pobres* is to detach ourselves from power structures and go back to the option for *los pobres* in accordance with the gospel of Jesús. In the CEBs we try and we want to follow the example of the first Christian communities, where we all see each other as equals and we all share the same utopia of the reign of God among us.[59]

The biblical and historical key to understanding the church of *lxs pobres* and its decolonial turn toward God's reign is what Tere references here as the *opción por los pobres*, the option for the poor[60] whereby *lxs pobres* refuse to accept the received narratives about themselves and choose to live in committed solidarity with one another in pursuit of God's reign. For *lxs pobres* to "opt for the poor" requires a conscious and critical turn away from the colonial negation of their very being—a negation too often instigated or exacerbated by the institutional Roman Catholic church—and toward the collective power that is latent in their self-affirmation and organization as liberated communities of decolonial faith, hope, and love. Naming themselves as the church of *lxs pobres*, and insisting that there is and should be no shame in being the church of *lxs pobres*, is a foundational expression of this liberating option, this decolonial turn.

Anita Landaverde, a founding member of the urban base community Pueblo de Dios en Camino, expresses the fundamental distinction of the CEBs as the church of *lxs pobres* in her reflections on the two types of churches and the Spirit-driven freedom that exists for *lxs pobres* in the church of *lxs pobres*:

> There are two types of churches! There is one church in which we, *los pobres*, do not fit. Only someone who becomes like the poor and becomes the voice of *los pobres* is going to understand. And so we consider ourselves the church of *los pobres*, a church of the base. But we are not the base of the institutional church. Because we are not *masa* [the masses/dough]. *Masa* can be moved this way or that, but not the ecclesial base communities. *Masa* is manipulated by the hierarchy. The institutional church calls all Catholics to show up as united. But we feel like we are the church on the move. Because we believe in the Spirit, in that Spirit of Jesús, of Monseñor Romero, of our martyrs, it's there. And so we don't fit within the institution because we feel like we are in prison. We are free.[61]

Here we can see that the Spirit of Jesús, of San Romero, of other Salvadoran heroes and martyrs, and indeed the Spirit of the church of *lxs pobres* itself, is a spirit of freedom that empowers *lxs pobres* to believe not only in the God of Life, but also in themselves and their own abilities to discern God's will and God's liberating presence in the historical and ecclesial signs of the times.

One member of the Segundo Montes community[62] puts it this way:

> The good news that God gave us is that we believe in God the liberator, who brought us the good news, and that we believe in ourselves, in *la pobre* or in *el pobre*, right? That we don't just believe [God is] in the priest who comes from somewhere else or in other people who come from somewhere else, but within our very own selves.[63]

The theological imagination behind such an assertion is deeply sacramental. Base community members often profess to find God all around them—in nature and within *lxs pobres*, but also and often most especially within their own communal efforts to build the reign of God. Bosch highlights this sacramentality of the CEBs in his insistence on their status as a place of salvific encounter with the divine in the stories of the people, whose experience of

God in themselves has too often been repressed by the way in which the coloniality of power despises the people's culture:

> Many of our communities . . . have felt that there is no beauty to be found in their history, that revelation always comes from afar and from above. Therefore, valuing their own trajectories as a place where God passes through is a blessed event that lets loose a torrent of inexhaustible creativity, an endless series of histories that make ready the stew of stories with which God feeds us.[64]

Herein lies the sacramental, even eucharistic nature of the CEBs' decolonial turn as the church of *lxs pobres*: These communities not only understand themselves to be a historical sacrament of God's presence and liberating action in history (in other words, a sacrament of God's reign), they also experience life together in community to be an effective site of God's presence, which feeds them and fills them with the grace of God's dream for creation.

To make this decolonial turn and believe in themselves as a sacrament of God's reign, the CEBs speak of the need to become incarnate in *la realidad* and to face reality for what it is—in one community leader's words, "*jodido*,"[65] or "screwed," but also and more fundamentally what Ellacuría calls "theologal," or infused with God's creative, salvific, and recreative presence.[66] Joseph Drexler-Dreis defines decolonial love as precisely this: "an orientation by which to make sense of one's place in the world and face up to reality" and "an historical sign that expresses something decisive about the divine, opening up the possibility of encounter with divine mystery, and thus salvation."[67] An overriding thesis in this book is that, in and through their decolonial turn, the CEBs open up the possibility of encounter with the divine and thus illuminate reality as sacraments of the reign of God. From this decolonial place of opening to the divine within reality, the CEBs both denounce that which is *jodido* in reality—where the divine is crucified in human beings and the natural world—and announce where the divine is present and active in historical healing and liberation. Where Maldonado-Torres calls this simultaneous yes and no, this decolonial love and rage, a characteristic of the decolonial turn, the CEBs as church of *lxs pobres* use the religious language of prophecy to express their alternative consciousness, self-expression, and action on behalf of God's liberative will for humanity and creation. We will explore this prophetic essence of the CEBs' decolonial praxis more fully in the following chapter on decolonial epistemology.

Maldonado-Torres posits that the decolonial turn unfolds as a collective project in which the *damnés* of the world emerge as agents of *epistemological, aesthetic*, and *social* transformation.[68] The Salvadoran CEBs embody each of these dimensions of transformative decolonial praxis in their three main dimensions of ecclesial praxis: *profecía*, or prophetic memory of suffering and martyrdom, denunciation of injustice, and annunciation of an-other possible world; *liturgia*, or liturgical celebrations and other creative rituals and artistic visions of liberation; and *diaconía*, which is a term borrowed from the Greek to roughly mean service and struggle for communal well-being, social transformation, and political liberation. Living out their baptismal anointing as prophets, priests, and organized advocates for liberation and God's reign of life, the CEBs are perpetually creating spaces where decolonial existence breaks through in the church and society. Let us now turn to the decolonization of knowledge, being, and power in each of these three dimensions of the CEBs' ecclesial praxis.

NOTES

1. Anita testifies to the resurgence of the CEBs among the repatriated communities of Cacaopera in "Acts of the Repatriated," §4. Octavio's story is told in "The Gospel according to the Zacamil," §8–9.

2. This language of re-membering has been used elsewhere to name the work of healing and liberating a broken and unjust world through reckoning with the past and cultivating communities of care and mutual relation. For example, see the work of two pioneering thinkers in feminist and womanist theologies: white feminist theologian Carter Heyward in *The Redemption of God: A Theology of Mutual Relation* (New York: University Press of America, 1982) and womanist anthropologist Linda E. Thomas in "Remember and Re-member," *Journal of Supervision and Training in Ministry* 14 (1992–1993): 241–252. Connections can also be drawn between the connotations of "re-membering" employed here and Toni Morrison's use of her term "rememory" in the novel *Beloved* (New York: Random House, 1987).

3. Anibal Quijano identifies four domains in this matrix, and Walter Mignolo adds a fifth at the insistence of Edgardo Lander, drawing on his work and that of Vandana Shiva. See Anibal Quijano, "Coloniality of Power, Eurocentrism, and Latin America," *Nepantla: Views from the South* 1, no. 3 (2000): 533–580 and "Coloniality and Modernity/Rationality," reprinted in *Cultural Studies* 21, nos. 2–3 (2007): 168–178; Walter D. Mignolo, "De-Linking," *Cultural Studies* 21, nos. 2–3 (2007), 478 and *Desobediencia Epistémica: Retórica de la Modernidad, Lógica de la Colonialidad, y Gramática de la Descolonialidad* (Buenos Aires: Ediciones del Signo, 2010), 12 and 79–80; and Edgardo Lander and Mariana Past, "Eurocentrism, Modern Knowledges, and the 'Natural' Order of Global Capital," in *Nepantla: Views from South* 3, no. 2 (2002): 245–268.

4. See Lander and Past, "Eurocentrism," 247.

5. Nelson Maldonado-Torres argues that the violence and destruction perpetrated within modernity/coloniality effects "the naturalization of extermination, expropriation, domination, exploitation, early death, and conditions that are worse than death, such as torture and rape." See Maldonado-Torres, "Outline of Ten Theses

on Coloniality and Decoloniality," 16, http://caribbeanstudiesassociation.org/docs/ Maldonado-Torres_Outline_Ten_Theses-10.23.16.pdf, accessed February 8, 2019. See also Nelson Maldonado-Torres, *Against War: Views from the Underside of Modernity* (Durham, NC: Duke University Press, 2008).

6. Maldonado-Torres, "Ten Theses," 23. For more on decolonial love, see Chela Sandoval, *Methodology of the Oppressed* (Minneapolis, MN: University of Minnesota Press, 2000). Joseph Drexler-Dreis has theorized decolonial love drawing on the theological pedagogy of Frantz Fanon and James Baldwin in *Decolonial Love: Salvation in Colonial Modernity* (New York: Fordham University Press, 2018).

7. Maldonado-Torres, "Outline of Ten Theses," 24.

8. Once again, we take inspiration for this turn of phrase from the Zapatista movement of Southern Mexico, which expresses and embodies a desire for a world "*donde quepan muchos mundos.*" See "Introduction," n28.

9. Francisco Bosch, ed., *Bendita mezcla: Hermanxs escuchadorxs, comunidades palabreras* (Montevideo, Uruguay: Fundación Amerindia, 2020), 6.

10. Articulación Continental Comunidades Eclesiales de Base, "Comunidades Eclesiales de Base: Identidad," www.cebcontinental.org, accessed October 10, 2019.

11. Comunidades Eclesiales de Base de El Salvador (CEBES), *Una Experiencia de Iglesia: Mística y Metodología* (Managua, Nicaragua: CEBES, n.d.), 11.

12. These words appear in a series of pamphlets designed for the CEBs to study the identity and mission of the church as "People of God" in and through twenty workshop sessions dedicated to a detailed engagement with the themes found in José Comblín's book *People of God* (Maryknoll, NY: Orbis Books, 2004).

13. FUNDAHMER, "Historia," https://fundahmerespanol.wordpress.com/quienes-somos/historia/, accessed October 10, 2020.

14. Grupo Libre, "Las CEBES," *Las CEBs Cantamos*, 2017, compact disc. NB: We have made the decision to include the Spanish lyrics to all of the songs we quote in part II in order to allow for those who are able to read the lyrics in the original language to do so. The English translation of these songs conveys the basic meaning of the lyrics, but not the poetry of their expression in Spanish.

15. Laurel Anne Marshall, "Un gesto vale más que mil palabras: las comunidades eclesiales de base de El Salvador en la construcción de celebraciones eucarísticas y bautismales" ("Actions Speak Louder than Words: Base Ecclesial Communities in El Salvador in the Construction of Eucharistic and Baptismal Celebrations") (master's thesis, San Salvador: Universidad Centroamericana "José Simeón Cañas," 2015), Appendix 1, xxxiii.

16. Marshall, xlii.

17. In addition to the description of these events in the *librito* "Colonio-Genesis," see Pope Alexander VI, *Inter Caetera* (1493), https://www.papalencyclicals.net/alex06/alex06inter.htm; Council of Castile, "The Requirement" (1510), http://nationalhumanitiescenter.org/pds/amerbegin/contact/text7/requirement.pdf; and King Phillip II, "Ordinances for the Discovery, Population, and Pacification of the Indies" (1573), http://codesproject.asu.edu/sites/default/files/THE%20LAWS%20OF%20THE%20INDIEStranslated.pdf. All accessed June 9, 2020.

Sacramento histórico del reino de Dios   209

18. Ada María Isasi-Díaz, "Solidarity: Love of Neighbors in the 1980s," in *Lift Every Voice: Constructing Christian Theologies from the Underside*, ed. Susan Brooks Thistlethwaite and Mary Potter Engel (San Francisco, CA: Harper & Row, 1990), 34. See also Isasi-Díaz, *En La Lucha: Elaborating a Mujerista Theology*, 10th Anniversary Edition (Minneapolis, MN: Fortress Press, 2004) and *Mujerista Theology: A Theology for the Twenty-First Century* (Maryknoll, NY: Orbis Books, 1996).

19. Walter Mignolo, *The Darker Side of Western Modernity: Global Futures, Decolonial Options* (Durham, NC: Duke University Press, 2011), 38.

20. Mignolo, xiv.

21. Mignolo, xxii.

22. Mignolo is also inspired by the Zapatistas in his vision of universal pluriversality. See "Introduction," n28.

23. Mignolo, 23. See also p. 54.

24. Mignolo, 70. *Sumak Kawsay* is an ancient Quechua phrase that means "good living" and implies harmonious relationships within and among human communities and with the natural world (Pachamama), https://www.pachamama.org/sumak-kawsay, accessed June 18, 2020.

25. Quijano, "Coloniality and Modernity/Rationality," 177.

26. See Agustín Luna's interview in *Sigue porque la vida sigue: Voces de las comunidades eclesiales de base ayer y hoy*, ed. José Gómez Martínez and Laurel Anne Marshall (Winston-Salem, NC: Library Partners Press, 2020), 138.

27. Luis Coto, Presentation on the History of the Salvadoran Ecclesial Base Communities at the CEBs' 50th Anniversary Celebration in Zacamil, February 2019.

28. Marshall, *Un gesto vale mas que mil palabras*, Appendices 6, 9, 10.3, and 11.

29. Maldonado-Torres, "Outline of Ten Theses," p. 23.

30. See David A. Sánchez, *From Patmos to the Barrio: Subverting Imperial Myths* (Minneapolis, MN: Fortress Press, 2008).

31. Many thanks to the grassroots Salvadoran theologian and founding member of FUNDAHMER, Armando Márquez Ochoa, for his reminder that this Greek term characterizes the communion sought by the CEBs in each of the forms of ecclesial praxis that we will feature in the following three chapters on decolonial knowledge, being, and power.

32. Interview with Avelino Castro in Gómez and Marshall, *Sigue porque la vida sigue*, 93–94.

33. See interview with Miguel Zepeda in Gómez and Marshall, *Sigue porque la vida sigue*, 165.

34. See Letter to the Hierarchy III, §2, in part I.

35. Popular hymn, unwritten, unpublished, and author unknown.

36. A whole host of literature in biblical studies and theology argues this same point, that Jesús's vision and praxis of the reign of God were a direct affront to the Roman Empire and form the basis for prophetic Christian critique of all forms of empire. See, for example, William R. Herzog II, *Jesus, Justice, and the Reign of God: A Ministry of Liberation* (Louisville, KY: Westminster John Knox Press, 2000);

Richard A. Horsley, *Jesus and Empire: The Kingdom of God and the New World Disorder* (Minneapolis, MN: Fortress Press, 2003); and Antonio González, *God's Reign and the End of Empires* (Miami, FL: Convivium Press, 2012). Wes Howard-Brook traces the historical movement from the biblical witness against empire to the Christian tradition's embrace of it in his two books: *"Come Out, My People!": God's Call Out of Empire in the Bible and Beyond* (Maryknoll, NY: Orbis Books, 2010) and *Empire Baptized: How the Church Embraced What Jesus Rejected, 2nd–5th Centuries* (Maryknoll, NY: Orbis Books, 2016).

37. *Lo cotidiano* as a *locus* of divine presence, sustenance, healing, and liberation is a concept that is central to Latina feminist and *mujerista* theologies. See Ada María Isasi-Díaz, "*Lo Cotidiano*: A Key Element of Mujerista Theology," *Journal of Hispanic/Latino Theology* 10, no. 1 (2002): 5–17.

38. Teresa Moreno de Melendez, "La Iglesia de los Pobres—Reino de Dios," presentation at Wake Forest University research symposium, "Does Church of the Poor Discourse Matter to the Marginalized?" Marietta, South Carolina, October 2019. This text is also cited as part of "Letter from the Community 'Nuevo Amanecer,'" §4.

39. Gómez and Marshall, *Sigue porque la vida sigue*, 88.

40. "Monseñor Romero" network of CEBs in La Libertad, "Sueño Comunidad," on *Las CEBs Cantamos*, 2017, compact disc.

41. We choose to translate *"razón"* as "verdicts" to preserve the sense of the systemic influence and efficacy of the kind of reason employed by colonial agents, by virtue of their money and power.

42. María Elena was a research consultant at our October 2019 research symposium on the Salvadoran Church of *lxs Pobres* that was sponsored by Wake Forest University. During our discussion on the reign of God, she spoke of and made note of these points on her *hoja de trabajo*.

43. §9.

44. From the Magnificat: "He has filled the hungry with good things, and sent the rich away empty" (Luke 1:53).

45. This insight was raised during the Wake Forest University Church of *lxs Pobres* Research Symposium, October 2019.

46. See interviews in Gómez and Marshall, *Sigue porque la vida sigue*, 67 and 99.

47. Maldonado-Torres, "Outline of Ten Theses," 30.

48. See Ignacio Ellacuría, "Church of the Poor, Historical Sacrament of Liberation," in *Ignacio Ellacuría: Essays on History, Liberation, and Salvation*, ed. Michael E. Lee (Maryknoll, NY: Orbis Books, 2013), 227–253.

49. Ellacuría, 246.

50. This quotation is invoked in many writings on the church of *lxs pobres*, just one of them being Jon Sobrino, "The Church of the Poor from John XXIII to Oscar Romero," *Concilium*, Issue 1 (2013): 99–107.

51. *EN*, §58. The document's characterization of extra-parroquial base communities as unequivocally possessing a "spirit of bitter criticism" and "an attitude of fault-finding and rejection" without giving voice to the Latin American CEBs' own self-understanding as committed to making manifest a church of *lxs pobres* whose

ecclesial communion is responsible to the oppressed, popular majorities is brash and imprudent. The document declines to call base communities outside of the parish structure "ecclesial" and establishes unilateral criteria that include

- that they avoid the ever-present temptation of systematic protest and a hypercritical attitude, under the pretext of authenticity and a spirit of collaboration;
- that they remain firmly attached to the local Church in which they are inserted, and to the universal Church . . . ;
- that they maintain a sincere communion with the pastors whom the Lord gives to His Church, and with the magisterium which the Spirit of Christ has entrusted to these pastors.

52. Consejo Episcopal Latinoamericano, "Conclusiones de la III Conferencia General Del Episcopado Latinoamericana (Puebla)," in *Las Cinco Conferencias Generales Del Episcopado Latinoamericano* (Bogotá: CELAM, 2014), §98, 279.

53. *EG*, §111 ff. *EG* relies on the people of God metaphor for the church and only mentions hierarchy in the context of qualifying the nature of the hierarchy's call to serve the whole people of God, the majority of which consists of the laity.

54. "An initiative of Pope Francis, the World Meeting of Popular Movements' (WMPM) purpose is to create an 'encounter' between Church leadership and grass-roots organizations working to address the 'economy of exclusion and inequality' (*Joy of the Gospel*, nos. 53–54) by working for structural changes that promote social, economic and racial justice." See http://popularmovements.org/about/.

55. *EG*, §198.

56. For example, the final document of the 2019 Synod on the Amazon suggested consideration of the priestly ordination of married, male community elders and the ordination of women deacons. In *Querida Amazonia*, Pope Francis ignores these recommendations entirely. See Leonardo Boff, "¿Para quiénes es, o no es querida la «Querida Amazonía»?" Servicios Koinonia Website, March 2, 2020, http://www.servicioskoinonia.org/boff/articulo.php?num=970 and Jamie Manson, "In 'Querida Amazonia,' Francis' Sacramental Imagination Stops Short of Women," *National Catholic Reporter*, February 18, 2020, https://www.ncronline.org/news/opinion/grace-margins/querida-amazonia-francis-sacramental-imagination-stops-short-women. Both Accessed June 17, 2020. We return to this issue in chapter 4 in our discussion of ecclesial governing authority. See also the excellent critiques of Pope Francis's enduring coloniality in Melissa Pagán, "Cultivating a Decolonial Feminist Integral Ecology: Extractive Zones and the Nexus of the Coloniality of Being/Coloniality of Gender" in *Journal of Hispanic/Latino Theology* Vol. 22 : No. 1, Article 6. (2020).

57. Pablo Richard explores the relationship between the CEBs, popular movements, and popular religious consciousness in "The Church of the Poor within the Popular Movement (*Movimiento Popular*)," in *Concilium* Volume 176 [*La Iglesia Popular: Between Fear and Hope*], ed. Leonardo Boff et al. (Edinburgh: T&T Clark, 1984), 10–16. "The Church of the Poor does not simply consist of the sum total of all Basic Ecclesial Communities, but includes all the liberating influence of these Basic Ecclesial Communities within the very nucleus of the people. These Basic Ecclesial

Communities, those who work in the pastoral field and certain other ecclesial institutions are—to employ the common metaphor—only the tip of the iceberg; the invisible mass of the Church of the Poor is hidden in the depths of that sea which consists of the popular movement and religious consciousness" (10).

58. Ellacuría, "Church of the Poor," 234.
59. Moreno de Melendez, "La Iglesia de los pobres—Reino de Dios."
60. Joseph Drexler-Dreis argues that the option for *lxs pobres* can be considered a decolonial option in his article, "The Option for the Poor as a Decolonial Option: Latin American Liberation Theology in Conversation with Teología India and Womanist Theology," *Political Theology* 18, no. 3 (2017): 269–86.
61. Laurel Anne Marshall, "Un gesto," Appendix 1, ii.
62. See "Act of the Repatriated," §2–3.
63. Marshall, "Un gesto," Appendix 6, xxix.
64. Bosch, *Bendita Mezcla*, 27.
65. See Gómez and Marshall, eds., *Sigue porque la vida sigue*, 138.
66. See "Introduction," n42.
67. Joseph Drexler-Dreis, *Decolonial Love: Salvation in Colonial Modernity* (New York: Fordham University Press, 2018), 119 and 153.
68. See Maldonado-Torres, "Outline of Ten Theses."

Chapter 2

Tomamos la palabra
Decolonial Knowledge in the Salvadoran Church of lxs Pobres

We are asleep. The system has us so complacent. To wake up, first we need to think with empathy, put ourselves in someone else's shoes, become aware of what others are suffering. Second, we need to think: is this what you want for your family, for your neighbors? No! You have to start to think critically, to study. If we don't, then we'll just stay asleep, saying Amen, Amen, and Amen. I believe in God. I believe. But not in a God like the Catholic Church has sold us.
—Ángela from the CEBs in Cacaopera[1]

In the small Christian communities of El Salvador's church of *lxs pobres*,[2] members young and old often join together in singing the protest songs of the twentieth-century *nueva trova* movement, traditional Salvadoran folk music, new songs written by the communities themselves, and the music of the renowned Central American popular masses.[3] These songs reverberate through rural chapels, urban community centers, family homes, under mango trees, and in town plazas during almost every gathering that the base communities organize, from weekly Celebrations of the Word and/or Eucharist, to Bible studies, youth group meetings, popular education sessions, political protests, and Salvadoran martyrs' anniversary celebrations. One of the songs that is often sung in full voice and with great pride during these gatherings is the *canto de despedida* of the Salvadoran Popular Mass, composed by Guillermo Cuéllar and entitled "Cuando el pobre crea en el pobre" ("When *el pobre* believes in *el pobre*").[4] The chorus of this song proclaims

Cuando el pobre crea en el pobre ya podremos cantar libertad. Cuando el pobre crea en el pobre construiremos la fraternidad.	When *el pobre* believes in *el pobre* Then we will be able to sing of freedom, When *el pobre* believes in *el pobre* We will construct fraternity.

These lyrics reveal the "decolonial turn" described in chapter 1; this decoloniality comes to creative expression in the base communities' insistence that the historically forgotten ones, the marginalized of the church and society, are the ones who hold the key to their own epistemological, ontological, and material liberation. The song's final verse fleshes out this decolonizing conviction in explicitly theological terms:

Cuando el pobre busca al pobre y nace la organización es que empieza nuestra liberación. Cuando el pobre anuncia al pobre la esperanza que Él nos dio, es que el reino entre nosotros nació.	When *el pobre* seeks out *el pobre* and organization is born, that's the beginning of our liberation. When *el pobre* announces to *el pobre* the hope that God gave us, that's the reign [of God] born among us.

Here the in-breaking of the reign of God, arguably a decolonial historical reality, depends on the knowledge that emerges from the process of *lxs pobres* entering into solidarity with *lxs pobres* and sharing the hope born of God's presence in their organized struggles for solidarity, survival, and liberation. The reign of God does not originate or end in places of economic affluence, political power, or institutional ecclesial authority, but from below—from the presence of God recognized, honored, and embodied in the historical dignity and solidarity of the marginalized.

Nelson Maldonado-Torres identifies epistemology, aesthetics, and activism as three realms in which the *damnés* of the earth collectively engage in forms of praxis that decolonize oppressive modes of knowledge, being, and power in culture, religion, and society.[5] This chapter and the two that follow flesh out key elements of the CEBs' decolonial ecclesiology as it has emerged from their ongoing struggles to uproot the enduring effects of coloniality in each of these three realms. In these communities, *lxs pobres* have been engaged in the evolving and ongoing process of waking up to reality and "believing in *lxs pobres*"—in themselves and their communities—for over fifty years. This has been a decolonial process of recovering human dignity and capacity for critical thought and creative subjectivity, as well as a rediscovering of the Christian vocation to engage in decolonial action for the transformation of an unjust world. This process has been facilitated by praxes of dialogue and prophetic memory, aesthetic and liturgical creativity, and committed action for mutual aid and social change. In and through these overlapping dimensions of the CEBs' pastoral praxis, the small communities at the heart of the Salvadoran church of *lxs pobres* live out their threefold baptismal anointing, decolonize the church and society, and thereby participate in the construction of God's reign as prophetic producers of knowledge, priestly cocreators of being and beauty, and divinely empowered subjects of social and historical transformation.[6]

This current chapter focuses on the decolonization of knowledge production that has taken place in the CEBs over the past fifty years. Maldonado-Torres identifies epistemology and the production of knowledge as foundational to the decolonial turn described in chapter 1. In his words, "decoloniality involves a decolonial epistemic turn whereby the *damné* emerges as a questioner, thinker, theorist, writer, and communicator."[7] Walter Mignolo calls this process—exemplified in the remarks of the Ángela in the epigraphs above—epistemic "delinking" or "disobedience." Yazmín from the CEB "San Romero" offers similar sentiments:

> I think that the church itself has never really called to me and I've never really understood it. . . . But I think that they have been mutilating it. They have been mutilating the gospel. . . . They've just held onto what is most convenient for them. Which is to keep the people asleep.[8]

In Mignolo's view, this process of waking up to and delinking from the hegemonic epistemology of Christian supremacy and modern rationality requires "learning to unlearn" the illusion of disembodied universality at the heart of Western theo- and ego-politics of knowledge.[9] It requires unveiling the contextuality and, therefore, the partiality of Western epistemology and critiquing its claims to universality for what they are—a farce. But delinking also requires the affirmation that other epistemologies exist in multiple forms in multiple places and in multiple embodied subjectivities around the world. Mignolo calls this affirmation of epistemic multiplicity the "geo- and body-politics of knowledge."[10] Knowledge is always and everywhere geo-graphical and em-bodied, contingent on both one's historical place and bodily experience in the world. Decoloniality points its scholars and practitioners toward knowledge emerging from geo-graphical "locations of the world that endured the effects and consequences of Western imperial and capitalist expansion,"[11] along with knowledge emerging from historically colonized bodies, particularly Black, Indigenous, and other bodies of color. Decoloniality works from the bottom up, from the re-vindication of "languages and subjectivities that have [been] denied the possibility of participating in the production, distribution, and organization of knowledge."[12]

It is important to note that decolonial epistemology changes not only the content of the conversation but also the terms themselves. As Mignolo puts it, "de-linking cannot be performed, obviously, within the frame of the theo- and the ego-logical [viz., Christian and modern] politics of knowledge and understanding. For, how can you de-link within the epistemic frame from where you want to de-link?"[13] Given the impossibility of such a task, he claims that the Christian framework—even when it is recast by liberation theology—is not capable of producing or practicing decoloniality. In the famous words of Audre Lorde, "the master's tools will never dismantle the master's house. They may allow us temporarily to beat him at his own game, but they will never enable us to bring about genuine change."[14] The CEBs consider themselves to be Christian communities (indeed, they consider themselves to be church!). However, we contend that their geo- and body-politics of knowledge delink from the "master's tools" of colonial Catholicism and reconnect them with the anti-imperial geo- and body-politics—the tools, so to speak—of a first century, colonized Palestinian Jewish *tekton*—in Aramaic, a *negara*; in Spanish, *un hacelotodo*; and in English, a menial laborer, handyman, or jack-of-all-trades.[15] Some CEBs are retrieving the rich wisdom of their Indigenous heritage, which we will discuss below, but even when they are not, they are performing the decolonial work of what Gloria Anzaldúa calls "border thinking," which in decolonial terms refers to ways of knowing that exist on the margins and connect with different geographies and bodies that have been subjected to imperialism and coloniality throughout modern history.[16] There is a self-recognition between the CEBs and the wounds and struggles of the Hebrew people in the Exodus, Israel in exile, Jesús in Nazareth, and the first communities of disciples following the Way of the One who preached and made manifest an anti-imperial reign of God[17]—arguably a world in which many worlds can flourish and all people are free to live life in abundance. The church of *lxs pobres* is a decolonial church insofar as its relinking with the story of Jesús is accompanied by a delinking from colonial frameworks of theological knowledge and ecclesial authority.

The epistemic delinking that the CEBs perform when they "believe in *lxs pobres*" and come together to produce knowledge collectively is best understood in correlation with their praxis of prophetic ministry. The CEBs understand *profecía* to be a fundamental Christian vocation to both denounce the oppressive systems and values of the *anti-reino* and announce the good news of the reign of God.[18] In this chapter, we locate the decolonial building blocks of the CEBs' prophetic ecclesial ministry in their dialogical pastoral method and their praxis of historical memory, both of which are productive of decolonial knowledge and, as a result, what the CEBs often refer to as "adult faith." We conclude that, in and through these prophetic praxes of decolonial dialogue and historical memory, the CEBs embody a decolonial faith that re-members and reimagines the role of tradition and authority in Catholic ecclesiology.

Tomamos la palabra 217

THE DECOLONIALITY OF PROPHETIC KNOWLEDGE PRODUCTION: FROM METHOD TO MEMORY

A Decolonial Method

The *ver-juzgar-actuar* (see-judge-act) method of pastoral work and theological reflection is perhaps best known in academic theology and religious studies for its use by the Latin American bishops at Medellín and Puebla and by liberation theologians who both influenced and were influenced by these landmark conferences. Its roots, however, lie in Europe and the work of a Belgian priest named Fr. Joseph Cardijn, who, prior to World War II, coined the methodology and its name and inspired the reflection and action of many Catholic social action groups such as the Young Christian Workers, Young Christian Students, and the Christian Family Movement. In the 1940s, Latin American Catholic Action groups, precursors to the earliest ecclesial base communities, especially in Brazil, were increasingly influenced by Cardijn's see-judge-act method, and farmers, workers, and students were motivated by it to influence the secular world in which they lived.[19]

Methodologically speaking, in both their initial formation and their everyday activities, the CEBs typically begin their reflections with observation and analysis of their concrete situation of oppression and injustice (see), they proceed to read that situation in the light of resources from their understanding of the Christian faith tradition (judge), and then they determine how to struggle for transformation of the unjust situation in accordance with the liberating will of God (act). The novelty of this method is that, rather than deductively applying universal (i.e., colonial) doctrinal or theological principles to their particular circumstances, these communities employ an inductive method in which "the situations themselves become theological loci of a discernment which must be made by way of reading the 'signs of the times'" in light of the Word of God.[20] It is important to note that this is not a linear process, but rather a dynamic and dialectical method of continual movement in which each stage of the process is related to the others: "In a certain sense, judgment and action are part of seeing. On the other hand, action helps us to move to a new seeing and judgment which are much more profound and illuminating."[21] Prior judgments and actions influence what and how the community sees and, in turn, what they see then leads to a new round of judgment and action. In recent decades, the Salvadoran CEBs have named *celebrar* (celebrate) as part of this methodological dynamism, and chapter 3 will engage the decolonization of being and creative expression that takes place in this now explicitly recognized step.[22]

The CEBs' see-judge-act pastoral methodology has facilitated and cultivated their decolonial epistemic turn, for wherever and whenever it is implemented, the members of the CEBs themselves are engaged in the process of knowledge production. It is important to note here, however, that the see-judge-act method is not inherently decolonial. While the CEBs begin with naming and analyzing their concrete situation in the first step, the entire pastoral-hermeneutical circle of see-judge-act is bathed in the light of a decidedly decolonial faith—a faith that first makes an option for *lxs pobres*. What the community members see or neglect to see in the first step depends on prior judgments about what is important to see and from what perspective it should be seen. Depending on one's social location within the colonial matrix of power, a colonized or colonizing subject might see only that which reinscribes their positionality in the power matrix. As Luis Rivera-Pagán points out, the colonized themselves can be imbued with a colonial mindset, for

> colonial discourse mystifies imperial dominion. It crafts by persuasion what the mechanisms of coercion are unable to achieve: the fine-tuned consent and admiration of the colonized subjects. It diffuses and affirms imperial ideological hegemony. Its greatest creation is what V. S. Naipaul has called mimic men.[23]

Imperial hegemony makes it difficult to see anything but that which reinforces hegemony.

What makes the CEBs' pastoral method decolonial is that it is founded in a prior stance of decolonial faith and faith-filled decolonial commitment to participate in the preferential option for *lxs pobres* made by God throughout salvation history and definitively in Jesús of Nazareth. While *lxs pobres*, their concrete situation, and their experiences as the church of *lxs pobres* represent the *material* starting point for the CEBs' pastoral/theological reflection, faith is still the *formal* starting point. As Clodovis Boff maintains in his reflections on the methodology of liberation theology, "it is only methodologically that one begins with 'seeing' or 'reality,' when in fact faith is always present as the alpha and the omega of the entire process."[24] A decolonial Christian faith requires a prior prophetic commitment to seeing, naming, and denouncing that which had previously been obscured and naturalized by the colonial power matrix: the reality of oppression of and violence against the colonized, that is, the reality of coloniality. The CEBs, in their most foundational reflections on their faith and identity as the church of *lxs pobres* at the base of the church and society, perform what Enrique Dussel maintains is already a decolonizing of epistemology and the fundamental condition for the possibility of decolonial theology:

> To think theologically from the oppressed *colonial* subjectivity, and having *critical* consciousness that this "being colonial" is in fact the theme of this reflection; that is already an act of adopting the perspective of an *epistemological*

Tomamos la palabra

de-colonizing of theology. And it is already the transcendental presupposition that conditions the possibility of *all* theological reflection.²⁵

Through the see-judge-act method, the CEBs then cultivate decolonial critical consciousness of and reflection on the reality of "being colonial," which they have historically named as being *lxs pobres*—a social, economic, racial, and theological class at the base of unjustly imposed secular and religious hierarchies.

Within this decolonial consciousness, the CEBs cultivate the aforementioned sense of "believing in" themselves, *lxs pobres*, the peripheral ones, as legitimate and necessary producers of knowledge and subjects of historical reality. This belief in the epistemological authority of the periphery and the "power of the poor in history"²⁶ stems from the decolonial faith commitments described above, but it is cultivated and embodied in and through the practice of *dialogue* as an integral component of the see-judge-act pastoral method. Indeed, another aspect of the CEBs' implementation of the see-judge-act method that makes it decolonial is the fact that it is implemented as a dialogical process, and not imposed from above. The people's active participation in the collective process, not their submission to imposed observations and interpretations, is what allows for and facilitates their formation of communities with decolonial critical consciousness and faith-filled commitment to the transformation of the world.²⁷ In and through such participation in the dialogical process of knowledge production and social action, the communal and individual dignity of base communities and their members is affirmed. As individuals and communities, they are able to *tomar la palabra*—to speak a word, to take the microphone—and offer their questions, insights, and wisdom to the communal process of discernment.

A key component of this dialogical process, and its decolonizing potential, is simply the freedom to ask questions, express doubts, and raise *inquietudes*. Consider, for example, the depth of questioning at work in reflections offered by Gustavo, a leader and musician from the CEB Pueblo de Dios en Camino:

> We are in another stage in history where we are obligated to reflect on Jesús from outside of the temple. This has caused me to deepen in restlessness, and I wonder about the following questions:
>
> - Why call ourselves *ecclesial* base communities if this new reality contrasts with the canons and norms of the church where I grew up?
> - Why be Christian, if this is a name that is too big for us, compared to the ideal of Jesús and the reality we see every day of injustice, of death, of rape, of abuse, of discrimination, and the religious representatives of Christian churches do not say anything, so approving of injustice and war?

- How are we to transform this reality that destroys our being, and [causes] the slow death of the natural world from our small Christian community?
- Why should we follow a Hebraic religious culture that comes from other very different ways of thinking, if we, too, come from cultures that are rich in a philosophy that loves all living things?
- Why won't the Catholic Church stop conquering other aboriginal cultures to inculcate them about the Hebrew God and all of the canons and norms?

As Christians, we speak of God, we exalt him, we worship him, we make him omnipresent, omniscient, all-powerful, invincible, we applaud him, we have him saved away in the temple, we take him flowers, we bow down, we celebrate his *fiestas*, but what do we do for the common good of all?[28]

Gustavo's questions here not only are indicative of epistemic delinking from the persistent coloniality of Roman Catholicism but break open the possibility of constructing new forms of knowledge that are more reflective of the reign of God as an-other world in which many worlds are free to coexist. Indeed, he also remarks that while Jesús shows us a way to become more fully human,

> The Catholic Church is not the official sponsor of the Spirit. As if it were Coca-Cola. No way. That's why we also believe that the Spirit is in the evangelical churches, too. Not just in the Catholic Church. And in people who are atheists. We believe that Jesús is there. And often, with much more presence than in those who raise hosts.[29]

The dialogical process of expressing *inquietudes* and *tomando la palabra* is not an easy one. It is important to remember here that the dignity and divine vocations of *lxs pobres*, the marginalized, the colonized, have been depreciated throughout history. Colonialism and coloniality operate on the assumption that all that the colonized have to offer that is of worth is their land (which was promptly stolen from them under colonialism) and their labor (which continues to be exploited through the coloniality of neoliberal global capitalism). Within this logic, the word of *lxs pobres* is worth naught, while the word of the rich is worth everything. As the wisdom writer Sirach states, "A rich man speaks and all are silent, his wisdom they extol to the clouds. A poor man speaks and they say, 'Who is that?'" (Sirach 13:22). This has led Salvadorans living in poverty to embody a lack of esteem for what they, their own neighbors, and their communities have to contribute. Oftentimes, among *lxs pobres* themselves, "what a laborer says has no weight beside the word of an engineer or a priest." They may say to one another, "at least they have studied. You are like us, you know nothing."[30] According to Dominique Barbé, this is why each base community is founded through a gentle and gradual pedagogy, which teaches the humble once again to listen to each other and speak to each other *in community*; to *give worth* to what they have to say as they express themselves to each other. It is really the miracle of the healing of the deaf-mute once again.[31]

Similarly, the CEBs of El Salvador are challenged with this same habit of low self-worth among their members, which hinders full participation. As one priest observes,

> it is not easy for *los pobres* to participate. They have always been told that they can't, that they don't know anything, that they are nothing. They have always been told that sacred things are not for them. One man said to me: "Father, I can't come, I'm not going to get up and embarrass myself!"[32]

Having been dispossessed and despised for so long has left its mark on those who often have little faith in their own ability to contribute something positive to the construction of a better world. The place of dialogue in the base communities' see-judge-act method, therefore, has opened up space for decolonizing the reigning epistemology of ecclesiastical authority, expert knowledge, and elitist educational standards. When members of the CEBs tell their stories, they often highlight what a transformative experience participation in the community has been for them as individuals who had been socialized to remain silent and submissive to authority. They narrate a decolonial movement from embarrassment, discomfort, and self-consciousness at the prospect of speaking their mind to courage, confidence, and excitement at the opportunity to actively and vocally *tomar la palabra* in communal conversations and decision-making, as well as biblical study, theological reflection, and prophetic speech acts. This is especially true for young people and rural women. In part I, young Adonay introduces himself by describing how being active in the CEBs helped him overcome his fear of public speaking and of sharing his opinions in a group:

> I went to the front. . . . My knees were shaking at the beginning, but then everything was okay. That was the first time I stopped being nervous, and it was a beautiful feeling, because not being nervous is a big challenge for me.[33]

Rosa Elvira Moya, too, relates how her participation in the Mothers' Congregations of the CEBs in the north of Morazán was like breaking free from a cage:

> I began to feel my value as a woman, and now I can even attend to children and young people and I participate in all the activities. But before I was really shy.

I couldn't say what I was thinking or feeling. I just listened. Thanks be to God that today, now that I am grown, I have lost some of my fear.[34]

On a communal level, the CEB Pueblo de Dios en Camino tells of their not inconsequential interaction with a new parish priest in the year 2000:

> We were working with a very verticalist and powerful ecclesial vision, where we lay people had no voice and made no decisions. We just had to get on board and say, "Yes, Father. Yes, Father." But since we had learned from our past, we could not be subdued. And we knew we had dignity, too. We couldn't let ourselves be disrespected by them. So we began to question the priest. And he said it was better for us to be out than in.[35]

Here we can see how the courage to *tomar la palabra* is not limited to internal dialogue within the CEBs themselves, but vis-à-vis other ecclesial authorities and actors.

Informed and liberated from fear by their preferential option for *lxs pobres* and their commitment to dialogue, the CEBs have taken concrete steps toward constructing a decolonial epistemology and thereby producing prophetic knowledge. Within the see-judge-act method, the CEBs practice seeing—seeking out and listening to—voices that have been obscured or silenced in secular and salvation history, including their own. For example, in the story of Jesús feeding the 5,000,[36] the CEBs reflect on their own experiences of traveling in groups and consider that if there were 5,000 men, there must have been at least that many women and children also traveling in the group. Women who cooked for combatants in the mountains during the war affirm that the number of troops in the area never reflected the numbers of cooks, messengers, and female medics holding the camps together. The CEBs specifically look to the margins of the scriptural accounts and to the social dynamics that affect their own reality to paint a complete picture and to "see" as accurately as possible. In judging, the CEBs use traditional ecclesial sources to discern the presence and judgment of God in history as well as sources that have been forgotten, pushed aside, or explicitly disavowed. They seek out marginalized and noncanonical theological sources precisely out of their own experience of being marginalized and discredited. They have found authority in their own voice and perspective, so they are open to hearing from discredited sources like Indigenous religious texts, poetry, and those who have been persecuted by the church and government in order to discern how to act in their own situations. Finally, the CEBs' practice of shared homilies during liturgy reflects their commitment to dialogue and the practice of believing in their own ability to interpret scripture.[37] Each community member is encouraged to share what he or she hears in the day's readings, to put their perspective in common and to be nuanced by others' views. The stress is not on who has the most correct or authoritative interpretation. The CEBs believe that in a diversity of opinions, guided always by the Holy Spirit and measured against the criteria of the Jesús of the scriptures and the God of Life they have come to know, a more genuinely liberating and life-giving understanding can emerge.

While this dialogical methodology permeates all that the CEBs do, the work of epistemic delinking is most evident in their explicitly self-declared "prophetic" activity. In most organized Salvadoran CEBs, members explicitly articulate their prophetic vocation to analyze their national and communal reality critically in light of the Word of God and to speak out on social and political issues affecting their societies. The fact that the members of the CEBs themselves are doing this analysis, not waiting for a word from a priest or bishop (or even a pope like Francis!), indicates that an epistemic turn has taken place here. From their earliest inception, collective interpretation of the Bible facilitated this epistemological revolution in the CEBs. Today, their prophetic activities of lay-led popular education, consciousness-raising, theological reflection, remembering martyrdom, and public protest of injustice are all examples of delinking from the colonial epistemology of the institutional church, in favor of a knowledge base *at the base* of the church and society. We explore the implications of this for how the CEBs conceive of ecclesial tradition and authority below. First, however, we turn to a decolonial analysis of one of the CEBs' most salient praxes of prophetic knowledge production: historical memory of suffering and martyrdom.

Historical Memory

In and through their pastoral method, the CEBs have been decolonizing epistemology at the base of the church and society for over fifty years. One fundamental aspect of this process has been their epistemic delinking from the coloniality of historical knowledge through their praxis of constructing their own *memoria histórica*, which forms the basis both for the historical narratives highlighted in part I of this book and the re-membering of the hoped-for reign of God that guides the pilgrim CEBs in their ecclesial praxis. Refusing to accept the colonial version of the past, a history of the victors, and its implicit vision for the future, the CEBs have reclaimed their own historical memory as an integral component of their identity and a necessary ingredient in their resistance to the violence of imperial hegemony. As one of the Salvadoran base communities puts it in a post on their Facebook page: "*Si no tenemos memoria, no existimos*" ("If we do not have memory, we do not exist"). [38]

To begin with, as part I made evident, the CEBs remember the conquest and colonization of Latin America precisely as conquest, not discovery, and, with the collaboration of popular educators and publications from groups like *Equipo Maíz* in San Salvador,[39] they deliberately uncover the coloniality of their history. As Gustavo puts it,

> if we are talking about the identity of the CEBs, clearly, we have Jesús as a reference point, and we have other women and men who are martyrs, but we also have to make a study of "who am I" in this land called America. We have to analyze "where do I come from?"[40]

In this vein, base community members are generally very cognizant of their Indigenous history and critical of the way in which land ownership was concentrated in the hands of the creole oligarchy throughout the course of the nineteenth century. They are cognizant and critical of President Maximiliano Hernández Martínez's violent repression of an Indigenous uprising seeking the redistribution of land in Western El Salvador in 1932.[41] And they are cognizant and critical of how this massacre of more than 10,000 Indigenous people is somehow linked with the near extinction of Indigenous identity in twentieth-century El Salvador.[42] Most of all, though, the base communities are producers of historical knowledge with regard to the history of the late twentieth-century armed conflict in their country. In particular, the CEBs ritually remember the civilian massacres and disappearances, as well as the heroes and martyrs of that conflict, in which nearly 75,000 civilians were killed, mostly by government forces.

For example, the base communities take part in yearly anniversary rituals dedicated to commemorating massacres committed by the Salvadoran armed forces, including Tres Calles (†1975, five victims); Río Sumpul (†1980, over 600 victims); and El Mozote (†1980, nearly 1,000 victims). Some CEBs also remember El Calabozo (†1982, over 200 victims); Tenango and Guadalupe (†1983, about 250 victims); and Copapayo (†1983, 142 victims). They also ritually remember the priests and religious women of the Salvadoran popular church, who gave their lives for the people's liberation struggles, such as Rutilio Grande (†1977), Alfonso Navarro (†1977), Ernesto Barrera (†1978), Octavio Ortiz (†1979), Rafael Palacios (†1979), Alirio Napoleón Macías (†1979), Silvia Maribel Arriola (†1981), and the "UCA martyrs," six Jesuit priests and two laywomen who worked at the University of Central America (†1989).[43] Saint Óscar Romero (†1980) holds pride of place among these martyrs, and evidence of his memory is ubiquitous in the CEBs, due to the powerful and very public platform he occupied as the prophetic archbishop of San Salvador from 1977 until he was assassinated by a government-sponsored death squad in 1980.[44] Countless lay catechists and other leaders and members of the CEBs themselves were also targeted, tortured, and murdered by military and paramilitary forces during the years leading up to and during

El Salvador's Civil War (1980–1992). These martyrs are less widely recognized and remembered, but many base communities are making efforts to recuperate the memory of their own communities' stories from the war years, including the stories of their leaders and other loved ones who were killed. For example, in the hamlets of Cacaopera, in the northeastern Department of Morazán, the women of the base communities have recently undertaken a process of recording and reflecting on their memories of suffering and communal resistance to violence and oppression before, during, and after the war. The annual commemorations of the massacre at El Chupadero (†1981, 70 victims), described in the introduction of this book, began as a result of this re-membering.

The memory of Romero, other clergy and churchwomen contains traces of coloniality in the primacy afforded to privileged male clerics and women religious, especially the slain North American churchwomen—Ita Ford, Maura Clark, Dorothy Kazel, and Jean Donovan.[45] However, increasing local memory efforts contribute to the ongoing decolonization of history and the reclaiming of historical knowledge production by those whom colonial history has tried to erase. In the case of the massacre at El Mozote, for example, the Salvadoran government and the U.S. State Department denied the account of the sole survivor, Rufina Amaya, a campesina woman who had just witnessed the brutal murder of her entire family, until years after the war. According to official accounts, the massacre had been staged by guerilla forces to make the government look bad.[46] Similarly, Bishop Aparicio allegedly claimed to the international press that the civilians being disappeared leading up to the war in El Salvador were just hiding, with the same goal of undermining the government.[47] The claims of the Salvadoran government, the U.S. State Department, and Bishop Aparicio have been accepted until proven false, while Rufina's claims, and the claims of many other traumatized, mourning families, have been questioned until proven true. The burden of proof always weighs on the shoulders of the *lxs pobres*.

The CEBs' memory of the massacre of El Mozote and other practices of remembering suffering and resistance in the base communities of El Salvador have been a means of both interrupting the dominant narratives of imperial hegemony and forming the CEBs in their communal and individual identities as moral agents of resistance to violence and oppression in the past and present.[48] Furthermore, this practice of "dangerous memory"[49] both nurtures an alternative imagination within the CEBs and inspires them to action for an alternative future based on that imagination. Each of these elements and effects of the base communities' historical memory contribute to their epistemic delinking from colonized accounts of the past in which their heroes, martyrs, and lost loved ones are erased from history or dehumanized and blamed for their own demise (as terrorists, communists, etc.). In and through their practices of remembering the suffering of the colonized, the CEBs engage in epistemological decolonization of not only the past, but also of visions for a more just future in which an-other world is possible. This is healing and liberating work. The stories of the CEBs will undoubtedly contribute to fulfilling Chinua Achebe's hope, cited by Luis Rivera-Pagán in his work on decolonial theology, that the twenty-first century "will see the first fruits . . . of the process of 're-storying' peoples who had been knocked silent by the trauma of all kinds of dispossession."[50]

The CEBs not only look back on the past to denounce their historical dispossession and announce the good news of their martyrs and Indigenous ancestors. They are constantly vigilant within and critical of their present reality and are committed to forging ahead in their annunciation and construction of the reign of God for present and future generations. As the prophetic people of God, the CEBs denounce the injustices and violence of coloniality and announce the good news of liberation in each of the dimensions of the colonial matrix of power, specifically in the realms of religion, economics, politics, gender relations, and ecology. This extensive scope of the CEBs' prophetic activity will become more evident in the chapters that follow. For now, let us consider the prophetic nature of the CEBs' epistemic delinking from conceptions of tradition and authority as they operate within the coloniality of Roman Catholic ecclesiology.

HORIZONS IN DECOLONIAL ECCLESIOLOGY: TRADITION AND TEACHING AUTHORITY

The Decolonial Danger of Adult Faith for Catholic Ecclesiology

The decolonial method of prophetic knowledge production that we have just described not only begins with the decolonial starting point of faith in the God of *lxs pobres* and belief in the worth and dignity of the colonized as epistemological and historical subjects; this method is also an ongoing and dialectical process that results in what members of the CEBs often call an "adult faith." For over 500 years, the impoverished and marginalized majorities of the land that is now known as El Salvador have been told how and what to think and believe. They have been infantilized and indeed dehumanized by the Roman Catholic church insofar as they have been cast as passive recipients of a faith tradition that required strict adherence to doctrine and to canonical and social norms and that, as we saw earlier, discouraged common people from questioning anything. Consider the CEBs' own description of traditional Salvadoran religious life prior to the advent of Salvadoran social conflicts of the mid- to late twentieth century:

In the municipalities and local communities, there was an intense religious life. Peasants participated in Catholic ceremonies, as much in the Sunday masses as in special celebrations, such as Holy Week and patron saints' feast days. The values and conceptions that these religious activities reproduced tended to create the predisposition in peasants to resignedly accept the conditions of their social life, the conditions of poverty and social domination in which they lived. The discourse of the priests was predominated by the spiritualistic conception that Catholics should conform themselves to the life that they were given and offer their sufferings to God, because in this way they would enter into the Kingdom of Heaven.[51]

This form of religiosity still pervades many Salvadoran parishes, and most adult members of the CEBs grew up with this kind of Catholic faith in which clerics held the keys not only to knowledge, but salvation itself. It is important to note that not all of the baptized always bought into this passive religiosity and many participated in anti-colonial and decolonial resistance movements throughout Salvadoran history. And yet, while the vast majority of Salvadoran Catholics have always been impoverished, the Catholic Church in El Salvador has not always been a church of *lxs pobres*.

In the CEBs, the church of *lxs pobres* is a historical sacrament of God's reign insofar as it forms its members as individuals and as communities to relate to God, one another, and all of creation as free and conscious subjects who can think for themselves and make their own decisions in *koinonia*, as a community, without desire for reward or fear of punishment by the church or by God. Free and conscious subjects do not accept the faith that has been handed to them naively or uncritically, as Western Christian culture has typically assumed a child would or should do.[52] Free and conscious subjects who commit themselves to the Christian faith are communally formed and are committed to life in community, but they are also autonomous adults who do not allow themselves to be indoctrinated or manipulated by anyone. Herein lies the connection between decolonial epistemology and what the CEBs call "adult faith"—its most recognizable feature is the capacity to think for oneself and publicly question received knowledge, particularly from the vantage point of solidarity with those who have historically been marginalized and silenced by the coloniality of knowledge. For the CEBs, however, the capacity to think, question, and actively participate in this process of knowledge production lies in a more profound, divine source—that is, in the experience of God within oneself, within one's community, within other human communities, and within creation as a whole. An adult faith has its basis in this experience of encounter with the divine and in a resultant revolution in one's understanding of and relationship with the divine, whose image and likeness are no longer equated with the *terrateniente*, the wealthy white male, the bishop, or the ordained priest. This image of God that the adult faith of the CEBs holds up is a God who is in all things, and especially in the struggles of suffering and oppressed humanity and creation: *el Dios de lxs pobres*. In this vision, God is not like an *hacendado* who rewards and punishes according to "His" whim or human merit, nor is God a benevolent power broker who will step in to resolve your problems if your faith is strong enough. The God of the CEBs is the God of the Bible—the God of Life, the God of *lxs pobres*, who suffers with and in them and who accompanies them in their struggles for survival, dignity, and liberation. Adult faith in this God—that which we might also call decolonial faith—requires making a commitment, *un compromiso*, to active solidarity with and participation in these struggles. For the church of *lxs pobres* in El Salvador, that commitment is suffused with constant, conscious efforts to critically assess all processes of knowledge production and to humbly, yet confidently and courageously make public the prophetic knowledge that is produced among the colonized in the CEBs. This includes prophetic critique of the church itself, and its penchant for overrepresentation of itself as the means and measure of knowledge and truth.

Sylvia Wynter argues that the "struggle of our times" is the struggle against the coloniality of being/power/truth/freedom that has ensued from the Western overrepresentation of "Man" as the optimally economic bourgeois subject.[53] This neoliberal iteration of "Man" is a descriptive statement about humanity that claims the extra-human authorship of the natural and social sciences, particularly biology and economics. This anthropological overrepresentation has evolved, Wynter posits, from the "True Christian Self," articulated by the premodern Latin Christian Church, and from the degodded, first iteration of Man that came about in Renaissance Humanism and the Enlightenment, when the European laity rebelled against the exclusive claim to salvific power by the clergy. Against this epistemic and ontological overrepresentation of one, colonial and contextual but purportedly "universal" conception of the human, Wynter challenges the colonized to represent themselves in her insistence that "the buck stops with us."[54] Arguably, this is what the CEBs are also saying and embodying as they struggle to practice an "adult faith" that corrects the overrepresentation of all three layers of Western Christian descriptive statements about humanity—premodern, modern, and neoliberal. In El Salvador, the buck stops with the church of *lxs pobres*. The epistemic struggle of the Salvadoran church of *lxs pobres* is a struggle to redefine and relativize the Christian self, reconceptualize what it means to be a rational subject, and reconfigure the economics of neoliberal capitalism. In and through that struggle and the "adult faith" that it produces, the base communities tip the scales of overrepresentation and assert their right to represent themselves not only in the realms of politics and economics, but in the realms of church tradition and ecclesial authority as well. The exercise of a decolonial adult faith in the CEBs, then, has particular implications for their role, especially within the teaching office of the Roman Catholic church, that reveal the continuing ambiguity of post-conciliar Catholic ecclesiology and challenge popular and canonical understandings of ecclesial authority.

The Coloniality of Tradition and Authority in Roman Catholic Ecclesiology

In order to critically engage normative Roman Catholic conceptions of tradition and authority, we must first take a step back and define the Catholic concept of revelation. To be more precise, we must discuss the different understandings of revelation that exist in tension in the church today. Before the Second Vatican Council, the magisterium of the Catholic Church considered itself to play the "teaching" role in the church, the *ecclesia docens*, while the faithful were exclusively the ones being taught, the *ecclesia discens*. These strictly separated roles reflected a neoscholastic, propositional model of revelation that was challenged by Vatican II's "Dogmatic Constitution on Divine Revelation," *Dei Verbum*. Instead of understanding revelation to be a series of doctrinal statements entrusted to the magisterium to be memorized and uncritically parroted by the faithful, this document offers a relational, Trinitarian understanding of revelation as the gratuitous self-communication of God to humanity for the sake of human salvation:

> It pleased God, in his goodness and wisdom, to reveal himself and to make known the mystery of his will (see Eph. 1:9), which was that people can draw near to the Father, through Christ, the Word made flesh, in the Holy Spirit, and thus become sharers in the divine nature (see Eph. 2:18; 2 Peter 1:4). By this revelation, then, the invisible God (see Col 1:15; 1 Tim. 17), from the fullness of his love, addresses men and women as his friends (see Ex. 33:11; John 15:14–15) and lives among them (see Bar. 3:38), in order to invite and receive them into his own company. [. . .] The most intimate truth about God and human salvation shines forth for us in Christ, who is himself both the mediator and the sum total of revelation.[55]

While the light of human reason is capable of providing knowledge of and encounter with God in and through encounter with created reality, according to *Dei Verbum*, God has chosen to reveal Godself to humanity so that the divine will to save "can, in the present condition of the human race, be known by all with ease, with firm certainty, and without the contamination of error."[56] With the coming of Christ and the preaching of Christ's gospel by the apostles, the revelation of God comes to its fulfillment, its completion. The apostles recorded their salvific encounter with Christ and the gospel message of Christ in sacred scripture. The ongoing tradition of the church encompasses the church's ever-evolving interpretation and application of the scriptural witness to divine revelation that was handed down by the apostles, particularly through the apostolic succession of bishops.

Dei Verbum therefore identifies sacred scripture and tradition as the means by which God has ordained that the church hand on the salvific knowledge encountered in divine revelation to all peoples, across time and space. In other words, scripture and tradition are not properly understood as revelation *itself*, but rather as the *means* by which the church passes on the good news of divine revelation from person to person, from people to people, and from generation to generation. Tradition, then, goes hand in hand with sacred scripture to function as

> a mirror in which the church, during its pilgrim journey here on earth, contemplates, from whom it receives everything, until such a time as it is brought to see him face to face as he really is (see 1 John 3:2).[57]

While the *content* of tradition is divine revelation, tradition itself is the *process* of handing on, receiving, and incorporating revelation into the life of the church.

Given the baptismal anointing of the whole people of God that informs conciliar ecclesiology, it comes as no surprise that the church's understanding of tradition here encompasses more than simply the deposit of teachings passed down via the teaching office of the magisterium. Rather, the church is guided by the Holy Spirit in its development of tradition, and the Spirit-filled development of tradition is informed by the faith and life of all believers, from the lay faithful to the ordained clergy and the bishops:

> The tradition that comes from the apostles makes progress in the church, with the help of the holy Spirit. There is a growth in insight into the realities and words that are being passed on. This comes about through the contemplation and study of believers who ponder these things in their hearts (see Luke, 2:19, 51). It comes from the intimate sense of spiritual realities which they experience. And it comes from the preaching of those who, on succeeding to the office bishop, have received the sure charism of truth. Thus, as the centuries go by, the church is always advancing towards the plenitude of divine truth, until eventually the words of God are fulfilled in it.[58]

Two paragraphs further on, *Dei Verbum* reiterates this comprehensive understanding of how tradition develops over time and is handed on through not only by the apostolic magisterium, but by all of the faithful:

Tomamos la palabra 231

Tradition and scripture make up a single sacred deposit of the word of God, which is entrusted to the church. By adhering to it the entire holy people, united to its pastors, remains always faithful to the teaching of the apostles, to the communion of life, to the breaking of bread and the prayers (see Acts 2:42, Greek). So, in maintaining, practicing, and professing the faith that has been handed on there is a unique interplay between the bishops and the faithful.[59]

What Sylvia Wynter might call the "overrepresentation" of the clergy and hierarchy is mitigated to a certain extent here by the emphasis on the role of the whole people of God in the development and handing on of tradition. However, further down in this same paragraph, the document affirms that

the task of giving an authentic interpretation of the word of God, whether in its written form or in the form of tradition, has been entrusted to the living teaching office of the church alone. Its authority in this matter is exercised in the name of Jesus Christ. The magisterium is not superior to the word of God, but is rather its servant. It teaches only what has been handed on to it. At the divine command and with the help of the holy Spirit, it listens to this devoutly, guards it reverently, and expounds it faithfully. All that it proposes for belief as being divinely revealed, it draws from this sole deposit of faith.[60]

Immediately after affirming that the whole people of God together develop the tradition of the church, the document reserves ultimate authority for authentically interpreting the Word of God to the "teaching office" of the church, the magisterium, which holds the "sure charism of truth."

One important detail in this paragraph is that *Dei Verbum* ascribes "listening" to this teaching office, blurring the line between *ecclesia docens* and *ecclesia discens*. It implies that even within the teaching office of the church, there may be different interpretations of revelation, each of which must be carefully listened to in order to teach authentically. The reception of this document contributed greatly to empowering lay ecclesial movements like the CEBs in Latin America because it opened space to dialogue about different interpretations of divine revelation among the people of God. However, the document does not decisively adjudicate the tension between different interpretations of revelation and the ultimate authority of the magisterium to make normative doctrinal statements. That is, the overrepresentation of the clergy and hierarchy is not entirely overcome in Vatican II. *Dei Verbum* attributes the "sure charism of truth" not to the laity, but to the apostolic teaching office of the church, the episcopal magisterium with its "unending succession of preachers"—that is, the hierarchy. The eschatological proviso latent in the document does relativize the extent to which the hierarchy is humanly able to express and embody the fullness of truth in human history, but the task of authentic interpretation of divinely revealed truth is entrusted to the church magisterium, whose authority is exercised in the name of Jesus Christ.[61] Indeed, the council asserts that scripture and tradition are so linked to the teaching authority of the church magisterium that "one of them cannot stand without the others. Working together, each in its own way under the action of the holy Spirit, they all contribute effectively to the salvation of souls."[62] As much as progressive Catholic scholars of Vatican II are justified in their inclusion of the laity in this teaching office as part of the whole prophetic people of God that hands on the faith tradition, the council and the canons of the church ultimately locate the epistemological authority to define the authentic tradition in the apostolic succession of bishops. Hence, the bishops of El Salvador maintain the authority to cast the base communities' ecclesial life and praxis beyond the pale of Catholic ecclesial existence.

Similarly, while the conciliar endorsement of the *sensus fidei fidelium* can function as an affirmation of the profound and enduring faith of the entire people of God, it is still the bishops who possess the ecclesial authority to define who the faithful are and what sense of faith fits within the bounds of the authoritative Catholic tradition. It is up to the bishops to prevent the faith tradition expressed and embodied by the lay faithful from falling into error. In *Lumen Gentium*, the council's "Dogmatic Constitution on the Church," the whole people of God prophetically witnesses to the overarching faith tradition, which cannot be mistaken in belief when "the entire people's supernatural sense of the faith . . . 'from the bishops to the last of the faithful' . . . manifests a universal consensus in matters of faith and morals."[63] The authority of the whole people's faith tradition here is powerful; the gates of Hell will not prevail against it (Matt. 16:18). And yet, the *sensus fidei fidelium* must be guided by the "sacred magisterium," which the people "faithfully obeys." The same *Lumen Gentium* affirms that

> bishops are heralds of the faith, who draw new disciples to Christ; they are authentic teachers, that is, teachers endowed with the authority of Christ, who preach to the people assigned to them the faith which is to be believed and applied in practice.[64]

Although the whole people of God carries forth the apostolic tradition of the church, and the laity actively collaborate with the clergy and hierarchy to do so, the hierarchical magisterium still affirms its own identity as *ecclesia docens* and retains the epistemological key to authentic knowledge and interpretation of the divine mysteries.[65] Again, it is for this reason that the bishops of El Salvador have been able to promulgate their authoritative judgment of many CEBs as either antithetical or irrelevant to the true tradition of the Catholic Church.

Contemporary theologies of revelation, like the works of Francis Sullivan or Ormond Rush, do address these ambiguities of the council's legacy. Sullivan, following the reflections of the International Theological Commission, a Vatican-appointed body of theologians, suggests that in an "ecclesiology of communion," different authorities within the one "teaching office" should be recognized—namely, the magisterium, professional theologians, and the sense of the faithful. These three authorities should dialogue with each other to receive revelation most authentically.[66] Rush further develops this model, describing the particular wisdom that each of these authorities brings to the conversation and emphasizing how each party is called to be the teaching and listening church, both *ecclesia docens* and *discens*.[67] Despite these positive theological contributions, the hierarchical authority of the magisterium still has the last word, and therefore ultimate epistemic authority, in many church debates in El Salvador and elsewhere. The church of *lxs pobres* does not have time to wait for theologians and the magisterium to deliberate among themselves what authentic interpretation of revelation is before acting. In the more than fifty-five years since the end of the council, the CEBs have had to make decisions for themselves, decisions that have practical consequences. Their discernment, the wisdom of their sense of the faith, and their practical commitment to the gospel are informative for the rest of the church as we continue to receive the ambiguous legacy of *Dei Verbum*.

In addition to the continued episcopal monopoly on the ultimate authority to interpret revelation and define the tradition, contemporary Catholic ecclesiology retains traces of coloniality in (a) its minimization of the extent to which the magisterium has systematically and institutionally wielded its authority to aid and abet crimes against humanity, such as conquest, forced conversion, inquisition, and persecution of non-Christians; and in (b) its lack of critical consciousness regarding the epistemological and, indeed, Christological, centrality of the church of *lxs pobres* as *ecclesia docens* in embodying and carrying forth the Christian tradition. We will address the first of these enduring dimensions of ecclesial coloniality here in this section, and then will make way for the witness of CEBs as teachers of the whole people of God in general, and of the magisterium specifically, to model decolonial ecclesial knowledge and prophetic preaching.

With regard to glossing over the historical evil and trauma inflicted and/or silently witnessed by the church, even the sincere apologies offered by recent popes and even the most progressive documents issued by Latin American bishops, including the first Latin American pope, neglect to engage or question the theological roots and systemic nature of ecclesial complicity in the conquest, colonization, and enduring coloniality of Latin America. For example, the closing documents of the Latin American Episcopal Conference at Medellín in 1968 offer only a brief and weak acknowledgment of the church's ecclesial complicity in the history of Latin American oppression, relying on the "bad apple" argument that blames whatever abuses that took place on the "frailty" of those messengers who were not "faithful to the Holy Spirit."[68] Furthermore, in his 1987 address to the Indigenous peoples of the Americas, Pope John Paul II acknowledged the harsh realities faced by native inhabitants of the Americas in their encounter with "the European way of life," but he jumps quickly to remind his audience that,

> in order to be objective, history must record the deeply positive aspects of your people's encounter with the culture that came from Europe. Among these positive aspects I wish to recall the work of *the many missionaries who strenuously defended the rights of the original inhabitants of this land.*[69]

Pride of place among these missionaries goes to Fray Junípero Serra, the Spanish Franciscan beatified by Pope John Paul II in 1988 and canonized by Pope Francis in 2015. The general acclaim for missionaries who "defended" the Indigenous peoples of the Americas and the particular praise for a man like Serra belie the institutional and theological innocence that the church would like to claim over and against its "bad apple" involvement in the conquest, colonization, and forced Christianization of the American continent. Many, if not most colonial missionaries, including Serra and the Jesuit missionaries of South America immortalized in the 1986 Roland Joffé film *The Mission*, may not have advocated or condoned open war on recalcitrant Indigenous peoples who refused to convert, but they often employed physically abusive, economically exploitative, and psychologically paternalistic methods of "pacific" conversion.[70] One must also question whether or not peaceful conversion was even a possibility in a context so drenched in the coloniality of military, political, economic, and other material power dynamics between the Spanish invaders and Indigenous peoples.

The Mass and prayers for forgiveness over which John Paul II presided during the Jubilee year on March 12, 2000, were far more repentant and comprehensive than this 1987 address, but they too left much to be desired. For instance, the first of the prayer of penitence, read by then cardinal Joseph Ratzinger, confessed the sins of violence that the church has committed "in the service of truth."[71] Like the contradictory nature of "peaceful conversion" during a violent conquest and its colonial aftermath, the assertion that violent conversion was carried out in the service of truth is an impossibility. A decolonial analysis reveals the theo-logic of totalizing violence at work even in the assertion that the church possesses a Christian truth that requires any means of coercing or persuading the conversion of non-Christian peoples, especially when those peoples have been dispossessed and oppressed by ruling Christian powers.

During his 2015 address in Bolivia to the second WMPM, Pope Francis echoes his predecessor's remorse for the role of the church in the violent conquest of the Americas:

> Here I wish to bring up an important issue. Some may rightly say, "When the Pope speaks of colonialism, he overlooks certain actions of the Church." I say this to you with regret: many grave sins were committed against the native peoples of America in the name of God. My predecessors acknowledged this, CELAM, the Council of Latin American Bishops, has said it, and I too wish to say it. Like Saint John Paul II, I ask that the Church—I repeat what he said— "kneel before God and implore forgiveness for the past and present sins of her sons and daughters." I would also say, and here I wish to be quite clear, as was Saint John Paul II: I humbly ask forgiveness, not only for the offenses of the Church herself, but also for crimes committed against the native peoples during the so-called conquest of America.[72]

Also like his predecessors, however, Francis immediately qualifies his apology with gratitude for those missionaries who evangelized by peaceful means and defended the rights of Indigenous peoples.

> Together with this request for forgiveness and in order to be just, I also would like us to remember the thousands of priests and bishops who strongly opposed the logic of the sword with the power of the Cross. There was sin, a great deal of it, for which we did not ask pardon. So for this, we ask forgiveness, I ask forgiveness. But here also, where there was sin, great sin, grace abounded through the men and women who defended the rights of indigenous peoples.

We would do well to bear in mind that these words are set within the context of a powerful and prophetic speech critiquing new and old forms of colonialism, as well as within the context of Francis's wider advocacy for economic and ecological justice and within the context of his broader calls for ecclesial self-critique and dismantling of clericalism. It is tempting to overlook the traces of coloniality in a religious leader as progressive and charismatic as Pope Francis. But the familiar refrain of a qualified apology that does not critically engage the coloniality of even the most just and peaceful missionary efforts is one among several factors that compromise the broader decolonial potential of Francis's papacy.

More recently in 2020, Pope Francis's post-synodal apostolic exhortation, *Querida Amazonia*, followed this same pattern of pairing confession and apology with a reminder of all the good that the church has also accomplished in the Americas in and through its missionaries and subsequent pastors:

> It is encouraging to remember that amid the grave excesses of the colonization of the Amazon region, so full of "contradictions and suffering," many missionaries came to bring the Gospel, leaving their homes and leading an austere and demanding life alongside those who were most defenceless. We know that not all of them were exemplary, yet the work of those who remained faithful to the Gospel also inspired "a legislation like the Laws of the Indies, which defended the dignity of the indigenous peoples from violence against their peoples and territories." Since it was often the priests who protected the indigenous peoples from their plunderers and abusers, the missionaries recounted that "they begged insistently that we not abandon them and they extorted from us the promise that we would return."[73]

Pope Francis's references here to the Laws of the Indies and the protection afforded to Indigenous peoples by some missionaries overlook the extent to which such ameliorative efforts were set squarely within, were made necessary by, and did not challenge the overarching colonial power matrix.

To drive this point home, consider the following perspective on the matter: the hierarchical magisterium of the Roman Catholic church—made up of the apostolic teachers who are purportedly graced with the "charism of truth"—has never repudiated the Doctrine of Discovery set in motion by the Spanish conquest and colonization of the Americas and theologically justified by Pope Alexander VI and many of his successors. We'll say it again for those in the back: the magisterium of the Roman Catholic church has never revoked the Doctrine of Discovery. This refusal to truly repent of the church's role in the conquest and colonization of the Americas persists despite numerous pleas by Indigenous peoples and their allies in recent decades, especially since the 500th anniversary of Cristobal Colón's invasion of the continent in 1492.[74] When it comes to upholding the tradition of the church and the teaching authority of the hierarchical magisterium, it seems that the Roman Catholic church is epistemologically unable to (a) admit to the full extent of its systemic involvement in the evils of colonialism or (b) call its own teaching authority into question, even when it commits such grievous and sinful errors. This refusal is characteristic of the continued coloniality of knowledge that plagues Roman Catholic ecclesiology and its overrepresentation of the true Christian self, particularly the ordained and episcopal Christian self, as epistemically and ontologically normative. It is a refusal to admit that the Christianization of the Americas was deeply flawed on a moral and theological level, not just in individual cases of violence and abuse. It is a refusal to admit that the Indigenous peoples of the Americas, along with other colonized peoples, existed and continue to exist as fully human subjects capable and deserving of exercising their own forms of knowledge production, creative spiritual expression, and social and ecclesial organization. While the CEBs do not tackle the ambiguous legacies of colonial missionaries or the Doctrine of Discovery head on, they are willing to question the authority of a tradition that was violently imposed on their ancestors and that continues to suppress their own affirmations of knowledge, being, and power. Indeed, the CEBs' decolonial critique of tradition and authority offers possibilities for delinking from colonial Catholicism and reimagining a church in which *no one* possesses the *sure* charism of truth, and in which privileged epistemological authority is granted not to those at the top of colonial hierarchies, but at the bottom, among the *damnés* on the underside of colonial history and religion.

The CEBs Decolonize Tradition and Authority

The Salvadoran base communities are not prone to using the terms tradition and authority very much in their own self-descriptions, everyday discourse, or theological reflections. In general, the term tradition comes up in their critiques of "traditional" Catholic churches in El Salvador and the term authority rarely comes up at all, other than in reference to political and ecclesial authorities—*las autoridades*—that exercise their power in oppressive and violent ways. In fact, from the perspective of the CEBs' eschatology and the criteria of the reign of God, normative Catholic tradition as ratified by the religious authorities has built the *anti-reino* in Salvadoran history and in the lived reality of many impoverished communities. The CEBs are thus deeply suspicious of tradition and authority in both the church and society. And yet they do identify with the tradition and authority of Jesús and the apostolic witness of the first Christian communities. They also appreciate and locate themselves within the liberative tradition of late twentieth-century Roman Catholicism, during which time many priests, bishops, and women religious were inspired to enter into radical solidarity with the world of *lxs pobres* by the reforms of the Second Vatican Council and by the documents of the CELAM that emerged from their meetings at Medellín (1968) and Puebla (1979).

However, the communities conceive of their role not only as receivers of magisterial pronouncements, "who treasure these things in their hearts" as *ecclesia discens*, even when they agree with such pronouncements. Rather, they understand themselves to be participative members of the people of God, as professors of an adult faith who are responsible for speaking from their experience for the good of the church, as *ecclesia docens*. Indeed, throughout the CEBs' several decades of communal ecclesial praxis, their faithfulness to listening *and speaking* has resulted in positive contributions to the tradition, as is the task of the whole people of God. In part I of this book, the CEBs testify to their refusal to dutifully receive the bishops' letter about the closure of the National University, signed by Monseñor Romero, without dialogue.[75] When Romero came to their communities to celebrate eucharist, they began to ask questions, to speak. Romero "accused us of disobedience to ecclesial authorities," and left without concluding the eucharistic celebration. Romero, then, first as auxiliary bishop and later as archbishop of San Salvador, treasured that encounter in his heart until he returned to reconcile with the community.

In his homilies and in interviews, Romero repeatedly attributes the development of his own pastoral sensibilities to the education given him by the church of *lxs pobres* in their role as *ecclesia docens*. "I feel that the people are my prophet," he preached in a 1979 homily,

> and with the anointing that they received from the Spirit of God at the time of their baptism, you are teaching me. The Spirit also makes the people of God incapable of accepting an erroneous or mistaken doctrine. You, as a people, would reject such a doctrine.... It is beautiful to think that with great fidelity I try to bring the gospel to you and to preach the gospel to you and that you desire to be faithful to Christ and not to me.[76]

It is not difficult to imagine that Romero's earlier experiences with the CEBs prepared him, at least in part, to preach this homily. Here, he recognizes that while he as bishop is responsible for teaching the gospel, he himself has been taught by the lay faithful and encourages their criteria, not of obedience to him, their bishop, but to Christ.

When Romero recognizes that the commitment that *lxs pobres* have to Christ may contradict his own interpretation of the gospel as archbishop, he recognizes the truth of their decolonial knowledge. This knowledge is born of their experiences as colonized peoples, or, as Ignacio Ellacuría and Jon Sobrino christologically put it, "crucified peoples"—the *damnés* whose bodies Empire has deemed threatening and has sought to eliminate. They, however, maintain faith in the ultimate victory of a God of Life, despite overwhelming evidence to the contrary and commit in their lives to living into the reality of God's dream for creation. In a reality of enduring coloniality, to "take the crucified down from their crosses" requires heeding the decolonial knowledge "from below" that prophetically denounces and seeks to dismantle the crosses of the *anti-reino*, while also announcing the reign of God.

San Romero's episcopal motto, *sentir con la iglesia*[77]—to think and feel with the church—represented his preferential option for feeling, thinking, and acting in solidarity with the suffering of Christ's crucified body in the midst of Salvadoran historical reality. After Romero's assassination, and especially as the Salvadoran hierarchy became increasingly hostile to the *sentir* of the CEBs, their questions and critiques were not received by a magisterium ready to listen. As presented in part I, especially in the "Letters from the Hierarchy" and in the accounts of contemporary CEBs like Nuevo Amanecer and Comunidad Rutilio Grande (from Nahuizalco), the CEBs' contributions to the continued interpretation of divine revelation have not been welcomed by the Salvadoran hierarchy in the past several decades. However, they have continued to write, speak, sing, and create their sense of their faith out loud through press releases on political issues like food sovereignty, health care, water management, and the privatization of pensions, through their own reflections in liturgical celebrations, through new songs and poems, murals, and participation in marches and protests, together with other organizations in civil society.

As a result of this conflict, and as a result of the ultimatums laid down by different members of the Salvadoran clergy and hierarchy, many Salvadoran base communities now operate outside of the parish structure—or parallel to it. Because of this new ecclesial reality, they express a vigilantly critical consciousness of the epistemic power of the church as an institution. This includes trenchant critiques of clericalism and a deliberate commitment to communal autonomy:

> We teach ourselves to not depend on priests. Oftentimes we get comfortable and just do what the priest says. That's much easier than being in community, thinking about what we should do. The parish often does us the "favor" of recognizing us and then it absorbs us completely and we aren't able to walk for ourselves and we end up not being autonomous, but we end up doing what the parish imposes on us, the program that the parish has.[78]

This is not to say that the CEBs reject the priesthood or the hierarchy altogether. Rather, they maintain that "the priest should have to walk with us and not us behind the priest."[79] The people of the base communities have great love and respect for those priests and bishops who are epistemically humble enough to exercise their ministry in *solidarity* with the people, with respect for the epistemic authority of the church of *lxs pobres*. For the CEBs, a priest or bishop should be in constant dialogue and partnership *with* the people, and not the purveyor of wisdom and knowledge from on high. Similarly, it is not that the magisterial teachings of the Catholic hierarchy are entirely irrelevant to the CEBs' decolonial knowledge base—certainly Archbishop Romero's and, to a lesser extent, Pope Francis's wisdom are given authoritative weight, as are some of the more recent, socially conscious pronouncements of the current archbishop José Luis Escobar Alas.[80] But the CEBs' epistemological priority is to view and analyze reality *from the perspective of the colonized.*

The CEBs' commitment to the dialectic of listening and speaking, of being *ecclesia discens* and *ecclesia docens*, and of trusting that there is a time for each is a way of being church, not only between the lay faithful and the hierarchy, but on a daily basis within the communities themselves. Members of the CEBs listen to and teach each other, including young people, women, the elderly, those without much formal education, those who just began participating in a community, and those who have grown up in a CEB. The experience of sharing knowledge and learning from others within the community is a foundation for the trust they have in this same process with their pastors and bishops, even when it does not go well in a particular instance. Francisco Bosch, upon publishing reflections on his experience of facilitating over thirty *"mingas,"*[81] popular and theological community workshops, among ecclesial base communities throughout Latin America between 2016 and 2020, puts it this way:

> From that path of forming ourselves as listeners, the sap began to flow among us: we began a dialogue about the stories of our faith, with a long root that unites us to the exodus of the Hebrew people and their struggle for freedom, land, and justice. At the same time, we dialogued about the movement of disposable and impure people that formed around the loving movement of Jesús, and we perceived there the potency of the journey between the book[s] of our communities and the book[s] of the Bible. From this flow of sap, we emerged stronger, and these pages are the first fruits of the tree. Because in América, we are more than seeds of the Word; we have enormous trees with fruits that narrate our faith.[82]

Bosch speaks here of the communities he visited as *"palabreras"*—as "worders" or wordsmiths, producers of words, of speech, of narrative. These words are born of a long process of listening, not only to the magisterium, but also to each other: *lxs pobres* listening to and teaching *lxs pobres*. The verb *"palabrear"* also has a sense of "giving one's word," of commitment, of speaking something true and lasting. The epistemic commitment of the CEBs is to both *tomar la palabra*, as rightful heirs of a vocation to subjectivity in the construction of God's reign, and to listen for the *palabra de Dios* in one another, their communities, the church more broadly, and creation as a whole.

The CEBs, therefore, decolonize and re-center the meaning of "tradition" and "authority" on a healing and liberating encounter with the divine light of the Spirit of God in themselves and all peoples, on compassion for the suffering of the crucified people in themselves and others, and on experiencing and embodying the resurrection of Jesús in their personal and communal struggles to overcome suffering and injustice with persistent and courageous protest. This means that the CEBs embody the tradition of Jesús not by intellectual assent to authoritative doctrine, but as an affective, visceral, existential, and embodied reality—as a *felt* and *lived* and *critically considered* commitment to and experience of the preferential option for the poor and participation in the construction of God's reign in human history. The CEBs discern authentic commitments to and experiences of these things decolonially—in dialogue as a community, in loving and active memory of their heroes and martyrs, and in hopeful commitment to the healing and liberation of their people that their adult faith requires. *Cuando el pobre crea en el pobre, cuando tomen la palabra*, the decolonial tradition and authority of the church of *lxs pobres* is born. And not even the gates of hell can prevail against it. In the words of Rosalina Martínez, a member of the CEBs' Mothers' Congregations in the north of Morazán, *"Estamos contando el cuento. . . . Estábamos en guerra y no hemos perdido nuestra fe"*—"We are telling the story. . . . We were in a war and we have not lost our faith."[83] The creative and liturgical praxis of the CEBs that has sustained their faith on this decolonial journey is the subject of our next chapter.

NOTES

1. Gómez and Marshall, eds., *Sigue porque la vida sigue*, 194–195. Ángela is the subject of "The *Librito* of the Prophet María Ángela Domínguez Pérez" in part I.
2. The first half of this chapter is a revised and expanded version of Elizabeth O'Donnell Gandolfo, "*Cuando el pobre crea en el pobre*: Decolonial Epistemology in the Ecclesial Base Communities of El Salvador," in *Decolonial Christianities: Latinx and Latin American Perspectives*, eds. Raimundo Barreto and Roberto Sirvent (New York: Palgrave Macmillan, 2019), 241–254.
3. These include the *Misa Popular Nicaragüense*, the *Misa Campesina Nicaragüense*, the *Misa Popular Salvadoreña*, and the more recently composed *Misa Mesoamericana*. See J. M. Vigil and A. Torrellas, *Misas Centroamericanas: Transcripción y Comentario Teológico* (Managua, Nicaragua: CAV-CEBES, 1988), https://cfones.jesuitas.cl/wp-content/uploads/2013/09/misascentroamericanas.pdf, accessed October 10, 2018.
4. Guillermo Cuéllar, "Cuando el pobre crea en el pobre," closing hymn of the "Salvadoran Popular Mass." To listen to the version of this song as it was recorded by the Salvadoran folk group, Yolocamba I Ta, visit https://www.youtube.com/watch?v=Ha3bxZ1NofE. For a recording that sounds closer to the way it is sung in the base communities, visit https://www.youtube.com/watch?v=euFVcTlsbM4. Both accessed October 10, 2018.
5. See Nelson Maldonado-Torres, "Outline of Ten Theses on Coloniality and Decoloniality," Frantz Fanon Foundation, http://caribbeanstudiesassociation.org/docs/Maldonado-Torres_Outline_Ten_Theses-10.23.16.pdf, accessed July 16, 2020.
6. The categories of decolonial epistemology, aesthetics, and power each correlate roughly with the Christian baptismal offices of prophet, priest, and king. It is within these baptismal functions of the whole people of God that CELAM promotes the CEBs in the final documents of Medellín. See "Pastoral de Conjunto" (no. 15, par. III.11): "Los miembros de estas comunidades, 'viviendo conforme a la vocación a que han sido llamados, ejerciten las funciones que Dios les ha confiado, sacerdotal,

profética y real,' y hagan así de su comunidad 'un signo de la presencia de Dios en el mundo' [*AG*, 15]."

7. Maldonado-Torres, "Outline of Ten Theses," 24.

8. Marshall, "Un gesto vale más que mil palabras," Appendix 9, xlvi.

9. The expression "learning to unlearn" emerged from the *Universidad Intercultural de los Pueblos Indígenas del Ecuador*. See Walter Mignolo, "Delinking," *Cultural Studies* 21, no. 2 (2007): 485.

10. Mignolo, "Delinking," 463, 484–485.

11. Mignolo, 463.

12. Mignolo, 492.

13. Mignolo, 461.

14. Audre Lorde, "The Master's Tools Will Never Dismantle the Master's House," in *Sister Outsider: Essays and Speeches* (Berkeley, CA: Crossing Press, 1984), 110–114.

15. See Roque Dalton's love poem to the colonized *tektons, negaras, hacelotodos,* and jacks-of-all-trades of El Salvador in "Nuevo-Exodus," §1.

16. See Gloria Anzaldua, *Borderlands/La Frontera: The New Mestiza* (San Francisco, CA: Aunt Lute Books, 1987). Mignolo develops this concept, describing border thinking as "the connector between the diversity of locales that were subjected as colonies of the modern empires [. . .] or that as empires had to respond to Western expansion. Border thinking is not grounded in Greek thinkers but in the colonial wounds and imperial subordination and, as such, it should become the connector between the diversity of subaltern histories . . . and corresponding subjectivities . . . [that] want to include the perspective and in the foundation of knowledge subjectivities that have been subjected in and by the colonial matrix of power. The diversity of actual manifestations and practices of border thinking make up what I have described as an-other paradigm." See Mignolo, "Delinking," 493. See also Walter D. Mignolo and Medina V. Tlostanova, "Theorizing from the Borders: Shifting to Geo- and Body-Politics of Knowledge," *European Journal of Social Theory* 9, no. 2 (2006): 205–221.

17. See the robust body of literature in which biblical scholars and theologians argue that the God of the Bible, the mission of Jesús, and the reign of God are diametrically opposed to Empire: for example, Richard A. Horsley, *Jesus and Empire: The Kingdom of God and the New World Disorder* (Minneapolis, MN: Fortress Press, 2002); John Dominic Crossan, *God and Empire: Jesus Against Rome, Then and Now* (New York: HarperCollins, 2008); and Antonio Gonzalez, *God's Reign and the End of Empires* (Miami, FL: Convivium Press, 2012).

18. Prophetic praxis understood in terms of denunciation and annunciation is central to much of Latin American liberation theology and can be seen in foundational texts such as Gustavo Gutierrez, *A Theology of Liberation*, 15th Anniversary Edition (Maryknoll, NY: Orbis Books, 1988). For a biblical argument for the dual task of the prophetic vocation, see Walter Brueggemann, *The Prophetic Imagination*, 40th Anniversary Edition (Minneapolis, MN: Fortress Press, 2018).

19. For a helpful source on the pastoral method of Catholic Action in Latin America and its relationship with liberation theology, see Ana María Bidegain, "From Catholic Action to Liberation Theology. Historical Process of the Laity in Latin

America in the Twentieth Century," Working Paper # 48, The Helen Kellogg Institute for International Studies, University of Notre Dame, 1985. For more on Joseph Cardijn and the application of his pastoral method in the context of the United States, see Mary Irene Zotti, "The Young Christian Workers," *U.S. Catholic Historian* 9, no. 4 (Fall 1990): 387–400. For an account of how Cardijn's methodology was influential for social movements in other parts of the world, see Austin F. Cerejo, "Cardijn's methodology and its relevance for social and structural change," in *Indian Church in the Struggle for a New Society*, ed. D. S. Amalorpavadass (Bangalore, India: Nat Biblical, Catechetical & Liturgical Centre, 1981), 402–421. For a more contemporary application, see Justin Sands, "Introducing Cardinal Cardijn's See–Judge–Act as an Interdisciplinary Method to Move Theory into Practice," *Religions* 9 (2018): 129.

20. Gregorio Iriarte, *Que es una Comunidad Eclesial de Base* (Bogotá: Ediciones Paulinas, 1991), 31–32.

21. Iriarte, 34.

22. NB: The *celebrar* dimension of the CEBs methodology appears in the *Acompañando la Vida* series of workbooks published in the 2000s by the ecclesial base communities of the Bajo Lempa region of El Salvador.

23. Luis Rivera-Pagán, "Towards a Decolonial Theology: Perspectives from the Caribbean," in *Decolonial Christianities: Latinx and Latin American Perspectives*, eds. Raimundo Barreto and Roberto Sirvent (New York: Palgrave Macmillan, 2019), 43.

24. Clodovis Boff, "Epistemología y Método de la Teología de la Liberación," in *Mysterium Liberationis: Conceptos Fundamentales de la Teología de la Liberación, Tomo I*, eds. Jon Sobrino and Ignacio Ellacuría (San Salvador: UCA Editores, 1993), 82. In *Decolonial Love*, Joseph Drexler-Dreis analyzes Boff's method through a decolonial lens and concludes that Boff's strict reliance on the European disciplines of the social sciences in this first step of his methodology prevents him from allowing for the world of *lxs pobres* to be theologically pedagogic. However, Boff's method in *Feet on the Ground Theology* (Maryknoll, NY: Orbis Books, 1987) has little to do with the social sciences and much more to do with encountering (and learning from) the presence of the divine in the Brazilian people. Nevertheless, one is left to wonder whether the original and enduring coloniality of Boff's method is what led him to repudiate liberation theology later in life.

25. Enrique Dussel, "Epistemological Decolonization of Theology," in *Decolonial Christianities: Latinx and Latin American Perspectives*, 32. Emphasis in the original.

26. See Gustavo Gutiérrez, *The Power of the Poor in History* (Maryknoll, NY: Orbis, 1983).

27. The pedagogy of the CEBs has much in common with and has arguably been influenced by the work of Paulo Freire, a groundbreaking educator in Brazil who critiqued traditional (colonial) methods of adult education and developed popular education techniques for literacy training based on concrete, everyday reality of the people. He and his pedagogy became influential worldwide and fell on especially fertile ground in ecclesial base communities and other popular organizations throughout Latin America. See Paulo Freire, *Pedagogy of the Oppressed* (New York: Continuum, 1981).

28. See "Letter from the Community 'Pueblo de Dios en Camino,'" §2, in part I; Gómez and Marshall, *Sigue*, 81–82.

29. See "Letter from the Community 'Pueblo de Dios en Camino,'" §5, in part I; Marshall, *Un gesto vale más*, Appendix 2, vi–vii.

30. Dominique Barbé, "Church Base Communities," in *Liberation Theology: An Introductory Reader*, eds. Curt Cadorette et al. (Maryknoll, NY: Orbis Books, 1992), 185.

31. Barbé. Emphasis in the original.

32. Comunidades Eclesiales de Base de El Salvador, *Mística y Metodología*, 85.

33. See "The *Librito* of the Prophet José Adonay Pérez Pérez," §1, in part I. Gómez and Marshall, *Sigue porque la vida sigue*, 207.

34. Comunidades Eclesiales de Base del Norte de Morazán, *Tomamos la Palabra* (Perquín, El Salvador: CEBES, 2000), 20.

35. See "Letter from the Community 'Pueblo de Dios en Camino,'" §1, in part I. Marshall, *Un gesto vale más*, Appendix 2, ii–iii.

36. This story appears in Matthew 14:13–21, Mark 6:31–44, Luke 9:12–17, and John 6:1–14.

37. See "The *Librito* of the Prophet Reina Greisi Leiva," §1, in part I.

38. See "CEBs San Romero" Facebook post, November 14, 2018,
    https://www.facebook.com/cebssanromero2006/photos/a.10156159720918825/10157145628878825/?type=3&theater, accessed February 19, 2019.

39. See the Equipo Maiz website at www.equipomaiz.org.sv.

40. Marshall, "Un gesto vale más que mil palabras," Appendix 2, ii–iii.

41. See "Colonio-Genesis," §9, and "The *Librito* of the Prophet Farabundo Martí" in part I.

42. See "Colonio-Genesis," §10, in part I.

43. Originally referred to as the "Jesuit martyrs," this group was renamed the "UCA martyrs" by popular consensus so as not to imply a distinction between the martyrdom of the priests and that of the two laywomen.

44. See "The *Librito* of the Prophet Óscar Romero" in part I.

45. Ford and Clark were Maryknoll sisters, Kazel was an Ursuline sister, and Donovan was a lay missioner. For a feminist analysis of patriarchal preference in the memory of Latin American martyrdom, see Elizabeth O'Donnell Gandolfo, "Women and Martyrdom: Feminist Liberation Theology in Dialogue with a Latin American Paradigm," *Horizons* 34, no. 1 (Spring 2007): 26–53.

46. This cover-up is detailed in the account by Mark Danner, *The Massacre at El Mozote: A Parable of the Cold War* (New York: Vintage Books, 1993), 85–139.

47. See "Letter from the Hierarchy II," §3, in part I.

48. See Elizabeth O'Donnell Gandolfo, "Remembering the Massacre at El Mozote: A Case for Dangerous Memory of Suffering as Christian Formation in Hope," *International Journal of Practical Theology* 17, no. 1 (2013): 62–87.

49. This term is borrowed from Johann Baptist Metz, *Faith in History and Society: Towards a Practical Fundamental Theology* (New York: Crossroad, 2007).

50. Luis Rivera-Pagán, "Towards a Decolonial Theology," 50, citing Chinua Achebe, *Home and Exile* (New York: Anchor Books, 2000), 79.

51. CEB Continental Webpage, "Camino Histórico CEBs Región Centroamérica," http://cebcontinental.org/index.php/quienes-somos/historia-de-las-ceb/region-centroamerica, accessed October 12, 2018.

52. We recognize that our use of infantilization and childhood as conceptual metaphors is problematic here, but these terms do convey the attitude with which Christian religious leaders have often "evangelized" in the Americas. These metaphors reflect more the anti-childhood bias of coloniality than the views of childhood that we hold as authors or that the CEBs hold as Christian communities. We recognize that not all cultures treat children as empty vessels to be filled with knowledge by authority figures, nor is it true that all children always naively or uncritically accept what their "superiors" teach them to be true about the world. Some members of the CEBs also question this "adult-centric" view of knowledge and authority. For example, Miguel Zepeda, who is a leader cited as a prophet in part I, describes a conversation with his stepdaughter in which she tells him that kids should have a say in the decisions that involve them. Miguel's humble and reflective reaction to this conversation led him to remain quiet and simply listen to his stepdaughter's concerns. He subsequently reflects that "if we had a culture of listening to girls and boys and young people, then the world would change." See *Sigue porque la vida sigue*, ed. Gómez and Marshall, 172. For a decolonial treatment of childhood, see Manfred Liebel, *Decolonizing Childhoods: From Exclusion to Dignity* (Bristol: Policy Press, 2020).

53. Sylvia Wynter, "Unsettling the Coloniality of Being/Power/Truth/Freedom: Towards the Human, After Man, Its Overrepresentation—An Argument," *New Centennial Review* 3, no. 3 (Fall 2003): 262.

54. Wynter, 317 and 331.

55. *DV*, §2.

56. *DV*, §6.

57. *DV*, §7.

58. *DV*, §8.

59. *DV*, §10.

60. *DV*.

61. *DV*.

62. *DV*.

63. *LG*, §12.

64. *LG*, §25.

65. The International Theological Commission's 2014 document "*Sensus Fidei* in the Life of the Church" reiterates this guiding criterion for identifying true manifestations of the *sensus fidei*: adherence to the magisterium.

66. Francis A. Sullivan, "Authority in an Ecclesiology of Communion," *New Theology Review* 10 (1997): 18–30.

67. Ormond Rush, *The Eyes of Faith: The Sense of the Faithful and the Church's Reception of Revelation* (Washington, DC: Catholic University of America Press, 2009). See especially 175–292.

68. CELAM, "Introduction to the Final Documents," §2. This is one of the points that Elizabeth O'Donnell Gandolfo makes in her critique of CELAM on questions of racial injustice. See Gandolfo, "Medellín and the Problem of Whiteness: An

Ambiguous Legacy," in *Medellín and Its Significance for the Church in the United States: Memories, Theologies, and Legacies*, eds. O. Ernesto Valiente et al. (Miami, FL: Convivium Press, 2018).

69. Pope John Paul II, "Meeting with the Native Peoples of the Americas: Address of His Holiness John Paul II," September 14, 1987. Emphasis in the original.

70. Indigenous critiques of Serra have been amplified in recent years, particularly since his canonization and again amid the widespread toppling of monuments to colonial figures in the summer of 2020. See, for example, J. Weston Phippin and National Journal, "Why Native Americans Oppose Junipero Serra's Sainthood," *Atlantic*, September 22, 2015, https://www.theatlantic.com/politics/archive/2015/09/why-native-americans-oppose-junipero-serras-sainthood/432876/. For a scholarly historical perspective, see also David Hurst Thomas, "The Life and Times of Junípero Serra: A Pan-Borderlands Perspective," *The Americas* 71, no. 2 (October 2014): 185–225. For a critical scholarly assessment of the Jesuit missions featured in Joffé's film, see James Schofield Saeger, "*The Mission* and Historical Missions: Film and the Writing of History," *The Americas* 74, no. S2 (2017): 393–415.

71. See "Solemn Prayer of the Faithful Confessing Sins and Requesting God's Pardon" from John Paul II's Day of Pardon Mass: First Sunday of Lent, March 12, 2000.

72. Pope Francis, "Participation at the Second World Meeting of Popular Movements, Address of the Holy Father," July 9, 2015, Bolivia.

73. *QA*, §18.

74. See, for example, Indian Country Today Website, "A 1993 Open Letter to Pope John Paul II," originally published August 11, 1993, https://indiancountrytoday.com/archive/a-1993-open-letter-to-pope-john-paul-ii-IE70yG6pVESYCa0pmQm-Cg, accessed July 14, 2020. More recently, a delegation of Indigenous peoples from Canada brought their own plea to Pope Francis in May 2016. See Humko Kaps Kap, "Historic Indigenous Mission Asks Pope Francis to Revoke the Paper Bulls of Discovery," http://longmarchtorome.com/the-creator-has-been-heard/, accessed July 14, 2020. In 2015, *National Catholic Reporter* published a series of articles on the Doctrine of Discovery, all of which can be accessed at https://www.ncronline.org/feature-series/the-trail-of-history/stories.

75. See "The *Librito* of the Prophet Óscar Romero," §1, in part I.

76. Archbishop Óscar Romero, Homily, July 8, 1979, The Archbishop Romero Trust, http://www.romerotrust.org.uk/homilies-and-writings.

77. *Sentir con la Iglesia*—to think and feel with the church—is a phrase that comes from the Spiritual Exercises of St. Ignatius Loyola. See Douglas Marcoullier, SJ, "Archbishop with an Attitude: Oscar Romero's *Sentir con la Iglesia*," *Studies in the Spirituality of the Jesuits* 35, no. 3 (May 2003): 2–3.

78. Marshall, "Un gesto vale más que mil palabras," Appendix 1, ii.

79. Marshall.

80. See "Letter from the Hierarchy III" in part I. See also the positions that Escobar Alas has taken against metallic mining and the privatization of water, and in favor of a reform of the state pension system and an increased minimum wage. Yaneth Estrada, "Arzobispo Escobar Alas llama a Gobernar a favor del pueblo," *Diario CoLatino*,

February 11, 2019, https://www.diariocolatino.com/arzobispo-escobar-alas-llama-a-gobernar-a-favor-del-pueblo/, accessed February 12, 2019.

81. Bosch defines *"minga"* as "a term that comes from Quechua, an Andean practice of communal work, born of needs that demand collaboration. *El minguero* [the facilitator of the *minga*] calls people together, depending on the needs of the community, to work. Each member supplies their own wisdom, strength, and tools, and the *minguero* gets the workspace ready so that nothing is lacking. This practice is common for community house-raisings, and the *minguero* prepares food for everybody" (Bosch, *Bendita Mezcla*, 22). He also refers to a *minga* with the shorthand "popular theology workshops."

82. Francisco J. Bosch, *Bendita Mezcla: Hermanxs escuchadorxs, comunidades palabreras* (Montevideo: Fundación Ameríndia, 2020), 10.

83. Comunidades Eclesiales de Base del Norte de Morazán, *Tomamos la Palabra*, 34.

Chapter 3

Celebramos la vida
Decolonial Being in the Salvadoran Church of lxs Pobres

There is no other way but to create and to sing.
—Chamba from the Bajo Lempa[1]

In Central America, Holy Week is a time of richly beautiful popular expression in song, dance, processions, the *via crucis*, and intricately designed *alfombras*, or large "carpets" made of dyed salt or sawdust, depicting a religious scene or simply a beautiful image. The story of another CEB that, like Pueblo de Dios en Camino, has been pushed out of their parish is infused with the decolonial salt of one particular *alfombra* designed by Andrea, a first generation university student majoring in psychology, and other members of her youth group, while they still formed part of a parish.[2] Their *alfombra* consisted of three images: the first was a barcode superimposed over the face of a child, symbolizing that "for society, we are just a number, a number that consumes, a number that isn't worth anything, that doesn't have any rights"; the second was a scale with money and an image of a pope on one side and a crucified *campesino* on the other, representing "religious power that distances itself from *campesinos*, from its true vocation to struggle for and support [the people]"; the third part took the form of a woman's hand, with words like "rape, abuse, and other situations of violence" written on each finger. This final section of the *alfombra* also included the symbols for male and female united to indicate that women and men should be equal and should work together for equal rights. When the time came for Andrea to speak to the people gathered at the parish about the section with the scale, the pope, and the crucified *campesino*, the priest took the microphone from Andrea's hand as soon as she began to speak. From that point on, the youth group was no longer allowed to create *alfombras*, which Andrea remarks had been "the only opportunity we had in the parish to express ourselves."[3] As it turns out,

Andrea's small community and their *alfombra* made of salt were not only the salt of the earth in terms of the flavor that their self-expression could provide to a meaningful religious ritual. They were the salt of the church, in the sense that salt burns when it is rubbed into a wound.[4] The salt from Andrea's *alfombra* creatively revealed the wounds inflicted by the colonial church in El Salvador and that church was not pleased.

The story of Andrea's *alfombra* is a telling example of what decolonial scholars today are calling decolonial aesthetics, which encompasses realms of human creativity that have been marginalized and devalued in the canons, museums, and philosophies of Western art and theology.[5] In this dimension of decolonial praxis, Nelson Maldonado-Torres states, "the embodied subject emerges as someone who can not only reflect about but also mold, shape, and reshape subjectivity, space, and time."[6] Coloniality imposes what Maldonado-Torres calls both "metaphysical catastrophe" and "ontological separation" on the colonized, negating (or attempting to negate) their very being by erasing (or attempting to erase) their spiritual, cultural, and artistic imaginary. The colonial church in Central America was the primary agent of this ontological-aesthetic negation in its imposition of not only Catholic doctrine but also Catholic sacraments, devotions, and other ritual practices on the colonized Indigenous and Afro-descendant peoples of El Salvador, who were stripped of their cosmovisions and sacred rituals when the church participated in the conquest and colonization of their lands. Alongside economic exploitation by the landholding oligarchy and periods of violent repression by the state, the church contributed to a veritable ethnocide in which Indigenous and African identities were nearly eliminated from El Salvador altogether and were replaced by *mestizo* (or mixed) identity.[7] This is not to say that the colonized subjects of Latin American Catholicism exercised no agency in their cultural, religious, and spiritual practices. To be sure, *mestizaje, mulatez*, and the accompanying religious syncretism between Indigenous, African, and/ or Iberian Catholic practices do contain many direct and indirect aesthetic elements of decolonial resistance within them.[8] However, our task here is to identify the decolonial creative praxis of the Salvadoran CEBs as a conscious, direct, and often explicit attempt to subversively "mold, shape, and reshape" the colonized subjectivity, time, and space of the church that has been handed down to them. In the words of the CEBs themselves, "artistic and cultural richness is one of the greatest forms of expression in the Salvadoran CEBs."[9] Their practices of decolonial creativity represent aesthetic contributions to not only survival and resistance within the colonial power matrix, but also liberation from that matrix and its destructive technologies of metaphysical catastrophe and ontological separation.

The praxis of decolonial creativity described and analyzed in this chapter represents "a shift away from the coloniality of established meanings, of sensing, of feeling, of vision, of gender and other modern/colonial conceptions of the body, as well as a rejection of the modern/colonial hierarchy of human experiences." It reveals an-other way of sensing or feeling the world and thus another way of producing the decolonial forms of knowledge described in chapter 2, along with another way of imagining and exercising the decolonial forms of power that will be explored in chapter 4. Indeed, according to Maldonado-Torres, the emergence of the *damnés* as creator

> is a key aspect of the decolonization of being, including the decolonization of time, space, and embodied subjectivity, but also of power and knowledge. Since aesthetics is so closely connected to embodied subjectivity and this subjectivity is at the crux of the coloniality of knowledge, power, and being, decolonial aesthetics very directly challenges, not only each basic coordinate of modernity/coloniality, but its most visceral foundations and overall scope.[10]

Perhaps most importantly, the decolonial aesthetic turn in the realms of creativity and spirituality opens up the body and the mind to questioning the world and connecting with other bodies and minds in organized movements of solidarity to construct an-other world: "Decolonial aesthetic creation, including decolonial performances of self and subjectivity are, among other things, rituals that seek to keep the body open as a continued source of questions, as a bridge to connect to others, and as prepared to act."[11] In the CEBs, this is true with regard to connecting not only with other human beings, but also with the nonhuman created world, and with the divine source of all being. The creative praxis of the Salvadoran base communities described and analyzed below, therefore, does not function as an isolated instance of decoloniality. Rather, it serves to open the communities up to interrogating reality and acting to transform reality in relationships of solidarity with one another and with other agents of decolonial and liberative struggle in the church and world.

The creative expressions that make up decolonial aesthetics can take many forms. Maldonado-Torres's list includes narrative, visual art, music, dancing, and other modes of performance. One might also add to this list the creativity of food production that takes place in decolonial forms of agriculture and culinary arts. We would include the CEBs' liturgical and sacramental praxis in this litany as well. These multiple forms of self-expression work together to form an inseparable whole, from which it is difficult to systematize or extract one category or example from all others. Taken together, they are practices that affirm the existence, dignity, and value of the church of *lxs pobres* both within and beyond its colonized context. For the sake of clarity and brevity, this chapter will focus on the CEBs' decolonial creativity as it shows up in the following four realms of praxis:

(1) personal/communal narrative and narrative theology, (2) visual arts and *artesanía*, (3) music and song, and (4) liturgy and sacrament. Following our description and analysis of these four realms of the communities' decolonial creativity, we turn to the ways in which these practices, coupled with the CEBs' theological reflection on them, contribute to the decolonization of how the ontology and aesthetics of priesthood and eucharistic celebrations are construed in Roman Catholic ecclesiology and practiced in the Salvadoran church. The sacramentality of the CEBs' creativity points to the ways in which sensing, perceiving, and encountering God's presence and God's reign are experienced and embodied differently in the church of *lxs pobres* than the colonial church.

DECOLONIZING THE COLONIALITY OF BEING: THE CREATIVE-LITURGICAL PRAXIS OF THE CEBS

Decolonial Narrative

The creative praxis of decolonial narrative, "a powerful means to challenge the coloniality of time,"[12] is woven throughout the CEBs' pastoral activities. The historical memory of suffering, martyrdom, and resistance that part I narrated and that we discussed in relation to decolonial epistemology is replete with this aesthetic form of decolonial praxis. From public testimony of survivors, to life stories recorded in tattered notebooks; from popular retellings of the gospel stories to the dramatized accounts of massacres and martyrdom—the gatherings and celebrations of the CEBs manifest not only an epistemological delinking from colonial history, but a creative engagement with historical narratives that bring the communities together, affirm their very being, and reclaim their stories as evidence of their right to exist and reclaim their relationship to time as agents of history.

However, we posit that the narratives of the CEBs challenge more than the coloniality of time understood as historical *chronos*. They also challenge the coloniality of being in time understood as *kairos*, insofar as they affirm and manifest the deep rootedness of historical existence in divine love, justice, and beauty. The CEBs construct not only historical narratives of historical human agency, but narrative and poetic theologies of divine presence and con-spiration with the cosmos and in the historical lives and liberation struggles of *lxs pobres*, the oppressed. The theological narratives of the CEBs are replete with both language of lament and language about God's presence in the natural world, in their neighbors, and even in the midst of the suffering that they endured during the armed conflict and continue to endure today. Francisco Bosch highlights this penchant for popular mysticism in his account of a theopoetic moment that occurred during a popular theology *minga*[13] held in the base community of Jardines de Colón:

> In a cement room, in a city made of cement, in a deforested country, is the little cement *casita* of the CEBs in the community Jardines de Colon. More than 30 folks have come together to *minguear*. It's 2017, the war between the gangs and the government stifles the air. We begin at the beginning, by listening to the earth, searching amongst the walls, the brick, the barbed wire, for a word that God might give us in the cosmos. A little piece of life, which rivals the grey for space: What does it have to say to us? And so, we look like we're out of our minds, leaning over a flower in the pathway, feeling the humidity of the ground, pressing stones firmly into the palms of our hands. Until one sister speaks up when we get back into our circle, "The secret that the earth told me was in the *izote* flower—mutilated a thousand times, but still wanting to live. Apparently, the instinct to live is greater than mutilation."[14]

An entire decolonial aesthetic is wrapped up in this simple, yet profoundly poetic and prophetic reflection on the *terquedad*—the obstinacy, or resilience—of the *izote* flower. To reflect on the presence of the divine in the *izote* as a metaphor for the presence of the divine in the Salvadoran people is a creative act that affirms, reimagines, and re-members the image of God and the *telos* of God's reign in the lives of those on the margins and undersides of coloniality. The CEBs are like the early communities of Jesús followers "that cried out at the death of the carpenter of Nazareth, but were also inspired to narrate the story of the beauty of his life." The CEBs too are determined to fulfill this task:

> that the beauty of the God of life, who accompanies the communities from below, might be narrated by the voices of the wretched of the earth, the ones who have been discarded by the system of death that is now imposed upon us.[15]

Not only does the performance of this task reaffirm the epistemological and creative subjectivity of *lxs pobres*; it also re-members the core of their being as participants in the eternal story of divine beauty.

Decolonial Art and Artesanía

As the story of Andrea's *alfombra* illustrates so powerfully, decolonial visual art and material *artesanía* also contribute to this reclamation of subjectivity and being insofar as they "directly impact the terrain of the coloniality of place and space."[16] Most communities have access to a chapel or other sacred space in which murals, altars, and other forms of material culture adorn the space. These adornments create a setting in which the historically vulnerable and marginalized place the existence and narratives of vulnerable and marginalized persons and communities at the center of their own encounters with the divine. While such visual art is sometimes commissioned in the form of projects like murals on chapel walls, community members themselves more often engage in the production of artwork that facilitates the liberating and healing expression of the people's stories, their struggles, and their deepest longings.

One example of this kind of communal self-expression through visual art and material culture is the construction of temporary altars as sacred spaces at the center of circular meetings, liturgies, or other activities. Usually, the foundation of the altar is a decorative cloth, often woven in a style characteristic of Indigenous textiles of the region, laid out on the floor of the meeting space. Upon this cloth altar, community members place items of sacred significance, such as photos of Salvadoran martyrs, a cross, a candle, fruits of the harvest like corn and beans, and other natural elements like water and earth. Adonay Pérez, one of the contemporary prophets of the CEBs, describes how he leads his community in preparing an altar to center and signify their time together:

> And in every meeting, I always bring the picture of Monseñor Romero, I put it in the center, and people who bring flowers put them there, and we'll put out a light, a candle, and I'll put something else appropriate, a little plant or something, a glass of water, that's a very typical CEBs altar. . . . And people bring their small symbols, too. I'll put, for example, the calendar "Faces Not To Forget" or a song book, you know, important things.[17]

Things of importance, sacred objects, are arranged in a meaningful way at the center of a community meeting space. There is a decolonial beauty to this repeated process of creatively signifying and sacralizing shared identity, struggle, life, and joy. Such beauty often connects explicitly with the communities' *memoria de Jesús* in many ways, especially when a community also places eucharistic elements on the altar and shares them in a common meal, a sacramental act that we will return to momentarily.

Another striking, though not singular, example of the CEBs' identity-forming and being-affirming visual art can be found in the rural community of La Hacienda in Morazán. La Hacienda was resettled in the early 1990s by families returning from the refugee camp in Colomoncagua, Honduras, where some of them had lived for over a decade.[18] A triptych of three murals was created in 2008 by the women of the community with the help of Mercedes Sánchez, a Salvadoran artist who has worked with different CEBs throughout the country to create participative murals and other forms of public art that represent their histories, identities, and dreams. As the women tell it, they met regularly with Mercedes for over a year, sharing their stories from childhood, fleeing the war, and returning to rebuild. Mercedes lived in their houses and participated in the women's daily life, attending community meetings, cooking alongside them in their smoky kitchens, playing with their children, listening to community gossip and conflict, and celebrating liturgy with the community on Sundays. After spending time with Mercedes and with each other, sharing and building trust, the women designed the three murals and painted them on canvas that still hangs in the community chapel.

The first mural is full of dark greens, blues, and blacks, with a full moon overhead scarcely illuminating the forest, wildlife, and tents and cooking fires in the wilderness. It represents the time when the women and their families first returned to La Hacienda after the war. Nothing remained of the old houses; they had to start over from scratch. The second mural is a scene set at dawn, the emerging sun casting its rays on a few humble homes, a school, the chapel, some cultivated fields and chicken pens, and a water pump in the creek. This mural depicts the community as it was at the time the murals were painted and shows how far the women and their families had come since those first dark days. The women describe this mural with pride, pointing out that their children have a proper school to attend and detailing how the water pump distributes water through rubber hoses to every house in the community, even during the dry season. In the third mural, the sun is at its midday peak, fully illuminating the community. Trees and wildlife continue to be plentiful, and the blue of the creek matches the sky. Electricity poles line the dirt road, and a water purification system connects the pump to the plumbing hoses. Adults sit in circles reading and talking, while pigs, cows, and chickens laze next to lush corn and bean plots. Children are playing soccer on their own leveled and painted field, and a medical clinic sits at the top of the road that leads into the community by the chapel. This idyllic scene represents the dreams that the women's group has for their community; it represents the world they want to create together.

These three canvases hang in the community chapel as the women's promise to themselves, their families, and their God about who they are and where they are bound. Their own imaginations and values define who they are as daughters of God and as a community, over and against their erasure from history and marginalization in the contemporary church and world. The murals hang in the chapel because the group believes that the Spirit of the God has accompanied them on every stage of their journey and continues to walk with them toward a future of abundant life. From a place of faith, the women of La Hacienda have created a vision that affirms their full humanity, despite the dehumanizing conditions of their contemporary situation. The mural serves to document their progress and inspire them to work toward what is left to do. In the time since the murals were painted, the people have worked together and with the local authorities to install electricity and build and staff a medical clinic in their community. This faith-inspired process of self-articulation and creativity, far from making the community complacent, enables them to take practical steps toward making their visions evermore real.

One other significant dimension of decolonial creativity that bears mentioning here is the individual and communal production of *artesanía* in the CEBs. *Artesanía* are crafts and tools that are at once artistic self-expression and useful, everyday household goods. They are ordinary items that are handcrafted and decorated with care and precision, not mass-produced, though tourist markets often create demand for cheaply made, unjustly trafficked imitations. Examples of *artesanía* include hammocks, woven bags and purses, embroidery, and leather cases for machetes. These items represent a dense intersection of the (de)coloniality of knowledge, being, and power, since they are at once products created through traditional ways of making passed down through generations, aesthetically beautiful pieces that express the preferences and vision of the artisan, and economic and household goods that can be bought and sold and that use local natural and synthetic resources. Bosch describes how participants in *mingas* participate in community reflections through this form of artistic expression:

> In the back of the room, three women. When I ask a question, they lower their heads. They are attentive, following everything with their gaze, connected with our purpose, but in silence. On the second day they began to weave. On the morning of the third day, everyone asked them if they could take pictures, they had made beautiful tapestries. They had their craft. They were women and Indigenous. Their text was woven. And they didn't think to keep that word to themselves. At that moment, we were all silent. . . . Text and textiles, tangling and untangling, *trama y desenlace*. To weave is to compose a text.[19]

In refugee camps in Honduras during the war, women embroidered scenes of the massacres from which they fled, selecting the shade of green they remember for the military helicopters and the dark red blood mixed with mud in the river. Their aesthetic choices communicate not only the individual point of view of the artisan herself, but also explain effectively why her community lives as it does and where they come from. The fabric that carries these stories is not framed on a wall or preserved in a drawer of memorabilia. It wraps tortillas for a meal and covers food from flies. Life, food, art, and history are all one. The beauty of these items' creation is inseparable from the beauty of their everyday function.

The creation of *artesanía* in El Salvador today, like all examples in this book, is a decolonial struggle to persevere against colonial conditions that have changed the craft but not entirely suppressed it. For example, a hammock is traditionally made out of spun *henequén*, a species of agave. The fibers are harvested, spun on trails of wheels lining rural roads and cornfields, and woven between two upright poles to create the final product, which serves as chairs, cradles, and beds in rural homes. Today, *henequén* has largely been replaced by thin plastic strands that campesino women buy from a middleman in town in (most commonly) blue, orange, yellow, green, and pink. Four thin strands are spun together to create a strong plastic string that is then woven in the traditional style and sold back to the middleman at a set price. The economic control the middleman-merchant has over the price of the work makes hammock-weaving *just* worth it; a plastic hammock can be made in a couple of days of working over the standing loom for 12–14 hours a day and makes the weaver a profit of about $11. The merchant sells it for $25 in town. If a merchant realizes that one of his clients is selling finished hammocks elsewhere for a better price, he stops selling her the unwoven plastic. Despite this lack of control over the raw materials (decades-old *henequén* fields were burned during the war), the pressure to produce a cheap product (consumers are used to the set $25 price tag), and the strain on a weaver's back and eyes when she works fast enough to earn between $20 and $30 per week,[20] hammock weaving is a specialized art form that rural women share and practice with pride. They talk about their preferred color combinations, compare notes about different suppliers' prices and color availability, and teach their children how to weave.

For the CEBs, creating alternative *artesanía* markets has been essential to continuing to produce the hammocks, woven bags, and embroidered *mantas* that keep their makers' individual and communal stories alive. In the late 1980s and early 1990s, the embroidery works created by refugees mentioned above were sold by aid workers to foreign solidarity groups to raise funds for communities in need of building materials, clothes, and food, like Segundo Montes or the communities in the Bajo Lempa region. For many CEBs, an action to which they consistently circle back in their pastoral method is to encourage and promote local artisans and to recover and practice traditional ways of making and trading. Their repertoire has expanded to include soaps and shampoos, traditional medicines and tinctures, quilts, skirts and other clothing, different types of sweet bread, woven backpacks and pencil cases, earrings, necklaces, musical instruments, and greeting cards. There is significant crossover with agricultural production as well, as organized groups of artisan women use seeds and nuts as beads, keep beehives and sell infused honey as a homeopathic remedy, and use their own corn and milk in their breads and sweets. Youth in the CEBs have increasingly developed a taste for silkscreening, often producing their own shirts for different celebrations and events with homemade designs depicting martyrs on their anniversaries; quotes from Romero's homilies; or cornfields, trees, and other images of the natural world. The night before a major celebration, the central chapel in one canton in Cacaopera is often strewn with hand-screened shirts drying on lines for the next day's festivities. When participants rise from their woven hammocks the next morning, share breakfast tortillas from an embroidered *manta*, and meet at the chapel to don a shirt and arrange an altar with photos, scripture, fabric, and fruits and branches—the Creator's own *artesanía*—they craft a community that is freely chosen, like the colors for a hammock, to be both functional and beautiful.

Decolonial Song

Decolonial music is a similarly healing, liberating, and empowering creative-aesthetic activity of the Salvadoran church of *lxs pobres*. In Maldonado-Torres's words again, decolonial music "can interrupt the logic of space and make subjects experience multiple forms of time through various rhythms."[21] Decolonial lyrics also inspire the body and mind to question and critique the established norms of coloniality in the realms of politics, economics, culture, gender, race, and theology. Through both music and lyrics, decolonial song connects colonized bodies and minds across time and space in a collective dance away from the coloniality of being and toward the full flourishing of life in abundance. As mentioned in the introduction to chapter 2, the CEBs' liturgical, cultural, and even recreational activities are replete with the alternative, liberationist lyrics and decolonial rhythms of the Latin American *nueva trova* movement that flourished in the 1960s,[22] the Salvadoran and Nicaraguan popular masses written during the 1970s–1980s,[23] the *campesino*-composed *corridos* dedicated to heroes and martyrs of the Salvadoran armed conflict,[24] and the more recent songs written by members of the CEBs themselves.

In 2017, the national network of ecclesial base communities in El Salvador recorded a compact disc with twenty-six original songs that they describe in the CD liner notes as

> our best option for expressing our ideals as CEBs, in accordance with our posture of seeing, judging, acting, and celebrating in the face of the reality that is happening every day in our country, voicing diverse appeals to change our reality and also remembering so many men and women, martyrs who gave their lives to defend the lives of others, desiring to follow the example of every one of them.[25]

Chamba, the community leader and musician in the Bajo Lempa region cited in chapter 1, observes that the music of the CEBs—what he calls the CEBs' *canto popular*, or music of the people—is an "instrument of conscientization and liberation" and an "invaluable ingredient for the daily activities of the ecclesial base communities in El Salvador."[26] Gustavo, the artist and singer-songwriter in the Pueblo de Dios en Camino community discussed in chapter 2, stresses the profound connection between this music and the very being, the soul of the communities:

> The songs of the CEBs have been constructed in conjunction with our history; they have emerged from the depths of our being, from the consciousness that comes from reality; the lyrics and music settle deep in the souls of our Christian communities.[27]

As this music emerges from and settles deep into the soul of the church of *lxs pobres*, the base communities affirm the dignity of their existence in an embodied way.

In this section, we highlight the decoloniality of the new songs written by and for the CEBs themselves. Many of these songs describe, lament, and denounce the interrelated realities of suffering and martyrdom in Salvadoran history, neoliberal economics and the accumulation of wealth in the hands of a few *acaparadores* (hoarders), the incursion of metallic mining and hydroelectric dams in the region, ecological devastation and climate change due to deforestation and conventional agriculture, the separation of families due to the necessity of migration, and the apathy of the institutional church in the face of such inhuman realities. For example, the song "Quejas a Monseñor" ("Grievances for Monseñor [Romero]") is based on a poem composed by a community leader that includes denunciations of many of these realities. The poem is structured around several grievances or complaints directed at the CEBs' beloved San Romero, beginning with a grievance about his own church:

Esta mañana te traigo mis quejas,	This morning I bring you my complaints,
unas quejas sobre tu iglesia,	some complaints about your church,
que cada día más se aleja, de los pobres, nuestra Iglesia.	which distances itself more and more every day from *los pobres*, from our church.
Es así Monseñor, cuántas cosas están pasando,	That's how it is, *Monseñor*, so many things are happening,
a mí me da dolor, porque solos estamos quedando.	it hurts me so much, because we are being left alone.[28]

The poem goes on to lament the realities of food insecurity and malnutrition; the exclusion of young people from an economy founded on neoliberal capitalism; violence against women and the church's complicity in women's suffering; the destruction of rivers and contamination of water sources by big business; and, again, the apathy of the institutional church, which remains silent in the face of such suffering.

Members of the CEBs are adamant that their music should not participate in this silence. Their songs, they say, should reflect reality, not the "*calles de oro, mar de cristal*," the "streets of gold and crystal seas," of traditional Catholic hymns.[29] In Gustavo's words,

> Our songs have to speak of real-life situations. Not of heaven. Because heaven is up above and there is also a here below. Here where there is so much suffering. In this world, where there is so much hunger. In this world, where every minute many children are dying. We speak about and we sing songs that have to do with reality. *That's* theology.[30]

By facing and denouncing the injustices of this world directly, the CEBs creatively express their epistemic delinking from coloniality, name reality for what it is, and thus engage in decolonial theological knowledge production. In the process, a decolonial consciousness is nurtured for confronting reality in other realms of praxis. As Gustavo puts it, "our consciousness is formed in and through our songs."[31]

On the other hand, the music of the CEBs is also celebratory—it announces the good news of liberation and calls the communities to participate in the construction of God's reign of peace, justice, and ecological well-being. For example, "Aunque sea a chuña" ("Even if we're barefoot") is a joyful tune with an upbeat rhythm that begins with a call to unity and celebration:

Con el pueblo unido, vamos a cantar,	United with the people, we are going to sing
Esta cachimbona, danza popular	This great tune, this people's dance
Canta la guitarra, también el tambor	The guitar is singing, and so is the drum
Que nadie se agüeve, que agarre el valor.	Nobody hold back, have some courage.
Aunque sea a chuña le vamos a entrar	Even if we're barefoot we're going to get in there
Quitando las piedras y no trompezar,	Clearing away the stones and not tripping up,
Un paso adelante, y uno para atrás	One step forward, and one step back
Será nuestra lema para caminar.	Will be our motto for the journey.

This song does not speak of joyful celebration as an apolitical opiate, though. Rather, it draws energy from shared celebration in order to call for

Celebramos la vida   261

the community to come together in a common struggle against the forces of oppression and for the rebirth of a new society:

La mera macolla es el pueblo unido,	The very heart of the matter is the people united
Nadie lo detiene, es un aguerrido	No one can stop them, they are battle-worn
contra el que chinga, tiene que luchar	Against anyone who messes with them, they
Y montar su vuelo a la libertad.	must fight and take flight towards freedom.
Trabajando juntos, vamos a lograr	Working together, we are going to succeed
Esta gran tarea, pronto va a acabar	This great task will soon be over
Y el maíz nuevo ya florecerá	And the new maize will soon blossom
Y el frijol del campo ya renacerá.	And the beans of the field will be born anew.[32]

Dozens, if not hundreds of songs, contain these prophetic-decolonial elements of denunciation, annunciation, celebration, and call to action.

Humor is another decolonial strategy that the CEBs employ in their creative activity more broadly, including in their music. One particularly notable song that combines prophetic denunciation with celebratory rhythm and decolonial humor is "A la chingada," written and performed by Grupo Libre in the CEBs of Cacaopera, Morazán.[33] This song was written in response to the incursion of hydroelectric dams and metallic mining in the rural and mountainous northeastern region of El Salvador. The lyrics call on local and national communities to raise popular consciousness of these issues and take action in defense of the land and water that sustains the lives and well-being of not only local *campesinos* and *campesinas* but entire ecosystems throughout the region. The song declares that neither the Torola River nor the land is for sale, and it proceeds to tell the invested public and private parties[34] where to go with their profit-driven plans for Morazán: *a la chingada*. This popular expression could be translated as "fuck off," "screw off," or "go to hell," but the CEBs sing these words with humor. The song thus takes a decolonially humorous approach to their denunciation of social, economic, and ecological exploitation. The song's composer, Agustín Luna, remarks that he felt compelled to write this song and why it occurred to him to use such provocative language:

Because if we don't [really] get into it, then we would also have problems, right. [We needed] a multitude, but if we don't enter into the consciousness that we have to struggle, then they were going to win. And so that's why I was thinking about those lyrics. And then later on, some [other lyrics come from] posters with sayings from when the company arrived at the soccer field in El Rodeo [for a meeting]. So some of those same sayings, I took up those sayings, and I just put them in the song.[35]

The provocative and humorous language of "*a la chingada*" conveys not only the rage of communities in response to the exploitation of their communities, lands, and waterways. It also conveys the subversive power of rage-filled, decolonial humor and the way in which that rage and that humor are intertwined and oriented toward decolonial love for the colonized and the land on which they dwell. Such means of creative expression fills the communities with the joy and strength necessary for resistance to Empire and the construction of God's reign.

The "Corrido de las Comunidades" ("The Ballad of the Communities") is another example from the new repertoire of the Salvadoran CEBs in which the lyrics celebrate the joy and strength that comes from communal struggle for a better world:

Compartimos los frutos, de vivir en comunidad	We share the fruits of living together in community
Llegamos con alegría a fortalecer la unidad	We arrive with joy to strengthen our unity
Hagamos vida el Evangelio para que en el	Let's make the Gospel come alive so that in the
Pueblo haya más dignidad	People there is more dignity.[36]

This song draws on the historical inspiration of the martyrs of the Salvadoran popular church, calling the CEBs to join their prophet, San Romero, in the struggle against ecological destruction, the privatization of water, and the incursion of metallic mining in Central America. Like many of the CEBs' songs, this one is replete with imagery drawn from the life-giving agricultural work of the CEBs, ending with words of encouragement: "*Adelante compañeras a sembrar la tierra con todo el amor*" ("Let's keep moving forward, comrades, sowing the earth with all our love"). With these songs and so many others, the CEBs are reclaiming subjectivity, time, space, and even the land itself as a realm of decolonial love—in other words, as the place of God's reign—in which they are called to participate.

Decolonial Liturgy and Sacraments

Finally, we would add to Maldonado-Torres's litany of decolonial creative praxis the liturgical and sacramental life of the CEBs. In a move that explicitly recognizes the centrality of liturgy in their communities, which often includes many of the creative elements detailed above, the CEBs of El Salvador have included "celebration" as an additional step in their see-judge-act pastoral method. Most base communities organize themselves to carry out some form of Sunday service, including some elements of both the Liturgy of the Word and/or the eucharist, whether lay-led or with a sympathetic priest to either preside or co-preside with the people. The CEBs also coordinate baptismal, funeral, and communal penance services; preparation for community festivals and anniversaries of the communities' martyrs; adaptation of liturgy to popular culture; and critical appropriation of popular religiosity. In recent years, some CEBs have also been reincorporating Indigenous ritual, linguistic, and artistic elements as part of their liturgical ministries. Whether it is a folk Mass held at the site of a civil war massacre or an Indigenous-inspired ritual of thanksgiving for the fruits of the land, the CEBs assert their subjectivity as creators of decolonial beauty, whereby they reclaim their own existence, along with time, space, and place.

One significant area in which the liturgical life of the CEBs has taken a decidedly decolonial turn in recent years is in the realm of the sacraments. When the CEBs began in the 1970s and 1980s, their understanding of the Bible and their practice of faith underwent radical transformation, but their sacramental practices remained more or less the same. In recent years, however, the CEBs have been engaged in the decolonial construction of liberating sacraments that they see as an important means of cultivating their commitment to a life of communal struggle for and construction of the reign of God.[37] Members of the CEBs are vocally critical of the way in which the institutional church implements the sacraments, especially baptism and eucharist. They denounce the commodification of these sacraments, which come with a monetary price tag, and some members describe the institutional sacraments as a "business" and as "inventions" of the church that are very "egoistic," "empty," "without meaning," "fear-filled," and even "*anti-reino*" (i.e., the antithesis of the reign of God).[38] However, the CEBs do not reject the sacraments—rather, they have a rich sacramental life in which eucharistic celebrations play a central role, sometimes with a sympathetic priest presiding alongside the community and other times with community leaders and/or the whole assembled congregation presiding. These communities refuse to allow the distance of the institutional church to deprive them of this sacrament, which they see, "*mirándolo desde Jesús*,"[39] from the perspective of Jesús, as a powerful manifestation of their commitment to *lxs pobres* and to the reign of God.

The CEBs' eucharistic celebrations are decidedly egalitarian and inclusive. Women are often leaders of the liturgical celebration, preachers of the Word, and/or even preside over the communion table. Furthermore, the CEBs generally practice an open table when they break and share bread together during liturgy. As Roni, from the CEB "Mons. Romero" in Altavista, observes: at Jesús's Last Supper, "everyone ate, even Judas."[40] Furthermore, the CEBs often depart from using the canonically approved Roman elements of unleavened bread and wine in order to create a eucharistic celebration in which typical Salvadoran food and drink are offered. Gustavo observes that this culturally decolonial practice is deeply theological: "theology *is* tortilla and hot chocolate" and "that's why we celebrate the eucharist with sweet bread, cookies, *pupusas*, with tortillas, with tamales."[41] The CEBs have little time for metaphysical explanations of the canonical regulations on eucharistic elements. Their decolonial sacramentology cuts to the heart of the meaning of the sacraments as that which gives life to the people and the earth, that which manifests and nurtures the memory of Jesús and the presence of God's reign among them.

Before moving on to consider how the CEBs are decolonizing Catholic ecclesiology in and through these praxes of creativity, it is important to note that in recent years the base communities have been incorporating more and more of their Indigenous heritage into their spirituality, creative activities, and liturgical life. Some members of the CEBs are investigating a reclamation of the Indigenous languages of El Salvador, which is evident in the song "Lengua Cacahuira" ("Kakawira Language"). The Spanish lyrics of the song announce the originality and complexity of the Kakawira language:

Señores, oigan lo que les voy a cantar,	[Ladies and] gentlemen, listen to what I am going to sing to you,
Como hablaba, nuestra gente ancestral.	how our ancestral people spoke.
Tenían el idioma buen original,	They had a language that was really original,
Un tanto complicao que ahora yo se los voy a contar.	A little complicated, but now I am going to tell you.
. . .	. . .
¡Es la lengua de mi pueblo!	It's the language of my people!
¡Es la lengua original!	It's the original language!
. . .	. . .
¡Es la lengua original, de los kakawiras!	It's the original language, of the Kakawiras!

The rest of the song is a prayer of thanksgiving, sung in the Kakawiran language, for the gifts of creation.

Other members of the CEBs speak of the importance of reclaiming Indigenous ceremonies, which are increasingly incorporated into communal celebrations. A heightened awareness of the Indigenous roots of Salvadoran popular religion is also taking hold in the Salvadoran church of *lxs pobres*. For example, every year on May 3, Salvadorans celebrate the "Day of the Cross" by placing sweet fruits typically in season in May around a wooden cross to coincide with traditional planting times for the growing/rainy season. While the ritual has definite origins in Spanish Catholicism, it also coincides with and incorporates elements of the Indigenous ceremony of offering gifts to the gods and to the Earth in celebration of and thanksgiving for the rebirth of the land in the rainy season. Furthermore, some community leaders are looking for ways to celebrate other lost Indigenous rituals, such as a ceremony for the Indigenous new year, a ritual of thanksgiving for water, and the celebrations of *El Pago de la Tierra* (Offering to the Earth) and *El Dia del Fuego* (The Day of Fire). Agustín, the composer of "A la chingada" and "Lengua Cacahuira," is a community leader in the region of El Salvador once inhabited by the Kakawira people. He observes that such reclamation of Indigenous faith and culture can be "very liberating."[42] In the language of decoloniality, these endeavors are liberating because they provide creative means of both resisting the erasure of Indigenous being under coloniality and affirming the dignity and worth of that being for the people of the base communities. The CEBs' recovery of indigeneity is an incipient and ongoing process that merits further investigation and research. The scope of our research and argument here, however, compels us to turn to the ways in which the CEBs' decolonial creativity points toward decolonial horizons in Catholic ecclesiology. It is to this question that we now turn.

HORIZONS IN DECOLONIAL ECCLESIOLOGY: PRIESTHOOD AND EUCHARISTIC THEOLOGY

The Coloniality of Priesthood in Roman Catholicism

Within the ecclesiology of the late medieval Catholicism that arrived in the Americas, ordained clergy not only held the epistemological authority to discern and define the divine will for human reality but also held the ontological keys to salvation. It was in and through the sacramental life of the church—especially the sacraments of baptism and eucharist—that salvation was gained, and these sacraments could only be performed by ordained priests, on the authority of their bishop. The ontological status of the ordained priest so united him with Christ that it was through his ritual action that the saving grace of Christ might be conferred upon the faithful. The coloniality of being that began in the conquest and colonization of Latin America and that continues to this day is multifaceted and complex, but a significant dimension of it was and continues to be the ontological separation of the "true Christian self" from the non-Christian other, along with the ontological separation of the ordained clergy from the laity.[43] We touched on how the CEBs tend to reject the former separation in chapter 1, but we have chosen to locate the latter separation here in this chapter on the decoloniality of being because the emphasis on the cultic functions of the ordained and thus ontologically separate priesthood play a significant role in the metaphysical catastrophe that results from stripping the colonized of their aesthetic and creative expressions and sacramental embodiments of the divine presence in human life. The coloniality of being in Latin American Catholicism results in large part from how the sacramental power of dispensing grace is concentrated in the hands of certain men, anointed with an ontological mark that sets them apart from the rest of the Christian faithful, and, all the more, from the rest of humanity. What's more, for centuries, these ordained men were almost exclusively European or of European descent.[44] All other aesthetic, creative, and liturgical modes of sensing, perceiving, and participating in the divine life are rendered suspect, primitive, superstitious, and, in colonial times, even criminal under this ontological separation.

The Second Vatican Council made great strides toward reducing the gap between the clergy and laity, and toward affirming and encouraging the full participation of the laity in the sacramental life of the church. As chapter 2 indicates, conciliar ecclesiology recovered the biblical understanding of the church as the people of God, with its members all anointed in baptism as a priestly, prophetic, and royal people called to holiness and apostolic mission in the church and world. In this vision, all of the faithful participate in the priesthood of the baptized. The laity are distinguished from the clergy primarily by their secular function, for "it is the special vocation of the laity to seek the kingdom of God by engaging in temporal affairs and directing them according to God's will."[45] It is this call to active involvement in matters of social concern that impelled much of the Latin American popular church to enter into solidarity with *lxs pobres*, the oppressed, in their daily struggles for survival and their social movements for liberation. Furthermore, the council encouraged the full participation of the laity in the liturgy and sacraments, thus opening up new vistas for lay Catholic involvement in liturgical ministry and sacramental life (e.g., in the roles of lector, acolyte, musician, and more). The lay-clergy binary thus came to be cast in primarily functional terms, with the common priesthood of the faithful and the ministerial or hierarchical priesthood each sharing, in their own special way, "in the one priesthood of Christ."[46] As such, the lay faithful and the ordained clergy are liturgical, prophetic, and political cocreators with the divine, collaborating with one another in a perpetual offering of priestly, prophetic, and royal service to the coming of God's reign. In fact, the conciliar documents insist that the ordained priesthood exists not to dominate but to serve the church as the whole people of God in this mission of building up the reign of God in the world. Here yet another crack in the colonial crust of the church opens up to allow for aesthetic and liturgical creativity among the laity, which comes to such full expression in communities like the CEBs in El Salvador's church of *lxs pobres*.

However, for the most part, the hierarchy and clergy of the Salvadoran church have not allowed space for lay ministry to come fully into its own as a site of creative affirmation of being, let alone sacramental efficacy. The stories of Andrea's *alfombra* above and in part I and of Romero's beatification in part I illustrate the fact that the creative expressions of the laity, even outside the realm of sacramental ministry, are often devalued at best and vilified at worst. The continued ontological separation of the clergy and hierarchy from the laity invests the former with the authority (chapter 2) and the power (chapter 4) to determine and officially sanction only those forms of creativity and liturgical devotion that they deem appropriate to the Catholic tradition as they define it. This practice runs counter to the spirit of Vatican II and has serious colonial implications for the sacraments and liturgical inculturation, which we will explore further below. More relevant and pressing here is the underlying issue of how, even alongside the council's more functional approach, priestly ordination effects an ontological change in the ordinand such that he (yes, always he!) is essentially marked by a new assimilation to Christ's own person.

Indeed, even the most progressive corners of post-conciliar Roman Catholicism cannot escape the fact that the magisterium has defined the difference between the common and ordained priesthood not simply as one of function; rather, it is still officially defined as an essential, ontological difference. Not only did the council not reject the ontological difference, it affirmed that the functions of lay and ordained priesthood continue to differ from one another "essentially and not only in degree."[47] In 2002, the Congregation for Clergy doubled down on this difference, insisting that the essence of the ordained ministry is ontological assimilation to Christ. It is precisely this essential transformation that confers on the ordained priest the power to fulfill his function as representative or icon of Christ the Head, acting *in persona Christi capitis*, in the transmission of divine grace (God's saving presence) to the whole people of God. The Sacrament of Holy Orders "configures the priest to Christ so as to enable him to act in the person of Christ, the Head, and to exercise the *potestas sacra* to *offer Sacrifice and forgive sins.*"[48] The ordained priesthood, then, retains its ontological status as the divinely sealed conduit of the recreative and redemptive grace made available in the liturgical life of the church, especially in the sacraments, and most especially in the sacrament of the eucharist, over which an ordained priest alone may preside *in persona Christi capitis*. The coloniality of this arrangement is glaringly self-evident: the ontological separation of ordained men from lay women and men feeds into a power matrix in which the Christian laity depend on the clergy for the "essential salvific actions" that effect the ontological affirmation and salvation of the faithful. The CEBs, though, refuse to accept the ontological designation of passive and dependent recipients of divine life, which they see as the freely given birthright of all human beings as children of God. "We are not *masa* [the masses/dough]. *Masa* is moved around this way and that, but not the ecclesial base communities, no."[49]

The CEBs Decolonize the Lay-Clergy Binary

The very first ecclesial base communities in El Salvador understood themselves to be on a path of formation to become a priestly people, a people of God conformed to the priesthood of Jesús. The communities began by passing through the various steps that make up the stages of priestly ordination, becoming porters, exorcists, lectors, acolytes, and deacons in their own communal and political realities. They opened the doors of the church and their homes to the marginalized and excluded; exorcised demons of alcoholism, machismo, and individualism; read the Bible together in community and preached the good news; served and supported one another and their neighbors in solidarity and love. Throughout this process, ordained priests and laity together were *becoming priests in everyday life*, preparing themselves together for offering the commitment and the sacrifice of their lives to God in the service of their people's liberation.[50] This chapter has fleshed out a sampling of the myriad ways in which contemporary CEBs celebrate the beauty of life, creatively embody their faith in the God of Life, and offer the sacrament of their very being to God and one another in search of God's reign of abundant life. In and through their aesthetic, creative, and sacramental praxis, the CEBs have come into their own as a priestly people—a people fully capable of facilitating a diversity of "salvific acts" that manifest the efficacious presence and love of God as the ground and essence of their very being, the being of all humanity, and the being of all creation. This process, coupled with the subsequent rejection of the CEBs by the Salvadoran hierarchy and vast majority of clergy, has led the CEBs to a new place of theological reflection on their ecclesial status as laity and the role of the ordained priesthood in the life of the church.

The Salvadoran base communities, as the church of *lxs pobres* on the move in history, carry out their pastoral ministry in the context of what has been called *"la hora de lxs laicxs"* ("the hour of the laity") in diverse circles of contemporary Roman Catholicism. On the one hand, the CEBs are a decolonial embodiment of this appellation brought to life and given flesh and bones in the church today. These are communities in which the laity are the lifeblood of the church, or rather the veins through which the blood of *el divino salvador del mundo*[51] runs with vigor, passion, and commitment to the full flourishing of humanity and creation in the reign of God. Agustín stresses the central ecclesial role of the laity as vigilantly attentive to the needs of the community. He remarks that "the role of the lay person is, I think this—to be more *pendiente* [attentive and unsettled], or to work harder, or to highlight what needs to be done, right? For others. It's to be looking out for others."[52] He notes that it is difficult to maintain this role in the church and society, especially when community life is destabilized by realities like internal migration and emigration to the North, but "the role of the laity always should be there; it needs to be working, motivating, or doing something as an example for others." As a farmer, lay leader, community organizer, environmental activist, singer-songwriter, and musician, Agustín faithfully does all of these things. In the realm of decolonial creativity in particular, when Agustín writes his music, works the land, or engages in Indigenous ritual actions, he is living out his baptismal vocation to participate in the priesthood of the One whose creative and recreative work gives and restores existence to all created life, especially those who are marginalized and oppressed in any way.

When Agustín's community in Cacaopera gathers in their chapel to break bread together, the nearest priest is often a two-to-three hour walk away at the parish residence in the town. The people of the community gather to reflect on the Word of God and meditate on the presence of the holy among them, convoked by the Creator, made present in the re-membering of the crucifixions of *lxs pobres* throughout the history of the people of Israel and in their reality today, and sent forth by the Spirit which animates their daily lives. The walls are adorned with pieces of murals of Jesús, of San Romero, of their own cornfields, and of holy words and phrases, and the altar is created anew each week. Holy words, some in the ancestral language of the Kakawira, others in locally accented Spanish, are read from the pages of scripture or sung in the form of songs of *Grupo Libre* and others from the hymnal *El Pueblo Canta*. Bread is shared, either tortilla, or *pan de torta* that someone made in their clay oven with the fruits and milks of the land. The shared homily discusses the mayor's most recent decision about agricultural aid this spring; or President Trump's most recent threat for ICE detainees, some of whom are their own children or brothers; or how to protect both the teacher, who travels in to the community's K–6 school from town every week, and the students, their children, present and vocal at the celebration, from COVID-19. In this community-directed memorial and resurrection of Jesús, the CEBs are living out their baptismal vocation to embody the real presence of the divine in their communal commitment to the shared banquet of God's reign. Their life goes on, whether the priest is busy attending to other communities or refusing to visit because of a political difference with the people, and the community will not let time go by without calling on God to be present among them and to give thanks for the life they are tasked with continuing to live in faith. The prolific and creative role of lay ministry in this emergent "hour of the laity" is, to a certain extent, a decolonial manner of making visible the dignity of the whole people of God, especially those whose creative capacity and basic right to exist have been historically degraded. Here we see the latent decolonial possibilities of Vatican II brought to life in the church of *lxs pobres*.

On the other hand, the autonomy of the CEBs' creative, celebratory, and sacramental praxis points to the possibility of deconstructing and thus decolonizing the lay-clergy binary altogether. Indeed, some members of the CEBs have begun to question the fundamental separation between the ordained priesthood and the laity, reflecting that "laity" is a "colonial and degrading word."[53] For Tere and her community Nuevo Amanecer, the concept of "laity" is too closely tied to the passive and dependent status described above:

> It's the people that only listens and doesn't give an opinion because it's only the consecrated [priest] who has the power of God and knows everything. . . . That word means nothing to me and I think we should get rid of it.[54]

Gustavo, from Pueblo de Dios en Camino, similarly reflects that

> it's good to examine this concept of "the laity." Laity is a concept that is part of a hierarchical structure. Should we use it, or shouldn't we use it? I don't think that we should use the concept of "laity." . . . Jesús said, "Now I am going to call you friends. Brothers and sisters." He didn't say "laity." "Laity" is a concept that comes from the church structure. And so we in the communities keep walking and we keep organizing ourselves too. And we are free to take up certain concepts or not.[55]

What Gustavo is expressing here aligns with the decoloniality of knowledge explored in chapter 2—that is, the epistemological freedom to examine the theological concepts of the church with a critical consciousness based on the experience of communities that have suffered harmful effects of such concepts and guided by the criteria of God's reign, as heralded by Jesús. The prophetic nature of the CEBs' engagement with colonial Catholicism thus becomes evident in their denouncement of that which the institutional church has harmfully imposed on the faithful and announcement of an egalitarian alternative based on Jesús's own message and praxis of the reign of God. This prophetic and decolonial knowledge production that takes place in the CEBs goes hand in hand with the decolonization of being, expressed in creative and liturgical praxis that we described above. When members of the CEBs choose to reject the lay-clergy binary in their creative, celebratory, and sacramental praxis, they reclaim and re-member the full dignity and sacred power of their existence. They delink from the ontological separation and hierarchy that characterizes the colonial power matrix. The reign of God thus breaks into history with a beauty that can only be perceived from below. This will also carry with it implications for the decolonization of power in the church and society, which we will explore at length in chapter 4.

What, then, is the role of the ordained priest in the church according to the CEBs? There does not seem to be a significant difference on this question between those who retain and those who reject the concept of the laity. Rather, most members of the CEBs refuse to accept a hierarchical role for the ordained clergy and most also insist on their own communal capacity to preside over their own lay-led sacraments, especially the breaking of the bread. However, we would do well to remember that the Salvadoran CEBs have often been forced into this position due to the rejection that they have experienced within parish and diocesan structures. If a sympathetic priest is committed to the values of the church of *lxs pobres* as sacrament of God's reign, then he is loved and accepted by the communities as one of their own. Certainly the myriad images of priests that adorn the walls of chapel and homes of the CEBs—some martyred, others not—point to a deep love and appreciation for the role of ordained priests in their history. The CEBs' continued appreciation for the role that ordained priests can play in the church of *lxs pobres* is further evidenced in the recent outpouring of love and grief at the 2015 death of Padre Pedro Declercq, one of the Belgian missionaries who helped to form the first Salvadoran CEBs in 1969, and at the 2020 death of Dom Pedro Casaldàliga, the Catalan-born Brazilian bishop and poet of *lxs pobres* extraordinaire. The CEBs proclaim that they want bishops (and priests) who are on the side of *lxs pobres*, not that they don't want bishops or priests at all. But by no means are priests or bishops granted a special, ontologically separate status as the only person in the community with the power to "confect the Body and Blood of the Redeemer."[56]

The Coloniality of Roman Catholic Sacramental Practice[57]

In a sentence, one specifically colonial problem with Roman Catholic theologies of the sacraments (besides the ontological status of ministers as discussed above) is that since the time when sacramental practices were universalized at the Council of Trent in the mid-sixteenth century, very little progress has been made to incorporate the experience of the clear majority of the contemporary world's faithful who live in Latin America.[58] If, as many liberation theologians emphasize, theology is a second moment of reflection on an experience of God in a concrete reality,[59] then theology—and ultimately magisterial teaching—should be flexible enough to incorporate the critiques and lived experiences of the Latin American sacramental imagination. However, the Euro-centric sacramental practices that were the ecclesial front of colonial invasions and the eventual concretization of Trent's canons in the Latin American context have, in many cases, become the last word on what "sacrament" means. The bread and wine that the magisterium affirms become the Body and Blood of Christ during Mass are the same bread and wine that marked the "right" kinds of Indigenous converts and indicated submission to the Spanish crown. Baptism was juxtaposed with the threat of

Spanish invasion; to belong to the Roman Catholic church during colonial times was to be saved from the worst kind of Spanish domination. The symbols which are meant to effectively put the faithful in touch with the grace of the God of Life are the same symbols that have historically and practically signified subjugation, colonization, and death.

In addition to this impasse of symbolic signification, colonial clericalism and Euro-centrism have held the faithful back from taking "that full, conscious, and active part in liturgical celebrations which is demanded by the very nature of the liturgy,"[60] called for by the Second Vatican Council's Constitution on the Sacred Liturgy. Although "any appearance of trafficking or trading is to be excluded entirely from the offering for Masses,"[61] CEBs report being charged for the celebration of sacraments like baptism, marriage, or funeral masses:

> It is a business. We have had that experience. When we were with the Maryknoll priests, that group invited anyone who wanted to be baptized to receive the proper formation. They never asked for money. But as soon as other priests came, we had to pay $5 per baptism. So. And that's true in lots of churches, not just in El Salvador. It is the business of the sacraments. It's not faithful.[62]

While the financial disparity between foreign missionary orders and Salvadoran diocesan priests brings an entirely separate layer of colonial analysis to the reality of charging money for the celebration of Mass or other sacraments,[63] it remains the case that these practices meant that *lxs pobres* have rarely been able to celebrate different moments of their life—the birth of a child, coming-of-age, marriage, death—with the witness of their church.

Relatedly, Catholic culture in El Salvador, as elsewhere, implies moralistic traditions that restrict who can serve as acceptable godparents for a newborn or who can receive communion during Mass. According to the Catechism, godparents should be "firm believers, able and ready to help the newly baptized—child or adult on the road of Christian life,"[64] but in El Salvador, godparents are often sought primarily for their financial wealth or social esteem. In a skit about baptism created by children in the community of Segundo Montes in 2014, the mother of a newborn asks the local owner of a store to be the godmother of her child because she can pay the offering to the church. The store owner asks the mother "what she has to do" to be the child's godmother, and the mother replies that she only has to go to a couple of short talks at the church and attend the ceremony. The rest of the skit detailed the mother's preparations for the lunch she would offer to the godmother and the priest after the ritual, worrying about what food to prepare and setting a nice table. In a discussion afterward, the community criticized how they have been educated to focus on the material aspects of the sacrament without focusing on the reasons why, according to them, Jesús himself chose to be baptized: to emphasize his commitment to God, to inaugurate his own mission, to make a commitment with his whole life, and to put his five senses (his body) at the disposition of God's work in the world.[65] Even children recognize this distinction, and are able to articulate, through play-acting, what is wrong with the status quo of baptism in their experience.

Similarly, when celebrating the eucharist during Mass, many who were raised Catholic do not file forward to receive the sacrament unless they have confessed immediately before the celebration begins. In countless conversations and questions with communities about this tendency, many admit to feeling unworthy of confessing and communing, or reveal a self-consciousness that a *pobre* receiving eucharist is considered to be "*creído*," thinking too highly of themself. Marriage, baptism, eucharist—that is, fully conscious and active participation in the life of the church—is not for the *damnés*.

As we suggest at the beginning of this section, the normative sacramental theology threateningly imposed upon the colonized peoples of the Americas and elsewhere was *inherently* colonial because it was imposed in a symbolic and historical context that was not shared by the colonized. The accumulated diversity of sacramental traditions from the time of the Apostles and the first Christian communities upon which the magisterium drew in order to articulate universal norms for sacramental practice at the Council of Trent was not delicately and consensually placed in dialogue with Indigenous understandings about divinity at work in the world that the Nahua, Kakawira, or Lenca people may have negotiated over generations and held dear at the time of the conquest. Rather, the flawed but Spirit-led traditioning of the church was cheapened, honed into propositional commands, and used as a weapon to convert Indigenous peoples into colonized *damnés* not even worthy of the sacraments they were forced to accept as necessary for salvation.

There are, then, two levels to the contemporary coloniality of the Sacraments in El Salvador today. One is represented by the clerical, needlessly controlling, at times noncanonical practices of the Salvadoran hierarchy, including charging for sacraments and focusing on moralistic criteria for participants instead of the criteria of conversion and discipleship. The second layer is the lack of sacramental inculturation and historic non-reception of the sacraments by many participants. The CEBs are well aware of these problems, especially the second. Héctor, from Pueblo de Dios en Camino, asks rhetorically

> I ask you, today, do you think that in the prison in Mariona, that there aren't people who are baptized? How many people in the Mariona prison are baptized, huh? All of them. Have they really committed themselves to the gospel? Or are they there because of what good people they are? I mean, the Church has done a

bad job with the Sacraments. And that's just in one prison. But if we go nationally, to all the prisons. . . . However, for us in San Ramón, [the sacrament] has to be something that moves you, that makes your heart of stone soften when you see the needs of others.⁶⁶

This off-the-cuff example is rife with potential misinterpretations. Héctor is not saying that being in prison categorically makes you a bad person, nor is he saying that all of the baptized have to be perfect people. Rather, he is trying to illustrate how being baptized in the church according to hierarchical rubrics generally does not inspire a person to live a more Christian life. This same tension was the reason given for so much delay in Romero's beatification and canonization. Because the ones who authorized his murder and physically shot him were baptized Christians, the church was unwilling to declare him a martyr *in odium fidei*. How, Rome argued, could Romero have been killed for standing up for his faith if those who killed him were also baptized believers?⁶⁷ The CEBs heard this refrain over and over again and saw in their daily lives how many people who benefitted from the marginalization of *lxs pobres* also professed to be Christians. What money-laundering president wasn't baptized? What army general who became a corrupt senator didn't go to church on Sunday? What gang leader extorting neighborhood businesses wasn't wearing a crucifix? What the CEBs try to point out with their criticism of sacramental practices is that the visible signs that the Roman Catholic church insists are guaranteed to confer grace do not in fact appear to confer grace in their lives and experience.

In response, the CEBs have begun to probe sacramental practices, desiring both to excise what does not give life or promote conversion and to recreate visible signs of the faith they profess in the God of scripture and the reign of life that God promises.

The CEBs Decolonize Liturgy and Sacrament

Much of the art, music, *artesanía*, altar-building, and liturgical practices already described in this chapter are, in large part, what comprise the CEBs' decolonial sacramental practices. These practices work to decolonize the non-canonical, clerical, and Eurocentric norms of Salvadoran sacramental practice because they seek to inculturate the liturgy evermore into the Salvadoran context, specifically the context of *lxs pobres*. Liturgical inculturation, while not mentioned explicitly in Vatican II, grows out of the council's insistence that

> the Church has no wish to impose a rigid uniformity in matters which do not implicate the faith or the good of the whole community; rather does she respect and foster the genius and talents of the various races and peoples. Anything in these peoples' way of life which is not indissolubly bound up with superstition

and error she studies with sympathy and, if possible, preserves intact. Sometimes in fact she admits such things into the liturgy itself, so long as they harmonize with its true and authentic spirit.[68]

This process is referred to in the council documents as "cultural adaptation."[69] Later commenters begin to speak of "inculturation" to promote the sense that non-European cultures are not simply donned as a costume by a static, given (inherently European) liturgical formulation, but rather that the liturgy, like the church as a whole, should have as its goal to become so deeply enmeshed in a given human culture that it becomes one with the innate cultural expressions of a people. Nevertheless, proposals for liturgical inculturation did not characterize the reception of the council in Latin America. Indeed, for the first ecclesial base communities, the Celebrations of the Word facilitated by *delegadxs de la Palabra* were essentially communal celebrations of the Liturgy of the Word. They often ended with the prayers of the faithful or the sign of peace, or, when consecrated hosts were available, the *delegado* or *delegada* would also serve as an extraordinary minister of the eucharist. The Liturgy of the Eucharist itself, with the consecration of the bread and wine, was only on the table, so to speak, when a priest was present. Because the first experiences of the CEBs focused so heavily on biblical literacy with an eye to the political and social upheavals of the time, it makes sense that scripture and the question of faith and politics were the more pressing facets of Christian life taken up by the church of *lxs pobres* and the liberation theologians who reflected on their experiences.

However, in the decades since the Peace Accords were signed, as the Salvadoran hierarchy distanced itself from the CEBs and as less priests were willing or able to celebrate the eucharist and other sacraments with the communities, the question of sacramental celebration became more and more urgent. Without celebrating eucharist regularly, and without the ability to baptize their children, confirm young people, or marry in the church, the ecclesial life of *lxs pobres* remained incomplete, and they noticed. The CEBs feel that they run the risk of becoming just a charity organization without their social action being partnered with a rich sacramental life. They are adamant that this not be the case; as Gustavo puts it,

> What we do is not social work. Service work, the church calls it. I have always maintained that, rather, it is the true work of Jesús. Neither Jesús nor Monseñor Romero did service work. What they did was the true praxis of the ideal of Jesús in the gospels . . . the true sacrament is the gospels.

That is, they inductively came to the same conclusion as the council, that "the liturgy is the summit toward which the activity of the Church is directed; at the same time it is the font from which all her power flows."[70] At the same time, they were unwilling to submit to the authority of a priest who would ask them to refrain from participating in politics and society out of their faith convictions in order for him to deign to administer the sacraments in their community. This tension is untenable.

Spanish theologian José María Castillo posits,

> If there are people who do not see worship as the most preeminent and effective task that the Church can carry out in order to humanize our society and to reduce the suffering in the world, then we have the most clear proof that Christian worship is not celebrated as God wants and as God commands. . . . Precisely because we want to be more radical and more effective in our liberating service to humanity, that is why we should be more demanding in our fidelity to Christian worship.[71]

This is the dynamic in the CEBs. Colonial sacramental practice has *not* been the source from which has flown their liberating praxis of the gospel of Jesús; we know this because they simply have not been included in the sacramental life of the church now for years! By that same token, they are unwilling to sacrifice their evangelical praxis to conform to the criteria of priests who have exclusive authority to administer valid sacraments.

Today, the CEBs re-member Jesús in their liturgies, which often include a ritual they call "the sharing of bread." In addition to their traditional reading of scripture (together with other "texts of life," such as poetry, dance, biographies of prophets and martyrs, San Romero's diaries and homilies, or their own communities' histories) and communal reflections, many CEBs bring tortillas, simple white bread, sweet breads, or even *pupusas* together with fruit wine or coffee to share at the end of their celebration in place of the rubrics of eucharist. Alternatively, especially at larger celebrations where various CEBs participate, a potluck style meal can punctuate the end of the liturgy. This meal is explicitly described as sacramental, as the kind of table over which Jesús presided at the Last Supper, a meal among friends of culturally significant and common foods.

The use of alternative "material," to use magisterial language, in a eucharistic celebration is, for the CEBs, a sign that their own bodies, culture, and foods are beloved of God, human enough to bear the significance of the sacrament. They affirm that Jesús promises to be truly present "when two or three are gathered in my name," and they have faith that their foods, too, are examples of continued gospel table fellowship. For some CEBs around San Salvador, the recovery of their Indigenous Nahua heritage has informed and fortified this conviction:

> The human being is spiritual by nature, independent of being religious or not—the sunbeam, the sun, the moon, trees, fruit, your relationship with all of this,

we've had this for thousands of years. It's a given. And there have been ways of manifesting this through rituals. For example, chilate was one of the symbolic beverages that our ancestors had. . . . *Chilate* is normally white. For our ancestors, white is summer. And there is a *chilate* that is dark, too. A drink that is dark, which is winter. They had their own worldview expressed historically through different forms, symbols, that we could see.[72]

Theologian Philippe Rouillard observes how using alternatives to wheat hosts and grape wine as eucharistic elements may actually revive sacramental practices outside of Europe. He says,

> Bread and wine are foreign words for many Christians of Africa and the Far East who do not use them as food and drink. One can very legitimately wonder whether it is in accord with Christ's intention to employ signs which in these regions really do not signify anything and if it would be better to adopt instead some food and beverage in use in the region in question.[73]

In addition to the symbolic emptiness of bread and wine when compared to something like *chilate* or tortilla, hosts and wine continue to carry actively negative colonial significance, far from the fellowship, solidarity, and divine presence they intend to communicate. The eucharist that members of the CEBs have experienced in their parishes is individualistic:

> [when] Jesús says "do this in memory of me," it was all the same food, everyone eating together, and the Church currently, I see that everybody has their own individual host, and it's a very individual moment for each person. It's not like we are sharing food.[74]

They also see the sacrament as exclusive, marginalizing:

> The way we do it in our community is pretty distinct because nobody is excluded. Instead, in the Church, if you are not baptized, you cannot receive communion. They also exclude children, and in the community, we do not. We all know the significance that communion has for us.[75]

That is, the way the CEBs celebrate the "sharing of the bread" in memory of Jesús not only uses different "material" as if to make a point; the fruits of the local soil effectively convoke the community and re-member Jesús in a way that is aligned with the gospels, in a way that canonical sacraments do not.

We understand the CEBs' sacramental practices, which do not conform to a local priest's whims or to the symbolically ambiguous rubric of the Roman Catholic magisterium, to be profoundly decolonial. To be clear, we do not presume to claim that their worship is a uniquely or universally stable conduit of encounter with God in the same way that the magisterium presumes to claim the sacraments to be. The official teaching office of the church has not deigned to enter into dialogue with the CEBs to a degree that suggests any kind of legitimate listening to the *sensus fidei* of the communities, and the CEBs appear to be uninterested in promoting their worship as required practice for the whole church. In fact, within the CEBs themselves there are different opinions about how to best celebrate. Some communities use bread and wine because they value the symbolic unity with the universal church, even as others feel strongly that any local food serves well to facilitate a true encounter with Jesús and a commitment to seeking the reign of God.[76] Nevertheless, these differences are relativized to the CEBs' desire to celebrate together and do not prevent shared celebrations between communities. Indeed, some symbols have become standard for all CEBs, even while other details vary: the table always has a Bible, a cross, photos of martyrs, a lit candle, and, most recently, elements of the natural world.[77] Ultimately, the criteria for eucharistic celebrations in the CEBs are not the sacramental rubrics, nor the threats of a local cleric. Rather, the CEBs judge the efficacy of the sacraments *ex opere operantis*, by virtue of the fruits of the community that celebrates.

These aesthetic, creative, and liturgical practices of the church of *lxs pobres* contribute to the construction of an-other church in which the memory of Jesús and the presence of the reign of God that he announced are celebrated in a manner fashioned by and recognizable to *lxs pobres* as a priestly people of God. The capacity for such creativity to contribute to the decolonial transformation of not only the church but also the world will become evident in our next chapter, which describes and analyzes the decolonial praxis of the CEBs in the realms of both secular and ecclesial power.

NOTES

1. José Salvador Cornejo Ruíz, "*Canto Popular*," presentation at Wake Forest University Church of the Poor Research Symposium, October 2019.
2. The following story is told in Andrea's own words in "Letter from the Community Nuevo Amanecer," §3, in part I.
3. Ibid.; Gómez and Marshall, eds., *Sigue porque la vida sigue*, 201.
4. Liz first encountered this interpretation of the "salt of the earth" metaphor from Matthew 5:13 in a shared homily in the "Mons. Romero" base community of Jardines de Colón in 2002–2003.
5. In contrast with modern/colonial "aestheTics," Walter Mignolo and Rolando Vazquez rename the creative modes of perception that decolonize the senses as forms of "aestheSis," which "starts from the consciousness that the modern/colonial project has implied not only control of the economy, the political, and knowledge, but also

control over the senses and perception. Modern aestheTics have played a key role in configuring a canon, a normativity that enabled the disdain and the rejection of other forms of aesthetic practices, or, more precisely, other forms of aestheSis, of sensing and perceiving. Decolonial aestheSis is an option that delivers a radical critique to modern, postmodern, and altermodern aestheTics and, simultaneously, contributes to making visible decolonial subjectivities at the confluence of popular practices of re-existence, artistic installations, theatrical and musical performances, literature and poetry, sculpture and other visual arts." See Walter Mignolo and Rolando Vazquez, "Decolonial AestheSis: Colonial Wounds/Decolonial Healings," *Social Text Journal Online*, July 15, 2013, https://socialtextjournal.org/periscope_article/decolonial-aesthesis-colonial-woundsdecolonial-healings/.

6. Maldonado-Torres, "Outline of Ten Theses," 27.

7. *Mestizaje* has been a foundational cultural and theological *locus* of reflection for Latinx scholars of theology and religion in the United States. Néstor Medina critically engages this *locus* with a hermeneutic of both appreciation and suspicion. He reminds his readers and interlocutors in the field of Hispanic/Latinx theology that the romanticization of *mestizaje* elides the violence that produced *mestizaje* in the first place. See Néstor Medina, *Mestizaje: Remapping Race, Culture, and Faith in Latino/a Catholicism* (Maryknoll, NY: Orbis Books, 2009). In El Salvador, *mestizo* identity also erases any traces of African heritage.

8. Jennifer Scheper Hughes calls these strategies of resistance the "*contraconquista*" (counter-conquest). See "The Sacred Art of Counter-Conquest: Material Christianity in Latin America," in *The Oxford Handbook of Latin American Christianity*, eds. David Thomas Orique, O.P., Susan Fitzpatrick-Behrens, and Virginia Garrard (New York: Oxford University Press, 2020).

9. Articulación Nacional de CEBs en El Salvador, liner notes, *Las CEBs Cantamos*, 2017, compact disc.

10. Maldonado-Torres, "Outline of Ten Theses," 25–26.

11. Maldonado-Torres, 26.

12. Maldonado-Torres, 27.

13. See chapter 2, n81.

14. Bosch, *Bendita Mezcla*, 23. The stubbornness of the *izote* in the face of adversity is a metaphor that shows up elsewhere in popular interpretations of Salvadoran history. See, for example, the historical account of the FMLN's radio station in Carlos Enriquez Consalvi, *La Terquedad Del Izote: La Historia de Radio Venceremos* (San Salvador: Ediciones MUPI, 2003).

15. Bosch, 27.

16. Maldonado-Torres, "Outline of Ten Theses," 27.

17. See "The *Librito* of the Prophet José Adonay Pérez Pérez" §4, in part I; Gómez and Marshall, *Sigue*, 211.

18. La Hacienda is one of the many communities visited by Anita and her father in "Acts of the Repatriated," §4 in part I.

19. Bosch, *Bendita Mezcla*, 68. *Trama* can mean both the plot of a narrative and the weft in weaving. *Desenlace* refers to the denouement of a narrative, but the word's root, *enlace*, connotes linkages, connection, relationship. So *trama y desenlace*

could be translated as something like either plot and denouement or weaving and unweaving.

20. This breakneck pace is reminiscent of the work of women weavers in "Colonio-Genesis," §3, in part I, who had to weave even during Mass to meet their quotas. It is the same struggle shared by textile workers in urban *maquiladoras*, the majority of whom are women.

21. Maldonado-Torres, "Outline of Ten Theses." In a special issue of *Toronto Journal of Theology* dedicated to decolonial theology, Becca Whitla also argues that singing can be a way of embodying decoloniality. See Becca Whitla, "Singing as *Un Saber del Sur*, or Another Way of Knowing," *Toronto Journal of Theology* 33, no. 2 (Fall 2017): 289–294.

22. Just a few examples of artists from the *nueva trova* movement include Victor Jara of Chile, Alí Primera of Venezuela, Mercedes Sosa of Argentina, and Los Guaraguao of Venezuela.

23. See chapter 2, n4. In 2012, the Belgian missionary who helped to found the original CEBs, Padre Pedro Declercq, and the singer-songwriter who composed many of these songs, Guillermo Cuéllar, put together a four-disc set of CDs that contains dozens of these songs, along with other religious and secular music of the *canto popular Salvadoreño*. It is entitled *Canciones de Lucha y Esperanza: Cancionero histórico de las comunidades eclesiales de base de El Salvador* ("Songs of Struggle and Hope: Historical songbook of the ecclesial base communities of El Salvador"). The liner notes of the set also contain a lengthy essay by Godofredo Echeverría on the role of this music in the base communities, entitled "Canción y comunidad en la riada de un Pueblo" ("Song and community in the stream of a people").

24. One example of this category of Salvadoran song is the musical group Los Torogoces de Morazán: "Formed in 1981 in conjunction with the FMLN's Radio Venceremos, these guerrilla musicians were using their artistic work as a weapon of war by serving as a voice of truth during the worst years of the conflict when mainstream media obscured the facts about the United States' and the Salvadoran governments' involvement in mass killings and other gross human rights violations." Christina Azahar, "Sounds and Memories of El Salvador's Civil War in the Songs of Los Torogoces de Morazán," *Lucero* 24 (2015): 28.

25. Articulación Nacional, *Las CEBs Cantamos*, liner notes.

26. José Salvador Cornejo Ruíz, "*Canto Popular*" (presentation, Wake Forest University research symposium, October 2019).

27. Articulación Nacional, *Las CEBs Cantamos*, liner notes.

28. The original poem "Quejas a Monseñor" was written by Miguel Ernesto Guevara Gris. It was recorded by "Monseñor Romero" network of CEBs in La Libertad, on *Las CEBs Cantamos*. Compact Disc. 2017.

29. See interview with Agustín Luna in Gómez and Marshall, eds., *Sigue porque la vida sigue*, 137–138.

30. Marshall, "Un gesto vale," Appendix 2, vi. Emphasis in the original.

31. Marshall, "Un gesto vale," Appendix 3, viii.

32. CEBs Pueblo de Dios en Camino y Nuevo Amanecer, San Salvador, "Aunque sea a chuña" on Las CEBs Cantamos. Compact Disc. 2017.

33. Grupo Libre, Cacaopera, "A la chingada" on Las CEBs Cantamos. Compact Disc. 2017.

34. The song specifically calls out the CEL (*Comisión Ejecutiva Hidroeléctrica del Río Lempa*) and ASTALDI (construction firm), the Salvadoran private-public partnerships that were behind the construction of the dam. Agustín and his community resisted the construction of this dam at "La Maroma" because they consider it to be a mismanagement of the river, because they would not necessarily have benefitted from the electricity it was slated to produce, and because it would have flooded out their homes, forcing them to leave their land for the second time in their lives (after the war).

35. Gómez and Marshall, *Sigue porque la vida sigue*, 140.

36. "Monseñor Romero" network of CEBs in La Libertad, "Corrido de las Comunidades" on Las CEBs Cantamos. Compact Disc. 2017.

37. This is the fundamental argument laid out in Marshall, "Un gesto vale más que mil palabras."

38. See Marshall, "Un gesto vale," Appendices.

39. Ibid., Appendix 2, p. iii.

40. Ibid., Appendix 9, p. l.

41. Ibid., Appendix 2, p. vi. Emphasis in the original.

42. See Gómez and Marshall, eds., *Sigue porque la vida sigue*, 142.

43. See Sylvia Wynter, "Unsettling the Coloniality of Being/Power/Truth/Freedom."

44. For a history of Indigenous ordination in Catholic Latin American, see M. Lundberg, "The Ordination of Indians in Colonial Spanish America: Law, Prejudice, and Practice During Three Centuries," *Swedish Missiological Themes* 91, no. 2 (2003): 297–317. As recently as the 1990s–2000s, Pope John Paul II banned the ordination of Indigenous deacons in Chiapas, Mexico. See D. Cevallos, "Mexico: Bishop Seeks Lifting on Ban of Naming Indigenous Deacons," Inter Press Service News Agency Website, May 20, 2002, http://www.ipsnews.net/2002/05/mexico-bishop-seeks-lifting-of-ban-on-naming-indigenous-deacons/, accessed November 22, 2017.

45. *LG*, § 31.

46. *LG*, § 10.

47. *LG*.

48. Congregation for the Clergy, "The Priest: Pastor and Leader of the Parish Community," August 4, 2002. Emphasis in the original.

49. Marshall, "Un gesto vale," Appendix 2, p. 137.

50. Pedro Declercq, a Belgian priest who committed his life to the CEBs, lays out this process in the book *La fe de un pueblo: historia de una comunidad cristiana en El Salvador* (1970–1980) (San Salvador: UCA Editores, 1983). *La fe de un pueblo* was published without mentioning a single author and it was translated and published in English under a pseudonym. See Pablo Galdámez, *The Faith of a People*, trans. Robert R. Barr (Maryknoll, NY: Orbis Books, 1986).

51. The namesake and patron of El Salvador, "the Divine Savior of the World," celebrated on the Feast of the Transfiguration on August 6.

52. Gómez and Marshall, eds., *Sigue porque la vida sigue*, 141–142.

53. Remarks made by José Salvador (Chamba) Ruíz Cornejo during discussion at WFU Research Symposium on the church of *Lxs Pobres*, October 2019.

54. Remarks made by Teresa Inmaculada (Tere) Moreno de Melendez during discussion at WFU Research Symposium on the church of *Lxs Pobres*, October 2019.

55. Marshall, "Un gesto vale," Appendix 2, p. vii.

56. Congregation for the Clergy, "The Priest: Pastor and Leader of the Parish Community," §8.

57. Much of this section comes from Laurel's work for her master's thesis, which used qualitative research methods to investigate sacramental practices among different CEBs from different parts of the country. See Marshall, "Un gesto vale mas."

58. Thirty-nine percent of Catholics were Latin American and 24% were European in 2010, compared to 65% European and 24% Latin American in 1910, according to the Pew Research Center's study "The Global Catholic Population," February 13, 2013, http://www.pewforum.org/2013/02/13/the-global-catholic-population/.

59. This definition is well-founded in the works of Gustavo Gutiérrez: "Belief in God is borne of a particular historical situation; the believer forms part . . . of a cultural and social fabric" (*El Dios de la Vida* [Salamanca: Sígueme, 1992], 17). This is also found in Clodovis Boff: "Before doing any theology, it is important to 'do' liberation . . . this nexus with practice found in the root of the method of liberation theology" ("Epistemología y método," *Mysterium Liberationis, Tomo I* [San Salvador: UCA Editores, 1991], 99). The primacy of praxis is also a fundamental concept for scholars working from El Salvador, like Ignacio Ellacuría and Jon Sobrino.

60. *SC*, §14.

61. *CCL*, can. 947.

62. Marshall, "Un gesto vale," Appendix 2, iv.

63. Indeed, at the Second Vatican Council, Latin American bishops strongly petitioned to be considered "mission countries" despite the Catholic Church being an established institution in most Latin American societies, in *AG*, 6, n15. This appeal was made primarily in order to be able to continue to access the mission funding administered by the *Propaganda Fide* and to receive the pastoral attention of missionary orders from "non-mission" territories, which was of essential importance for the functioning and humanitarian efforts of local churches. However necessary this funding was for important humanitarian and community-building work, continuing to call the Roman Catholic church's work in these regions "missionary" in the strict sense reinforces the tendency to think of the world in terms of a duality between "mission countries" and Christendom proper, that is, in Maldonado-Torres's terms, between Europe and the colonized, between zones of being and nonbeing.

64. *CCC*, 1255.

65. Marshall, "Un gesto vale," Appendix 10, lxviii.

66. Marshall, "Un gesto vale," Apéndice 3, xiv.

67. "This last point, then, [whether Romero's death was imposed out of a hatred of the faith], was identified as the key question in Romero's case" (Michael Lee, *Revolutionary Saint*, 186).

68. *SC*, §37.

69. *SC*, §24, 38, 39, 40, 44, 107.

70. *SC*, §10.
71. José María Castillo, *Símbolos de libertad* (Salamanca: Sígueme, 2001), 114.
72. Marshall, "Un gesto vale," Appendix 3, xiii.
73. Philippe Rouillard, "From Human Meal to Christian Sacrifice," in *Living Bread, Saving Cup: Readings on the Eucharist*, ed. R. Kevin Seasoltz (Collegeville, MN: Liturgical Press, 1982), 132.
74. Marshall, "Un gesto vale," Appendix 9, xlv.
75. Marshall, xlix.
76. These topics are debated respectfully but passionately among the CEBs. During our research symposium at Wake Forest University in October 2019, CEB members were pretty equally split on this issue. Nevertheless, these differences are relativized to the CEBs' desire to celebrate together and do not prevent shared celebrations between communities.
77. This observation was made by María Elena Sanabria during our research symposium. María Elena works at FUNDAHMER and helps coordinate the CEBs' weekly radio program. She has a wide range of experience documenting the CEBs' network meetings and liturgical celebrations, and we consider this opinion to be fairly well-founded.

Chapter 4

Luchamos por la justicia
Decolonial Power in the Salvadoran Church of lxs Pobres

We have to work together in the struggle! Because if it's just me, then none of this makes any sense. We're not going to see any change. . . . Those who don't join the struggle are the ones who are messing it up for everyone else, putting obstacles in our path, putting stones in our path so we can't. And if I'm neutral, then it's as if I'm dead, I'm not even alive. If you're going to live a neutral life, then it's better not to live at all. . . . If you're going to stand there with your arms crossed, then why the hell are we even here? . . . This world can change; clearly, it can be different, if we all see ourselves as part of the struggle.
—Ángela from the CEBs in Cacaopera[1]

"¡Queremos obispos al lado de los pobres! . . . ¡Queremos obispos al lado de las pobres!"
—Salvadoran church of *lxs Pobres*

"We want bishops on the side of *lxs pobres*!" The Salvadoran base communities, together with other members of the church of *lxs pobres* and popular organizations in civil society, often chant this phrase at rallies and vigils as a prophetic challenge to the coloniality of power that continues to infect the institutional church in El Salvador and beyond. The resonance of this phrase was especially poignant during the vigil held at San Salvador's metropolitan cathedral on the occasion of the twenty-fifth anniversary of Archbishop Óscar Romero's assassination in 2005. The archbishop at the time, Fernando Sáenz Lacalle, had taken the podium to pay his respects to the crowd and offer a few obligatory words in honor of his martyred predecessor. Sáenz Lacalle, however, was no Romero. For reasons alluded to in previous chapters, he was notorious for siding, not with *lxs pobres*, but with the powerful; not with the humble, but with the haughty, secure as he was in his honorary rank of general in the Salvadoran Armed Forces. He was a religious leader who distanced himself from the people's struggles and whom the popular church therefore might have described in Ángela's words as "messing it up for everyone else, putting obstacles in our path, putting stones in our path so we can't."[2] So when the church of *lxs pobres* gathered at the cathedral and had his ear, they did not miss the rare opportunity to speak the truth to "his Eminence." And their words rang out as a prophetic denunciation of his abandonment of El Salvador's impoverished and oppressed majorities. In turn, when Auxiliary Bishop (now cardinal) Rosa Chávez entered the scene, the words *"queremos obispos al lado de los pobres"* rang out with an entirely different sentiment, because Chávez, more like Romero, was and is a bishop (and now a cardinal) who speaks and acts deliberately, though imperfectly, on behalf of solidarity with *lxs pobres* in their struggles for justice and liberation.

What the CEBs express when they clamor for bishops who side with *lxs pobres* is a decolonial desire for the institutional church to use its power for the sake of service to and accompaniment of the Salvadoran people in their struggles for justice, equity, peace, and a more dignified life. The people's church chants ¡*queremos obispos al lado de los/las pobres!* as a means of using their own collective power to challenge the institutional church to both (a) recognize and honor the knowledge and creativity of *lxs pobres* and (b) renounce its colonial alliance with the powerful in favor of an alliance with the power that lies in the commitment of the church of *lxs pobres* to forms of social transformation compatible with God's reign. The decolonial epistemology and creativity of El Salvador's church of *lxs pobres*, explored in the previous two chapters, are oriented toward committed action for social transformation, understood theologically as the construction of God's reign in human history, here and now. But because "thinking and creating cannot by themselves change the world," Maldonado-Torres argues that "decoloniality involves an activist decolonial turn whereby the *damné* emerges as an agent of social change." While decolonial knowledge and being are liberating in and of themselves, much more is needed to undo the colonial matrix of power. Indeed,

> the *damné* needs to try to take hold of multiple such activities, thinking, creating, etc., and make them part of strategies and efforts to effectively decolonize power, knowledge, and being. This requires the emergence of the *damné* as an agent of social change.[3]

In the CEBs, this emergence is nurtured by raising communal consciousness of oppression and creatively imagining an-other world, and is fulfilled in their committed action within a collective struggle for life and liberation. The epistemic praxis of the CEBs, especially their praxis of prophetic memory, comes together with song, dance, celebration, liturgy, and art to inspire and inform action aligned with the reign of God and therefore against the *anti-reino*. As Agustín observes, for example, the people's music of the CEBs has "inspired me to see reality" and is a "help for strengthening our protest."[4] And the CEBs' understanding of the sacrament of breaking bread together signifies their shared commitment to the struggle to bring about God's reign. Decolonial knowledge production and creativity nurture committed social action aimed at decolonization of the power matrix.

In an effort to transform the intersecting nodes of the reigning power structures in the church and world, the CEBs organize many of their activities around a commitment to *diaconía*, a term that some CEBs utilize to signify action in the everyday service of human and ecological promotion. More broadly, they see their service to their people and the earth as part of *la lucha*, or the larger struggle of their people for liberation. In and through their collective service and struggle, the CEBs are engaged in the process of transforming each of the nodes of the colonial matrix of power: control of subjectivity, economics/labor, authority/politics, gender relations/sexuality, and ecology. Taken together, these dimensions of the CEBs' shared struggle coalesce with their internal organizational structures to form a decolonial challenge to the coloniality of ecclesial governing authority in Roman Catholicism. In what follows, we work our way through how the CEBs confront each of the nodes of the colonial power matrix in their ecclesial praxis, and we then turn to a brief analysis of how the CEBs' praxis of decolonial power points the church toward new horizons for articulating an explicitly decolonial ecclesiology.

THE PRAXIS OF DECOLONIAL POWER IN THE SALVADORAN CEBS

From Colonial Control of Subjectivity to the Decoloniality of Collective Struggle

Control of subjectivity is a foundational dimension of the colonial power matrix and the decolonization of subjectivity in the realms of knowledge, being, and power is central to the decolonial project. Under coloniality, each of these dimensions of human subjectivity is reserved for white, wealthy, Western men (and the white women and poor white men who benefit from and too often align themselves with the colonial paradigm). Decolonial subjectivity involves not only an epistemic and aesthetic/spiritual break with the coloniality of knowledge and being; it also requires historical action in favor of transformation in the realm of local and global power structures.

It is important to note, however, that the praxis of decolonial subjectivity does not mirror the subjectivism and libertarianism characteristic of modern, rational individualism. Rather, decolonial subjectivity is always collective and intersubjective.[5]

The epistemological and creative praxis of the CEBs discussed throughout the previous two chapters already represents their collective and intersubjective commitment to action that combats the power of colonial subjectivity. There is a transformation of power taking place in the simple fact of the CEBs coming together and organizing themselves as communities of *lxs pobres*, as subjects at the base of the church and society. As the song cited at the beginning of chapter 2 proclaims, "when *el pobre* seeks out *el pobre*, and organization is born, that's how our liberation begins." Identifying as "*pobre*" and claiming agency rooted in the God of Life and aimed at the construction of the reign of God are at the heart of the CEBs' claim to constitute the church of *lxs pobres*. In addition to decolonial knowledge production and creative expression, the CEBs work to activate the social power in collective, organized communities that is foundational for becoming agents of social change. As Avelino, an ex-combatant in the Salvadoran revolution, puts it:

> They [the rich] have their power, their wealth, but the communities have an advantage. It's just a question of doing the work. The popular struggle, which is rather passive right now, could explode. They [the rich] have all that money, but I believe that popular struggle has more weight in this country.[6]

The level of organization within the CEBs is, in and of itself, the beginning of their decolonial power in the realm of subjectivity and beyond. This is why the early CEBs, and any other popular groups that organized themselves, were so violently persecuted by the reigning power structure in the 1970s and 1980s. The potential threat that organized and critically conscious communities posed to coloniality was too great to allow to exist. This was especially true when organized and critically conscious communities moved to organized and committed action for change. We will return to the centrality of *organización* when we turn to explicit ecclesiological proposals below.

Since the CEBs' inception in the late twentieth century, their see-judge-act methodology has emphasized empowered action for social change as an essential part of who the CEBs are, as subjects of not only knowledge and creativity, but history itself. The first CEBs assumed national leadership roles in organizing rural farming cooperatives and urban workers' unions, denouncing state violence, and petitioning for universal access to health care and education. These actions witness to the historical commitment of the church of *lxs pobres* not only to verbally announce the reign of God, but work concretely toward dignified life for all out of the convictions of their faith.

For the contemporary CEBs, organized participation in collective struggles for a dignified life on earth for all continues to be a defining characteristic of their "new way of being church."[7]

The first generation of base communities in El Salvador were, out of stark necessity, primarily concerned with subjectivity and power surrounding economic issues of justice and equity in their society. *Lxs pobres* were primarily understood to be the economically impoverished, and the CEBs denounced the violent ways in which economic poverty strips human beings of their most basic needs: for food, for clean water, for clothes, for health care and shelter. This litany of essential human needs—reminiscent of the way Jesús demands that we care for each other and, thus, for him in Matthew 25—is the most fundamental expression of poverty and, for the CEBs, this is the first injustice to be addressed when triaging the signs of the times. We will explore this realm of economic subjectivity further in the section that follows. On the other hand, for decolonial scholars and activists, too narrow of a focus on economic poverty, without adequate attention to the entire colonial matrix of power, is a limited way of seeing reality, insufficient for decolonizing subjectivity and tackling the complicated interwoven oppressions of enduring coloniality. Mignolo, for example, argues that liberation theology—because of its continued dependence on a Christian theo-logical framework—is not broad or complex enough in its critiques of modernity and coloniality.[8] The "decency" of such a framework leads to upholding the romantic ideal of the valiant *campesino*. Such an ideal re-objectifies human subjects and fails to critique the colonial (hetero)sexism, racism, or anthropocentrism that may lie behind a facade of noble rural poverty.[9] Indeed, the theology associated with the first CEBs hardly addresses issues of gender equality, Indigenous identity, or ecology, much less sexual diversity, disability, or questions of race and colorism. For Mignolo and others, these oversights stick liberation theology, together with the whole of Christianity, squarely onto the colonial ball of wax.

However, the evolving experience of subjectivity in the contemporary CEBs critiques both the exclusive option for economic poverty and Mignolo's dismissive analysis of liberation theology. As the signs of the times in El Salvador have changed, the CEBs' attention to and reflection on their sociopolitical context has resulted not only in increasingly decolonial epistemological and creative tendencies, but also in a decidedly decolonial praxis that is unafraid to be "honest with the real"[10] in order to combat interrelated injustices that permeate Salvadoran society today. The contemporary CEBs are still the church of *lxs pobres*, but their commitments reveal an increasingly intersectional understanding of poverty that recognizes the manifold ways the colonial matrix of power affects the knowledge, being, and power of the colonized. Indeed, their knowledge production and creative expression are protagonized in and through the subjectivity of humanized *damnés* like Andrea and her group of young people or the women of La Hacienda. So too are their intersubjective struggles for transformation in the realms of economy, politics, gender relations, and ecology.

From Colonial Control of Economics to a Decolonial Economics of Solidarity

In the realm of economics, Sylvia Wynter argues that the contemporary, neoliberal iteration of Man dehumanizes Black, non-white, non-male, and impoverished bodies as those who have been "dysselected" by the free market system (with Black bodies at the very bottom of this hierarchy). Man, defined in late modernity as the successful economic "Breadwinner," is optimally human and it is the power of the free market that mediates his salvation in an atomized world of economic scarcity. The free market is also posited as the only potential salvation for those who have been dysselected, resulting in a power structure that simultaneously destroys lives and purports to save them. Under globalized, neoliberal capitalism, the colonial control of labor not only chews up the lives of laborers, it spits out those whose lack of productivity renders them worthless and disposable.[11] The Salvadoran church of *lxs pobres* "unsettles" the coloniality of power here by striving to embody an economics of solidarity at both the micro-level, within and among their own communities, and at the macro-level, nationally and internationally.

At the micro-level, the CEBs engage in the *diaconía* of mutual aid and shared resources within their own communities and in relationship with other communities as well. In this vein, contemporary CEBs form and support agricultural and artisan cooperatives; they raise funds for scholarships, for the sick, and for the burial of the dead; they dig wells as sources of potable water; and so on. For example, when excessive rain or drought plagues communities in a particular region, CEBs from other parts of the country organize to donate corn and beans where the crops have failed. In recent years, CEBs in Cacaopera have begun having festivals at the end of the year, to which each hyperlocal community brings the *artesanía* or other (agri)cultural products they've been developing for sale or trade. These communities also manage collective grain silos: with a small, community-managed seed fund, the "silo committee" buys corn, beans, and in some cases sorghum from local families who have excess harvest and sells it at cost to families that have less. This way, the grain doesn't go to the market in town, where middlemen raise the prices for poor families to make profit for themselves. In this area of praxis, where "members jointly take on the essential struggles for survival or for the improvement of living [conditions],"[12] the CEBs seek to address the immediate needs of their communities. Theologically, members of these communities understand the sharing, or *compartir*, of resources here as the real meaning of the eucharistic celebration, and see their efforts as a commitment to follow in the way of Jesús and imitate the first communities of disciples in the Acts of the Apostles (see Acts 2:42–47). In the words of one community member from the CEB San Romero de las Américas in Altavista,

> There's a saying, right? "Either we're all in the bed or we're all on the floor." I feel like it's a commitment that we have, because we do it from the heart, and we do it with faith in Jesús, which is at the center for all of us and he is the one who moves us in our faith. And so I feel like it's really important that we [share] in our community, but not only in our community.... We've learned a lot about sharing in this community, to have this commitment as a community, but not only for ourselves but for others too.[13]

Another member of the same community remarks that this practice of *compartir*, or sharing, is really what it means to remember Jesús when he said, "Do this in memory of me." Even as the economically poor themselves, the CEBs stress that this sharing is not charity, but solidarity, to be done "*del mismo pan que tiene uno*,"[14] from one's own bread and not from one's excess. Here the decolonial transformation of economic power lies in the grassroots solidarity of *lxs pobres* with *lxs pobres* for the sake of communal survival and well-being.

However, the CEBs are savvy to the structures of economic injustice and thus recognize that communal *diaconía* through sharing and mutual aid is not enough. Therefore, they are committed to concerted struggle for macro-level, systemic change aimed at the transformation of an unjust and exclusionary local and global economy. At this level, the CEBs are involved in regional and national movements that address the underlying social and economic structures that conspire against meeting the basic needs and hopes of the people. For example, over the past twenty years alone, the CEBs have been consistently involved in collective action against neoliberal economic projects like dollarization, the Central American Free Trade Agreement, the privatization of the state pension system, and, currently, the privatization of water. They have also actively advocated for legislative advancement of social goods, such as food sovereignty and security. Far from the colonial church's historical exhortation to passive acceptance of suffering as God's will in hopes of a reward in heaven, the CEBs' decolonial *diaconía* involves a committed struggle to create an-other world in which all people have access to an economy that facilitates a dignified life for all.

From Colonial Control of Authority to a Decolonial Politics of Justice and Peace

In the contemporary colonial matrix of power, what Quijano calls the colonial "control of authority" is located in the nation-state, with its "public power and its violent mechanisms."[15] The European colonization of the Americas in the fifteenth to nineteenth centuries concentrated social, economic, and political authority in the hands of monarchies, viceroyalties, and royal military forces. In the nineteenth century, Latin American independence movements transferred control of political and military authority in the newly formed nation-states to the hands of wealthy Euro-descendent landowners. The subsequent history of political control and violent repression of colonized races and classes in the land that came to be known as El Salvador is intricately woven into the way the CEBs' tell their story,[16] and one hallmark of the CEBs is their decolonial and faith-inspired praxis of struggling to transform power structures through their politics of justice and peace.

In the mid- to late twentieth century, political authority was dominated by the Salvadoran oligarchy, enforced by repressive military regimes, supported by Catholic ecclesial power, and backed by the foreign policy of the United States. As the CEBs emerged during this time, many members joined the armed resistance and/or supported the Salvadoran revolution in some other way. Others joined in or collaborated with student movements, worker unions, and other organizations in civil society that sought to transform the structures of political and military authority in El Salvador. Looking back on the decade of the 1970s, they describe the events that culminated in the civil war as the "elimination of a political option."[17] The 1992 Peace Accords opened up political options and, in the postwar years, while the CEBs as such are not partisan organizations, most members have had some affiliation with or affinity toward to the leftist party that grew out of the armed struggle of the Salvadoran revolution, the FMLN.[18] While many members of the CEBs supported a socialist revolution during the 1970s and 1980s, and while many have supported the FMLN as a political party, most members also maintain a critical consciousness vis-à-vis the corruption and indifference to suffering that tend to come hand in hand with political power in the modern nation-state. Party leaders have visibly profited from their positions in the Legislative Assembly or as members of the presidential cabinet, which garners criticism from folks in the grassroots whose conditions have not improved as dramatically, if at all.

Anita, whose reflections on *re-cordar*/re-membering in chapter 1 grew out of her experience losing all five of her brothers during the armed conflict, questions this elitist embrace of political power on the Salvadoran left. She reflects on how she doesn't complain to God about the horrors that her family went through during the war, but she does regret the ways in which political power has compromised the cause for which her brothers died:

> What I do resent now is when I see politicians, and I am talking about people who were with my brothers, when I see them in government positions, in big events, and the women are so elegant, the men are so elegant, and somewhat distanced from the *gente pobre* [poor people] and even from those who were their comrades in the war. That saddens me, since they speak so little of those who had to die so that others could get to where they are and have the positions that they have now. And it's not that getting there is bad, it's letting yourself get absorbed into those spaces of power that are already fixed and all that we see today. But above all, the problem is forgetting the whole process that took place and the suffering and sacrifice of twelve years, hoping to see the ideal changes needed for a life of dignity on the part of *los pobres*. And so, that's what leaves a bad taste in my mouth, that they've forgotten about the *familias pobres* [poor families], including those who gave their lives.[19]

The embrace of party politics, with all the power and prestige that it entails, becomes all the more troublesome to members of the CEBs when elitism slides toward corruption, including theft of public funds for personal gain. Miguel Zepeda Santos calls on not only the CEBs, but all of civil society to get organized and rise up against corruption:

> But we're not going to achieve this going out there with just us, the ecclesial base communities, we'll never achieve it. And that's why our marches and demonstrations don't work. It won't work if it's just the evangelicals or just the youth, either! We're only going to achieve it when we do it the way it was done in the past. There was a strike that paralyzed all of San Salvador. If all of us, *los pobres*, take off the colors of our political parties, if we take off the colors of the Catholic Church, of the evangelicals, and we got out there in the same struggle in the street, then yes, we would put an end to this corruption. We'd put an end to the corrupt. As long as that doesn't happen, we'll still be screwed. That's why we need to get out into the street.[20]

As these comments suggest, the CEBs' contemporary efforts in the area of transforming political power include their prophetic denunciations of political corruption, but they are equally committed to resisting continued impunity for human rights violations committed during and after the armed conflict, and to protesting contemporary brutal policing tactics.

In and through these efforts, the Salvadoran church of *lxs pobres* has continually used its collective power to defy and decolonize the traditional marriage between the church and the reigning political and military powers that be. While San Romero, the patron saint of the church of *lxs pobres*, made a decisive break with those powers when he was archbishop of San Salvador, the rest of the Roman Catholic hierarchy in El Salvador was by no means on board with his prophetic ministry. Under the papacy of John Paul II, the conservative backlash in the Salvadoran hierarchy solidified even further, especially under the aforementioned 1995–2008 Archbishopric of Fernando Sáenz Lacalle, who was so beloved by the Salvadoran elite that he was offered (and accepted) the title of Brigadier General in the Salvadoran military. The CEBs were highly critical of Archbishop Sáenz and his return to the "apolitical" religiosity of colonial Catholicism, which they recognized for what it was: implicit, and sometimes even explicit, support for the unjust status quo and the powerful Salvadorans who benefit from that status quo. The current archbishop of San Salvador, José Luis Escobar Alas, began his archdiocesan ministry with a similar understanding of the relationship between the church and political authority. However, it appears that the example of San Romero and the witness of the Salvadoran church of *lxs pobres* have been gradually transforming Escobar Alas's approach.[21]

To gain an appreciation for the dynamics of this process, which is deeply interrelated with the CEBs' transformation of subjectivity, we will take a closer look at the evolving relationship between the base communities and Archbishop Escobar Alas over the course of the past decade. A first incident is the case of the Metropolitan Cathedral in downtown San Salvador, whose front face used to be adorned with a tile mural installed by Salvadoran popular artist Fernando Llort. Llort's signature style includes line-drawn, brightly colored icons of Salvadoran life—cornstalks, birds, flowers, simple houses, farm and forest animals, the sun, and men and women working the land—that represent a society of dignified and just living.[22] The mural on the facade of the cathedral was titled *Harmonia de mi pueblo* (Harmony of My People) and was installed in 1997 as a "monument to the everyday Salvadoran who had persevered through the struggle; it was a celebration of peace."[23] In early January 2012, the mural disappeared overnight, and Salvadorans woke up to a pile of ceramic dust and rubble at the foot of the cathedral. Archbishop Escobar Alas, who had ordered the removal of the work, gave myriad reasons—for example, that art signed by the artist represented a hubris that had no place in or on a church, that the mural contained masonic imagery, that tiles were falling off the mural and might hurt somebody—none of which held up to analysis.[24] The CEBs, together with other sectors of the church and civil society, publicly lamented the loss of this collective cultural patrimony and bemoaned the exercise of ecclesial authority that made such an aesthetic decision that did not reflect, and in fact negated, their own creative expression and identity. They felt that this exercise of ecclesial power was out of line and demonstrated publicly to make their voices heard. Furthermore, the archbishop's disdain for this particular artistic expression of the people's hopes for justice and peace indicates a disconnect between his exercise of power and the people's struggles for the kind of abundant life depicted in the mural.

A second incident in the CEBs' relationship with the archbishop and his approach to ecclesial and political authority was the closure of Tutela Legal in 2013. Tutela Legal was the Archdiocesan Office for Human Rights established by Archbishop Romero and María Julía Hernández that had been documenting cases of human rights abuses from prewar times forward, many of which had never been brought to justice, either because of the Amnesty Law of 1992 or a lack of attention from overwhelmed and partisan federal prosecutors. The office's archives contained unique testimonies of victims of government violence, of disappeared and murdered civilians' family members, of communities whose water sources had been polluted by commercial enterprises after the war, and cases of discrimination, profiling, and police abuse of young people suspected of belonging to gangs. After it was closed from one day to the next by Escobar Alas, additional reports of unmarked SUVs removing boxes of documents in the cover of night during the following weeks again sparked protest among the CEBs and other sectors. This time, the CEBs issued a public statement expressing "Christian indignation" over the incident:

> Dear Archbishop of San Salvador, we feel so indignant over your actions towards Tutela Legal (that is, towards the life of the victims), that we can only offer you the holy words of Monseñor Romero, applying them to the situation in which we currently find ourselves: "In the name of God, then, and in the name of this suffering people, whose laments rise to the heavens more tumultuously every day, we ask you, [dear Archbishop], we beseech you, we order you, in the name of God": recognize your mistake and your error, ask God and the victims for forgiveness, and reverse your decision, reinstalling Tutela Legal and its staff, in this way strengthening and widening this office to be present in every parish and community, like the open arms and heart of solidarity of our Mother Church that, following Mary, was under the cross of her Son and received his destroyed and murdered body in her arms.[25]

Projecting their voice into the public arena, the CEBs assert their authority to speak as the people of God who have a stake in their church, to claim status as members, to re-member the ecclesial body, and to direct the exercise of its power on behalf of the "destroyed and murdered" bodies of the victims. In the rest of the statement, they also decry the complicity of the institutional church in protecting the victimizers and preventing justice in the cases Tutela Legal was established to defend. This contemporary example of the church's collusion with oligarchic secular power is the kind of colonial control of authority that the CEBs use their public voice to denounce. Not only do the CEBs call the church to exercise its authority on behalf of *lxs pobres* in society; they abhor any support the church lends to the exercise of oppressive and unjust secular political power.

Nevertheless, as the documents in "Letter from the Hierarchy III" in part I attest, the relationship between the CEBs and Monseñor Escobar Alas is evolving, and it appears that he is gaining a better understanding of what it means to be the church of *lxs pobres*. For example, he has lent an ear to the voice of the church of *lxs pobres* in the concrete circumstances of the process of St. Oscar Romero's beatification and canonization.[26] For the beatification ceremony in 2015, the CEBs were not invited to be represented at the vigil or the beatification Mass in the city center, nor were they consulted in planning any of the activities. The CEBs held their own overnight vigil across the city from the Archdiocesan beatification events and marched down to join the thousands of bystanders the following day. For the canonization events in 2018, however, Archbishop Escobar Alas invited the CEBs for a meeting at his offices to help plan the vigil Mass and cultural activities at the Cathedral in San Salvador. During this meeting, according to the witness of members of the CEBs in attendance, the archbishop apologized to the CEBs for the lack of pastoral accompaniment they had received from the archdiocese over the past decades and indicated a desire to work *with* the CEBs to plan for Romero's canonization. Together, archdiocesan officials and CEBs leadership negotiated the music, readings, lectors, liturgical dance, and cultural celebration in a spirit of greater dialogue and fraternity that hinted back to the ministry of Romero himself. Since that time, Escobar Alas has concelebrated Mass to mark the CEBs' fiftieth anniversary celebration in February 2019, and has collaborated with Armando Márquez, the grassroots Salvadoran theologian who works closely with the CEBs, to facilitate a workshop about his most recent pastoral letter.

In addition to these hopeful signs in intraecclesial solidarity, Archbishop Escobar Alas has made some prophetic moves vis-à-vis the control of political authority in El Salvador. He was involved in the nationwide campaign to prohibit metallic mining in the country, which culminated successfully in the 2017 legislative ban on mining for gold and other metals.[27] Furthermore, he has also been involved in *la lucha* against the privatization of water in El Salvador, making his own public statement on the matter after a Sunday Mass in 2017. Surrounded by reporters, he protests: "[Access to] water is so important that it can't be only in the hands of a group of people. This cannot be! It needs to be in the hands of the people."[28] This struggle to protect the water rights of Salvadorans is still in process, with advocates hoping for an explicit legislative protection of water as a human right and a ban on water privatization. In these examples, we can see that Escobar Alas has begun to accompany the church of *lxs pobres* and Salvadoran civil society in their struggles to transform political authority for the sake of human rights and communal well-being. Could it be that encounters with San Romero throughout the beatification and canonization process, facilitated through his meetings with Romero's people, inspired this shift in the use of ecclesial power to transform rather than justify political authority? According to Escobar Alas himself, he sees Romero as "without a doubt, a role model for us. . . . He is the one who marked a turning point in our history, when the [Salvadoran] Church became preoccupied with human rights."[29] This seems to mark a decisive change in attitude from the 2012 removal of the mural and the 2013 closure of Tutela Legal. It appears as if the CEBs' proclamations, appeals to Romero, and the exercise of ecclesial humility and fraternal dialogue are able to affect change in the use of ecclesial power in a real way. This praxis of influencing the use of institutional ecclesial power is a significant contemporary example of the CEBs' work against colonial control of political authority.

From Control of Gender and Sexuality to the Decolonization of Gender Roles and Resistance to Sexual Violence

Though the CEBs' explicit understanding of poverty was primarily economic/material throughout the 1960s and 1970s, in practice, the very earliest formation of ecclesial base communities hinged on delinking from the colonial control of gender and sexuality as it existed within heterosexual marriage and the relationship between husbands and wives. In the experience of the Zacamil communities, re-membering how to be men and women outside the rules of *machismo* and rigid gender roles were some of the first challenges the Zacamil communities addressed:

> *Machismo* had destroyed families in El Salvador, as in many of our Latin American countries. From colonial times, the male had always been the conqueror who had all the rights, and women were the suffering victims of men's whims. This mission of each one repeated generation after generation: the man was to engender children—through pleasure or force—children the woman was to raise and who were, for her, a sort of life insurance, since nothing was ever sure with the man. While she cared for the children, he had the right to all the adventures he desired, any kind of shamelessness . . . that's how the *machista* framework operates.[30]
>
> The sacrament of marriage in El Salvador seems, rather, to be an anti-sacrament. In many cases, it is no more than a classist ritual because only those who have money can participate. Social pressure is so great that *los pobres* do not dare ask for marriage in the Church. They associate it with a new dress and new

expenditures: flowers for the altar, a rental car, a party, music, an *alfombra* . . . if there isn't money to pay for all that, it seems like a third-class marriage and *los más pobres* feel humiliated. Instead, *campesinos* who have married in the Church often have done it during a "mission," with a priest who blesses multiple marriages at a time.[31]

And so the pastoral team organized retreats for married couples and celebrated vow renewals and new marriages, which became foundational experiences of community building:

> From within all of these problems and concerns, we discovered anew the true sense of marriage in our ecclesial communities. Couples discovered that for their [pastoral] work to be credible, they needed to witness to their fidelity in front of the community. They discovered that they were not only spouses but also mutual supports for their Christian work. And they wanted to be happy. What would later become fidelity to the people, even unto death, began as fidelity in married life.
>
> And so we began to celebrate marriages. Not everybody got married at once. Some needed much more time to prepare and to work through any series of problems and situations. Others were ready much sooner. Those first marriages were unforgettable festivals. The whole community was in attendance, including the children of the married couple. They were not scandalized. For those children, it was an honor to see how their parents promised each other mutual love. And for the communities, attendance was a commitment: they would defend that love forever. Those festivals were also a sign of God's fidelity, that God was committed to God's *pueblo pobre*. It was truly a sacrament.[32]

In addition to the experience of preparing and celebrating these marriages, many rural women in the first generation of CEBs were involved in *"Congregaciones de Madres"* or organized mothers' groups that came together as women for biblical reflection and to organize to secure food for their families in guerilla territory or in refugee camps.[33] After the war, they continued many communal projects, such as forming artisan cooperatives that produce much of the *artesanía* described in the previous chapter. Women's involvement in these activities gave them the confidence and the skills to become empowered leaders in their communities, participating in not only the production of knowledge and creation of beauty, but in the power to make decisions and guide their communities toward paths of economic and gender justice.[34] Over time, women of the CEBs became critically conscious of their oppression and marginalization as *pobres* and as women, and they began to demand equality and respect not only in their communities and the larger society, but in their homes and in their relationships with their male companions and spouses. They also began to recognize the reproduction of patriarchy in themselves and have come to question the many subtle and complex ways in which boys and men are socialized into their prescribed roles as well.

The prophetic voices of the current generation of CEBs continue to speak out against *machismo* and to push the definitions of acceptable gender and sexual expression in their communities. In section 5 of Ángela Domínguez's testimony in part I of this book, for example, she laments how *machismo* continues to affect her life and her relationship with her sons:

> Because they raised us in a *machista* way, that women have to be submissive, and women have to be obedient, and women have to be everything that is opposite men. And so when we raise our children, many times we commit the error of saying, "Behave like a young man."[35]

This lament results in a strengthened commitment to the kind of anti-patriarchal work that she and other women in the CEBs are doing. When asked about what happens when one attempts to break with *machismo*, she remarks:

> Oh, boy. You are standing against a whole system that, shit, you're fighting against something that just doesn't budge. Many times, I've gone through this, when I have struggled against it within my own family, or in my community, or at work. The consequences: you will be repressed, you will have limits put on you, you will be restricted in certain things, they try to get on your nerves, they will try to tie your hands, cover your mouth, so that you can't speak or do anything. And it's this way because it's a *machista* system that we live in and everything in our system is powered by *machismo*, and that's why we don't see the efforts that so many women have made, just like me. I haven't done anything really great, but from the very moment that I start thinking differently or start being conscious that I have to think differently and act differently and start treating my son differently, I think I'm doing something. Of course! I know that I've won no Nobel Peace Prize, and I'm not sitting around waiting for that to happen. But at least I will have the satisfaction of knowing that I struggled against a whole system, and that I could do something, even if only with my own son. That is my hope.[36]

Clearly, women of the contemporary CEBs still express frustration with this area of transformation in their lives, families, and communities, but together with other women and other members of their communities, they are committed to struggling for equality, recognition, and the full dignity of their humanity. And the struggles of women from the original Mothers' Congregations and of younger women like Ángela have paid off in many ways. The transformation of power dynamics between men and women within the CEBs has opened up spaces for women's voices and leadership to take center stage. It has also transformed the consciousness, positionality, and practices of some men in the communities, to the point where sometimes it is the men who open up space for dialogue and encourage the women of the community to take their rightful place in creating an egalitarian power structure in the community or in their homes.[37]

Furthermore, some of the CEBs both recognize and advocate for women's leadership in the church and in their faith communities and support struggles for women's rights and well-being in the broader Salvadoran society. For example, some members of the CEBs have been involved in the struggle to change El Salvador's draconian abortion laws, which have condemned dozens of women to prison for decades because they suffered miscarriages under "suspicious" circumstances.[38] Furthermore, some members of the CEBs are also moving toward involvement in the struggle against heterosexism and homophobia in their communities and the broader culture. These decolonial advances are quite recent and only in their nascent stages. There is much work to be done here as the CEBs move toward greater decolonization of power in this domain of coloniality.

In addition to the transformation of gender roles in secular society as part of their social praxis, the CEBs also see women's leadership as essential to their ecclesial praxis, including their liturgical celebrations. Women and men share in the planning, facilitation, and evaluation of community celebrations, and often women are given priority in recognition of the long history of women's exclusion from leadership roles in the church. The insight, gleaned from the *experience* of women's liturgical leadership, that liturgy is celebrated more richly when all the people of God are invited to bring their concerns and full lives to its facilitation, has precipitated the intentional inclusion of other disempowered demographics, like young people and children, into the liturgical life of the communities. The decolonial dynamic at work here points toward ever greater inclusion of those who exist on the margins of not only the larger church and society but also the communities themselves. We will return to this dynamic of inclusion and empowerment below.

From Colonial Control of Nature toward a New Heaven and a New Earth

Finally, the Salvadoran CEBs of the twenty-first century have exercised agency for transformation of power in the realm of ecology and the relationship between human beings and the earth, seeking as a model the promise in the book of Revelation of a new heaven and a new earth (Rev. 21:1). This promise recognizes the unity of Creation and the connection between earthly and spiritual life. In the late twentieth century, the struggle for access to arable land was one of the driving forces behind the Salvadoran revolution. Today, the problem of unjust land distribution is by no means resolved, but the primary struggle of rural base communities lies in the transformation of how subsistence farmers use the land to meet their families' basic needs. These communities have recognized the ecological degradation wrought by conventional agriculture methods like monoculture and over-weeding and by commercial agriculture supplies like synthetic herbicides and pesticides, as well as the threat that mono-genetic, copyrighted modified seeds represent in light of the climate crisis facing tropical farmers today. They remember, and lament the passing of a time when the rivers were swimming with fish, when

> the rivers were abundant because there were so many fish of all kinds. In just a moment, [your] net would be full. There were *mojadas*, there were *guabinas*, there were *tepemechines*, *filines*, *mojarras*, *chacalines*, *camarones*, there was another one that we called *golomina* . . . yes, the fish were abundant. Not anymore. Today the fish have been lost and there are very few. A whole variety of fish that were lost.[39]

In light of the degradation of their lands and waters, many rural CEBs have sought to transform their farming practices to harness the power of sustainable and ancestral agriculture. One avenue for such transformation for the CEBs in the department of Morazán has been a program called *Escuela Campesina*, which is an agroecological curriculum for students from the postwar generations who have discontinued their formal education.[40] Ecological transformation is not the prerogative of only the rural CEBs, however. Both rural and urban CEBs are involved in reforestation campaigns and coordinated struggles against systemic threats to Creation, including metallic mining and hydroelectric dams, which would devastate the health of local ecosystems and the human beings that live in them.

Just as the CEBs' decolonial epistemology and creative expressions root their subversion of colonial control of subjectivity and makes resistance to the other nodes of the colonial matrix of power possible, so too their service and social agency find expression in *lxs pobres* partnering with *lxs pobres* in popular art, song, dance, and worship. Recent expression around a decolonial relationship with the natural world is particularly striking, as demonstrated in one of the CEBs' new songs that we highlighted in chapter 3, which tells the transnational hydroelectric and mining companies to "go to hell."

Vamos compañeros y el pueblo en general	Come on, companions, and everyone in general
A tomar conciencia para poder enfrentar	To raise our consciousness to be able to confront
Tenemos la amenaza que nos quieren inundar	The threat against us, that they want to flood us out
Con la represa en la Maroma Morazán.	With the Maroma dam in Morazán.
El río Torola nos está en venta,	The Torola River is not for sale,
Ni mucho menos nuestras propiedades.	Much less our properties.
. . .	. . .
Pa' colmo de eso nos quieren contaminar	On top of everything else, they want to pollute us
Con las minerías ¡miren qué barbaridad![41]	With mining. Isn't it ridiculous!?

Other songs lament the realities of climate change and conventional agriculture, calling for a better way to live in harmony with the planet. By encouraging their communities to raise consciousness through lively, danceable songs and accessible lyrics, the CEBs hope to act in a way that moves toward the creation of a new kind of world. This fusion of a decolonial praxis of knowledge, being, and power is grounded in the CEBs' explicitly Christian faith, a graceful response to the God of Life that ever reveals the divine self to these particular people in this particular place through the power of the Holy Spirit, according to the pattern of Jesús the Christ, who proclaimed the reign of God.

HORIZONS IN DECOLONIAL ECCLESIOLOGY: GOVERNING AUTHORITY

The Coloniality of Power in Ecclesial Governing Authority

The CEBs' decolonial praxis of social transformation in the interrelated realms explored above is a paradigmatic expression of how the Second Vatican Council envisions the mission of the church in and for the life of the world. Recall that, in conciliar and post-conciliar Catholic ecclesiology, the laity are especially called to apostolic mission in the secular world, acting as leaven in the dough of society and becoming a people of God that illumines and responds to the joys and hopes, sufferings and anxieties of *el pueblo* in general. While the church's historical relationship to coloniality too often has been and continues to be one of alliance with the powerful and privileged members of society, the Council Fathers, the CELAM, and now Pope Francis have made it clear that a break with that historical alliance is in order. Jesús of Nazareth's prophetic, anti-imperial praxis of the reign of God has finally made its way back into official Roman Catholic ecclesiology when it comes to the church's mission *ad extra*. Unfortunately, far too many priests, bishops, and even popes have reacted to this prophetic turn with what Jon Sobrino calls a *marcha atrás*,[42] putting the church into reverse gear and clinging to the power and privilege that continued coloniality affords. Too many religious leaders espouse either a blatant desire to return to the theocratic politics of Christendom and/or a latent desire to preserve an unjust status quo through adherence to an "apolitical" and otherworldly spiritualism. The Salvadoran church of *lxs pobres* resists both of these tendencies, actively calling the Roman Catholic hierarchy to conversion and to commitment to *lxs pobres* in pursuit of God's reign. The evolution of the CEBs' relationship with Archbishop Escobar Alas described above indicates that they are seeing some of the fruits of their labor. The Salvadoran hierarchy, along with much of the Latin American hierarchy, is beginning to re-member its promises at the Pact of the Catacombs, to become a church of and for *lxs pobres*, a church that uses its power in the service of God's reign of justice, peace, and ecological well-being for all people and the planet as a whole.[43]

The mission of the church to build up the reign of God in the world cannot be bifurcated into *ad extra* and *ad intra* movements. And yet the supposed hierarchical nature of the church has maintained a division between these two missional impulses; the laity are designated to work out "in the world," while clergy are tasked with the maintenance of the "church itself." Practically, this means that while some progress has been made toward the decolonization of Roman Catholic ecclesiology *ad extra* (albeit in fits and starts), the state of Roman Catholic ecclesiology *ad intra* remains mired in the muck of colonial power dynamics. Not only does the hierarchy retain a colonial hold on teaching and sacramental authority (as explored in chapters 2 and 3), the internal structures of governing authority in the church mirror the coloniality of power. In short, the power structures of the church *ad intra* are decidedly *anti-reino*. They contradict Jesús's vision of the beloved community, in which leaders do not "lord it over" their people, but relate to one another in mutuality, service, and love (cf. Matt. 20:25). Indeed, together with the CEBs, and as students of their ecclesial praxis, we maintain that the coloniality of power inherent in the church's hierarchical structure inhibits the perfection of the ecclesial mission in and for the world. Below we uncover the coloniality of power in Roman Catholic structures of governing authority, and we conclude with a summation of how the Salvadoran CEBs decolonize these structures in and through their praxis of *organización*.

As the reader will now be well aware, with the ecclesiology of Vatican II and its reception in Latin America, the Roman Catholic church made significant advances toward more communal and egalitarian models of the whole church as *communio*, sacrament of salvation, and people of God on pilgrimage to the reign of God. Previous chapters have critically engaged with how these models of communion ecclesiology have decolonial potential, but are too often compromised by the continued coloniality of the church's centralized and hierarchical governance, exactly the topic of the present chapter. Roman Catholic theologies and structures of governing authority are so prohibitively and persistently colonial in their reservation of such authority to the clergy and hierarchy that they disallow for the adoption of decolonial praxes in the realms of knowledge and creativity.

Certainly, interpretations of the church as "hierarchical communion" fall prey to the continued coloniality of Roman Catholic ecclesiology. While the church as communion requires "participation and responsibility at all . . . levels," Richard McBrien notes that

> some Catholics interpret the ecclesiology of communion more narrowly. For them, communion has only a vertical dimension. It refers exclusively to the Church's union in grace with the triune God and to the union of the local churches and their bishops with the Holy See. Such an ecclesiology views the Church primarily in otherworldly and hierarchical categories.[44]

Many prelates within the Salvadoran hierarchy over the past fifty years have counted themselves among those committed to this hierarchical vision of the ecclesial communion, including Archbishop Romero prior to his evolution toward an ecclesiology of the people of God.[45] Local priests also espouse and embody this view when they literally lock the doors of the church and prohibit the CEBs' access to important material resources such as chapel space, community centers, and even parish vehicles.[46] To understand and structure the church as a hierarchical communion not only concentrates epistemic and aesthetic/cultic authority in the hands of a select few ontologically separate (and until recently, mostly European or Euro-descendent) men but also concentrates the power to make decisions and shape the material conditions of the church in their hands as well.

One of the more egalitarian alternatives to the coloniality of hierarchical communion is articulated by some post-conciliar theologians in terms of structured or ordered communion, which is a model that attempts to balance the mutuality of the whole people of God with a legitimate need for structure and visible unity. This model, following *Lumen Gentium*, and referenced briefly in chapter 2, takes baptism as the starting point for ecclesial belonging, underscoring the fundamental equality of the whole people of God, *qua* church. Among others, Richard Gaillardetz proposes that "hierarchical communion" ought not be understood or exercised according to pyramidal conceptions of power, as it is in the models referenced above, but rather as a "sacred order" that draws the church into participation in the eternal ordering of the self-giving communion of the triune God. The whole church is thereby called internally and sent externally to fulfill its mission to the world in the service of God's reign. Gaillardetz envisions the embodiment of this ecclesial mission in a diversity of ministries that correspond with the diversity of charisms given by God to all the faithful.

While all the faithful are gifted by the Holy Spirit with charisms that contribute to the mission of the church, there are specific ecclesial charisms that he argues require formal communal and ritual recognition at the local parish and/or diocesan level. Such ministries position an individual in a new relationship to the ecclesial body, and she is empowered by the Holy Spirit to fulfill the responsibilities that her ministry requires. Gaillardetz's understanding of power here is not power over but power to *"fulfill one's baptismal call and engage in effective action in service of the Church's life and mission."*[47] He looks to the early church for a model of diverse ministries that include ordained bishops, presbyters, and deacons, but that also include the addition of installed and commissioned ministries open to lay women and men. The designation of "lay ministry" is problematic for Gaillardetz, though, because "it is only with difficulty shorn of its past historical associations with a kind of ecclesial passivity." In fact, he argues that "qualifying ministry as 'lay' tends to vitiate the construction" of a theology affirms the church as a communion of *"all the baptized,* the *Christifideles,* as followers of Jesus and members of the People of God."[48] Here we sense strong resonances with the CEBs' increasing hermeneutic of suspicion around the concept of the laity that was particularly highlighted in chapter 3. This should not be surprising, perhaps, given the similarity between the guiding principle and starting point of the CEBs in the "the community of the baptized called to share a common mission to proclaim, serve, and realize the coming reign of God." Indeed, Gaillardetz's proposal has profound possibilities for a decolonial theology of ministry, mission, and church authority. However, the decolonial potential of his ministerial model of ordered communion is compromised by hierarchical governing structures that allow for authoritative suppression of the very ministries Gaillardetz recognizes as central to the life and mission of the church. That is, the proposal is hindered by an ecclesial governing structure that has the power to suppress the very mission of the church as sacrament of God's reign and the ecclesial praxes or ministries that support this mission.

Even more radically egalitarian interpretations of communion ecclesiology, like the ecclesiology of Leonardo Boff, arise from the experience of and participation in ecclesial expressions like the CEBs. These interpretations also hold decolonial promise, especially when they are inspired by and organized in favor of participation in building up the reign of God *desde lxs pobres.* They contribute to the decolonization of ecclesial power *ad intra* insofar as they place governing authority of local churches in the collective hands of local lay people in horizontal relationships of dialogue and collaboration with the clergy and hierarchy. The problem, however, is that these decolonial moves are also structurally impossible, or at least unsustainable, within the reigning institutional power structures of Roman Catholicism. The church affirms that members of the lay faithful participate in Christ's "kingly function" and are permitted to

> "cooperate in the exercise of this power [of governance] in accord with the norm of the law." And so the Church provides for their presence at particular councils, diocesan synods, pastoral councils; the exercise of the pastoral care of a parish, collaboration in finance committees, and collaboration in ecclesiastical tribunals, etc.[49]

Lay involvement in church governance has vastly increased in the years since the council due to this approach, but lay participation in these avenues is generally limited to a consultative role.[50] The clergy and hierarchy retain decision-making power and material control of ecclesial resources.

Parishes are normatively administered by priests, who hold the power to decide how parochial resources are allotted and who is allowed to have access to those resources. Just recently—in fact, during the writing of this book—the Vatican's Congregation for Clergy issued guidelines stating as much in an instruction regarding the "Pastoral conversion of the Parish community in the service of the evangelizing mission of the church."[51] This instruction indicates that the norm for pastoral care of parishes is administration by ordained priests, with administration by deacons, lay persons, or religious women reserved only for cases of shortages of ordained priests. Administration of parish goods should involve the laity through the establishment of a parish finance council, but it is the priest who "presides" over that council. While parish goods belong to the parish and not to the priest, he is the "steward" of these goods and thus holds a great deal of governing authority over their use. The lay involvement here is laudable, but limited. Real, material power lies in the hands of the priest. Similarly, the Parish Council is a consultative body. It

> highlights and realizes the centrality of the People of God as the subject and active protagonist of the evangelizing mission, in virtue of the fact that every member of the faithful has received the gifts of the Spirit through Baptism and Confirmation.[52]

And yet, lay leadership is limited here as well: "The Parish Pastoral Council '*possesses a consultative vote only,*' in the sense that its proposals must be accepted favorably by the Parish priest to become operative."[53] The priest is bound to take the recommendations of the pastoral council seriously and enter into communal discernment with them, but he has the last word. While the instruction warns against the extreme use of power, in reality the priest has the power to make final decisions that affect the spiritual and material well-being of the parish and its local community. A progressive and collaborative priest who "sides with *lxs pobres*" might preside over a parish in what the CEBs call a "horizontal" fashion, but when he is transferred, retires, or dies, there is no structural impediment to new parish priests implementing a "vertical" approach. The reader will recall that this was the case with several CEBs that have been forced out of their parishes over the past twenty some years. In some cases, these communities were literally locked out of parish facilities by priests who were well within their canonical rights to do so.[54]

At the diocesan, regional, and global level, the return to synodality as a collegial means of governing the church is similarly ambiguous. On the one hand, the synod normalizes a dialogical method of governance that lends itself to a humbler hierarchy, more open to learning from and exercising power in mutual relationship with one another and with the broader *sensus fidelium* among the whole people of God. For example, the preparation for the 2019 Synod of Bishops for the Pan-Amazonian region included extensive consultation with local church communities, Indigenous communities, scientists, and other experts in the region. As a result, the *Instrumentum Laboris* for the Synod and the sessions of the Synod itself included candid and robust discussion of the expressed desire of many Amazonian communities for church governance structures that include greater leadership roles for women, and pathways toward women deacons and married priests.

The bishops' final document included mention of these discussions for the pope's consideration, requesting "that an instituted ministry of 'women's community leadership' be created and recognized as part of meeting the changing demands of evangelization and care for communities." The bishops also noted that

> in the many consultations carried out in the Amazon, the fundamental role of religious and lay women in the Church of the Amazon and its communities was recognized and emphasized, given the wealth of services they provide. In a large number of these consultations, the permanent diaconate for women was requested.[55]

With regard to the promotion of married priests, the final document makes the following request:

> Considering that legitimate diversity does not harm the communion and unity of the Church, but rather expresses and serves it (cf. *LG*, 13; *OE*, 6), witness the plurality of existing rites and disciplines, we propose that criteria and dispositions be

established by the competent authority, within the framework of *Lumen Gentium* 26, to ordain as priests suitable and respected men of the community with a legitimately constituted and stable family, who have had a fruitful permanent diaconate and receive an adequate formation for the priesthood, in order to sustain the life of the Christian community through the preaching of the Word and the celebration of the Sacraments in the most remote areas of the Amazon region.[56]

Here we see that many of the bishops listened faithfully to their people and brought their communities' pastoral concerns and genuine ecclesial desires to the attention of the wider college of bishops and Pope Francis.

In his post-synodal apostolic exhortation, *Querida Amazonia*, Francis lays out four *"sueños"* (dreams) for the Amazon region that respond to the expressed desire of local communities for greater church presence in the areas of ecological, cultural, social, and ecclesial promotion. In the first three dreams, Francis responds beautifully to the "cry of the earth and the cry of the poor" for justice and ecological well-being. The document cites local participants in the preparatory process, quoting from their own words, for example, that

> we are water, air, earth and life of the environment created by God. For this reason, we demand an end to the mistreatment and destruction of mother Earth. The land has blood, and it is bleeding; the multinationals have cut the veins of our mother Earth.[57]

In *Querida Amazonia*, Francis uses the power of the institutional church to enter into solidarity with the Amazonian people and publicly denounce the powerful networks that plague the region with economic, ecological, and political coloniality and violence. This delinking from the coloniality of power is a genuinely decolonial transformation in the church's mission *ad extra*. However, in the fourth section of the document, the pope skirts around the women's diaconate and married priests as ecclesiological questions of church governance and power structures *ad intra*. This section begins in the pastoral and poetic style of the previous three, affirming lay ministries, but the rest of the section reverts to a more juridical approach to church discipline. In the words of Leonardo Boff, the document contains "three-and-a-half dreams, and a nightmare."[58]

This is the reality of Roman Catholic church governance. Even at its best and most beautiful expressions of parish life, the structures of power place ultimate authority in the hands of the parish priest. Even at its best and most beautiful synodal moments, the structures of power subject the laity to the authority of the bishops and ultimate authority lies in the hands of the pope. The Code of Canon Law states that it is for the synod of bishops to discuss the questions for consideration and express its wishes but not to resolve them or issue decrees about them unless in certain cases the Roman Pontiff has endowed it with deliberative power, in which case he ratifies the decisions of the synod.

Indeed, the synod of bishops is "directly subject to the authority of the Roman Pontiff."[59] More progressive interpretations of communion ecclesiology express a fervent hope for the evolution of more collegial and less clerical relationships of power and authority in the institutional church. And yet the ordering of church governance structures remains so mired in the coloniality of power that these hopes are inevitably dashed time and time again.

The Decoloniality of Power in the CEBs' Praxis of Ecclesial *Organización*

The CEBs do not pretend to offer a global blueprint for Roman Catholic ecclesial governance, nor do we as authors presume to do so. However, the decolonial witness of the CEBs both resists the reigning Roman Catholic paradigm of hierarchical communion and points toward the praxis of *organización* as a mode of ecclesial communion more aligned with the mission of being a sacrament of the reign of God not only in the broader world, but within the church itself. While the model of ordered communion referenced above holds decolonial promise, it is, as a proposal, missing a practical, lived element and, thus, is still situated within a governing structure that affords clergy and bishops the power to suppress the diversity of charisms and priority of God's reign in the mission of the church. Furthermore, the paradigm of "order" does not translate well into the context of the Spanish-speaking world, and in fact carries with it connotations of coloniality, especially in El Salvador.[60] In the historical context of the Salvadoran church of *lxs pobres*, the Spanish word for order—*orden*—was the acronym and common name for ORDEN, one of the most violently repressive paramilitary forces of the twentieth century.[61] The adjective "ordered"—translated as *ordenado*—is similarly problematic because it implies something that is commanded and thus imposed from above. This word also creates some confusion because it is the Spanish word for being ordained in the sacrament of Holy Orders. Overall, *orden* and *ordenado* imply a juridical and hierarchical authority structure that imposes, from above, certain economic, social, political, and ecclesial arrangements on the population below. From this perspective, a church that understands its internal structure as a *comunión ordenada* is too compatible with a power structure that insists on order and unity, at the expense of the freedom and diversity that characterize the equitably and universally distributed subjectivity of God's reign. *Orden* lends itself too easily to a situation in which those who hold positions of power reinscribe a colonial power structure by "lording it over" those who have been historically colonized and repressed within the church—especially people of color, people living in poverty, women, and sexual minorities. *Orden* dehumanizes and violates the God-given capacity and vocation of all human beings to represent themselves freely and to participate in communities of genuine diversity, dialogue, and deliberate action—in short, *orden* violates the human calling to "become subjects in God's presence."[62]

For the CEBs, ecclesial leadership and decision-making processes in the church of *lxs pobres* are not *ordenados* according to charisms and ministries that are limited by one's gender, age, class, race, or ontological status as laity or clergy. Rather, the CEBs structure the exercise of power in their communities in diverse and creative ways through community-based, participatory processes of *organización*. Members of the CEBs are human beings and, like all human beings, they can fall prey to temptations of usurping power and resources for individual and/or group self-interest. No structural paradigm will completely eliminate this human tendency toward egocentrism. However, the CEBs' active and dynamic principle of *organización* offers a paradigm that does not facilitate or codify these tendencies very easily because it is an organic, egalitarian, and participatory process without fixed structures or laws that define the way it operates. The CEBs' pursuit of organized ecclesial communion *ad intra* seeks fraternal solidarity and unity of purpose—namely, God's reign—while simultaneously leaving room for diversity of charisms and even divergent ecclesial practices.

In the history of the CEBs, the use of the term *organización* is rooted in the popular liberation movements afoot during the 1960s and 1970s. When a person became involved in the popular struggle or, later, in the armed revolutionary movements, they might say *"me organicé"*—a reflexive verb meaning "I organized myself" or "I got organized." A community that entered into these struggles collectively might say *"nos organizamos"*—"we organized ourselves" or "we got organized." This meant that a person or a community was entering into a critically conscious, collective process of struggle for subjectivity, life, and liberation. More concretely, it meant that a person or community was taking tangible steps of coordinated action toward these goals. At a more mundane but equally significant level, displaced persons in the refugee camps across the northern border in Honduras also used the verb *organizarse* to describe their processes of working together to provide basic necessities for themselves and their families, as well as their efforts at consciousness raising, communal celebrations, and other areas of decision-making. It exceeds the scope of our research to enter into an analysis of the power structures at work within Salvadoran popular organizations, guerrilla movements, or refugee camps in the late twentieth century. Our task here is to speak to the priority, significance, and praxis of *organización* as a process of power sharing in the base communities.

In *Sigue porque la vida sigue*, the book of twelve interviews of base community members that has served as an important primary source for this book, God and community are the most frequently used key terms, with 148 and 268 mentions each, respectively. After these two terms, the root word *organiz-/organic-* appears seventy-two times, followed closely by the terms *pueblo* and *iglesia*, which both garner seventy uses. *Organización* is clearly a key element of the CEBs' praxis, identity, and understanding of what it means to be church. Though the CEBs see a relationship between the emancipatory praxis of secular movements for liberation and the liberatory praxis of the Christian faith, the parameters of *organización* are rooted more deeply and consistently in the latter than in the former. For these Christian communities, the biblical witness to the reign of God embodied by Jesús of Nazareth and by the first Christian communities is of utmost importance in how they understand their organized relationships of power and vulnerability with one another and with the larger society. The Jesús of the CEBs is an organizer, an animator of communities, who brings them together to form organized collective relationships of love and solidarity in pursuit of God's reign. Gustavo puts it this way:

> I think that every idealistic and visionary person has their own philosophy in the world. Jesús was one of those people. He is born and lives in a determinate place, he has a father and he has a mother. They give him a name, he has brothers, sisters, cousins, aunts, and uncles. He eats and he grows and when he comes to realize his communitarian work, he chooses a small structure of people from his community for his project. They organize and they plan.[63]

In this understanding of the movement led by Jesús, Jesús is a visionary and is the one to call people together, but it is the community as a whole that works, organizes, and plans together. Recall from chapter 3 that Gustavo is also the commentator who points out that Jesús does not call the members of his community "laity." He calls them friends.

The egalitarian nature of the organized community becomes even clearer in the CEBs' frequent reference to the first Christian communities in Acts of the Apostles as their model for how to be church. Tomás Luna, one of the community mystics cited in the "Revelations after the Peace Accords" in part I, defines the CEBs with direct reference to these first communities, whose *organización* united them in love and equality. He remarks that, like the first Christian communities what we have discovered is that we should be united because God wants it that way, that we all might live and that we might all feel ourselves to be siblings; nobody is more or less than anybody else, you see. Not because of whatever colors we might be or languages we might speak, right. God loves us all as much as anybody. That is what God demands, right, that we live in love, that we are not fighting or feeling jealousy, no. And that we share the little that we have too. . . . We had to be united, we had to work together . . . we had to love one another, we had to get involved; or rather, we had to, as they say, get better organized.[64]

Getting involved in the community, getting organized—these have been ecclesial touchstones for how church operates in the CEBs: working together in unity to care for one another in love. As we saw in part I, a *campesino* from Suchitoto who came to Fr. Chencho for confession put it this way:

As usual, he began in the traditional way, "Forgive me, Father, for I have sinned." I asked him what his sins were, and he said, "I have sinned against love." To sin against love, in most cases, means the sexual abuse of a woman or a man, to be adulterous, and so on. I asked him to explain his sin and he said, "I have sinned against love, because I am not organized." His reply puzzled me. I did not expect it. I had not studied that kind of sin in morality coursework at the Gregorian Pontifical University of Rome, nor had I heard of it from the lips of the twentieth century's greatest professor of morality, Father Bernard Häring, at the Lumen Vitae Institute. My moral theology did not extend so far. I asked, "And why do you say you have sinned by not being organized?" His answer was swift and sure. "If I am not organized [as part of a farmworker association or labor union], it means I do not love my neighbor, that I do not care about my neighbor's life, that I am selfish." For that campesino and for many others, to organize is an obligation that has its roots in the commandment to love. It is an obligation that goes beyond political, economic, or social reasons.[65]

Just as this obligation to *organizarse* guided many in the early CEBs, it continues to guide their collective consciousness and individual consciences today. As Reina, who is one of the prophets cited in part I, puts it:

I'm not too worried about whether or not I make it to Mass each Sunday, but if I see someone around me who needs me, I'm telling you, I don't think twice. That's what I do and it's all about helping out. And if I don't have what's needed, I ask for assistance from someone else, but I know that help is possible. And I believe that great things can be done if we get organized and come together as one.[66]

This is the true meaning of ecclesial power for the CEBs: it is the power to do great things together in unity for the sake of abundant life for all God's people, especially those who are most in need. Moreover, the internal power at work here is not organized for the sake of the internal ecclesial community alone, but for the sake of building up God's reign in human history. The separation between the church *ad intra* and *ad extra*, while illustrative for our purposes of describing the direction of the church of *lxs pobres*' critical lens in recent years, is ultimately untenable. The singular mission of the church is to be a sacrament of salvation to the world, for which internal coherence is necessary.

What, then, do structures of ecclesial power and authority look like in the CEBs and, more broadly, in their connections with other communities and with the wider church? In chapter 2, we mentioned that the CEBs do not use the language of authority. But they do use the language of leadership. Generally speaking, the leaders of a base community work together as a team to organize all of the many activities we have detailed in these past three chapters: they lead biblical reflections and raise critical consciousness, they organize and lead the community in sacramental and cultural celebrations, and they organize mutual aid efforts and communal participation in political protest. Some communities have rotating "pastoral teams" of two to three people that share responsibility for planning the weekly celebration once per month. Others have organized teams related to liturgy or other ministries that the community has discerned to be essential to their shared life together, such as theological formation, mutual aid, or music ministry. Perhaps more importantly, though, most leaders in the base communities work together as *animadores* (animators) of the community, inspiring folks to come together and empowering them to become involved, get organized, and become leaders themselves.

Miguel Zepeda, another prophet cited in part I, is a community leader who reflects that the empowerment of new leadership fills him with great joy. When a young person in his community came forward one Sunday with proposals for new youth projects, he reacted with great enthusiasm:

> Man! I was just listening, sitting there. And that gave me such great joy, it gave me a lot of satisfaction. And I said, how interesting that I am not always going to be here all the time, and now there is someone else who can take this up and he is young and has energy, he has potential, he has capacity, he has a whole life ahead, he can make proposals, he can renew the community. He can give another style to it! And so, shit! That filled me with life.[67]

While Roman Catholic teaching regarding ecclesial governance contains these ideals of service and empowerment of the laity (at least theoretically), the reality delineated above is that the coloniality of ecclesial power structures contradicts these ideals and too often results in the opposite effect. The CEBs, in contrast, operate within the dynamic and organic nature of *organización*, where leadership is exercised communally and freely by all who wish to get involved. The result is not anarchy but empowerment; empowerment of the entire community for the exercise of subjectivity in pursuit of God's reign is precisely the goal of the CEBs' praxis of *organización*. This is true at the local level, as well as at national, regional, and continental levels, where the CEBs *se articulan*—assemble, come together, speak a joint word—as representative networks that bring local problems to a shared table and relay joint messages and proposals back to their communities. The *articulaciones* of CEBs are synodal in fact. There is no canon law governing them, and no higher committee approving or disapproving of their methods. The CEBs are responsible to and for themselves, and internally, each person to each other, such that what works is ratified in practice and problematic ways of proceeding do not endure. In the municipality of Cacaopera, for example, each community selects a representative or two to attend monthly departmental meetings. And two members are selected from the regional meeting to represent the CEBs of the department at the national meetings, together with two members from San Salvador, La Libertad, Usulután, Perquín, and Nahuizalco. News, invitations, questions, and concerns pass back and forth through these communicative nodes, with representatives sharing conclusions and enduring questions from the meetings at their community's weekly liturgy. The representatives' authority comes directly from the approval given them by the community, and the process works best when each member present participates fully and actively. The national *articulación* of CEBs in El Salvador sends representatives to neighboring countries' national retreats, as well as to regional meetings and the international continental meeting every four years.

The actual level of *organización* in Salvadoran CEBs varies and not every leader is as committed to equality and empowerment as Miguel. Some leaders may even attempt to mimic the coloniality of power that was instilled in them in more traditional church settings, and in Salvadoran society more broadly. But the principle of *organización* offers a structural openness that facilitates the cultivation of diverse subjectivities and empowers community members, including young people like Ángela and Adonay, who entered into a leadership role in his community in his early teens. His words witness to the subjectivity that he experiences and embodies in his work as an ecclesial agent of communal *organización*:

> I feel the responsibility I feel because the CEBs have awakened something in me that nobody else had awakened, not even the Catholic church, which is the traditional church. But really, yeah, I feel like it's something that motivates me and that interests me because I like to see the people organized. So it's

something that I feel like, yeah, really, I can do it, or I'm capable, or maybe because God asks it of me. Because that's how the CEBs are, it's all volunteer work leading a group or accompanying other groups and all that. And I feel like a leader, and I'm interested because, yeah, I want to see the community organized. The four communities here in Agua Blanca, totally organized in this sector, since we have the chapel here. I've always thought that in the future we should organize it to have greater coverage for the chapel since right now there is not as much support for the celebrations on Sunday and the youth don't do that many activities. But I want to take that back up because before there was a youth group that did activities. But right now, no, nobody had decided to take up the idea. So I decided to continue with this. And what I propose is to be able to fix up the chapel and build small spaces in our communities where we would have a place to meet, to reflect, so that there isn't so much disorganization in the communities, so much egoism, like we are right now with some families here, others there, and all that.[68]

Adonay's experience of ecclesial life in the CEBs has not only woken something up within him, but has motivated and empowered him to exercise his subjectivity by organizing his community for the sake of greater ecclesial unity and more widespread participation. *Organización* here refers not to an organization as a discrete entity unto itself, like a formal institution, a business, or a nonprofit organization. *Organización* is a process of coming together as a community to exercise subjectivity and collective power in favor of the universally and equitably distributed subjectivity of God's reign. The CEBs organize for the sake of such subjectivity *ad extra*—in and for the life of the world—but they also organize for the sake of such subjectivity within the church itself. There is unity and coherence in the mission. The CEBs sing that the reign of God is born when the people organize because the reign of God is a reality in which all people are free to be subjects, *con-spirando* in partnership with the God of Life. But like the CEBs' vision of the reign of God, *organización* as a process of cultivating subjectivity is not a totalizing process and the catholicity of this process is not a one-size-fits-all proposition. Rather, it's an open process in which all sizes belong. *Organización* includes all people who are committed to exercising subjectivity in egalitarian relationships of solidarity for the sake of abundant life for all human beings and creation itself. "Everyone who pulls up a chair has a place and a mission."[69] In our next and final chapter, we will turn to what these egalitarian relationships might look like across lines of power and how privileged Christians who benefit from coloniality might participate in re-imagining the table and re-membering the mission of the church in decolonial solidarity with the church of *lxs pobres*.

NOTES

1. Gómez and Marshall, eds., *Sigue porque la vida sigue*, 193–194.
2. Gómez and Marshall, 193.
3. Maldonado-Torres, "Outline of Ten Theses," 28.
4. Gómez and Marshall, eds., *Sigue porque la vida sigue*, 140.
5. See Aníbal Quijano, "Coloniality and Modernity/Rationality," *Cultural Studies* 21, no. 2–3 (2007): 168–178.
6. Gómez and Marshall, eds., *Sigue porque la vida sigue*, 99.
7. This is how the CEBs refer to themselves in the song *Nueva forma de ser Iglesia* ("A New Way of Being Church"), and this is also how Leonardo Boff reflects on the Latin American CEBs in *Ecclesiogenesis* (Maryknoll, NY: Orbis Books, 1986).
8. Walter Mignolo, *Desobediencia epistémica*, 33.
9. See also the work of Marcella Althaus-Reid, who critiques liberation theology for presenting a "decent," sanitized, and asexual image of the poor in *Indecent Theology: Theological Perversions in Sex, Gender, and Politics* (New York: Routledge, 2000).
10. See Jon Sobrino, *Where Is God? Earthquake, Terrorism, Barbarity, and Hope* (Maryknoll, NY: Orbis Books 2004).
11. See Sylvia Wynter, "Unsettling the Coloniality of Being/Power/Truth/Freedom: Towards the Human, After Man, Its Overrepresentation—An Argument," *New Centennial Review* 3, no. 3 (Fall 2003): 257–337. Pope Francis calls this phenomenon of rendering certain lives dispensable "throwaway culture." See *EG*, §53.
12. Barbé, "Church Base Communities," 181.
13. Marshall, "Un gesto vale más que mil palabras," Appendix 9, xlviii.
14. Marshall, Appendix 9, xlviii.
15. Aníbal Quijano, "Coloniality of Power, Eurocentrism, and Latin America," *Nepantla: Views from South* 1, no. 3 (2000): 533–580.
16. See part I, "Colonio-Genesis."
17. The Museum to the Revolution in Perquín, Morazán, titles one of its exhibit rooms "Reasons for the War." One of the reasons is, indeed, the elimination of a "political option," such as voting, petitioning, or protesting.
18. The inputs for this analysis are less clear after the 2019 presidential elections in which Nayib Bukele, former FMLN mayor of San Salvador, was ousted from the party despite popular support and went on to win the presidency in a landslide.
19. Gómez and Marshall, eds., *Sigue porque la vida sigue*, 128–129.
20. Gómez and Marshall, 174.
21. See "Letter from the Hierarchy III" in part I.
22. For more about Llort or for examples of his work, see https://www.fernando-llort.com/.
23. Rachel Heidenry, "Archbishop Orders Destruction of Salvadoran Mural," Pulitzer Center, January 6, 2012, accessed February 25, 2019, pulitzercenter.org/reporting/archbishop-orders-destruction-salvadoran-mural.

24. Patricia Carías, "Arzobispo dice mural de Llort no puede estar en catedral porque tiene símbolos masones," El Faro, February 6, 2012, accessed on February 25, 2019, www.elfaro.net/es/201202/noticias/7486/, cited in Marshall, "Un gesto vale," 6.
25. CEBs of El Salvador, "Ante el cierre de Tutela Legal y el despido de sus colaboradores/as . . . . ," October 4, 2013, fundahmer.files.wordpress.com/2013/10/comunicado-cebc2b4s-ante-decisic3b3n-de-cierre-de-tutela-legal.pdfv, accessed February 25, 2019.
26. For an account of these events, see "Letter from the Hierarchy III" in part I.
27. See Gene Palumbo and Elizabeth Malkin, "El Salvador, Prizing Water Over Gold, Bans All Metal Mining," New York Times, March 27, 2017, https://www.nytimes.com/2017/03/29/world/americas/el-salvador-prizing-water-over-gold-bans-all-metal-mining.html. See also Gene Palumbo, "Spurred by Catholic Leaders, El Salvador Becomes First Nation to Ban Mining," America, April 3, 2017, accessed February 25, 2019, https://www.americamagazine.org/politics-society/2017/04/03/spurred-catholic-leaders-el-salvador-becomes-first-nation-ban-mining. For a more comprehensive account of the struggle and sacrifice that precipitated the ban, see Robin Broad and John Cavanaugh, The Water Defenders: How Ordinary People Saved a Country from Corporate Greed (Boston, MA: Beacon Press, 2021).
28. "Arzobispo José Luis Escobar Alas se muestra en contra de la privatización del agua," Canal Genteve, June 20, 2017, www.youtube.com/watch?v=nIhXa88o7Gc&t=10s, accessed February 25, 2019.
29. Melissa Vida, "Church in El Salvador Backs Law Declaring Clean, Affordable Water as a Human Right," America, April 6, 2018, www.americamagazine.org/politics-society/2018/04/06/church-el-salvador-backs-law-declaring-clean-affordable-water-human, accessed on February 25, 2019.
30. Fe de un pueblo, 32.
31. Fe de un pueblo, 35–36.
32. Fe de un pueblo, 36.
33. See "The Gospel according to Morazán," §3, in part I.
34. See the book of women's testimonies published by the Ecclesial Base Communities of Northern Morazán, Tomamos la Palabra (Morazán, El Salvador: Talleres Gráficos UCA, 2001).
35. "The Librito of the Prophet María Ángela Domínguez Pérez," §5, in part I; Gómez and Marshall, eds., Sigue porque la vida sigue, 190–191.
36. "The Librito of the Prophet María Ángela Domínguez Pérez," §5, in part I.
37. See Miguel Zepeda's interview in Gómez and Marshall, eds., Sigue porque la vida sigue, 147–178.
38. See Elisabeth Malkin, "They Were Jailed for Miscarriages. Now, Campaign Aims to End Abortion Ban," New York Times, April 9, 2018, https://www.nytimes.com/2018/04/09/world/americas/el-salvador-abortion.html, accessed February 21, 2019.
39. "Colonio-Genesis," §1, in part I; Gómez and Marshall, eds., Sigue porque la vida sigue, 25.

40. See Laurel Marshall Potter, "*Campesina* School: Popular Agroecological Education in Ecclesial Base Communities in El Salvador," in *Valuing Lives, Healing Earth: Religion, Gender, and Life on Earth*, eds. Teresa Yugar et al. (Leuven: Peeters, 2021), 235–247. See also "Escuela Campesina," FUNDAHMER website, https://fundahmerespanol.wordpress.com/proyectos/desarrollo-humano/escuela-campesina/, accessed October 12, 2018.

41. Grupo Libre, CEBs Cacaopera, Morazán, "A La Chingada," *Las CEBs Cantamos: Articulación de CEBs en El Salvador*, 2017, compact disc.

42. See, for example, Jon Sobrino, *Resurección de la verdadera Iglesia: Los pobres, lugar teológico de la eclesiología* (Guevara, Spain: Ediciones Sal Terrae, 1984), 214 and 234.

43. See "Nuevo-Exodus," §2, in part I; Maria Clara Lucchetti Bingemer, *Latin American Theology: Roots and Branches* (Maryknoll: Orbis, 2016), 51–53.

44. Richard P. McBrien, *The Church: The Evolution of Catholicism* (New York: HarperOne, 2008), 283.

45. See Michael Lee's account of Romero's evolution in *Revolutionary Saint*.

46. See the three letters from contemporary CEBs in part I.

47. Richard R. Gaillardetz, "The Ecclesiological Foundations of Ministry within an Ordered Communion," in *Ordering of the Baptismal Priesthood*, ed. Susan Wood (Collegeville, MN: Liturgical Press, 2003), 41. For Gaillardetz's later applications of his ecclesiology of ordered communion, see *By What Authority: A Primer on Scripture, the Magisterium, and the Sense of the Faithful* (Minneapolis, MN: Liturgical Press, 2003), 66 ff; and *Ecclesiology for a Global Church: A People Called and Sent* (Maryknoll, NY: Orbis Books, 2008), 133. Emphasis in original.

48. Gaillardetz, "The Ecclesiological Foundations of Ministry," 44. Emphasis in original.

49. *CCC*, §911, citing the *CCL*.

50. Canon law is clear that in pastoral councils on the diocesan and parochial levels, "members of the Christian faithful outstanding in firm faith, good morals, and prudence" serve at the discretion of the local bishop (Can. 513 and 536). This is one of the very few formal avenues available to all of the baptized for participating in the governance of the church. Paul Lakeland comments that the laity have "no appropriate institutional vehicles for speaking out" in *A Council that Will Never End: Lumen Gentium and the Church Today* (Collegeville, MN: Liturgical Press, 2013).

51. Congregation for the Clergy, "Pastoral Conversion of the Parish Community in the Service of the Evangelising Mission of the Church," http://www.clerus.va/content/dam/clerus/Dox/Istruzione2020/Instruction_EN.pdf, accessed August 25, 2020. A summary of the document can be found at Joshua McElwee, "Vatican Reiterates: Catholic Parishes Should Be Led by Priests, not Laypeople," *National Catholic Reporter*, June 20, 2020, https://www.ncronline.org/news/parish/vatican-reiterates-catholic-parishes-should-be-led-priests-not-laypeople, accessed August 25, 2020.

52. Congregation for the Clergy, no. 110.

53. Congregation for the Clergy, no. 113. Emphasis in the original, citing *CCL*, can. 536, §2.

54. *CCL*, can. 1276 on the administration of goods states, "It is for the ordinary to exercise careful vigilance over the administration of all goods which belong to public juridic persons subject to him." Parroquial or diocesan pastoral councils, where lay people can "investigate, consider, and propose practical conclusions about those things which pertain to pastoral works in the diocese" (can. 512), are optional and consultative (can. 512).

55. Synod of Bishops for the Pan-Amazonian Region Final Document, "The Amazon: New Paths for the Church and for an Integral Ecology," October 26, 2019, §102 and 103, http://www.synod.va/content/sinodoamazonico/en/documents/final-document-of-the-amazon-synod.html, accessed August 26, 2020.

56. Synod of Bishops, §111.

57. *QA*, §42.

58. Leonardo Boff, "¿Para quiénes es, o no es querida la Querida Amazonia?" March 2, 2020, http://www.servicioskoinonia.org/boff/articulo.php?num=970.

59. *CCL*, Can. 343 and 344.

60. These connotations may apply in English as well. In our own context of the United States, the phrase "law and order" has been employed extensively in the past half century as coded language for racist and capitalist control of people of color, especially African Americans, and the poor and working classes more broadly. While we recognize that the word "order" has a rich history in the Christian tradition, hearkening even back to God's act of creation, giving order to the cosmos, we cannot ignore the cultural trappings of this word, this symbol, in our own place and times.

61. See "Colonio-Genesis," §11, in part I.

62. See Johannes Baptist Metz, *Faith in History and Society: Toward a Practical Fundamental Theology* (New York: Herder & Herder, 2007), 70–76.

63. Gómez and Marshall, eds., *Sigue porque la vida sigue*, 88.

64. Gómez and Marshall, 30.

65. José Inocencio Alas, *Land, Liberation and Death Squads: A Priest's Story, Suchitoto, El Salvador, 1968–1977*, trans. Robin Fazio and Emily Wade Will (Eugene: RESOURCE, 2016), 50. Cited in "The Gospel according to Suchitoto," §7, in part I.

66. Gómez and Marshall, eds., *Sigue porque la vida sigue*, 66.

67. Gómez and Marshall, 106.

68. "The *Librito* of the Prophet José Adonay Pérez Pérez," §5; Gómez and Marshall, *Sigue porque la vida sigue*, 213.

69. Guillermo Cuéllar, "Vamos todos al banquete." See "The Gospel according to Suchitoto," §9, in part I, n13.

Chapter 5

Si el grano de trigo no muere
The Challenge of Decolonial Solidarity

And yes, I believe that it is important to sow those seeds of solidarity because if I am not in solidarity with the other, if I am just for myself, for myself, then the universe is not going to be there for me, it closes itself off to me.
—Reina Greisi Leiva from La Libertad[1]

If we were to sum up the decolonial witness of El Salvador's church of the poor in just one word, that word might be solidarity. The reign of God is a world of abundant life and *koinonia*, a world in which many worlds are free to coexist. It is a communal reality in which all people are free to exercise intersubjectivity in communion with and empowered by the God of Life, particularly as God is present in and with human beings and all of creation. The fullness of this reality is not yet experienced or embodied in human history and, in fact, the powers and principalities of the *anti-reino*, which we correlate with the colonial matrix of power, actively work against the realization of God's reign with relentless violence that makes abundant life and free existence for all impossible. These structural powers and their individual manifestations destroy *koinonia* by violating the vocation of all people to be subjects in God's presence. These colonial principalities overrepresent the subjectivity of some human beings, while denying subjectivity to others. Solidarity, on the other hand, is the historical praxis in which the *reino*'s reality of intersubjectivity is "already" present and active, albeit imperfectly and partially, in the *koinonia* of egalitarian human communities of shared life and struggle. Solidarity is at the heart of the CEBs' praxis of decolonial knowledge, wherein *lxs pobres* believe in *lxs pobres* and come together to reclaim their epistemic authority as prophetic authors of historical memory, wisdom, and hope. Solidarity is at the heart of the CEBs' praxis of decolonial being, wherein *lxs pobres* re-member their communal subjectivity in priestly affirmations of creativity, beauty, celebration, and joy. And solidarity is at the heart of the CEBs' praxis of decolonial power, wherein *lxs pobres* bear one another's burdens in everyday life and struggle together for a church and a world in which there are *ni ricos, ni pobres*, neither rich nor poor—a world no longer structured according to the colonial logics of wealth and poverty, North and South, colonizers and colonized, subjects and objects.

In his tenth and final thesis on coloniality and decoloniality, Nelson Maldonado-Torres affirms, in the language of decolonial scholarship, what we have observed and analyzed at work in the intra- and intercommunal solidarity of the CEBs. He asserts that decoloniality is "not a project of individual salvation," but rather "a collective project" that must be undertaken by the colonized, together with other colonized subjects: "Thinking, creating, and acting are all done, not by looking for recognition by the masters, but while reaching out to other *damnés*." The reign of God is *de lxs pobres* and it is *lxs pobres* whose intersubjective solidarity manifests the sacramental inbreaking of God's reign in human history. And yet, both Maldonado-Torres and the CEBs affirm that it is not only the *damnés* or *lxs pobres* who take part in the decolonial project. "It is the damnés *and others who also resign from modernity/coloniality* who, thinking, creating, and acting together in various forms of community can seek to disrupt the coloniality of knowledge, power, and being and change the world."[2] This chapter inquires how those of us who are the "others" in this statement—that is, those of us who benefit from the colonial power matrix in various ways—might "resign from modernity/coloniality" and enter into decolonial solidarity with the *damnés/pobres*.

In the process of exploring this question, we seek to root out traces of coloniality that can often remain both in the solidarity of Roman Catholic church of the poor discourse and in the praxis of solidarity with Latin America by privileged Christians in North America. We argue that Christians who participate in and/or benefit from coloniality can only engage in decolonial solidarity by ceding the overrepresentation of our own subjectivity and recognizing that the subjects of solidarity in the church of *lxs pobres* are first and foremost *lxs pobres* themselves. Christians who are privileged by race, class, gender, sexuality, and/or citizenship in the colonial power matrix should not "look at" human beings on the underside of these privileges as indirect objects or passive recipients of solidarity (much less charity); rather we should look to and learn from communities like the CEBs as primary subjects of solidarity in their own right. The challenge of resigning from overrepresented subjectivity applies most obviously and most directly to predominantly white churches and white Christians because the colonial matrix of power is held together by racialized hierarchies that place white subjectivity above all others. However, some members of other racialized communities can and do benefit from coloniality in the realms of economics, ecclesial authority, political power, military might, gender, sexuality, and/or citizenship. Therefore, we hope that the insights we have learned from the CEBs can be helpful for anyone crossing lines of power and privilege to enter into solidarity with persons and communities whose subjectivity has been violated by the coloniality of power. Furthermore, we hope that lessons can be learned here for solidarity not only with Latin America, but with grassroots movements of marginalized communities in other parts of the world, including within our own context of the United States.

Resigning from the overrepresentation of one's subjectivity is a process of conversion that is not accomplished overnight, nor is it for the faint of heart. It is a lifelong process of purgation that requires renouncing the colonial overrepresentation of subjectivity; exorcizing the demons of epistemic and ontological hierarchies; and making peace with the vulnerability of human existence in a finite, interdependent, and ambiguous universe. We conclude this chapter with an extended reflection on this final requirement for decolonial solidarity because, without such an embrace of the vulnerability that comes with decolonial solidarity, we will never know the power of the universe or the grace of divine solidarity that is available to all humanity and creation at the heart of God's reign.

THE COLONIALITY OF SOLIDARITY

Pope Francis and Solidarity with the Church of the Poor

When Pope John XXIII, the signatories of the Pact of the Catacombs, the Latin American Bishops, and now Pope Francis call for "a church that is poor and for the poor,"[3] they are calling for a church that embodies human solidarity in and through a preferential option for the poor. Though its biblical and theological roots run deep, the concept of solidarity has been an explicitly salient feature of Catholic social thought for nearly a century, and Pope John Paul II made the promotion of human solidarity a hallmark of his papacy. But it is Pope Francis who has most insistently placed the poor at the center of this human and Christian calling to recognize the reality of human interdependence, to respond to the suffering of the "other" with compassion and assistance, and to concretize this compassion in the transformation of the economic and political structures of human life.[4] This call to solidarity with the poor is indeed at the heart of Francis's papacy and he himself has demonstrated such solidarity in word and in deed: choosing a more humble residence and attire than his predecessors, visiting with prisoners and refugees, promoting popular movements, supporting the Indigenous peoples of the Amazon region, and much more.

Nearly all of his writings promote solidarity, and his most recent encyclical, *Fratelli Tutti: On Fraternity and Social Friendship*, is an extended reflection on solidarity, particularly with the poor and marginalized. This renewed emphasis on solidarity with the poor is a significant and welcome step that the Roman Catholic church has made toward delinking from the coloniality of power, insofar as it urges the wealthy and powerful to renounce their privileges and enter into solidarity with those who are poor and powerless.

The concept and praxis of solidarity in Catholic social thought, especially as articulated by Pope Francis, also leans toward decoloniality in its move both away from simple acts of charity and toward the creation of a world in which the wealth of a few does not inhibit the life of the many:

> The word "solidarity" is a little worn and at times poorly understood, but it refers to something more than a few sporadic acts of generosity. It presumes the creation of a new mindset which thinks in terms of community and the priority of the life of all over the appropriation of goods by a few.[5]

Like decoloniality, the Catholic concept and praxis of solidarity encompasses both a transformation of power structures and a transformation of individual and communal ways of knowing and being in the world. It requires resigning from the modern/colonial worldview because it involves the "spontaneous reaction" (an embodied decolonial knowledge?) of "those who recognize that the social function of property and the universal destination of goods are realities which come before private property." Because private property is only justified in service to the common good, "solidarity must be lived as the decision to restore to the poor what belongs to them."[6] Here we detect a fundamental break with the colonial power matrix and the value it places on private ownership of capital over and against the universal destination of created goods, a precept that arguably supports the decolonial *telos* of a world in which all peoples are free to enjoy access to the goods that they need to exist. Furthermore,

> these convictions and habits of solidarity, when they are put into practice, open the way to other structural transformations and make them possible. Changing structures without generating new convictions and attitudes will only ensure that those same structures will become, sooner or later, corrupt, oppressive and ineffectual.[7]

In the language of decoloniality, without cultivating the foundational "convictions and habits" that result in delinking from the colonial paradigm of extractivism and capital accumulation, solidarity can simply degenerate into a new set of structures that reinscribe coloniality.

Another decolonial aspect of solidarity in Catholic social thought, and in Pope Francis's papacy more specifically, is the epistemic authority that it recognizes in the suffering and oppressed, who are understood to not only bear God's image but also share in the condition of poverty with which God united Godself in Christ. Pope Francis puts it thusly:

> They [the poor] have much to teach us. Not only do they share in the *sensus fidei*, but in their difficulties they know the suffering Christ. We need to let ourselves be evangelized by them. The new evangelization is an invitation to acknowledge the saving power at work in their lives and to put them at the center of the Church's pilgrim way. We are called to find Christ in them, to lend our voice to their causes, but also to be their friends, to listen to them, to speak for them, and to embrace the mysterious wisdom which God wishes to share with us through them.[8]

Here we can see that Francis proposes not only contemplating and learning from the suffering of Christ in the poor and vulnerable, he also champions their "causes," to which he calls the church to lend its voice. Most significantly, he has supported these causes by initiating and addressing the WMPM with support and encouragement for the solidarity that people living in poverty and on the margins of society embody in both their relationships with one another and the way in which they "address the 'economy of exclusion and inequality' by working for structural changes that promote social, economic and racial justice."[9]

This support for popular movements may in fact be one of the most decolonial moves of Pope Francis's papacy. In *Fratelli Tutti*, Francis quotes from his addresses to the WMPM several times (ten in all, by our count), applauding participants for their exercise of solidarity, not only as a virtue of everyday living in community, but, thereby, as a way of making history:

> Solidarity means much more than engaging in sporadic acts of generosity. It means thinking and acting in terms of community. It means that the lives of all are prior to the appropriation of goods by a few. It also means combatting the structural causes of poverty, inequality, the lack of work, land and housing, the denial of social and labor rights. It means confronting the destructive effects of the empire of money.... Solidarity, understood in its most profound meaning, is a way of making history, and this is what popular movements are doing.[10]

This message invites the church to learn from the solidarity of grassroots popular movements, particularly with regard to the importance of historical protagonism from below. Quoting again from his 2016 Address to the

WMPM in *Fratelli Tutti*, he remarks that in the midst of a world economic system that excludes participation from below,

> what is needed is a model of social, political and economic participation "that can include popular movements and invigorate local, national and international governing structures with that torrent of moral energy that springs from including the excluded in the building of a common destiny," while also ensuring that "these experiences of solidarity which grow up from below, from the subsoil of the planet—can come together, be more coordinated, keep on meeting one another."[11]

He goes on to warn, however, that the uniqueness and diversity of these movements not be flattened, because there is both a poetic beauty to popular protagonism and a necessity of their agency for the flourishing of democracy:

> This, however, must happen in a way that will not betray their distinctive way of acting as "sowers of change, promoters of a process involving millions of actions, great and small, creatively intertwined like words in a poem." In that sense, such movements are "social poets" that, in their own way, work, propose, promote and liberate. They help make possible an integral human development that goes beyond "the idea of social policies being a policy *for* the poor, but never *with* the poor and never *of* the poor, much less part of a project that reunites peoples." They may be troublesome, and certain "theorists" may find it hard to classify them, yet we must find the courage to acknowledge that, without them, "democracy atrophies, turns into a mere word, a formality; it loses its representative character and becomes disembodied, since it leaves out the people in their daily struggle for dignity, in the building of their future."[12]

The emphasis on a politics *of* the poor here is very much akin to the way in which the CEBs have made themselves primary, collective protagonists of God's reign in the church *of* the poor. Decolonial solidarity requires this re-centering of the agency of the *damnés/pobres* in the search for an-other world and an-other church in which many worlds fit.

In order to encourage the cultivation of a church that reimagines, listens to, and reaches out to the poor in solidarity, Pope Francis has instituted an annual "World Day of the Poor." In the Apostolic Letter that concluded the church's Extraordinary Jubilee of Mercy in 2016, Francis states that he intends the World Day of the Poor to function as an evangelizing challenge to the church "to reflect on how poverty is at the very heart of the Gospel and that, as long as Lazarus lies at the door of our homes (cf. Lk. 16:19–21), there can be no justice or social peace."[13] While we applaud this attempt to re-center impoverished peoples in the life of the church, we also posit that, by focusing in on this one aspect of Francis's ministry, we might come to a greater understanding of how the minimization of the subjectivity of *lxs pobres* unfortunately persists all too often in his papacy's approach to solidarity with the poor. Despite the decolonial impulses in Francis's understanding of solidarity, the overriding approach to the poor in his papacy too often tends to *minimize* rather than highlight the historical subjectivity of impoverished and colonized peoples who come together in organized solidarity with one another for the sake of transforming history.

For each of the four years since the World Day of the Poor was instituted, Francis has issued a special message reflecting on poverty, on the hope and faith of the poor, and on the urgent call to solidarity that the suffering of the poor places on the church. In general, these messages have been somewhat more romantic and less prophetic than the extended economic and ecological critiques that are woven throughout Francis's other writings and speeches. To be fair, though, the message for the fourth World Day of the Poor, organized around the theme "Stretch forth your hand to the poor," does issue a trenchant and prophetic critique of the individualism that plagues contemporary culture and inhibits solidarity, even in the midst of the COVID-19 pandemic. As Francis puts it,

> the command: "Stretch forth your hand to the poor" challenges the attitude of those who prefer to keep their hands in their pockets and to remain unmoved by situations of poverty in which they are often complicit. Indifference and cynicism are their daily food. . . . If they stretch out their hands, it is to touch computer keys to transfer sums of money from one part of the world to another, ensuring the wealth of an elite few and the dire poverty of millions and the ruin of entire nations. Some hands are outstretched to accumulate money by the sale of weapons that others, including those of children, use to sow death and poverty. Other hands are outstretched to deal doses of death in dark alleys in order to grow rich and live in luxury and excess, or to quietly pass a bribe for the sake of quick and corrupt gain. Others still, parading a sham respectability, lay down laws which they themselves do not observe.[14]

Conversely, Francis states that "a hand held out is a sign; a sign that immediately speaks of closeness, solidarity and love." These messages are designed to issue a moral challenge and a spiritual inspiration for believers to reach out to those who are suffering with a compassionate heart, a listening ear, helping hands, and a commitment to the transformation of society in favor of justice and abundant life for all.

Again, these are laudable goals, with some decolonial impulses to them, yet these World Day of the Poor messages tend to reinscribe the overrepresentation of colonial subjectivity by privileging more affluent and powerful individuals and communities as the primary subjects of solidarity in both the church and wider world. Despite Pope Francis's backing of grassroots popular movements elsewhere, these messages do not call the poor themselves to "believe in the poor" or to enter into relationships of organized solidarity with one another. Nor do they recognize or encourage in general or particular terms how *lxs pobres* already are the primary subjects of solidarity in grassroots popular movements, in local communities, or in ecclesial expressions like the CEBs. Rather, these messages are directed at encouraging the subjectivity of those who have the power, privilege, and resources to give up in the service of solidarity with the suffering "other." The poor are primarily cast here as passive sufferers whose only agency is in their "cry" for aid and their hands outstretched for help. The privileged agents of solidarity are the nonpoor, whose compassion and actions aimed at saving, liberating, and giving hope to the poor are correlated with God's own saving, liberating, and hope-giving actions. Theologically, the poor "belong to the Church by 'evangelical right'"[15] and the nonpoor are called to image and imitate the saving grace of God's active solidarity with humanity. Jesus inaugurated the reign of God with the poor at its center, but "he has entrusted to us, his disciples, the task of carrying it forward with responsibility for giving hope to the poor."[16] It seems that we, the nonpoor, are the disciples to whom this message is addressed and that we, the nonpoor, are the ones called to exercise our agency in imitation of the divine savior who gives hope and life to the poor. "If we want to help change history and promote real development, we need to hear the cry of the poor and commit ourselves to ending their marginalization."[17] While there is a call to diminishment of material wealth and economic power in this vision, there does not seem to be a corresponding diminishment of subjectivity among the nonpoor, whose overrepresentation here seems to crowd out the discipleship and subjectivity of *lxs pobres*. The solidarity encouraged here does not move the church toward becoming an *iglesia de lxs pobres*—a church *of* the poor—but rather runs the risk of reinscribing a colonial church *for* the poor.[18]

On the flip side of this theological coin, the poor are understood to image and imitate God primarily in their vulnerability and in the negation of their subjectivity as those who know the suffering of Christ in their flesh. They are not the church themselves, but rather they "need" a church that exists outside and above them for spiritual and temporal salvation, guidance, friendship, and hope. Although Pope Francis is careful to emphasize that the church's solidarity with the poor should not take the form of charity or material assistance alone, and that the poor should not be understood in passive terms, it is still the nonpoor church that the poor need to be "for" them. The poor are not primarily understood to be disciples here, but rather an inspiration for the nonpoor church to carry out its own vocation to discipleship. The poor "evangelize" and "save" the nonpoor "because they enable us to encounter the face of Jesus Christ." But the side of Jesus's face that the nonpoor encounter in the poor is the suffering side, the side that embodies an existential knowledge of what it means to be vulnerable and truly dependent on God. "With their trust and readiness to receive help, they show us in a quiet and often joyful way, how essential it is to live simply and abandon ourselves to God's providence."[19] *Lxs pobres* of El Salvador's church of the poor certainly do have faith and trust and hope in God's promises of deliverance. But they also image and imitate God's saving action in their solidarity with one another as subjects of God's reign in human history. Unfortunately the many decolonial possibilities of solidarity in the ministry of Pope Francis are too often overshadowed by this way in which he and the ecclesial tradition more broadly diminish rather than step aside and make way for *lxs pobres* to exercise their own subjectivity as disciples and agents of liberating knowledge, being, and power in the church and world.[20]

North American Christian Solidarity with Latin America

Similar to Francis's re-centering of the value of solidarity with the poor for the ecclesial imagination, "solidarity" has long been an important value and significant buzzword among activist groups in North America concerned with U.S. intervention in Latin America. These groups, both secular and faith-based, are politically active in raising awareness about unjust realities in Latin America while morally and financially supporting initiatives, often grassroots-led and run by Latin Americans, in search of *otro mundo posible*. A paradigmatic example is Witness for Peace (WFP), which began in 1983 in response to the U.S. funding of the Contras in Nicaragua. WFP activists first went to Nicaragua "to document the devastating effects of US-sponsored 'low intensity warfare,'"[21] which subsequently led to activist campaigns against Reagan's war on Central America more broadly and, beginning in 1990, accompaniment of Guatemalan and Mexican refugees back to their communities, among other initiatives in later years. "Solidarity" has always been a keyword of WFP's work, and in 2019, they reorganized as a "solidarity collective" committed to "horizontal solidarity . . . inspired by the analysis and vision of Berta Cáceres, including the need for movements to inherently reflect the intertwining struggles against capitalism, racism, and patriarchy."[22] Another enduring example of solidarity initiatives from the North with Latin America is the Sanctuary Movement, which was born in the late 1980s and reborn again in the Trump era, with the aim of providing safe haven for undocumented immigrants and refugees at risk of deportation.[23] While the aims and protagonists of solidarity movements have shifted over the last several years and vary widely between contexts and organizations, the word "solidarity" in these contexts continues to signify an identification with the Latin American left, a commitment to critical awareness of U.S. foreign policy, and, most importantly, a desire to "accompany" and "walk with" groups of marginalized and impoverished populations seeking their own liberation.

The church of *lxs pobres* in El Salvador has a long history of friendship and activism with these faith-based solidarity groups in the United States. When U.S. newspapers reported the assassination of Archbishop Romero in early 1980, followed later that year by the assassination of four North American pastoral workers, many faithful Christians, especially those interested in emerging liberation theologies and attuned to the triumph of the Nicaraguan revolution in July 1979, turned their attention to El Salvador. As the country became mired in war, the plight of internal and international Salvadoran refugees became a focus of Christian solidarity efforts, and many networks and nonprofits emerged to struggle against U.S. involvement in the conflict and to aid refugees fleeing violence. Churches and faith groups in the United States connected with Christian groups in El Salvador, and as refugees like the Segundo Montes community pushed for repatriation, these groups committed themselves to helping returning Salvadorans establish their new communities, both by fundraising and by physical protective presence, a literal "walking with."

One such group, Christians for Peace in El Salvador (CRISPAZ), was founded in 1984 by a Lutheran pastor, a Quaker activist, and a Catholic priest who were convinced that "the presence of U.S. citizens and their advocacy in the U.S. was seen to be important for ministry to the refugees, displaced from their communities and vulnerable to such abuse on the part of government agencies."[24] The following year, the new board of CRISPAZ traveled to El Salvador to learn about the situation in person and in depth, meeting with Catholic and Presbyterian aid workers and celebrating the anniversary of Monseñor Romero's martyrdom. This trip was a catalyst for CRISPAZ's continuing solidarity work, which endures to the present day. "Delegations" became a hallmark of CRISPAZ's efforts: as a result of connecting faithful, well-intentioned Christians from the United States with Salvadorans who were experiencing the effects of U.S.-funded state violence, the crucifixion of the Salvadoran people took on flesh and blood, faces and names of women and men with whom CRISPAZ members had met, eaten with, cried with, shared a song with, and embraced as friends. The Salvadoran conflict ceased being a remote, though horrible, news story from a faraway land and began to affect the hearts and minds of U.S. citizens who could share the story of the Salvadoran struggle with their own communities and churches, gather resources for refugee communities and aid workers accompanying them on the ground, and, not insignificantly, phone bank and otherwise petition their congressional representatives who were responsible for approving military funding.

After the war, the work of CRISPAZ and similar groups continued. These groups connected with the CEBs through CEBES and later FUNDAHMER, and concerned citizens in the United States began to develop relationships with emerging communities of repatriated Salvadorans and land cooperatives. These so-called sister community relationships "are built on the values of solidarity and accompaniment and work for the common good"[25] and aim to be relationships of mutuality, where both parties are transformed by long-term relationships of encounter; shared analysis of the signs of the times; and communication in the form of letters, emails, phone calls, and now even Zoom meetings throughout the year. Delegations and in-person visits remain essential to these relationships, too; many churches and solidarity groups visit their Salvadoran sister communities regularly, both to strengthen existing bonds of friendship and mutual commitment and to introduce new community members to the experience. Out of these relationships, small community-led initiatives have begun in many Salvadoran communities, including scholarship programs, support for community agriculture initiatives, continued pastoral formation, and emergency funds for natural disasters and food shortages. The support of sister communities has been essential for the CEBs, especially as support from the institutional church waned after the war and well into the new millennium.

Today, CRISPAZ and other U.S.-based solidarity groups also facilitate educational immersion trips for high school and university students during school vacations. Often, a school will send their students to the same community year after year, echoing the churches' sister community relationships, in search of creating a sustainable, long-lasting bond between the school and the community. For CRISPAZ, "a major focus of the encounter is to reflect on the meaning of working for justice rather than working for charity, understanding one's role as a global citizen and humanizing the different issues that are present in our societies."[26] While annual student encounters necessarily differ from churches' long-term sister community delegations and relationships, these visits all focus on allowing personal encounters to generate a commitment to justice in Latin America and in the participants' home communities.

While solidarity movements in the United States have certainly served as an important support for Salvadorans struggling to improve their communities and their country, nearly thirty years of postwar "solidarity" has generated significant reflection on and insightful critique of this model from both U.S. and Salvadoran participants. The growing body of research on "short term missions" (STMs) is a helpful starting point for beginning to understand these criticisms, especially since visits by North American "delegations" have become such an important part of maintaining the links between sister communities. Robert Ellis Haynes defines STMs as trips that last two weeks or less and typically include activities with children, building or repairing buildings, providing health care, or explicit evangelism.[27] An estimated 1.5 million Americans participate in international STMs every year,[28] constituting a "third wave" of Christian (Catholic and Protestant) missionary activity.[29] Because the "first wave" of such activity resulted in the coloniality from which the CEBs are still emerging, North American "solidarity" with the Salvadoran church of the poor must be willing to be self-critical and must actively seek feedback from the CEBs themselves.

STMs are vulnerable to many problems that have become the focus of study in recent years. The cultural (and linguistic) chasm that often separates churches and student communities in the United States from their partners in El Salvador is certainly too great to be overcome in a short visit; scholars question whether cultural gaps between communities allow for any meaningful relationship to be built and affirm that irreversible harm is often done without proper contextualization.[30] Some studies show that the intended effects of STMs on North American participants—namely, long-lasting commitments to justice work or reduced ethnocentrism—rarely take hold, and some STMs are even criticized as "religious tourism."[31] The Salvadoran CEBs' sister community relationships are both vulnerable to these criticisms and have developed some responses to these critiques over time. These relationships are often bridged and facilitated by the CEBs' own organizations, like FUNDAHMER or a regional pastoral team, and these potential difficulties are discussed explicitly between communities on both sides of the relationship. FUNDAHMER, for example, resists North American communities' often immediate proposals to establish some sort of humanitarian project after a first visit to a Salvadoran community. They insist that a sister community relationship takes at least two to three years of long-distance correspondence and in-person visits to be established solidly enough to undertake a joint project. Once these projects or small initiatives are established, the community articulates what their needs are; the North American community is discouraged from proposing their own solutions to perceived problems. In response to the potential for colonial evangelizing impulses, CRISPAZ staff has developed the language of "reverse mission," inviting participants in their delegations to begin their mission work when they *return* to their home communities, ready to share stories of the Salvadoran reality, and the way faith is interpreted and enacted in contexts beyond that of North America. Of course, mistakes slip through the cracks; interpersonal squabbles affect communities on both sides of the relationship, aging North American church communities have difficulty finding new leadership, and North American schools have not proven to be the most stable relationship partner as student turnover is constant and the staff person in charge of coordinating the relationship is responsible first to the school's administrative priorities, national travel policies, and her or his own personal life and career trajectory.

It remains difficult to conduct something like a cost-benefit analysis of these relationships. Ellen Moodie, in her critical reflections on accompanying a church group from Illinois to visit La Cruz, their sister community in rural Morazán, in 2010, recognizes many elements of the *hermanamiento* that surprise her:

> By now the communities share a kind of history. Father Dan has baptized babies in La Cruz who are now parents themselves. The delegations are led by people who (often informally) guide newcomers in the history and culture of El Salvador and La Cruz, as well as in respect for local customs and practices.[32]

Suspicious of STMs, but moved by her visit, Moodie senses that

> there is *something* going on. La Cruz, I decided, may well offer a glimpse of one possible way of interacting. It represents a sustained effort at contact between groups from radically different backgrounds. And yet at the same time, after my experience on the trip, I am not at all convinced that either "side" "gets" the other in terms of traditional frameworks we may have of how one knows. The dinner conversations, for example, were often quite awkward for me, as I sat between the Illinois women and the community members at the meal. The missioners one night, for example, discussed in English the number of calories in all the starchy food we were eating (spaghetti, french-fried potatoes and thick tortillas, along with truly free-range chicken), and whether or not we should be taking antibiotics preemptively (Linda, the nurse, had brought the drug Cipro for everyone), and why some North American parents refuse vaccinations for their children. . . . The schoolteachers and community leaders invited to the meal sat quietly or commented on the day's activities in Spanish. There was almost no interaction. When one side or the other laughed, I tried to translate the jokes—not easy.[33]

Another researcher that Moodie mentions, who is also familiar with the same *hermanamiento*, is likewise forthcoming with her doubts:

> She describes an uncomfortable hierarchy among the participants in the trips, with the visitors and APDES [the Salvadoran NGO that coordinates the relationship] "above" the community members. La Cruz residents provide free labor, in her view, guiding the visitors, protecting them (important in El Salvador, with one of the highest crime rates in the world), providing accommodations, and cooking for them (the per diem payments made by the

missioners pay for the food but not the preparation). They [the people of La Cruz] depend on the [Illinois] group's decisions on whether or not to support different initiatives. One interviewee told her, "We have to know how to care for this connection with the sister community, know how to stay in contact, never lose contact, because if we lose it, the children won't be able to study and we won't see the students moving up in life." Further, the resources can cause conflict.[34]

We are sensitive to this researcher's concern that North American visitors are taking advantage of the people of La Cruz—possibly to feel better about their own lives, to feel like do-gooders, or even just to have another interesting travel experience. But might this critique also paint the Salvadorans as the subjects of the arrangement, presenting these gawking, lumbering *gringos* with a romanticized sense of rural community life in order to influence them into sending $20,000–$30,000 per year for community projects?[35] Ultimately, there is a way to look at sister community relationships as either manipulative, calculated grabs for financial, social, or spiritual capital on both sides, or as ideal relationships of mutuality and Christian concern. The truth most likely differs for each relationship and lies somewhere in between.

From our own experience facilitating sister community visits among the CEBs in El Salvador and translating, mailing, and delivering letters, pictures, and emails throughout the years, we have countless interpretations of the positives and negatives of these relationships. We've raged against college students applying to come to El Salvador over spring break because it looks good on their resume. We've seen something change in the eyes of those same students when they put their feet in a bomb crater their government paid for a hundred yards away from the houses where they spent the night. We've seen those students go on to do incredible good while still being fallible human beings. We've seen some of their peers forget. We've seen young Salvadorans go to college because a church in Texas holds barbecues to raise money for their scholarships; not only do they become professionals, they also grow up and become young leaders in their communities with opinions and drive. We've seen community councils mired in conflict over whose house the sister community visitors will stay in. We've seen a generation of young people grow taller and stronger than their parents because they had eggs and soymilk to eat as babies. We've seen straight, married, upper-class, liberal white fathers from Boston who can't speak a lick of Spanish facilitate radical redistribution of wealth because of the love that has grown between him and a grandma who suffers from arthritis thousands of miles away. We've translated terrible, frustrating, offensive emails between community leaders and church treasurers when a project doesn't go as planned. These relationships themselves are ambiguous, unfinished, imperfect. But without them, we have to cede that our worlds would be smaller and even less attuned to the abundant life of God's reign.

These relationships seem to invite reflections that sound like reflections on the reign of God: they are already something like what relationships of true sister- or brotherhood should be, but they remain woefully not yet fulfilled. Moodie ends her analysis reflecting on the gaping inequality that separates each group from the other. Both the Salvadorans and the group from Illinois remain ultimately unknown by the other, she suggests, and this continued separation, willful or accidental, may "block bigger changes," even if some good does come from a trip.[36] Within the ambiguity and continued debate about the effect of these relationships, an obstinate truth lingers: the structures remain the same. Bigger changes *are* blocked, whether by an unwillingness to know more deeply, by conscious or subconscious allegiance to one's own culture and social power, or weariness of inventing new paths.

At the end of a visit between sister communities, the question always arises: *What should we do?* This question is especially prescient for first-time visitors, and it is the same question we all tend to ask when confronted with any of several difficult realities that come to us in headlines, on the radio, or in letters from a sister community. The rains washed out La Cruz's corn crop this year: *What should we do?* Marta's father needs dialysis and there's no machine close by: *What should we do?* Hive beetles took out all the beehives the women's group set up last year: *What should we do?*

We wrote a book about the decolonial promise of the ecclesiology of the Salvadoran church of the poor. Now, dear readers, *what should we do?*

Historically, the answer to this question has been to "walk with" the CEBs in their struggles, to accompany. The spirituality of accompaniment is easy to understand when you're literally walking miles between houses through cornfields with Salvadoran companions holding your arm so you don't fall, or sitting in a circle of plastic chairs listening to community elders tell your group about their time in refugee camps during the war. But it is much more difficult to transfer those moments back home. Students come back to new semesters, new classes, new to-do lists, extracurriculars, friends, family, service hours, homework, and peers who cannot understand their experiences. Church groups come back to family life, a week of work to catch up on, a thousand other ministries, and fitting worship into cherished weekend time. Even outside of the sister community dynamic, in our own contexts or given international conflict or ecological destruction, this question—*what should we do*—arises again and again, increasingly demanding and with diminishing returns. We are inspired by our Salvadoran siblings' *organización*, by their empowerment, by the true shining of their full selves coming to light. However, as inspired as we may be, nothing we have yet done has solved the structures of enduring coloniality, of inequality and injustice, that provoke tragedy after tragedy. Millions of STM visitors have not come back from their mission and changed the world. If Moodie's estimates are true, hundreds of thousands of dollars to La Cruz since 1990 has not fundamentally changed the economic structures that keep this and so many other communities impoverished. Book after book has been written about structural problems in the Catholic Church, and sexual abuse cases continue to surface. We have marched, we have called Congress, we have voted, we have shouted, we have reacted time and time again, and every day, someone else's son is in detention in Texas, or some new forest is ablaze.

Perhaps we have been asking the wrong question. If coloniality endures as the dominance of the knowledge, being, and power of relatively privileged and affluent citizens of the United States, among other global powers, whose foreign policies have invaded, plundered, and left for dead our human siblings and the natural world, then we who are privileged or affluent beneficiaries of coloniality should not keep asking *what should we do?* It is our own twisted sense of subjectivity, as if we could run the world for everybody, that is at the root of many of the world's problems. Practically, we cannot "walk with" our Salvadoran friends because we have shunned them to live in zones of nonbeing. We are not at the same starting point, and we must see that clearly.

Imagine a path. A path in the mountains, perhaps, like the one that ambles through La Cruz. Somewhere along the path is the house where you are bound and a table set with spaghetti, french fries, thick tortilla, and the hen whose egg-laying squawking woke you up in the morning. A hammock awaits you there, where you can take off your hiking boots and rest. At the other end of the path, bound for the same house, is your sister from La Cruz. She, too, is hungry, and hopes to arrive at the table. You both begin walking. Your path takes you through a deep river, you are almost swept away, and everything looks and feels very different on the other side. Her path takes her up a steep incline; her brow breaks a sweat. Your challenges are different, but your destination is the same.

We believe that decolonial solidarity functions something like this path. To be in solidarity with our siblings in La Cruz is to share a vision of the same final destination, but not to pretend that our paths are the same. For privileged Christians in North America, San Salvador, or Rome to be in solidarity with the Salvadoran church of *lxs pobres*, or with any other church or movement of the *damnés*, is to recognize that our pilgrimage should be bound for the same destination (a world in which many worlds fit), but that our paths will differ wildly in arriving. The path of those who benefit from coloniality, in whatever areas of our lives, is challenged to resign from definitions and systems that prioritize our knowledge, being, and power over and against the *damnés* and *pobres* of the world. For those condemned to non-knowledge, nonbeing, and powerlessness under the reign of coloniality, the challenge is to know, to be, and to act. Our "walking together" must be a walking toward each other, hoping to find the banquet along the way.

HORIZONS IN DECOLONIAL SOLIDARITY

Those of us who are protagonists and beneficiaries of coloniality have been mistaken about our path to the reign of God, at least in part because we have been *doing* too much. Instead, we should first ask: *what should be done to us?* How must we be transformed, worked on, changed, so that we may arrive at the banquet? Jesús answered in this way to the disciples:

> I tell you the truth, it will be hard for a rich person to enter the kingdom of heaven! Again I say, it is easier for a camel to go through the eye of a needle than for a rich person to enter into the kingdom of God.[37]

Jesús instructs the rich man to be transformed, to change, to no longer be rich. Of course, just as to be *pobre* is to experience dehumanization for reasons beyond economics, to be "rich" is to benefit from the matrix of colonial power beyond only material wealth. We believe that the call to privileged beneficiaries of coloniality is the same as Jesus's call to the rich young man. The path that we tread on pilgrimage to God's reign must transform our knowledge, being, and power such that we no longer overrepresent our own subjectivity or monopolize resources for our own self-protection and human flourishing. Our goal as church is the same—the universal and equitable distribution of subjectivity that characterizes God's reign. But the work of getting there—of growing in solidarity—is different.

Unsettling Solidarity

This new question—*what should be done to us?*—challenges those of us who benefit from and/or participate in coloniality to unsettle our practices of solidarity. Returning to Maldonado-Torres's invitation, the work of colonial subjects seeking transformation for the benefit of all is to *resign* from coloniality; to *delink* from our impulse to do, to act; and to *disrupt* the reigning structures of knowledge, being, and power that reify coloniality. It is an undoing of our categories, an apophatic and kenotic approach to all of our identity markers, to who we are, that requires shedding the layers of conspicuous overrepresentation that have asserted colonial subjectivity over and against the *damnés/pobres*. Again, Sylvia Wynter's categories are helpful:

> The struggle of our new millennium will be one between the ongoing imperative of securing the well-being of our present ethnoclass (i.e., Western bourgeois)

conception of the human, Man, which overrepresents itself as if it were the human itself, and that of securing the well-being, and therefore the full cognitive and behavioral autonomy of the human species itself/ourselves.[38]

To collaborate in securing the well-being of the whole human species (and all other beings that are woven into the web of Life), we must reduce our own self-assertion, our own representation, insofar as we participate in the overrepresentation of the colonial "Man" in our own lives and places.[39] This is how we understand the two different paths to be walked in the work of solidarity. For groups like the Salvadoran CEBs that have been systematically underrepresented as human and as church, their work is to affirm their subjectivity, their own knowledge, being, and power, to emerge from the zones of nonbeing as fully human. For groups whose ways of thinking, being, and exercising power have long been overrepresented as universal or totalizing, our work is to stop clinging to our own inflated sense of self and action in order to emerge from colonial zones of modernity as, similarly, only human. Our destination is the same. Both the Salvadoran church of *lxs pobres* and churches that benefit from and/or participate in coloniality have the same destination: to be fully and only human, to be the creatures God made us to be, children of the Creator and siblings to each other in a world where all of our worlds fit. But our paths are different.

To be concrete about this work, we find it helpful to apply a new grammar to our own ecclesial praxis, as suggested by the question above. In asking, *what should we do?*, the amorphous "we" is again the subject of the question, the one who "does," the one who acts and re-acts. By asking *what should be done to us?*, our own subjectivity is decentered without disallowing for the possibility of transformation; indeed, we ask for transformation, for *metanoia*. Perhaps this approach is hyperbolic; we certainly do not mean to condemn our own or any human knowledge, being, or power to zones of nonbeing, but this rhetorical exercise reframes the direction of our own praxis toward the eschatological banquet at which we hope to arrive. Appropriate subjectivity is the goal, so undoing the overrepresentation of our own subjectivity will feel reductive, risky, uncontrolled. Maldonado-Torres identifies this feeling in his first point about decolonial praxis:

> Colonialism, decolonization and related concepts generate anxiety and fear. . . . Anyone who introduces the question about the meaning and significance of colonialism and decolonization most likely faces a decadent and genocidal modern/colonial attitude of indifference, obfuscation, constant evasion, and aggression, typically in the guise of neutral and rational assessments, postracialism, and well-intentioned liberal values.[40]

Dipesh Chakrabarty provokes such reactions, for example, with the title of his work, *Provincializing Europe*, which aims to relegate the "global heritage" of

European thought to an appropriate place, relative to other thought-traditions that are invisibilized in their contributions to the contemporary world.[41] Ultimately, we believe that some grammatical objectification is a helpful medicine for reframing our praxis.

Spatially, preserving the metaphor of the path to the banquet, this new way of expressing solidarity as walking toward each other might look something like the following:

Colonial "Man" must reduce his own universal overrepresentation as human, and the *damnés* must take on increased representation as human beings. In terms of the grammatical subject-object relationship, we could say:

Those who have always been the subjects (of history, of war, of modernity) must experience a diminishment and fundamental transformation of subjectivity in order to find our way toward appropriate interrelational subjectivity. This might feel like a violation of subjectivity, or even an objectification of sorts, but it is really a process of becoming a real, incarnate, intersubject—a subject in community with other subjects. Conversely, those who have been historically objectified must insist on their own subjectivity, not as a mirror or mimesis of overrepresented colonial subjectivity, but in intersubjective community with other *damnés*, which is precisely what the CEBs are attempting to do in the Salvadoran church of *lxs pobres*.

Eschatologically, and in the language of Christian faith, our paths look something like this:

Churches and Christians who enjoy the benefits of and/or participate in the coloniality of knowledge, being, and power must turn back from the so-called progress that has served to justify so much destruction and must move toward *lxs pobres*. The banquet where we desire to rest and to be satisfied in communion with God, one another, and all creation, does not lie "ahead," on a superhighway of so-called progress that violently tramples the subjectivity and bodies of *lxs pobres* and the planet alike. Advancing along a path motivated by the frantic logic of modernity only further removes us from our fellow human siblings and from God's own dream for creation. It is a path of *anti-reino*. We must be willing to stop, to be known, re-formed, re-membered as beloved of the Creator and siblings of one another by virtue of our brother Jesús, the *hacelotodo* from Nazareth, who shared table fellowship with the *damnés* of his time. Meanwhile, *lxs pobres* continue along the path lined with the crosses of many historical crucifixions—El Mozote, the Middle Passage, domestic violence, detention centers, lynchings, rape, unjust criminalization and incarceration, hunger, wildfires, floods—not because the suffering is redemptive, but because the path, made treacherous by others and trod in solidarity by Jesús, is bound for the banquet. When the colonial church seeks to resign from coloniality and enter God's reign, it walks toward *lxs pobres*, and *lxs pobres*—accompanied by the Spirit of the resurrected, crucified One and the re-membered, crucified many—walk toward the banquet.

To be human, to have an appropriate sense and embodiment of our own subjectivity, and in our hope for the reign of God, in solidarity, we must be aware of our place relative to our goal. To provide some concrete examples, this exercise can be applied more precisely to the realms of knowledge, being, and power. The previous chapters have shown the CEBs' decolonial ecclesial praxis of asserting their own humanity, subjectivity, and pilgrimage toward the reign of God in these three areas. Let us now turn to the responses that decoloniality demands of those of us who benefit from coloniality and the overrepresentation of our own knowledge, being, and power.

To Be Known

The subjective thrust of the CEBs' decolonizing praxis in the realm of knowledge involves questioning, proposing, asserting alternative ways of knowing, and trusting their own knowledge. The title of chapter 2, "*Tomamos la palabra*," could be roughly translated as "Our turn to speak." *Lxs pobres*' ways of knowing, including the central praxis of *memory*, are central for the CEBs' ecclesiology, and they insist that this self-trust is the practice of an "adult faith." This confidence allows them to question the tradition they have been given with an eye to their context, and empowers them to become teachers, even of archbishops! In the realm of knowledge, the CEBs are growing in their own subjectivity: they question, they talk, they remember and tell their own story, and they teach.

In solidarity with this aspect of the CEBs' decolonial ecclesial praxis, then, churches with colonial power and/or privilege might ask ourselves, not *what do we know?* but *how are we known?* What happens when we become the objects of knowledge, the ones who do not know but are known? Indeed, we might seek not to question, but to be questioned; not to talk, but to listen; not to tell a universal story, but to have our histories and memories undone or corrected; not to teach but to be taught.

What a difficult challenge this poses for us. The re-membering of *lxs pobres* questions the histories, the stories, and the criteria for truth that we hold as canon; it is disorienting. When the CEBs re-member their Indigenous ancestors, we must dis-member our unblemished images of missionary saints like Junípero Serra, and we must dis-member a theological universe that *still* has not recanted the Doctrine of Discovery. When the CEBs re-member their martyrs and tell the story of how and why they were killed, we must dis-member our image of liberating U.S. foreign policy and unquestioning patriotism. When the CEBs re-member Jesús with tortilla and coffee during their weekly liturgies, we must dis-member our idols of form and material. Our idols will be known for what they are, and we will be revealed as idolators: of people, of country, of history, of doctrine. To be known from the perspective of *lxs pobres* is to encounter our own systemic sinfulness; it is a debt we cannot pay, a reckoning we feel that we cannot bear. And yet, to be known and to learn our history from the perspectives of *lxs pobres* is our hope.

To Be Created

In the realm of being, the CEBs emerge as creative subjects through the decolonial ecclesial praxis described in chapter 3. They celebrate, they create, they sing, they *are*. They emerge from nonbeing as beloved stewards of beauty and life, a priestly people, human, fully and flawed. They paint murals, create songs, weave hammocks, tell stories, imagine futures, tell jokes, and celebrate liturgy. They affirm their being as children of God, not a second-class laity, but fully church.

In solidarity with this facet of the CEBs' decolonial ecclesial praxis, then, those of us who benefit from and/or participate in coloniality might ask, not *what should we create*? but rather *how should we be (re-)created*? Instead of insisting on our creative power and potential, it may be fruitful to meditate on our createdness, on being creatures. We can also allow for the undoing of Western aesthetic and cultural controls of what is "beautiful," what our sacred spaces are, what images our sacred art depicts, and even what kinds of "polite" or civility discourses control our relationships in church and society. The call is to allow an-other aestheSis to form our attractions and values, to immerse ourselves in worlds of representation and signification that are marginal to the world that has been created around us, to let our desires be formed by a diversity of ways of being a human creature.

This, too, is a profound challenge to our ecclesial status quo. How great is the pull of aesthetic nostalgia in our ecclesial identity! When Notre-Dame de

Paris burned in April 2019, there was much wailing and gnashing of teeth, and millions of dollars of donations poured in overnight to rebuild the historic cathedral. To be sure, as a symbol of Christianity and French identity, and as a wealth of historic art and Catholic culture and legend, the loss of Notre-Dame is not insignificant. However, the scramble to preserve it, juxtaposed with the unmitigated burning of the Amazon rainforest[42] and the previously ignored fundraising campaign to rebuild Louisiana churches destroyed in acts of racist arson,[43] revealed the instinctive, aesthetic priorities of those with the power to preserve select Christian symbols. When the Salvadoran church of *lxs pobres* paints Romero on the inside of their chapels decades before he is recognized as a saint by the hierarchy, or when they lament the deliberate destruction of the Llort mural on the Metropolitan Cathedral, our task is to consider these and other marginalized, silenced, condemned, and destroyed images and to allow them re-create our own being as church in relationship to God, one another, and all of creation.

To Be Organized

The CEBs exercise decolonial ecclesial power by being empowered, *al organizarse*. They organize themselves to exert force on the political and cultural structures in their contexts toward a more just and equitable society, a world where many worlds fit, a church where many churches fit. They are active in their own political struggles, inspired by their faith, and they advocate, as church, for a world where all people may thrive. They also act out of their own empowerment for the good of the church as an effective sacrament of this hoped-for world, demonstrating an-other possible way to be an ecclesial communion. After decades of outright rejection from the Salvadoran hierarchy, their faithfulness to the power of the Spirit in their own communities has touched the heart of another archbishop and continues to challenge Salvadorans of faith to reconsider the colonial trappings of the ecclesial knowledge, being, and power that have been operative for centuries in that corner of creation.

The question, *what should be done to us?* is most proper to this third realm of the decolonial ecclesial praxis to which relatively privileged churches are called in solidarity with the CEBs' empowering *organización*. For so long, the impoverished faithful in El Salvador have been *ordenado/mandado*, ordered to celebrate and to profess faith according to the logic and expression of a colonial church, according to formulations going as far back as the sixteenth-century Council of Trent, whose conflicts and attempts at resolution were so foreign to the reality of the lands where they were imposed. Now it is time for the pendulum to swing back the other way, for the theological reflections and ecclesiological proposals of the church of *lxs pobres* to address the heirs of Trent.

What might be fair, justified even, is for the church of *lxs pobres* to have a chance to *ordenar*, to order, to ordain. Certainly, as Paulo Freire observed in his seminal work *Pedagogy of the Oppressed*, "at a certain point in their existential experience the oppressed feel an irresistible attraction towards the oppressors and their way of life. Sharing this way of life becomes an overpowering aspiration."[44] The concern that the "oppressed" may become the "oppressor" is certainly at the heart of the fear Maldonado-Torres identifies as the primary reactions to decoloniality. As Christians who benefit from coloniality are known and are reformed aesthetically, we may be tempted to look to the Salvadoran church of *lxs pobres*, and other churches and movements of the *damnés*, to ordain us, to tell us what to do, to tell us what sacrifices to make to erase our history of violence and overrepresentation. However, in grace, what we are offered is *organización*. We, too, are offered empowerment, the call to assume appropriate power in our local churches, the mission to take on responsibility for our own ecclesial praxis. The CEBs' model changes the terms of the game; we are not engaged in a tit-for-tat exchange of harm until all peoples are equally beaten down. Nor is it appropriate to lay the burden of decolonial subjectivity entirely on the shoulders of *lxs pobres*. Rather, in solidarity with the *organización* of the church of *lxs pobres*, we, too, are called to become appropriate ecclesial actors.

How does this call to *organización*, the same call that the CEBs respond to, fit into our metaphor of the divergent paths toward the shared banquet? Indeed, this call reveals the multiplicity and diversity of paths to the banquet, far more nuanced than one path for the Salvadoran church of *lxs pobres* and one path for churches that benefit from coloniality. Each ecclesial community—North and South; affluent and impoverished; white, Black, and brown—must first analyze their own intersectional realities, must identify where they are on their pilgrimage relative to the reign of God and discern together where they are overrepresented and where they have been objectified. Then, using the above questions as a guide, each church asks either, *what do we have to teach?* or *what do we have to learn?* Each church asks either *what can we create?* or *how must we be recreated?* Each church asks *what do we do?* or *what must be done to us?* All ecclesial communities are pilgrim; we are all on our own paths toward the banquet. What a decolonial lens helps us discern is which questions we should be asking, at what times, and in relation to whom.

A final reflection about the set of questions for colonial subjects seeking to delink or resign from coloniality: the calls we name here—to be known, to be re-created, and to be organized—all raise yet another question. *By whom?* To be known, to be recreated, and to be organized is not an individual activity; the passive voice looks for the other who will know, who will create, and who will organize. By whom should we be known, by whom should we be re-created, and according to whose pattern should we be organized? The answer is twofold: by God and by our neighbor, specifically by *lxs pobres*.

The identification between God and "the least of these" is apparent in Matthew 25:31–46, when Jesus separates the sheep and the goats and affirms that, for better or worse, "just as you did it to one of the least of these who are members of my family, you did it to me." This phrase is certainly applicable to the violence and metaphysical catastrophe of coloniality/modernity: "just as you colonized one of the least of these who are members of my family, you colonized me." We might also apply it to the tasks assigned to churches that benefit from coloniality more generally: "just as you are known by the one of the least of these who are members of my family, so are you known by me"; "just as you are re-created by the one of the least of these who are members of my family, so are you re-created by me"; "just as you are organized by one of the least of these who are members of my family, so are you organized by me." These tasks, which challenge privileged churches to cede the overrepresentation of our own subjectivity and to submit ourselves to the knowledge, being, and power of another, depend on the action of Christ and of *lxs pobres* to know, to create, and to act. To be known, influenced by, and worked on requires the other; it is not a solitary task. It requires the church to be a *koinonia*, a communion, a world where many worlds fit and are connected in bonds of existential solidarity. In our pilgrimage to the eschatological banquet, each ecclesial community, made of persons-in-communion, discerns our starting point and our path in relationship to others whom we seek to know and by whom we seek to be known. Only in this way can we arrive at our shared destination: "Just as you seek to arrive at the banquet to feast with one of the least of these who are members of my family, so do you seek to arrive at the banquet to feast with me."

A Concrete Example

Each ecclesial community, in their relationship to others, must choose a set of questions and discern an appropriate ecclesial praxis against the metaphysical catastrophe of an enduringly colonial church. Much of this book has been spent describing and celebrating the discernment and praxis of the Salvadoran church of *lxs pobres* in order to (1) help Christians that benefit from coloniality to relate to and locate themselves in relation to our Salvadoran siblings, along with other churches and movements of *lxs pobres* and *damnés*, in faith and (2) announce the good news of the continuity and evolution of liberating/decolonial ecclesial praxis in El Salvador. We have attempted to provide plentiful examples of the CEBs' own praxis in the realms of decolonial knowledge, being, and power and, positively, as a prophetic, priestly, and empowered people. We now turn to one story of ecclesial praxis in North

America in order to apply the tasks and questions proper to North American ecclesial solidarity and evaluate our own path.

In 1997, the first "Ignatian Teach-In" was held in a meeting tent about a mile away from Fort Benning near Columbus, Georgia. Fort Benning is the home of the Western Hemisphere Institute for Security Cooperation (WHINSEC, 2001), formerly the School of the Americas (SOA), a military school which, in its own words, "provides professional education and training for civilian, military and law enforcement students from nations throughout the Western Hemisphere."[45] Throughout the Salvadoran Civil War (1980–1992), officers in the Salvadoran government's armed forces trained at the SOA. These officers returned to El Salvador to commit some of the most horrific war crimes, including the massacre at El Mozote, the assassination of four North American pastoral workers, the assassination of Monseñor Romero, and the massacre at the UCA, the Jesuit university in San Salvador.[46] These events were cataloged in the report by the UN Truth Commission in 1993, and in 1996, the Pentagon declassified training manuals used at the SOA that advocated torture, extortion, and extrajudicial execution.[47] Many groups active in secular and political solidarity movements had already been protesting the SOA when these revelations came to light, and the following November, members and affiliates of Jesuit-run high schools, colleges, and parishes joined them at the gates of Fort Benning.[48] For Jesuit groups, participation in this protest was explicitly linked to the demand for justice for the assassination of the UCA martyrs.

For thirteen years, from 1996 to 2009, the "Ignatian Family Teach-In for Justice" (IFTJ), as it came to be called, gathered, first in a tent and subsequently in a conference center, to offer panel discussions, lectures, and workshops about immigration, global trade, feminism and LGBT ecclesial belonging and leadership, and ecology, among other topics central to the "reality" of the church in the United States (in retrospect, many of these topics are nodes of the colonial matrix of power). On the last day of the gathering, participants at the IFTJ joined other religious and secular solidarity collectives in marching to the gates of Fort Benning to demand the closure of SOA-WHINSEC. These events were organized by a group called the SOA Watch, and the road up to the gates was lined with tables, posters, artwork, and discussion fora hosted by partner organizations like the Beehive Design Collective, the Women's Ordination Conference, No Más Muertes, Veterans for Peace, and others. Almost all participants—some years as many as 25,000[49]—carried white crosses bearing the names and ages of victims of SOA graduates, and as the crowd circled up to the gates, they placed the crosses in the mesh fence. The names were also read out loud with the crowd responding, "*¡PRESENTE!*" Guest speakers, including many Salvadorans over the years, for example, Jon Sobrino and Rufina Amaya, offered words of remembrance and inspiration to the protestors, and the events appeared in Salvadoran newspapers every year.

Participating in the IFTJ and the protest at the gates of Fort Benning was a unique opportunity for Jesuit students and parishioners to be known, re-created, and organized. Often, a school would sponsor a trip through campus ministry, involving preparatory meetings facilitated by campus ministers and Jesuit postulants and pastors and overnight bus trips from all over the country to Columbus, Georgia, the weekend before Thanksgiving. The clarity of the critique of U.S. foreign policy and the encounter with victims of the U.S. military contradicted the story that many students and parishioners believed about the noble paternalism of their country and unmasked the facade of human rights and progress that justified such foreign involvement. At the same time, the organizations that marched at Fort Benning offered other dreams for our national reality. For many students—especially for middle to upper class, white, Christian U.S. citizens—it was our first real, embodied contact with the underbelly of modernity, and the first time we saw groups of organized, conscientious citizens and people of faith articulate alternatives to the status quo. It was exposure to the festering wound, the unhealed legacy of our unjust privilege. It was confusing, surprising, *unsettling*. It was also beautiful and poignant; the art and theater of some of the protesters, including street performances by clowns and mimes and the awkward, dancing *puppetistas*, made of *papier-mâché* heads and fabric operated by long poles held by a puppeteer, were unusual, unrefined, and, in some cases, uncomfortable. Pamphlets, stickers, and posters identifying the United States with a giant, tentacled sea monster or depicting Uncle Sam as a flesh-eating zombie awakened our critical minds and provoked questions. At many preparatory meetings, pastoral chaperones, anticipating the surge of emotions and indignation the encounter would provoke, would encourage students *not* to cross the fence onto the base, as many activists would every year. It was an introduction to faith-based direct action and civil disobedience in the tradition of the Plowshares Movement or the Catholic Worker, an education in the justice-oriented tradition of the North American church.

Most of all, the IFTJ and the protest at the gates of Fort Benning was a practical lesson in re-membering. As students and protestors approached the gates of the base, the cross in their hand bore the name of a human being whose life had been ended as a direct result of the training offered on the other side of the fence: "Ignacio Ellacuría, 59 years old"; "Óscar Romero, 62 years old"; "Cristino Amaya, 9 years old"; "Celina Ramos, 16 years old"; "Anonymous girl, 8 months." As the names of the crosses in the hands of each individual walking up to the gates was read aloud, the chorus of responses—"*¡PRESENTE!*"—took on a meditative, mantra-like quality. The fact that the previous days' workshops around contemporary issues in the church and the world culminated in a re-membering of the victims of past instances of violence and destruction set the tone for participants' dispersion back into the world toward the future. Surrounded by marginal and alternative creative expression, echoing the stories of the silenced, the event called on the gathered body to be transformed toward *lxs pobres*.

Beginning in 2010, the Ignatian Solidarity Network (ISN) decided to move the IFTJ—the series of panels, workshops, and lectures in the days before the protest at the gates of the SOA/WHINSEC—to Washington, DC. Today, the value of including legislative advocacy in their activism and engagement endures as the primary stated reason for the move.[50] Other reasons given at the time include (1) a desire to advocate for other peoples and other issues beyond *only* the murder of the UCA martyrs and the U.S. military's inhumane actions by way of trainings at the SOA and (2) a concern about the perceived inefficacy or misplaced nostalgia of the protest.[51] Surely, the IFTJ continues to be a valuable experience for students and an important moment of visibility for Catholic advocacy in the United States today. However, we cannot help but notice how this shift has eliminated so many important moments of discomfort, of challenge, and of encounter with the world of *lxs pobres* that happened outside the gates of Fort Benning. Instead of a meditative procession to the border of a military base while invoking the presence of the victims of imperial violence, students head to Capitol Hill for "Advocacy Day." Where once radically alternative Catholic adults modeled lifestyles that stand in stark contrast to the pictures of success given to students at Jesuit schools, now legislative representation in the national capital is the ideal, and students bring suits and other business attire for their meetings in the halls of power. The students are also removed from the other organizations and groups that showed up to the protest in Georgia. SOA Watch, the group which coordinates the protest that IFTJ participants supported, stayed at Fort Benning in 2010 without the involvement of the ISN and has continued to host their annual protests both there and at the U.S.-Mexico border through the present day.[52] As a separate initiative, the IFTJ as it stands now is no longer one of many partners in the SOA Watch network committed to both shutting down the SOA/WHINSEC and issuing radical critiques of U.S. foreign policy. Instead of imagining a movement for a better world where many worlds fit, the IFTJ as it stands now imagines Jesuit students as the primary protagonists of the world they desire; the dialogue is now more of a monologue. The opportunity for witnessing to a progressive Catholic faith is weakened, as well. While the ISN reported 3,000 attendees at the Saturday Mass at the convention center near Fort Benning in 2006, the record for Teach-In attendance in Washington, DC, is 1,700.[53] Whether the missing 1,300 souls are Jesuit students who are not able to attend the Teach-In in Washington, DC, or members of groups outside of the ISN in town for the protest at Fort Benning is impossible for us to determine; either way, it seems that the decision to move the IFTJ to Washington, DC, has not helped strengthen connections between Christian worship and political activism.

Let us compare the decision of the ISN to the praxis of the SOA Watch. As mentioned above, the SOA Watch continues to be present at Fort Benning and has also hosted three "Encuentros" at the U.S.-Mexico border at Nogales. This simple difference in the physical *spaces* where the SOA Watch stands is significant. By going to the border, the SOA Watch asks to listen to and be informed by migrants, those working in *albergues* to care for migrants, and the lawyers and social workers helping migrants navigate the impossibly messy system of courts and documentation. In response to the perceived nostalgia of the protest at Fort Benning, the SOA Watch has pivoted to be known and re-formed by *lxs pobres* of our age, the children and grandchildren of *lxs pobres* murdered by SOA graduates in the 1980s. The IFTJ, instead, has chosen to form its students at the hands of the heirs of the representative seats that approved the SOA budget in the 1980s and still approve the budget for WHINSEC. While it may be true that legislative advocacy can be an effective and even necessary strategy for making change in the United States, the approach of the IFTJ today is not the radical option it once was for re-informing and re-creating students' imaginaries away from worship of Caesar, upward mobility, and the reign of Congress.

Additionally, participating in the IFTJ today *benefits* students' ascent up the ladder of success in a culture of coloniality. It counts for students' required service hours for graduation,[54] promises "new professional development opportunities,"[55] and appears on students' resumés and applications for grants and admission to university, graduate school, or even jobs in Jesuit higher education. It teaches students not to be re-created according to the *logos* of the Creator through the perspective of *lxs pobres*, but rather how to succeed in the world as it is. Participating in the activities and events of the SOA Watch, on the other hand, promises no benefit in this world, and the SOA Watch has suffered a decline in notoriety and influence—and any hope of claiming to be efficacious—since the IFTJ moved to Washington, DC.

Another sinister detail, and perhaps the true nail in the coffin for the collaboration for *otros mundos posibles* between the SOA Watch and the ISN: the founder of the SOA Watch, Roy Bourgeois, was excommunicated from the Catholic Church in 2008 for concelebrating and delivering the homily at the ordination ceremony of Janice Sevre-Duszynska, of Roman Catholic Womenpriests. It is hard to ignore the timing of the IFTJ's move to Washington, DC, and Bourgeois's unyielding self-defense to the Congregation for the Doctrine of the Faith until his 2012 "canonical dismissal" from the Maryknoll order and the Roman Catholic priesthood—a punishment commonly referred to as, tellingly, "laicization." To be punished by a demotion to the status laity, to use canon law to strip away the pastoral commissioning of a man who spent a lifetime working for justice for the victims of SOA graduates, to frame support of women's ordination as more scandalous than weakening a movement that seeks to re-member the unjustified murder of human lives—these are the interlocking nodes of the coloniality of power at work.

This story has faded from the memory of Jesuit students and institutions today, and our ability to imagine a different kind of formation for future students is rapidly fading with it. A group that has not forgotten, however, is the Salvadoran church of *lxs pobres*. The "Escuela de las Américas" is an indelible presence in their memories, and they know that Jesuit universities, the partner universities of their UCA, showed up to re-member the victims of its graduates—and to be known, re-created, and re-fashioned from the underside of history, at least for a time.

CULTIVATING DECOLONIAL SOLIDARITY: VULNERABILITY AND THE GRACE OF RESILIENCE FOR THE WORK OF RESISTANCE

With its weapons of war like the SOA and a militarized U.S.-Mexico border, coloniality is designed to make those who benefit from its structures invulnerable to the finitude, interdependence, and ambiguity of human existence. The overrepresentation of subjectivity in the realms of knowledge, being, and power is like a coat of armor with violent and deadly spikes covering its every surface. Epistemological coloniality—with its totalizing claims to a monopoly on truth—violently shields its beneficiaries from the necessity of recognizing the limitations and contextuality of all human knowledge projects. Ontological coloniality—with its hierarchical binaries between spirit and matter, human and nonhuman, clergy and laity, male and female, pale-skinned Europeans and darker "others," and so on—violently shields its beneficiaries from facing the absolute dependence and interdependence of human beings on one another and the rest of creation. The coloniality of power—with the myriad forms of control that it grants its beneficiaries—is an especially effective and violent means of protection from the finitude and vicissitudes of life in the world. The coloniality of power grants seemingly unlimited resources to its beneficiaries in an attempt to not only meet basic human needs, but to stave off myriad forms of existential anxiety. If my subjectivity is privileged as universally normative and affirmed, and if not only my needs but manifold desires are privileged as normative and affirmed, then my existence is affirmed. These affirmations are illusions, of course, because they have no basis in the fundamental reality of human existence: absolute equality and utter dependence of all human beings before the divine gift of life as God's image bearers in this world. And yet investment in this illusion accrues and multiplies with exponential potency, paying colonial dividends, generation after generation. The beneficiaries of coloniality cling to this illusion for dear life, willing and even eager to sacrifice not only the truth but the embodied existence of the colonized for its sake.

These are high stakes and, therefore, any real or perceived threat to the coloniality of power provokes a range of reactions in its power brokers and beneficiaries. As mentioned above, Maldonado-Torres explicitly names the first thesis of the decolonial project to be that decolonial praxis causes reactions of fear and anxiety in the beneficiaries of coloniality:

> anxieties about the legitimacy of the normative citizen-subject and the social, political, and economic order that sustains it, and fears about the very presence and the potential action of those who typically address these topics in this way—that is, the colonized. These kinds of anxiety and fear lead to multiple forms of evasion, to micro-aggressions, and to open aggressive behavior.[56]

When the colonized question, denounce, and struggle to undo the unjust, unearned, and violently pillaged privileges that coloniality affords to the "winners" of modern world history, these "winners" often experience profound anxiety. The possibility of diminished subjectivity, not to mention material comfort, is terrifying for the winners of history because it threatens to unmask the existential illusions on which the invulnerability of life as we know it depends. To "resign from modernity/coloniality" and enter into decolonial solidarity with the struggles of those on the underside and peripheries of history does not come naturally to those of us whose very existence as modern, Western, "rational" subjects depends on the coloniality of power. As we discussed above, to resign from modernity/coloniality requires a transformation of subjectivity that unmasks, displaces, unmakes, re-creates, and re-members the subject according to an appropriate level of subjectivity that permits the fullest possible exercise of intersubjectivity for every human being and creation as a whole.

This process of conversion is not typically very comfortable or easy, as the story of the rich young man reminds us (Luke 18:25). The profound transformation required to enter into the fullness of life seems impossible, and the call to this transformation that is issued by colonized peoples is met with profound anxiety and even grief. Recall how the rich man "became sad" when Jesús invited him to sell all that he had and redistribute his wealth to the poor. The call to resign from modernity/coloniality produces a similar effect. This is because resignation from power, privilege, and overrepresentation requires that we lean into the risk of perceived and/or real loss, and that we embrace the vulnerability of living life without the real and perceived protections that power, privilege, and overrepresentation provide. Embracing this vulnerability is not easy for those of us whose existence has been fortified by structures and illusions of invulnerability. And yet it is the only way to enter into God's reign as it manifests itself historically in real relationships of decolonial solidarity.

Lxs pobres of the Salvadoran CEBs have no choice but to be vulnerable, since the coloniality of power has distributed vulnerability on their backs—disproportionately, unjustly, and violently—for centuries. The choice that the CEBs make in the face of this reality is to share the burdens of their vulnerability together in collective solidarity and to resist the unjust, colonial distribution of vulnerability in various realms of human existence. Some members of the CEBs, themselves *pobres*, made this choice even in the face of death. This book has sought to demonstrate and celebrate that the decolonial solidarity that the CEBs' practice as the church of *lxs pobres*, sacrament of God's reign, embodies a delinking from coloniality and a witness against the *anti-reino*, whereby the CEBs "disrupt the coloniality of knowledge, power, and being and [thereby] change the world."[57] However, we hope it has also been made clear in these pages that this embodied decolonial commitment has resulted in exposure to heightened vulnerability and violent persecution for the church of *lxs pobres*. Especially in their early years, the CEBs were subject to the anxious and rage-filled, calculated, and violent reactions of the powerful to the challenge they posed as the newly emergent popular church. Many members of the CEBs lost their lives—or rather, were murdered—for their resistance to the reigning power structures in Salvadoran society. In more recent years, the threat of political assassinations has waned, but vulnerability to the coloniality of power within the institutional church and other societal institutions has persisted in ever-evolving ways. And yet the CEBs too persist in their memory of the proclamation of the *reino* by Jesús, and they re-member the lives and deaths of their martyrs as paradigmatic examples of what it means to be a human being and Christian in the midst of a world that is ruled by the powers and principalities of the *anti-reino*. The CEBs make peace with vulnerability, not for its own sake or for the sake of surrender to God or self-abnegation, but for the sake of bearing one another's burdens and journeying together, in solidarity and love, toward the abundant life of God's reign. The experience of "fullness" that members of CEBs describe in their accounts of committed solidarity points to the power of divine grace that empowers and transforms their vulnerability into the fullness of life in God's presence. As folks in El Salvador might say, *vale la pena*—it's worth it. Or *no hay de otro*—there is no other way, even if the result of the struggle in one's lifetime is not the *victoria final*.

Not only are those of us who benefit from coloniality terrified of losing our power and privilege, we have a hard time letting go of messianic missions to save the world from its problems and thereby arrive at some final victory. We have a hard time accepting what the CEBs are forced to accept on a daily basis, that human existence is finite, that our efforts are limited, and that we can only do so much in one lifetime. Coloniality is uncomfortable with finitude, and it resists making peace with the limitations expressed by a leader even as dedicated and accomplished as community elder Santiago Portillo: "I feel like I haven't done everything, but I have done something. And that's why I feel happy and content."[58] Unlike Santiago, beneficiaries of coloniality can tend to cling to notions of a *victoria final* that we can and must bring about, or at least contribute to, by our own heroic efforts, here and now. The white supremacy culture at the heart of coloniality is characterized by this sense of urgency and absolutism, which violently reinscribes the overrepresentation of colonial subjectivity, even in its most liberal, progressive, and revolutionary forms. Even when our intentions are "good" and we try to "help," we cling to control and the invulnerability (and superiority) of our self-professed goodness, expertise, and rationality. We struggle with the vulnerability of letting go of control, which is precisely what decolonial solidarity requires. Our fragile egos can shatter when we are confronted with our finitude, our limitations, the ambiguity of even our best intentions, and the violence of even some of our most well-intentioned efforts at making the world a "better" place. What will it take for us to commit to a lifetime of giving up these illusions of invulnerability and control, thereby entering into decolonial solidarity with the collective struggle for a world in which many worlds are free to coexist?

Just as there is no way to "work" ourselves out of the anxiety that we experience as human beings in the face of our vulnerability, there is no way to "work" ourselves out of the fragility and obsession with control that those of us with any degree of power or privilege within the colonial power matrix experience when we are threatened with real or perceived diminishment of our subjectivity. It takes courage to allow marginal wisdom to guide our choices, but even this courage is not the result of our own herculean human efforts. If it were, it would simply be mimicking the self-made colonial "courage" of the invulnerable, rugged individual. Decolonial courage requires the grace of divine love opening our hearts and minds to the abundant life that is available when we resign from coloniality and enter into solidarity with the *damnés* in their struggles for an-other world. The grace that is available in this process of conversion to decolonial solidarity is far more life-giving than anything we could have imagined, acquired, or controlled for ourselves. This grace operates within us as a form of resilience that re-makes and re-members us as members in God's reign of abundant life for all.

Something that is fragile breaks easily, and a thesaurus might list the antonym of fragile as unbreakable, just as the opposite of vulnerable is invulnerable. But the grace that the beneficiaries of coloniality need in order to resign from coloniality and enter into the fullness of life is not to be made unbreakable or invulnerable (though it occurs to us as authors that perhaps this is exactly what colonial theologies have sought to do for their beneficiaries). Rather, what we need is the grace of resilience so that, when we are faced with perceived or real threats of harm to our power and privilege, we don't fall apart and harm colonized and impoverished peoples in the process. The American Psychological Association defines resilience as

> the process of adapting well in the face of adversity, trauma, tragedy, threats or significant sources of stress. . . . It means "bouncing back" from difficult experiences. . . . Being resilient does not mean that a person doesn't experience difficulty or distress. . . . In fact, the road to resilience is likely to involve considerable emotional distress.[59]

For one who benefits from coloniality in any number of ways, bouncing back from challenges to internal and external coloniality does not mean an easy return to the person one already was, but rather entails a difficult and distressing process of transformation in the direction of ever greater humility, courage, peace, and compassion. With the grace of resilience, we can be free and flexible[60] enough to not only tolerate but embrace threats to our place in the colonial power matrix. We can let them in and allow them to tear down the walls of our privilege and the preposterousness of our power. With the grace of resilience we can be confronted and challenged without running away, shutting down, or shutting up our challenger. With the grace of resilience, we can "bounce back" from the demise of our privilege with fortified hearts, minds, and bodies that are ready to learn from and humbly partner with *lxs pobres* in the work of decolonial solidarity and resistance.

We can be re-membered, but it is grace that accomplishes our re-membering, not our own human efforts, however well-intentioned they may be. And yet, while we can't work our way into the resilient courage required for the practice of decolonial solidarity, we can cultivate it by engaging in the spiritual and ecclesial work described above—of contemplative listening to and learning from the voice of the divine at work in the church of *lxs pobres*. Being made known, re-created, and re-fashioned by the divine grace of solidarity with *lxs pobres* and *damnés* of this world will transform our consciousness, our being, and our way of showing up and exercising power in the church and world. As the title and epigraph to this chapter suggest, continually planting these seeds of decolonial solidarity in ourselves and in our world is the only way to die to our former selves and open ourselves up to the grace that the universe, the divine gift of Creation, has to offer. This is the truth that the Salvadoran CEBs have learned and lived into for over fifty years: *Si el grano de trigo no muere*—"unless a grain of wheat falls into the earth and dies, it remains just a single grain; but if it dies, it bears much fruit" (John 12:24). Such is the task before us all, what we are called to *do* and how we are called to be *undone*—dying to the ways and means of coloniality in the church and world and being reborn as a new humanity, sharers in the divine life, and the universally and equitably distributed subjectivity of God's reign.

Que así sea: a banquet, the table set with spaghetti, french fries, chicken, and tortilla, together with food and drink from every corner of creation, the stuff of which our bodies and blood are made, *cada cual con su taburete*, as re-membered intersubjects, all of us *pobres* in relation to our Divine Creator, all of us *damnés* if coloniality continues to have its way. A bag of fried green plantains with *curtido* and salsa, bought from a roadside stand off the superhighway of coloniality/modernity, missed by the zooming cars and high-speed trains, accessible by foot or by haphazard bicycle, shared with others gathered while discussing clean water, pensions, and the rain. A march outside of a military base, police barracks, or detention center; dancing colors and singing names, a diversity of causes and struggles united in refusing to forget, invoking the divine promise of justice. A small chapel in El Jocote, with a dirt floor and a tile roof, an out-of-tune guitar and a dog-eared songbook, re-membering those silenced by the world. Already but not yet, we each turn on our own paths toward the music.

NOTES

1. Gómez and Marshall, *Sigue porque la vida sigue*, 75.
2. Maldonado-Torres, "Outline of Ten Theses," 29. Emphasis added.
3. *EG*, §198.
4. Gerald J. Beyer lays out these three "moments" of solidarity in "The Meaning of Solidarity in Catholic Social Teaching," *Political Theology* 15, no. 1 (2014), 15 ff.
5. *EG*, § 188.
6. *EG*, §189.
7. *EG*, §189.
8. *EG*, §198.
9. Quoting *EG*, §53–54. See the U.S. WMPM website at http://popularmovements.org/about/.
10. *FT*, §116 and "Address to the Participants in the World Meeting of Popular Movements," October 28, 2014.
11. *FT*, §169. Quoting both the 2014 address and his 2016 "Address to the Participants in the World Meeting of Popular Movements," *L'Osservatore Romano*, 7–8 (November 2016): 4–5.

12. *FT*, §169. Emphasis in the original.
13. *MM*, §21.
14. Pope Francis, "Message for the Fourth World Day of the Poor," November 15, 2020, §9.
15. Pope Francis, "Message for the First World Day of the Poor," November 19, 2017, §5.
16. Pope Francis, "Message for the Third World Day of the Poor," November 17, 2019, §5.
17. Pope Francis, "Message for the First World Day of the Poor," November 19, 2017, §4.
18. Many thanks to Armando Marquez Ochoa for helping us think through these distinctions at our Wake Forest University research symposium on the church of the poor in October 2019.
19. Pope Francis, "Message for the First World Day of the Poor," November 19, 2017, §8.
20. We rest our case here, but could certainly add to this argument an entire analysis of Francis's lack of solidarity with women and sexual minorities in the church and world.
21. "History," Witness for Peace Solidarity Collective, https://www.solidarityc ollective.org/history-mission, accessed September 7, 2020.
22. "Mission and Vision," Witness for Peace Solidarity Collective, https://www .solidaritycollective.org/our-mission, accessed September 7, 2020. See the *librito* of the Prophet Berta Cáceres in part I.
23. In his article on sanctuary in the Trump era, Elliot Young traces the history of the movement through the Sanctuary Movement for Central American refugees protagonized by Protestant, Catholic, and Jewish groups in the United States in the 1980s: "In the 1980s, religious groups revived the idea of providing safe haven by protecting some of the millions of Central Americans fleeing brutal dictators and civil war. By 1987, scores of cities and several states had declared themselves sanctuaries, prohibiting their employees from cooperating with federal immigration authorities." In "Sanctuary in the Trump Era," North American Congress on Latin America (NACLA), February 3, 2017, https://nacla.org/news/2017/02/07/sanctuary -trump-era.
24. "Our History," Christians for Peace in El Salvador (CRISPAZ), https://www .crispaz.org/about-us/our-history/, accessed September 7, 2020.
25. "Solidarity," Fundación Hermano Mercedes Ruíz (FUNDAHMER), https:// fundahmer.wordpress.com/programs/solidarity/, accessed September 7, 2020.
26. "El Salvador Encounter," Christians for Peace in El Salvador (CRISPAZ), https://www.crispaz.org/delegation-trips/el-salvador-encounter/, accessed September 7, 2020.
27. Robert Ellis Haynes, *Consuming Mission: Towards a Theology of Short-Term Mission and Pilgrimage* (Eugene, OR: Pickwick, 2018), 67.
28. Robert J. Priest, Terry Dischinger, Steve Rasmussen, and C. M. Brown, "Researching the Short-Term Mission Movement," *Missiology* 34, no. 4 (October 2006), 432.

29. Haynes, *Consuming Mission*, 68.
30. Haynes, 70.
31. Haynes, 70.
32. Ellen Moodie, "Inequality and Intimacy," 153.
33. Moodie, 154. Emphasis in the original.
34. Moodie, 154.
35. Moodie cites this number on page 153.
36. Moodie, 160.
37. Mt. 19:23–24, Lk. 18:24–25, NRSV.
38. Sylvia Wynter, "Unsettling the Coloniality of Being/Power/Truth/Freedom," 260.
39. True discernment about the intersectional nature of coloniality is necessary for this step. Our race, sex, class, ability, and other identity markers, culturally conditioned though they be, place pieces of ourselves on different sides of the coloniality/modernity divide in different circumstances.
40. Maldonado-Torres, "Outline of Ten Theses," 8.
41. Dipesh Chakrabarty, *Provincializing Europe* (Princeton, NJ: Princeton University Press, 2000), 4.
42. Christen Kerr McLean, "Yes, the Burning of Notre Dame Was Bad. The Amazon Fires Are So Much Worse," *Washington Post*, August 25, 2019, https://www.washingtonpost.com/opinions/yes-the-burning-of-notre-dame-was-bad-the-amazon-fires-are-so-much-worse/2019/08/25/c77a3716-c5bf-11e9-8bf7-cde2d9e09055_story.html.
43. P. R. Lockhart, "Black Churches in Louisiana See $1.9 Million Surge in Donations after Fire at Notre Dame Cathedral," *Vox*, April 19, 2019, https://www.vox.com/identities/2019/4/17/18412465/louisiana-black-churches-fire-donations-notre-dame.
44. Paulo Freire, *Pedagogy of the Oppressed*, 20th anniversary edition (Maryknoll: Orbis, 1993), 44.
45. "A Welcome from the Commandant," official website of the Western Hemisphere Institute for Security Cooperation (WHINSEC), July 1, 2019, https://www.benning.army.mil/tenant/WHINSEC/About-Institute.html.
46. "SOA Country Sheets: El Salvador," SOA Watch website, https://soaw.org/soa-country-sheets/, accessed September 30, 2020.
47. "About: SOA Watch," SOA Watch website, https://soaw.org/about/, accessed September 30, 2020.
48. This history draws on our own memories, the website of the Ignatian Family Teach-In for Justice ("Ignatian Family Teach-In for Justice History: From the Gates of Ft. Benning to the Halls of Congress," https://ignatiansolidarity.net/iftj/iftj-history/), the website of the SOA Watch (http://soawatch.org/), the website of the Jesuits ("Teach-In for Justice—The Commitment of the Ignatian Solidarity Network," https://www.jesuits.global/2020/09/03/teach-in-for-justice-the-commitment-of-the-ignatian-solidarity-network/, accessed September 30, 2020), and the website of the Schlegel Center for Service and Justice at Creighton University ("History of the

IFTJ," http://blogs.creighton.edu/ccsj/ignatianfamilyteachinforjustice/the-history/, accessed September 30, 2020).

49. SOA Watch, "25,000 Strong! Eleven Arrested for Nonviolent Civil Disobedience," *Latin America in Movement*, November 18, 2007, https://www.alainet.org/en/articulo/124346.

50. Ignatian Solidarity Network, "Ignatian Family Teach-In for Justice History"; Jesuits, "Teach-In for Justice—The Commitment of the Ignatian Solidarity Network."

51. This is, admittedly, based on Laurel's own memory of being a student at a Jesuit university in 2009–2010 and informal conversations she has had with friends and peers who were students or campus ministers at the time attempting to re-member these events.

52. Both the IFTJ and the SOA Watch commemorative events were held virtually in November 2020 and 2021 due to COVID-19.

53. Ignatian Solidarity Network, "Ignatian Family Teach-In for Justice History."

54. Ignatian Solidarity Network, "Ideas for Hosting and Recruiting for IFTJ 2020," https://ignatiansolidarity.net/iftj/prepare/, accessed September 30, 2020.

55. IFTJ homepage, https://ignatiansolidarity.net/iftj/, accessed September 30, 2020.

56. Maldonado-Torres, "Outline of Ten Theses," 8. See also the work of Robin DiAngelo, according to whom white fragility "is a state in which even a minimum amount of racial stress becomes intolerable, triggering a range of defensive moves. These moves include the outward display of emotions such as anger, fear, and guilt, and behaviors such as argumentation, silence, and leaving the stress-inducing situation. . . . This insulated environment of racial privilege builds white expectations for racial comfort while at the same time lowering the ability to tolerate racial stress." In "White Fragility," *International Journal of Critical Pedagogy* 3, no. 3 (2011): 54. See also *White Fragility: Why It's So Hard for White People to Talk About Racism* (Boston, MA: Beacon Press, 2018). For an important critique of DiAngelo's work as condescending toward Black people, see John McWhorter, "The Dehumanizing Condescension of White Fragility," *Atlantic* Website, July 15, 2020, https://www.theatlantic.com/ideas/archive/2020/07/dehumanizing-condescension-white-fragility/614146/.

57. Maldonado-Torres, "Outline of Ten Theses," 29. Emphasis ours.

58. Gómez and Marshall, *Sigue porque la vida sigue*, 34. Both Santiago and his wife Raquel passed away during the writing of this book, on June 11, 2020.

59. American Psychological Association, "The Road to Resilience," accessed June 4, 2018, http://www.apa.org/helpcenter/road-resilience.aspx. Elizabeth O'Donnell Gandolfo fleshes out the human need for resilience as a partner to resistance in *The Power and Vulnerability of Love: A Theological Anthropology* (Minneapolis, MN: Fortress Press, 2015).

60. Marcia Mount Shoop and Mary McClintock Fulkerson write about the need for the cultivation of flexibility in white Christian antiracism. See *A Body Broken, A Body Betrayed: Race, Memory, and Eucharist in White-Dominant Churches* (Eugene, OR: Cascade Books, 2015), 16 ff.

Bibliography

Alas, José Inocencio. *Land, Liberation and Death Squads: A Priest's Story, Suchitoto, El Salvador, 1968–1977*. Translated by Robin Fazio and Emily Wade Will. Eugene, OR: Resource, 2016.
Pope Alexander VI. *Inter Caetera*. 1493. Accessed at papalencyclicals.net/Alex06/ alex06inter.htm.
Althaus-Reid, Marcella. *Indecent Theology: Theological Perversions in Sex, Gender, and Politics*. New York: Routledge, 2000.
American Psychological Association. "The Road to Resilience." Official website of the American Psychological Association. Accessed June 4, 2018. http://www.apa.org/helpcenter/road-resilience.aspx.
Anzaldúa, Gloria. *Borderlands/La Frontera: The New Mestiza*. San Francisco, CA: Aunt Lute Books, 1987.
Archdiocese of San Salvador. "Reseña Histórica." Official website of the Archdiocese of San Salvador. Accessed August 28, 2020. http://www.arzobispadosansalvador.org/sobre-nosotros/resena-historica/.
Arévalo, Amaral Palevi Gómez. "Entre la Espada y la Pared: Movilidad Forzada de Personas Salvadoreñas LGBT." *Mediações* 22, no. 1 (2017): 130–155.
Articulación Continental Comunidades Eclesiales de Base. "Comunidades Eclesiales de Base: Identidad." Accessed October 10, 2019. www.cebcontinental.org.
Azahar, Christina. "Sounds and Memories of El Salvador's Civil War in the Songs of Los Torogoces de Morazán." *Lucero* 24 (2015).
Barbé, Dominique. "Church Base Communities." In *Liberation Theology: An Introductory Reader*, edited by Curt Cadorette et al. Maryknoll, NY: Orbis Books, 1992.
Beyer, Gerald J. "The Meaning of Solidarity in Catholic Social Teaching." *Political Theology* 15, no. 1 (2014): 7–25.
Bidegain, Ana María. "From Catholic Action to Liberation Theology. Historical Process of the Laity in Latin America in the Twentieth Century." Working Paper

#48, The Helen Kellogg Institute for International Studies, University of Notre Dame, 1985

Bingemer, Maria Clara Lucchetti. *Latin American Theology: Roots and Branches.* Maryknoll, NY: Orbis, 2016.

Boff, Clodovis. "Epistemología y Método de la Teología de la Liberación." In *Mysterium Liberationis: Conceptos Fundamentales de la Teología de la Liberación, Tomo I*, edited by Jon Sobrino and Ignacio Ellacuría. San Salvador: UCA Editores, 1993.

Boff, Clodovis. *Feet on the Ground Theology.* Maryknoll, NY: Orbis Books, 1987.

Boff, Leonardo. "¿Para quiénes es, o no es querida la 'Querida Amazonía'?" Servicios Koinonia Website, March 2, 2020. http://www.servicioskoinonia.org/boff/articulo.php?num=970.

Bosch, Fransico, ed. *Bendita Mezcla: Hermanxs escuchadorxs, comunidades palabreras.* Montevideo: Fundación Amerindia, 2020.

Broad, Robin and John Cavanaugh, *The Water Defenders: How Ordinary People Saved a Country from Corporate Greed.* Boston, MA: Beacon Press, 2021.

Brueggemann, Walter. *The Prophetic Imagination.* 40th anniversary ed. Minneapolis: Fortress Press, 2018.

Burke, Kevin. "The Crucified People as 'Light for the Nations': A Reflection on Ignacio Ellacuría." In *Rethinking Martyrdom*, edited by Teresa Okure et al., 120–130. London: SCM Press, 2003.

Burkholder, Mark A. "New Laws of 1542." In *Encyclopedia of Latin American History and Culture.* Vol. 4, edited by Barbara A. Tenenbaum and Georgette M. Dorn. New York: Charles Scribner's and Sons, 1996.

Cáceres, Berta. "Berta Caceres acceptance speech, 2015 Goldman Prize ceremony." YouTube, Goldman Environmental Prize, channel. April 22, 2015. https://www.youtube.com/watch?v=AR1kwx8b0ms&t=12s.

Cardenal, Ernesto. *The Gospel in Solentiname.* Maryknoll, NY: Orbis, 2010.

Cardenal, Rodolfo. *Historia de una esperanza: vida de Rutilio Grande.* San Salvador: UCA Editores, 1985.

Castillo, Álvar. "Símbolo de rebeldía." In *El Pueblo Canta: Libro de Cantos*, #491. San Salvador: Talleres de Imprenta Criterio, 1998.

Castillo, José María. *Símbolos de libertad.* Salamanca: Sígueme, 2001.

Cavada Díaz, Miguel. *La Biblia*, inter-lectionary hymn of the "Mesoamerican Mass."

Cerejo, Austin F. "Cardijin's Methodology and Its Relevance for Social and Structural Change." In *Indian Church in the Struggle for a New Society*, edited by D. S. Amalorpavadass, 402–421. Bangalore, India: National Biblical, Catechetical & Liturgical Centre, 1981.

Chakrabarty, Dipesh. *Provincializing Europe.* Princeton, NJ: Princeton University Press, 2000.

Christians for Peace in El Salvador (CRISPAZ). "El Salvador Encounter." Website of CRISPAZ. Accessed September 7, 2020. https://www.crispaz.org/delegation-trips/el-salvador-encounter/.

Christians for Peace in El Salvador (CRISPAZ). "Our History." Website of CRISPAZ. Accessed September 7, 2020. https://www.crispaz.org/about-us/our-history/.

Bibliography

CEB Continental. "Camino Histórico CEBs Región Centroamérica." Accessed October 12, 2018. http://cebcontinental.org/index.php/quienes-somos/historia-de-las-ceb/region-centroamerica.
Las CEBs Cantamos. 2018. San Salvador. Compact disc.
Code of Canon Law: Latin-English Edition. Washington, DC: Canon Law Society of America, 1998.
Colonnese, Louis Michael, ed. *The Church in the Present-Day Transformation of Latin America in the Light of the Council* (Medellín Conclusions). Bogotá: CELAM, 1970.
Comblín, José. *People of God*. Maryknoll, NY: Orbis Books, 2004.
Comité Clandestino Revolucionario Indígena-Comandancia General del Ejército Zapatista de Liberación Nacional. "Cuarta Declaración de la Selva Lacandona," January 1, 1996. http://enlacezapatista.ezln.org.mx/1996/01/01/cuarta-declaracion-de-la-selva-lacandona/.
Comunidades Eclesiales de Base de El Salvador. "Luz de Ocote." Managua, Nicaragua: no date or publisher.
Comunidades Eclesiales de Base de El Salvador. "Nuestro Centro Pastoral 'Hermano Mercedes Ruiz.'" San Salvador: CEBES, n.d.
Comunidades Eclesiales de Base de El Salvador. *Una Experiencia de Iglesia: Mística y Metodología*. San Salvador, El Salvador: CEBES, n.d.
Comunidades Eclesiales de Base del Norte de Morazán. *Tomamos la Palabra*. Morazán, El Salvador: Talleres Gráficos UCA, 2001.
Congregation for the Clergy. "Pastoral Conversion of the Parish Community in the Service of the Evangelising Mission of the Church." Accessed August 25, 2020. http://www.clerus.va/content/dam/clerus/Dox/Istruzione2020/Instruction_EN.pdf.
Congregation for the Clergy. "The Priest: Pastor and Leader of the Parish Community." August 4, 2002.
Congregation for the Doctrine of the Faith. "Notification on the Works of Jon Sobrino, SJ." November 26, 2006.
Consalvi, Carlos Enriquez. *La Terquedad Del Izote: La Historia de Radio Venceremos*. San Salvador: Ediciones MUPI, 2003.
Consejo Episcopal Latinoamericano. "Conclusiones de la III Conferencia General Del Episcopado Latinoamericana (Puebla)." In *Las Cinco Conferencias Generales Del Episcopado Latinoamericano*. Bogotá: CELAM, 2014.
Cornejo Ruíz, José Salvador. "Canto Popular." Presentation, Wake Forest University Research Symposium, October 2019.
Coto, Luis. "Una Historia de las Comunidades Eclesiales de Base en El Salvador." Keynote address given during the 50th anniversary celebration of the Salvadoran Base Ecclesial Communities in San Salvador, February 8, 2019.
Council of Castile. "The Requirement." 1510. Accessed June 9, 2020. http://nationalhumanitiescenter.org/pds/amerbegin/contact/text7/requirement.pdf; and
Crossan, John Dominic. *God and Empire: Jesus Against Rome, Then and Now*. New York: HarperCollins, 2008.
Cruces, Guillermo et al. "The Growth-Employment-Poverty Nexus in Latin America in the 2000s: El Salvador Country Study." World Institute for Development

Economics Research, United Nations University, September 2015. https://www.wider.unu.edu/sites/default/files/wp2015-077.pdf.

Cuéllar, Guillermo. "Vamos Todos al Banquete." In *El Pueblo Canta: Libro de Cantos*, #821. San Salvador: Talleres de Imprenta Criterio, 1998.

Dalton, Roque. "Anastasio Aquino, tu lucha . . ." In *La ventana en el rostro*. Mexico City: Ocean Sur, 2015.

Danner, Mark. *The Massacre at El Mozote: A Parable of the Cold War*. New York: Vintage Books, 1993.

De La Torre, Miguel. *The Politics of Jesús: A Hispanic Political Theology*. Lanham, MD: Rowman & Littlefield, 2015.

DiAngelo, Robin. "White Fragility." *International Journal of Critical Pedagogy* 3, no. 3 (2011): 54–70.

DiAngelo, Robin. *White Fragility: Why It's So Hard for White People to Talk About Racism*. Boston, MA: Beacon Press, 2018.

Dussel, Enrique. "Epistemological Decolonization of Theology." In *Decolonial Christianities: Latinx and Latin American Perspectives*, edited by Raimundo Barreto and Roberto Sirvent. New York: Palgrave Macmillan, 2019.

Drexler-Dreis, Joseph. *Decolonial Love: Salvation in Colonial Modernity*. New York: Fordham University Press, 2019.

Drexler-Dreis, Joseph. "The Option for the Poor as a Decolonial Option: Latin American Liberation Theology in Conversation with Teología India and Womanist Theology." *Political Theology* 18, no. 3 (2017): 269–286.

"El Ferrocarril, sus orígenes y su historia." Website of FENADESAL and the Salvadoran Port Authority, 2009. https://web.archive.org/web/20100308022920/http://www.fenadesal.gob.sv/contenido.php?cont=52&id=87.

El Pueblo Canta: Libro de Cantos, #161. San Salvador: Talleres de Imprenta Criterio, 1998.

Ellacuría, Ignacio. "Christian Spirituality." In *Ignacio Ellacuría: Essays on History, Liberation, and Salvation*, edited by Michael E. Lee. Maryknoll, NY: Orbis Books, 2013.

Ellacuría, Ignacio. "Church of the Poor, Historical Sacrament of Liberation." In *Ignacio Ellacuría: Essays on History, Liberation, and Salvation*, edited by Michael E. Lee, 227–253. Maryknoll, NY: Orbis Books, 2013.

Ellacuría, Ignacio. "The Crucified People." In *Mysterium Liberationis: Fundamental Concepts of Liberation Theology*, edited by Ignacio Ellacuría and Jon Sobrino, 580–603. Maryknoll, NY: Orbis, 1993.

Ellacuría, Ignacio. "The Historicity of Christian Salvation." In *Ignacio Ellacuría: Essays on History, Liberation, and Salvation*, edited by Michael E. Lee. Maryknoll, NY: Orbis Books, 2013.

Equipo Maíz, *Historia de El Salvador: de cómo la gente guanaca no sucumbó ante los infames ultrajes de españoles, criollos, gringos, y otras plagas*. 9th ed. San Salvador: Equipo Maiz, 2012.

Escobar, Alberto, Juan Gavidia, and Don Lito. "Cumbia de Monseñor Romero." Accessed October 12, 2020. https://www.youtube.com/watch?v=CCosBo7CjV0.

Escobar Alas, Monseñor José Luis. "Invito a todos que, siguiendo las huellas de nuestro Santo, luchemos por la justicia." Homily from St. Óscar Romero's canonization celebration in San Salvador on October 14, 2018 (final text, October 28, 2018).
Estrada, Yaneth. "Arzobispo Escobar Alas llama a Gobernar a favor del pueblo." *Diario CoLatino*, February 11, 2019. https://www.diariocolatino.com/arzobispo-escobar-alas-llama-a-gobernar-a-favor-del-pueblo/.
La fe de un pueblo: historia de una comunidad cristiana en el salvador (1970–1980). San Salvador: UCA Editores, 1983.
Fernández, José Antonio. *La huella colonial.* San Salvador: Banco Agrícola Comercial, 1996.
Flannery, Austin, O.P. *Vatican Council II: Constitutions, Decrees, Declarations.* New York: Costello Publishing Company, 1996.
Pope Francis. Chrism Mass Homily, March 28, 2013.
Pope Francis. "Message for the First World Day of the Poor." November 19, 2017.
Pope Francis. "Message for the Third World Day of the Poor." November 17, 2019.
Pope Francis. "Message for the Fourth World Day of the Poor." November 15, 2020.
Pope Francis. "Participation at the Second World Meeting of Popular Movements, Address of the Holy Father." July 9, 2015. Bolivia.
Freire, Paulo. *Pedagogy of the Oppressed.* 20th anniversary ed. Maryknoll, NY: Orbis, 1993.
FMLN. "An Interview with Ana María Leddy, Author of the Hymn of the *Frente*." Official website of the FMLN, February 23, 2010. https://fmln.org.sv/index.php/nuestro-partido/himno-del-fmln.
Fundación Hermano Mercedes Ruíz (FUNDAHMER). "Escuela Campesina." Accessed October 12, 2018. https://fundahmerespanol.wordpress.com/proyectos/desarrollo-humano/escuela-campesina/.
Fundación Hermano Mercedes Ruíz (FUNDAHMER). "Historia." Accessed October 10, 2020. https://fundahmerespanol.wordpress.com/quienes-somos/historia/.
Fundación Hermano Mercedes Ruíz (FUNDAHMER). "Solidarity." Accessed September 7, 2020. https://fundahmer.wordpress.com/programs/solidarity/.
Gaillardetz, Richard R. *By What Authority: A Primer on Scripture, the Magisterium, and the Sense of the Faithful.* Minneapolis, MN: Liturgical Press, 2003.
Gaillardetz, Richard R. "The Ecclesiological Foundations of Ministry within an Ordered Communion." In *Ordering of the Baptismal Priesthood*, edited by Susan Wood. Collegeville, MN: Liturgical Press, 2003.
Gaillardetz, Richard R. *Ecclesiology for a Global Church: A People Called and Sent.* Maryknoll, NY: Orbis Books, 2008.
Galdámez, Pablo. *Esperanza de un pueblo.* San Salvador: Equipo Maíz, 2012.
Gandolfo, Elizabeth O'Donnell. "*Cuando el pobre crea en el pobre*: Decolonial Epistemology in the Ecclesial Base Communities of El Salvador." In *Decolonial Christianities: Latinx and Latin American Perspectives*, edited by Raimundo Barreto and Roberto Sirvent, 241–254. New York: Palgrave Macmillan, 2019.

Gandolfo, Elizabeth O'Donnell. "Medellín and the Problem of Whiteness: An Ambiguous Legacy." In *Medellín and Its Significance for the Church in the United States: Memories, Theologies, and Legacies*, edited by O. Ernesto Valiente et al. Miami, FL: Convivium Press, 2018.

Gandolfo, Elizabeth O'Donnell. *The Power and Vulnerability of Love: A Theological Anthropology*. Minneapolis, MN: Fortress, 2015.

Gandolfo, Elizabeth O'Donnell. "Remembering the Massacre at El Mozote: A Case for Dangerous Memory of Suffering as Christian Formation in Hope." *International Journal of Practical Theology* 17, no. 1 (2013): 62–87.

Gandolfo, Elizabeth O'Donnell. "Women and Martyrdom: Feminist Liberation Theology in Dialogue with a Latin American Paradigm." *Horizons* 34, no. 1 (Spring 2007): 26–53.

García Dueñas, Lauri. "El Salvador: Ancianos de Izalco recuerdan masacre de miles de indígenas 1932." *Indymedia Argentina*, January 23, 2005. https://archivo.argentina.indymedia.org/news/2005/01/258611.php.

Goizueta, Adrián y el Experimental. "Farabundo Martí." Recorded 2016. On *Antología 80–83*. Compact disc.

Gómez Martínez, José and Laurel Anne Marshall, eds. *Sigue porque la vida sigue: Voces de las comunidades eclesiales de base de El Salvador ayer y hoy*. Winston-Salem, NC: Library Partners Press, 2020.

Gonzalez, Antonio. *God's Reign and the End of Empires*. Miami, FL: Convivium, 2012.

Gould, Jeffrey L. "Ignacio Ellacuría and the Salvadorean Revolution." *Journal of Latin American Studies* 47 (2015): 294–295.

Grupo Horizontes. "Monseñor Romero." In *El Pueblo Canta: Libro de Cantos*, #490. San Salvador: Talleres de Imprenta Criterio, 1998.

Grupo Horizontes. "Profeta Salvadoreño." Accessed October 12, 2020. https://www.youtube.com/watch?v=QPtobAQzz9k.

Grupo Libre. "Las CEBES." 2017. *Las CEBs Cantamos*. Compact disc.

Gutiérrez, Gustavo. *El Dios de la Vida*. Salamanca: Sígueme, 1992.

Gutiérrez, Gustavo. *The Power of the Poor in History*. Maryknoll, NY: Orbis, 1983.

Gutiérrez, Gustavo. *A Theology of Liberation, Revised Edition with a New Introduction*. Maryknoll, NY: Orbis, 1988.

Harvey, Jennifer. "What Would Zacchaeus Do?" In *Whiteness and Christology: What Would Jesus Do?*, edited by George Yancy, 84–100. New York: Routledge, 2012.

Haynes, Robert Ellis. *Consuming Mission: Towards a Theology of Short-Term Mission and Pilgrimage*. Eugene, OR: Pickwick, 2018.

Heidenry, Rachel. "Archbishop Orders Destruction of Salvadoran Mural." Pulitzer Center, January 6, 2012. Accessed February 25, 2019. pulitzercenter.org/reporting/archbishop-orders-destruction-salvadoran-mural.

Herzog, William R., II. *Jesus, Justice, and the Reign of God: A Ministry of Liberation*. Louisville, KY: Westminster John Knox Press, 2000.

Heyward, Carter. *The Redemption of God: A Theology of Mutual Relation*. New York: University Press of America, 1982.

Horsley, Richard A. *Jesus and Empire: The Kingdom of God and the New World Disorder*. Minneapolis, MN: Fortress, 2003.
Howard-Brook, Wes. *"Come Out, My People!": God's Call Out of Empire in the Bible and Beyond*. Maryknoll, NY: Orbis Books, 2010.
Howard-Brook, Wes. *Empire Baptized: How the Church Embraced What Jesus Rejected, 2nd–5th Centuries*. Maryknoll, NY: Orbis Books, 2016.
Hughes, Jennifer Scheper. "The Sacred Art of Counter-Conquest: Material Christianity in Latin America." In *The Oxford Handbook of Latin American Christianity*, edited Manuel A. Vasquez, Susan Fitzpatrick Behrens, and David Orique. New York: Oxford University Press, 2015.
"Hymn of the *Frente*." Official website of the FMLN. https://fmln.org.sv/index.php/nuestro-partido/himno-del-fmln.
Ignatian Solidarity Network. "Ideas for Hosting and Recruiting for IFTJ 2020." Website of Ignatian Solidarity Network. Accessed September 30, 2020. https://ignatiansolidarity.net/iftj/prepare/
Ignatian Solidarity Network. "Ignatian Family Teach-In for Justice History." Website of Ignatian Solidarity Network. https://ignatiansolidarity.net/iftj/iftj-history/.
Iriarte, Gregorio. *Que es una Comunidad Eclesial de Base*. Bogotá: Ediciones Paulinas, 1991.
Isasi-Díaz, Ada María. "Lo Cotidiano: A Key Element of Mujerista Theology." *Journal of Hispanic/Latino Theology* 10, no. 1 (2002): 5–17.
Isasi-Díaz, Ada María. *En La Lucha: Elaborating a Mujerista Theology*. 10th anniversary ed. Minneapolis, MN: Fortress Press, 2004.
Isasi-Díaz, Ada María. *Mujerista Theology: A Theology for the Twenty-First Century*. Maryknoll, NY: Orbis Books, 1996.
Isasi-Díaz, Ada María. "Solidarity: Love of Neighbors in the 1980s." In *Lift Every Voice: Constructing Christian Theologies from the Underside*, edited by Susan Brooks Thistlethwaite and Mary Potter Engel. San Francisco: Harper & Row, 1990.
Jackson, Laura, dir. *El Salvador: Portraits in a Revolution*. New York: Filmakers Library, 1994. DVD. Retrieved from https://video.alexanderstreet.com/watch/el-salvador-portraits-in-a-revolution.
Jennings, Willie James. *After Whiteness: An Education in Belonging*. Grand Rapids. MI: Eerdmans, 2020.
Jennings, Willie James. *The Christian Imagination: Theology and the Origins of Race*. New Haven, CT: Yale University Press, 2010.
Pope John Paul II. "Meeting with the Native Peoples of the Americas: Address of His Holiness John Paul II." September 14, 1987.
Pope John Paul II. "Solemn Prayer of the Faithful Confessing Sins and Requesting God's Pardon." From John Paul II's Day of Pardon Mass: First Sunday of Lent, March 12, 2000.
King Phillip II, "Ordinances for the Discovery, Population, and Pacification of the Indies" (1573), at http://codesproject.asu.edu/sites/default/files/THE%20LAWS%20OF%20THE%20INDIEStranslated.pdf.

Lakeland, Paul. *A Council That Will Never End: Lumen Gentium and the Church Today*. Collegeville, MN: Liturgical Press, 2013.

Lander, Edgardo and Mariana Past. "Eurocentrism, Modern Knowledges, and the 'Natural' Order of Global Capital." *Nepantla: Views from South* 3, no. 2 (2002): 245–268.

Lara-Martínez, Rafael. *Mitos en la lengua materna de los pipiles de Izalco en El Salvador: versión poética*. San Salvador: El Monstruo Editorial, 2012.

Lardé y Larín, Jorge. *El Salvador: descubrimiento, conquista, y colonización*. 2nd ed. San Salvador: Consejo Nacional para la Cultura y el Arte, 2000.

Lee, Michael. *Revolutionary Saint: The Theological Legacy of Óscar Romero*. Maryknoll, NY: Orbis, 2018.

Liebel, Manfred. *Decolonizing Childhoods: From Exclusion to Dignity*. Bristol: Policy Press, 2020.

López Vigil, María. *Muerte y vida en Morazán: testimonio de un sacerdote*. San Salvador: UCA Editores, 1987.

López Vigil, María. *Óscar Romero: Memories in Mosaic*. Translated by Kathy Ogle. Washington, DC: EPICA, 2000.

Lorde, Audre. "The Master's Tools Will Never Dismantle the Master's House." In *Sister Outsider: Essays and Speeches*, 110–114. Berkeley, CA: Crossing Press, 1984.

Lundberg, M. "The Ordination of Indians in Colonial Spanish America: Law, Prejudice, and Practice During Three Centuries." *Swedish Missiological Themes* 91, no. 2 (2003): 297–317.

Maldonado-Torres, Nelson. *Against War: Views from the Underside of Modernity*. Durham, NC: Duke University Press, 2008.

Maldonado-Torres, Nelson. "On the Coloniality of Being: Contributions to the Development of a Concept." *Cultural Studies* 21, nos. 2–3 (2007): 240–270.

Maldonado-Torres, Nelson. "Outline of Ten Theses on Coloniality and Decoloniality." Frantz Fanon Foundation. Accessed February 8, 2019. http://caribbeanstudiesassociation.org/docs/Maldonado-Torres_Outline_Ten_Theses-10.23.16.pdf.

Marcoullier, Douglas, SJ. "Archbishop with an Attitude: Oscar Romero's *Sentir con la Iglesia*." *Studies in the Spirituality of the Jesuits* 35, no. 3 (May 2003).

Mariz, Cecília Loreto. *Coping with Poverty: Pentecostals and Christian Base Communities in Brazil*. Philadelphia, PA: Temple University Press, 1994.

Marshall, Laurel Anne. "Un gesto vale más que mil palabras: las comunidades eclesiales de base de El Salvador en la construcción de celebraciones eucarísticas y bautismales" ("Actions Speak Louder than Words: Base Ecclesial Communities in El Salvador in the Construction of Eucharistic and Baptismal Celebrations"). Master's thesis, San Salvador: Universidad Centroamericana "José Simeón Cañas," 2015.

McBrien, Richard P. *The Church: The Evolution of Catholicism*. New York: HarperOne, 2008.

McWhorter, John. "The Dehumanizing Condescension of *White Fragility*." *Atlantic*, July 15, 2020. https://www.theatlantic.com/ideas/archive/2020/07/dehumanizing-condescension-white-fragility/614146/.

Medina, Néstor. *Mestizaje: Remapping Race, Culture, and Faith in Latino/a Catholicism*. Maryknoll, NY: Orbis Books, 2009.
Menjívar, Cecilia and Andrea Gómez Cervantes. "El Salvador: Civil War, Natural Disasters, and Gang Violence Drive Migration." *Migration Information Source*, Online Journal of the Migration Policy Institute, August 29, 2018.https://www.migrationpolicy.org/article/el-salvador-civil-war-natural-disasters-and-gang-violence-drive-migration.
Metz, Johann Baptist. *Faith in History and Society: Towards a Practical Fundamental Theology*. New York: Crossroad, 2007.
Middleton, Stephen et al., eds. *The Construction of Whiteness: An Interdisciplinary Analysis of Race Formation and the Meaning of White Identity*. Jackson, MS: University Press of Mississippi, 2018.
Mignolo, Walter. *The Darker Side of Western Modernity: Global Futures, Decolonial Options*. Durham: Duke University Press, 2011.
Mignolo, Walter. "Delinking." *Cultural Studies* 21, nos. 2–3 (2007): 449–514.
Mignolo, Walter. *Desobediencia Epistémica: Retórica de la Modernidad, Lógica de la Colonialidad, y Gramática de la Descolonialidad*. Buenos Aires: Ediciones del Signo, 2010.
Mignolo, Walter and Arturo Escobar, eds. *Globalization and the Decolonial Option*. London: Routledge, 2010.
Mignolo, Walter and Medina V. Tlostanova. "Theorizing from the Borders: Shifting to Geo- and Body-Politics of Knowledge." *European Journal of Social Theory* 9, no. 2 (2006): 205–221.
Mignolo, Walter and Rolando Vazquez. "Decolonial AestheSis: Colonial Wounds/Decolonial Healings." *Social Text Journal Online*, July 15, 2013, https://socialtextjournal.org/periscope_article/decolonial-aesthesis-colonial-woundsdecolonial-healings/.
Moodie, Ellen. "Democracy, Disenchantment, and the Future in El Salvador." In *Central America in the New Millennium: Living Transition and Reimagining Democracy*, edited by Jennifer L. Burell and Ellen Moodie, 96–112. New York: Berghahn Books, 2013.
Morana, Mabel, Enrique Dussel, and Carlos A. Jáuregui, eds. *Coloniality at Large: Latin America and the Postcolonial Debate*. Durham, NC: Duke University Press, 2008.
Moreno de Melendez, Teresa Inmaculada. "La Iglesia de los pobres—Reino de Dios." Presentation at Wake Forest University research symposium, "Does Church of the Poor Discourse Matter to the Marginalized?" Marietta, South Carolina, October 2019.
Muñoz, Ronaldo. "La Recepción de la Lumen Gentium en América Latina: a los cuarenta años de su promulgación." *Revista Latinoamericana de Teología* 21, no. 62 (2004): 268.
Museo de la Palabra y la Imagen (MUPI). "Humor Machista." *Prudencia Ayala: Presidenta*, museum exhibit, San Salvador, 2016. https://issuu.com/mupi/docs/exposicio__n_sobre_prudencia_ayala.
Museo de la Palabra y la Imagen (MUPI). "Prudencia Ayala (animación)." MUPI. March 9, 2017. https://www.youtube.com/watch?v=7Zqap0omZVA.

National Network of CEBs in El Salvador. "Pastoral Letter by the CEBs in El Salvador." July 2016.

Organization of American States. "Acta de Independencia." July 1956. Accessed at http://www.sice.oas.org/sica/Studies/DocUnionCentroamericana.pdf.

Pagán, Melissa. "Cultivating a Decolonial Feminist Integral Ecology: Extractive Zones and the Nexus of the Coloniality of Being/Coloniality of Gender." *Journal of Hispanic / Latino Theology* 22, no. 1 (2020): 1–28.

Peterson, Anna L. *Martyrdom and the Politics of Religion: Progressive Catholicism in El Salvador's Civil War*. Albany, NY: State University of New York Press, 1997.

Peterson, Anna L. *Seeds of the Kingdom: Utopian Communities in the Americas*. New York: Oxford University Press, 2005.

Pew Research Center."The Global Catholic Population." February 13, 2013. http://www.pewforum.org/2013/02/13/the-global-catholic-population/.

Phippin, J. Weston and National Journal. "Why Native Americans Oppose Junipero Serra's Sainthood." *Atlantic*, September 22, 2015. https://www.theatlantic.com/politics/archive/2015/09/why-native-americans-oppose-junipero-serras-sainthood/432876/

Polimédio, Chayenne. "The Rise of the Brazilian Evangelicals," *Atlantic*, January 24, 2018. https://www.theatlantic.com/international/archive/2018/01/the-evangelical-takeover-of-brazilian-politics/551423/.

Potter, Laurel Marshall. "*Campesina* School: Popular Agroecological Education in Ecclesial Base Communities in El Salvador." In *Valuing Lives, Healing Earth*, edited by Lilian Dube et al. Brussels: Peeters, forthcoming.

Priest, Robert J., Terry Dischinger, Steve Rasmussen, and C. M. Brown. "Researching the Short-Term Mission Movement." *Missiology* 34, no. 4 (October 2006): 431–450.

"Q & A with Berta Cáceres." The Goldman Environmental Prize website. May 12, 2015. https://www.goldmanprize.org/blog/qa-with-berta-caceres/.

Quijano, Anibal. "Coloniality and Modernity/Rationality." *Cultural Studies* 21, nos. 2–3 (2007): 168–178.

Quijano, Anibal. "Coloniality of Power, Eurocentrism, and Latin America." *Nepantla: Views from the South* 1, no. 3 (2000): 533–580.

Quijano, Anibal. "Keynote address at the III Latin American and Caribbean Congress for the Social Sciences," FLASCO Ecuador, August 25, 2015. https://www.youtube.com/watch?v=OxL5KwZGvdY.

Richard, Pablo. "The Church of the Poor within the Popular Movement (*Movimiento Popular*)." In *Concilium* 176 [*La Iglesia Popular: Between Fear and Hope*], edited by Leonardo Boff et al., 10–16. Edinburgh: T&T Clark, 1984.

Rieger, Jeorg. *Christ and Empire: From Paul to Postcolonial Times*. Minneapolis, MN: Fortress, 2007.

Rivas, Pedro Geoffroy. "Anastasio Aquino." In "Poemas a Anastasio Aquino," *Diario CoLatino*, October 8, 2016. https://www.diariocolatino.com/poemas-a-anastasio-aquino/.

Rivera-Pagán, Luis. "Towards a Decolonial Theology: Perspectives from the Caribbean." In *Decolonial Christianities: Latinx and Latin American Perspectives*, edited by Raimundo Barreto and Roberto Sirvent. New York: Palgrave Macmillan, 2019.

Rodríguez, José David and Loida I. Martell-Otero, eds. *Teología en Conjunto: A Collaborative Hispanic Protestant Theology*. Louisville, KY: Westminster John Knox, 1997.

Romero, St. Óscar. "The Church in the Service of Personal, Community, and Transcendent Liberation." Homily, March 23, 1980. The Archbishop Romero Trust. http://www.romerotrust.org.uk/homilies-and-writings/homilies/church-service-personal-community-and-transcendent-liberation.

Romero, St. Óscar. "The Final Homily of Archbishop Romero." Homily, March 24, 1980. The Archbishop Romero Trust. http://www.romerotrust.org.uk/homilies-and-writings/homilies/final-homily-archbishop-romero.

Romero, St. Óscar. Fourth Pastoral Letter, "The Church's Mission amid the National Crisis," August 6, 1979. In *Voice of the Voiceless: The Four Pastoral Letters and Other Statements*. Maryknoll, NY: Orbis Books, 2020.

Romero, St. Óscar. "The God of our Faith." Homily, May 21, 1978. The Archbishop Romero Trust. http://www.romerotrust.org.uk/homilies-and-writings/homilies/god-our-faith.

Romero, St. Óscar. "Homily," September 10, 1978. Servicios Koinonia Website. Accessed October 15, 2020. http://servicioskoinonia.org/romero/homilias/A/780910.htm.

Romero, St. Óscar. "Homily," July 8, 1979. The Archbishop Romero Trust. http://www.romerotrust.org.uk/homilies-and-writings.

Rouillard, Philippe. "From Human Meal to Christian Sacrifice." In *Living Bread, Saving Cup: Readings on the Eucharist*, edited by R. Kevin Seasoltz. Collegeville, MN: Liturgical Press, 1982.

Rush, Ormond. *The Eyes of Faith: The Sense of the Faithful and the Church's Reception of Revelation*. Washington, DC: Catholic University of America Press, 2009.

Saeger, James Schofield. "*The Mission* and Historical Missions: Film and the Writing of History." *The Americas* 74, no. S2 (2017): 393–415.

Sánchez, David A. *From Patmos to the Barrio: Subverting Imperial Myths*. Minneapolis, MN: Fortress Press, 2008.

Sánchez, Peter M. *Priest Under Fire: Padre David Rodríguez, the Catholic Church, and El Salvador's Revolutionary Movement*. Gainesville, FL: University Press of Florida, 2015.

Sancho, Eduardo. "Causa de la Violencia en El Salvador: El Apartheid Social." *Realidad y Reflexión* 38 (2015): 101–113.

Sandoval, Chela. *Methodology of the Oppressed*. Minneapolis, MN: University of Minnesota Press, 2000.

Sands, Justin. "Introducing Cardinal Cardijn's See–Judge–Act as an Interdisciplinary Method to Move Theory into Practice." *Religions* 9 (2018): 129.

La semilla que cayó en tierra fértil: testimonio de miembros de las comunidades cristianas. San Salvador: Consejo de Mujeres Misioneras por la Paz, 1996.

de Sepúlveda, Juan Ginés. *Demócrates segundo, o, Tratado sobre las justas causas de la guerra contra los indios.* 2nd ed. Madrid: Consejo Superior de Investigaciones Científicas, Instituto Francisco de Vitoria, 1984.

Shoop, Marcia Mount and Mary McClintock Fulkerson. *A Body Broken, A Body Betrayed: Race, Memory, and Eucharist in White-Dominant Churches.* Eugene, OR: Cascade Books, 2015.

Sibrián, Sergio, dir. *El tigre y el venado.* 2013. Accessed at https://www.youtube.com/watch?v=J4V5v5t2aHs&t=4s.

SOA Watch. "About: SOA Watch." SOA Watch website. Accessed September 30, 2020. https://soaw.org/about/.

SOA Watch. "SOA Country Sheets: El Salvador." SOA Watch website. Accessed September 30, 2020. https://soaw.org/soa-country-sheets/.

Sobrino, Jon. "Carta a Ellacu." Homily, October 31, 1992. In *Carta a las Iglesias.* November 1–15, 1992. http://www.uca.edu.sv/martires/new/memorias/cart3.htm.

Sobrino, Jon. "Carta a Ellacuría." In *Carta a las Iglesias.* October 27, 2011. http://www.uca.edu.sv/publica/cartas/media/archivo/520c88_2527cartaaellacu.pdf.

Sobrino, Jon. "Carta a Ellacuría: fineza y santidad." *Carta a las Iglesias*, # 523. November 2003. http://www.uca.edu.sv/publica/cartas/ci523.html #ELLACURIA.

Sobrino, Jon. "Carta a Ignacio Ellacuría." In *Carta a las Iglesias*, #413. November 1998. http://www.uca.edu.sv/publica/cartas/ci413.html.

Sobrino, Jon. "The Church of the Poor from John XXIII to Oscar Romero." *Concilium*, Issue 1 (2013): 99–107.

Sobrino, Jon. *Jesucristo Liberador.* San Salvador: UCA Editores, 1991.

Sobrino, Jon. *Jesus the Liberator: A Historical-Theological Reading of Jesus of Nazareth.* Maryknoll, NY: Orbis Books, 1993.

Sobrino, Jon. *Resurección de la verdadera Iglesia: Los pobres, lugar teológico de la eclesiología.* Guevara, Spain: Ediciones Sal Terrae, 1984.

Sobrino, Jon. *Where Is God? Earthquake, Terrorism, Barbarity, and Hope.* Maryknoll, NY: Orbis Books, 2004.

Sobrino, Jon. *Witnesses to the Kingdom: The Martyrs of El Salvador and the Crucified Peoples.* Maryknoll, NY: Orbis, 2003.

Smith, Gregory A. "Among White Evangelicals, Regular Churchgoers Are the Most Supportive of Trump." Pew Research Center, April 26, 2017. https://www.pewresearch.org/fact-tank/2017/04/26/among-white-evangelicals-regular-churchgoers-are-the-most-supportive-of-trump/.

Spadaro, Antonio, SJ. "A Big Heart Open to God: An Interview with Pope Francis." *America*, September 30, 2013. https://www.americamagazine.org/faith/2013/09/30/big-heart-open-god-interview-pope-francis.

Sullivan, Francis A. "Authority in an Ecclesiology of Communion." *New Theology Review* 10 (1997): 18–30.

Synod of Bishops for the Pan-Amazonian Region. "The Amazon: New Paths for the Church and for an Integral Ecology." October 26, 2019. Accessed August 26, 2020. http://www.synod.va/content/sinodoamazonico/en/documents/final-document-of-the-amazon-synod.html.

"Teach-In for Justice—The Commitment of the Ignatian Solidarity Network." Official website of the Society of Jesus. Accessed September 30, 2020. https://www.jesuits.global/2020/09/03/teach-in-for-justice-the-commitment-of-the-ignatian-solidarity-network/

Thomas, David Hurst. "The Life and Times of Junípero Serra: A Pan-Borderlands Perspective." *The Americas* 71, no. 2 (October 2014): 185–225.

Thomas, Linda E. "Remember and Re-member." *Journal of Supervision and Training in Ministry* 14 (1992–1993): 241–252.

Torres, Gilmer. "*Pueblo Mío, Tuyo, y Nuestro.*" Lyrics accessed February 13, 2020 at http://siembracanciones.blogspot.com/2008/09/este-pueblo-mo-tuyo-y-nuestro.html.

Trigo, Pedro. *Cómo relacionarnos humanizadoramente: relaciones humanas entre personas y en la sociedad.* Caracas: Centro Gumilla, 2014.

Trigo, Pedro. "Donde encontramos a Dios hoy en América Latina y lo que se le opone en esta época global." In *Desafíos de una teología iberoamericana inculturada en tiempos de globalización, interculturalidad y exclusión social: Actas del Primer Encuentro Iberoamericana de Teología*, edited by Luis Aranguren Gonzalo and Félix Palazzi. Miami, FL: Convivium Press, 2017.

United Nations' Commission on the Truth. "De la locura a la esperanza: la guerra de 12 años en El Salvador." San José: DEI, 1993.

Vigil, J. M. and A. Torrellas. *Misas Centroamericanas: Transcripción y Comentario Teológico.* Managua, Nicaragua: CAV-CEBES, 1988. Accessed October 10, 2018. https://cfones.jesuitas.cl/wp-content/uploads/2013/09/misascentroamericanas.pdf.

Walsh, Shannon Drysdale and Cecilia Menjívar. "Impunity and Multisided Violence in the Lives of Latin American Women: El Salvador in Comparative Perspective." *Current Sociology* 64, no. 4 (July 2016): 586–602.

WHINSEC. "A Welcome from the Commandant." Official website of the Western Hemisphere Institute for Security Cooperation (WHINSEC), July 1, 2019. https://www.benning.army.mil/tenant/WHINSEC/About-Institute.html.

Whitla, Becca. "Singing as *Un Saber del Sur*, or Another Way of Knowing." *Toronto Journal of Theology* 33, no. 2 (Fall 2017): 289–294.

Wingeier-Rayo, Philip D. *Where Are the Poor? A Comparison of the Ecclesial Base Communities and Pentecostalism—A Case Study in Cuernavaca, Mexico.* Eugene, OR: Pickwick Publications, 2011.

Wright, Scott, Minor Sinclair, Margaret Lyle, and David Scott, eds. *El Salvador: A Spring Whose Waters Never Run Dry.* Washington, DC: EPICA, 1990.

Wynter, Sylvia. "Unsettling the Coloniality of Being/Power/Truth/Freedom: Towards the Human, After Man, Its Overrepresentation—An Argument." *New Centennial Review* 3, no. 3 (2003): 257–337.

Yancy, George, ed. *Whiteness and Christology: What Would Jesus Do?* New York: Routledge, 2012.

Young, Elliot. "Sanctuary in the Trump Era." North American Congress on Latin America (NACLA), February 3, 2017. https://nacla.org/news/2017/02/07/sanctuary-trump-era.

Zotti, Mary Irene. "The Young Christian Workers." *U.S. Catholic Historian* 9, no. 4 (Fall 1990): 387–400.

Index

aesthetics, 20, 191, 206, 214, 241n6, 250–53, 256, 258, 265–66, 268, 278n5, 287, 294, 304, 341–43
agriculture, 4, 35, 37–38, 46, 76, 84–85, 92, 145, 147, 149, 165, 172n35, 195, 217, 251, 258–59, 262, 269, 288, 290, 301–2, 331
Alas, José Inocencio, 75–80, 312
Althaus-Reid, Marcella, 15, 316n9
Anzaldúa, Gloria, 216
Aquino, Anastasio, viii, 40, 51–54, 103, 141
ARENA, 2, 164–65
artesanía, 20, 33, 35, 42, 140, 149, 252–53, 256–58, 274, 290, 298, 341
Ayala, Prudencia, viii, 40, 55–57, 141

Bajo Lempa, 95–99, 119, 123–26, 178n159, 181n205, 200, 243n22, 249, 257–58
baptism, 95, 103, 178n163, 191, 207, 215, 230, 238, 241n6, 263, 265–66, 269, 271–73, 304–6
Bible, 8, 70, 86, 228, 242n17, 278; *lectura popular* of the, 15, 46, 70–71, 77, 83–84, 87–88, 99, 109, 141, 213, 223, 240, 263, 268
Boff, Clodovis, 27n50, 218, 282n59
Boff, Leonardo, 305, 308, 316n7

Bosch, Francisco, 106, 190–91, 205, 240, 247n81, 252, 256
Brueggemann, Walter, 7, 242n18
Bukele, Nayib, 23n5, 183n252, 316n18

Cacaopera, 22, 93–95, 148, 154–55, 213, 225, 258, 261, 269, 285, 290, 314
Cáceres, Berta, 159–63, 329
canto popular, 16, 46, 59, 64–66, 183n256, 191, 195–98, 213–14, 258–62, 264, 269, 280n23–4, 301–2
Cardijn, Joseph, 217, 242n19
CEBES (pastoral center), 41, 49, 90–91, 94–95, 140, 178n149, 331
CEDES. *See* Salvadoran Bishops' Conference
CELAM. *See* Latin American Bishops' Conference
Chávez y González, Monseñor Luis, 47, 114–15, 175n91–2, 177n126
church: as hierarchical communion, 21, 98, 116, 135, 202, 270, 303–5, 309; as people of God, 9, 14, 27n49, 42–45, 70, 92, 100, 115–17, 127–28, 131, 138–39, 189–91, 202–3, 208n12, 226, 230–33, 237–38, 266–69, 278, 295, 300, 302–7; as pilgrim, 3, 10, 191, 194, 200–1, 223,

230, 303, 325, 336–37, 340, 343–44;
of the poor/*de lxs pobres*, vii–iii, 3,
8–11, 13–17, 31, 41, 45–49, 61–62,
82, 91, 100, 115, 123–26, 129, 144,
169, 177n133, 178n148, 187, 201–7,
210n51, 218, 227–29, 233, 238–39,
271, 289–90, 293–94, 309–10, 323–
30, 339, 349. *See also* ecclesiology
clergy, 3, 9, 91, 110, 114–39, 225, 228,
230–32, 239, 265–71, 303–4, 306,
309–10, 349
clericalism, 8, 11, 17, 225, 227, 235,
239, 272–74, 309
coloniality, 3–7, 17, 31–39, 55, 188–89,
192, 206, 225, 233–37, 250–53, 265–
67, 271–73, 287–88, 302–9, 323–24
colonial matrix of power, 5–7, 10–12,
15–18, 31, 51, 187–88, 207n3, 218,
226, 236, 242n16, 250, 267, 270,
286–87, 289, 292, 301, 321–22, 324,
337, 345, 352–53
Communist Party of El Salvador (PCS),
38, 57
Congregations of (Christian) Mothers.
See Mothers' Congregations
conquest, 4–6, 32–33, 192–93, 223,
233–36, 250, 265, 273, 279n8
Cortés, Hernán, 34
cotidianidad (everyday life), vii, 14,
27n53, 36, 70, 187, 195, 202,
210n37, 268, 322, 325
CRISPAZ, 330–32
crucified people, 13–14, 111, 166–67,
170, 206, 238, 240, 249, 340

Dalton, Roque, 41–42, 52–54
damnés, 17, 189, 206, 214, 237, 238,
251, 273, 290, 322, 326, 336–37,
339–40, 343–44, 352–54
De Alvarado, Pedro, 32, 34
DeClerq, Fr. Pedro, viii, 70, 90, 123,
126, 131, 181n205, 271, 280n23,
281n50
Decoloniality, 3–7; of being, 252–65; as
de-linking, 216, 220, 223, 225–26,

237, 252, 260, 270, 297, 308, 324,
337, 351; of knowledge, 7, 237–41;
of power, 287–302, 309–15
Dei Verbum, 229–31, 233
De las Casas, Bartolomé, 35
Delgado, Fr. José Matías, 35–36, 51
De Mendoza, Antonio, 35
diaconía, 207, 287, 290–91
dialogue, 8, 11–13, 15–16, 21, 48, 63,
68, 97, 114, 136, 214, 216, 219,
221–22, 231, 233, 237, 239–40, 273,
278, 296–97, 300, 306, 310, 347
doctrine of discovery, 236–37, 341
Domínguez Pérez, María Ángela, 22,
148–53, 213, 215, 285–86, 299, 314
Drexler-Dreis, Joseph, 15, 206, 208n6,
243n24
Dussel, Enrique, 24n15, 218

ecclesiology, 9–10, 15, 20, 115–16,
169, 189, 202–4, 265–66, 335,
340, 342; authority, 20–21, 41,
115, 171n13, 214, 216, 221–23,
229–33, 236–37, 239–41, 265, 267,
276, 287, 294, 302–9, 313–14;
communion ecclesiology, 21, 44,
63, 98, 116, 118, 125–26, 130, 194,
202–3, 210n51, 233, 304–5, 309–10,
339, 342; *ecclesia discens/ecclesia
docens*, 229, 231–33, 237–39;
tradition, 20, 115–17, 216, 229–33,
236–37, 240–41, 273
ecology, 76, 132–33, 157–59, 161, 163,
179n176, 179n182, 195, 201, 203,
226, 235, 259–62, 287, 289–90,
300–1, 303, 308, 327, 335, 345
El Chupadero, massacre of, 2–4, 16,
225
Ellacuría, Ignacio, 15, 26n42, 27n50,
67, 164–70, 202, 204, 206, 238,
243n24, 346
El Mozote, massacre of, 4, 224–25, 340,
345
empire, 5, 11–12, 34, 36–37, 41, 66, 83,
137, 193, 195, 201, 238, 262, 325

epistemology, 6–8, 15, 201, 206, 214–16, 218, 221–23, 227, 241n6, 252, 286, 301, 324, 340
Equipo Maíz, 31, 51, 136, 182n242, 224, 244n39
eschatology, vii, 14, 20, 187, 189–90, 192–93, 200, 203, 231, 237, 338–39, 344
Escobar Alas, José Luis, 115, 130–34, 137–39, 239, 246n80, 294–97, 303
eucharist, vii, 42, 48, 62–63, 78–79, 87, 123, 126, 191, 194, 206, 213, 237–38, 252, 254, 263–65, 267, 269, 271–73, 275–78, 287, 291
eurocentrism, 5, 15, 27n50, 188, 193, 266, 274–75, 304, 338–39

faith: adult faith, 216, 226–29, 237, 241, 340; liberating/liberative, 8–9, 11; in oneself/in one's peers, 83, 85, 221; and politics, 105, 219, 275–76, 288, 292, 311, 332, 342, 346
FMLN, 2, 23n5, 58–60, 82, 88, 140, 165, 280n24, 292
Fratelli Tutti, 324–26
Fundación Hermano Mercedes Ruiz (FUNDAHMER), 22, 91, 95, 119, 140, 148, 154, 191, 198, 331–32

gender and sexuality, 4–6, 11, 18, 55–56, 85, 149, 188, 193, 197, 226, 251, 258, 287, 289–90, 297–300, 310, 316n9, 322–23
Ginés de Sepúlveda, Juan, 35
grace, 9, 63, 138–39, 200, 206, 235, 265–67, 272, 274, 302, 304, 323, 328, 343, 349, 351–53
Grande, Rutilio, 43–44, 75, 80–81, 105, 115, 117–18, 177n132–3, 198, 224, 239
Guatemala, 35–36, 38, 41, 45, 47, 55–56, 58, 77, 108, 144, 172n15, 329
Gutiérrez, Gustavo, 13, 15, 27n50, 242n18, 282n59

Hernández Martínez, Maximiliano, 38–39, 57, 173n42, 224
hierarchy (of the Roman Catholic church), 3, 9, 90–91, 98, 106, 114–39, 164, 175n95, 178n149, 181n202, 203, 205, 211n53, 231–32, 238–39, 266–68, 273, 294, 303–7, 342
Holy Spirit, 305
Honduras, 41, 50, 82–83, 90, 108, 149, 159–60, 163, 168, 254, 256, 310

Ignatian Family Teach-in for Justice, 345–49
inculturation, 20, 267, 273–77
indigeneity, 57, 265
Instituto Pastoral de América Latina (IPLA), 41, 43–45, 47, 75–77, 80, 174n57

Kakawira, 33, 163, 264–65, 269, 273
koinonia, 194–96, 227, 321, 344

laity, 8, 27n53, 40–42, 45–48, 67–68, 90–91, 99, 101, 108, 110, 117, 123, 126, 137–38, 173n52, 222–24, 228, 230–32, 238–39, 244n43, 263, 265–71, 302–3, 305–8, 310–11, 313, 318n50, 319n54, 341, 349
La Matanza of 1932, 38–39, 57
Larraín, Manuel, 43, 173n56, 174n57
Latin American Bishops' Conference (CELAM), 8, 10, 41, 43–44, 108, 120, 202–3, 217, 233, 235, 237, 302
Leiva, Reina Greisi, 22, 140–43, 321
Lempa River, 33, 97, 281n34
Lenca or Potón, 33, 159–63, 173n54, 273
liberation theology, 8, 10, 12–17, 115, 120–23, 128, 149, 166, 216–18, 242n19, 243n24, 271, 275, 289, 330
liturgy, viii, 9, 16, 20, 22, 35, 39, 42, 44, 46, 62–63, 68, 71–72, 78–80, 83, 86–88, 94, 96–98, 100–1, 105, 118, 122–24, 126, 136–37, 141, 154–55, 191, 194, 202, 207, 213–14, 222,

237–39, 241, 251–52, 254–55, 258, 262–67, 269–78, 280n20, 287, 291, 296, 298, 300, 308, 312–15, 341, 347s
locus theologicus, 8, 10, 12–15, 27n53, 210n37, 279n7
Lorde, Audre, 216
Lumen Gentium, 115, 202, 232, 304, 307–8

machismo, 8, 18, 144–46, 152–53, 158, 192, 197, 268, 289, 297, 299–300
magisterium, 99, 126, 211, 229–33, 236, 238–40, 245n65, 267, 271, 273, 277–78
Maldonado-Torres, Nelson, 7, 188–89, 201, 206, 207n5, 214–15, 250–51, 258, 262, 282n63, 286, 322, 337–38, 343, 350
marriage, 33–34, 48, 52, 70, 103, 142, 272–73, 275, 293, 297–98, 307–8, 334
Martí, Farabundo, viii, 40, 57–60, 141, 175n88
martyrdom, 43, 83, 102, 124, 128, 131–33, 166, 168–70, 176n104, 200–1, 205, 223–26, 244n45, 254, 257–59, 262–63, 274, 276, 278, 341, 351; of Romero, 61–66, 115, 119, 126, 138, 201, 330; stories of, 51–53, 58–59, 72–74, 81, 101, 159–64
Maya, 33
Medellín, CELAM meeting at, 8, 10, 41, 43–45, 47, 62, 114, 118, 119, 202, 217, 233; CEBs' appeal to, 62–63, 83, 100, 127, 237
memory: as dangerous memory, 225; historical memory, viii, 2–3, 19–20, 31–32, 57, 128, 132, 156, 187, 207, 214, 216, 223–26, 241, 252, 287, 321; memory of Jesús, 264, 276–78, 291, 351; as "re-membering," vii, viii, 2, 10, 17, 20, 21, 62, 187, 189, 199, 204, 207n2, 223, 253, 270, 295, 297, 322, 340–41, 346–47, 350–54

mestizaje, 57, 250, 279n7
methodology: pastoral method, 44, 79, 98–99, 217–23, 226, 242n19, 262, 307; theological method, 10–17, 243n24, 282n59
Mignolo, Walter, 5–7, 188, 192–93, 215, 242n16, 278n5, 289
migration: internal, 96, 268; to the United States, 4, 24n26, 139, 149, 164, 259, 269, 355n23
milpa, 37, 53, 85, 99, 144
modernity: and coloniality, 4–7, 188, 192, 200, 207n5, 215–16, 251, 288–90, 322, 340, 346
Montes, Segundo, 92–93, 166–67, 169
Morazán, Francisco, 36, 52
Mothers' Congregations, 82, 85, 140, 154, 221, 241, 296, 299
mutual aid, 21, 92, 196, 214, 290, 291, 313

Nahua-Pipil, 32–35, 273, 276
National Coordination of the Popular Church (CONIP), 49
National Democratic Organization (ORDEN), 39, 309
National Guard, 37, 56, 63, 78
National Network of Ecclesial Base Communities of El Salvador, 9, 50, 119, 123, 127, 130–33, 258, 314
National University of El Salvador (UES), closure of (1972), 62, 237
Neo-liberalism, 4, 7, 127, 164, 179n182, 188, 200, 220, 228, 259, 290–91
New Laws of 1542, 35
Nicaragua, 15, 45, 56, 329, 330
Nonualco, Indigenous uprising at, 51–53

Ontology: colonial, 6, 7; of the ordained priesthood, 20, 252
option for the poor, 13, 14, 20, 121, 122, 127, 128, 199, 204, 205, 218, 222, 240, 323

organización/organization, 303, 309–15, 335, 342–43; versus *órden*, 309
Ortiz, Anita, 22, 94–95, 187
Ortiz, Octavio, 67, 72–74, 94; anniversary of, 154–55

paternalism, 10, 12, 18, 346
patriarchy, 5, 11, 15, 18, 161, 188, 192, 197, 299, 329
people of God. *See* church
Pérez Pérez, José Adonay, 22, 154–58, 165, 170, 221, 254, 314–15
Ponselle, Rogelio, 22, 82–83, 88–89, 95, 155
Pope Francis, 3, 10, 119, 137, 203, 235, 236, 239, 302, 308, 323–29
Pope John XXIII, 10, 202, 323
Pope Paul VI, 43, 115, 202
popular movements, 8, 17, 39, 176n102, 211n57, 323, 325, 326; Pope Francis, support for, 323–26; world meeting of, 211n54
postcolonial theory, 4, 24n15
priesthood: common, 117, 118, 178n163, 266–67; of the CEBs, 268–70; ordained, 20, 117, 178n163, 239, 265–67, 308
Proaño, Leonidas, 43, 174n56–57
Puebla, CELAM meeting at, 10, 120, 127, 202–3, 217, 237

queer or LGBTQ+, 4, 15, 345
Querida Amazonia, 203, 211n56, 235, 308
Quijano, Anibal, 5–6, 171n12, 193, 207n3, 292

racism, 6, 8, 18, 188, 192, 289–90, 322–23, 329
Radio Venceremos, 59, 279n14, 280n24
reign of God, 112–13; in art, vii-viii; and ecclesiology, 201–7; versus Kingdom of God, 189; and

pluriversality, 193–94. *See also* solidarity
repatriation, 19, 90–99, 123, 164, 330–31
resilience, 9, 253, 349–53
revelation, theology of, 206, 229–33
Rivas, Pedro Geoffrey, 53
Rivera-Pagán, Luis, 218, 226
Rodríguez, David, 46
Romero, Oscar Arnulfo, 1, 17, 27n49, 49, 61–66, 73, 84, 118–23, 237–38; beatification of, 126–30, 296–97; canonization, 130, 136–39, 176n98, 296–97
Ruiz, Mercedes, 178n158

sacrament, church as, 189, 201–7
sacraments, 103, 117, 135, 191, 250, 262–67, 271–78
Saenz LaCalle, Fernando, 119, 122, 130, 165, 285, 294
Salvadoran Bishops' Conference (CEDES), 47–48, 116–17, 122
Salvadoran revolution, 59–60, 176n102, 194–95, 292, 301, 310
sensus fidei, 232, 245n65, 278, 307, 325
sexuality. *See* gender and sexuality
short term missions, 331–36
Sobrino, Jon, 13–14, 26n44–45, 121, 164–70, 238, 303
Solentiname, 15–16
solidarity: coloniality of, 3, 203, 323–37; of clergy with *lxs pobres*, 202, 203, 238–39, 286, 296, 308; decolonization of, 21, 322–23, 337–49; economics of, 290–91; of *lxs pobres* with *lxs pobres*, 96, 98, 127, 160–61, 204, 214, 251, 268, 277; of North American Christians with Latin America, 329–36; and the reign of God, 112, 196, 198, 200, 311, 321–22, 354
Suchitoto, 75–81, 312
sumak kawsay, 193, 209n24

Trigo, Pedro, 14

Universidad Centroamericana "José Simeón Cañas" (UCA), 164–65, 167; martyrs of, 224, 244n43, 345
Urioste, Ricardo, 45–46

Vatican II, 8, 10, 40–42, 266–67, 272, 274–75, 282n63, 302–3; Latin American reception of, 47, 83, 114–18, 135
Ventura, Miguel, 82, 88, 90
vulnerability, 323, 328, 349–52

whiteness, 5, 11, 24n26, 25n32, 26n35, 227, 245n68, 287, 322; unsettling of, 346; white fragility, 357n56; white savior complex, 17; white supremacy, 4, 12, 352
Wynter, Sylvia, 6–7, 228, 231, 290, 337–38

Zapatistas, 7–8, 25n29, 209n22
Zepeda Santos, Miguel, 144–47, 245n52, 293, 313

About the Authors

Elizabeth O'Donnell Gandolfo is the Edith B. and Arthur E. Earley Associate Professor of Catholic and Latin American Studies at Wake Forest University School of Divinity in Winston-Salem, North Carolina. Gandolfo is a constructive theologian in the Catholic tradition, whose scholarly and pedagogical work seeks theological and practical paths of hope, healing, and liberation for people and the planet. Her first book, *The Power and Vulnerability of Love: A Theological Anthropology* (Fortress, 2015), draws on women's experiences of maternity and natality to construct a theology of suffering and redemption that is anchored in the reality of human vulnerability. She is also coeditor of *Parenting as Spiritual Practice and Source for Theology: Mothering Matters* (Palgrave Macmillan, 2017), which brings together theological reflections on mothering by women scholars in theology, bible, and ethics. She has published scholarly articles and has offered academic and public presentations on the place of motherhood in theology and spirituality, the theological and political significance of remembering suffering and martyrdom in communal spaces, the problem of whiteness and its entanglement with Christian theology, the decolonial ecclesiology of ecclesial base communities in Latin America, and the phenomenon of eco-martyrdom in the Americas. Gandolfo has been in relationship with the Ecclesial Base Communities of El Salvador since living and working with them prior to graduate studies in the early 2000s.

Laurel Marshall Potter is a doctoral candidate in Systematic and Comparative Theology at Boston College and an instructor at the UCA in San Salvador. She earned her master's degree in Latin American Theology from the UCA in 2015 and enjoys over ten years of personal participation and professional relationship with Ecclesial Base Communities in Central America. Laurel's dissertation studies eucharistic celebrations and questions of interculturation in these and other liminal ecclesial communities in resistance and, as with her master's thesis, draws on participatory, dialogical, and community-directed research. Laurel is an coeditor of *Sigue porque la vida sigue: voces de las comunidades eclesiales de base de El Salvador ayer y hoy*, a collection of interviews with intergenerational members of contemporary ecclesial communities, and her writing can be found in the *NACLA Report* and in the collection *Valuing Lives, Healing Earth: Religion, Gender, and Life on Earth*.

www.ingramcontent.com/pod-product-compliance
Lightning Source LLC
Chambersburg PA
CBHW051250300426
44114CB00011B/961